the BINGE WATCHER'S guide

SUPERNATURAL

AN UNOFFICIAL COMPANION

Jessica Mason

For more information contact:
Riverdale Avenue Books
5676 Riverdale Avenue
Riverdale, NY 10471.

www.riverdaleavebooks.com
Design by www.formatting4U.com
Cover by Scott Carpenter

Digital ISBN: 9781626015975
Trade Paperback ISBN: 9781626015982

First Edition, October 2021

Table of Contents

Acknowledgments

This book is a love letter to a show that changed my life, and the opportunity to write it came at a pivotal moment. First, I have to thank Lori Perkins for her faith in me and making this happen, and thanks to Athena for guiding me on the way.

Thanks also to my wife, who endured many episodes asking "why is he a demon again?" and my daughter who begged to watched Sam and Dean all the time. Also, to my father, who proves the literary bug is genetic, and my mother who always believed in me.

Further, this book would not exist without Jules Wilkinson and her tireless work maintaining the *Supernatural* Wiki fan page (www.supernaturalwiki.com).

Thank you to my incredible *Supernatural* friends and family whose insight, passion and support made this book better: Ana, Emily, Amanda, Sarah, Laura, Davy, Steve, Jeremy, Ruthie, Os, Rachel, Kim, Michelle, Bobo, Lynn, Holly, Nicki, Suzanne, Rich, Rob, and especially Meghan and Meredith.

Thank you to Jared Padalecki, Jensen Ackles, and Misha Collins, as well as Eric Kripke, Robert Singer, Sera Gamble, Jeremy Carver and Andrew Dabb for making a show that means so much to so many of us.

During the writing of this book, many-time *Supernatural* director Charles Beeson passed away. The *Supernatural* family also lost Holli Dewees, a friend, mother and active volunteer with Random Acts, to cancer. This book is dedicated to their memory.

For Tam, my daughter, who would have been Dean if things had turned out differently.
One day, I'll let you watch the scary parts.

Introduction

It all started, as so many things do, with the internet. During the spring of 2012, I was spending a lot of time on the internet, and being a giant nerd meant a good deal of that was spent on a quaint little site called Tumblr. I first joined Tumblr to talk about musical theater and, like everyone in 2012, to fangirl over *The Avengers* and Tom Hiddleston. But being on Tumblr in 2012 also meant one thing was unavoidable: *Supernatural*.

Of course, I knew about *Supernatural* before Tumblr. I was aware when it first premiered in 2005, but had avoided it because it seemed like a boys-only version of my beloved *Buffy the Vampire Slayer*, whose loss I was still mourning. Over the years I'd caught bits and pieces and, thanks to the only episodes I'd seen being vampire themed, I was under the impression that's what it was all about. I guess Jacob from *Lost* showed up as the devil at one point? Maybe?

But people on Tumblr were obsessed with this show, and not just with the brothers or the sexy angel that often teamed up with them who I briefly thought was Spanish and named Castille. So, when my wife had to study for the bar exam over the summer of 2012, I figured why not see what all the fuss was about. It could at the very least keep me entertained while she studied. At the time, there were seven seasons available—surely that would take months to get through. Little did I know that this show about two brothers and their angel would change my whole life.

Nine years after my first episode, *Supernatural* has imprinted itself like a handprint on my soul. It got me through a terrible bout of depression, inspired me to write reams of fanfic and Tumblr posts, and maybe most importantly, it inspired me to take that passion and energy for the series and turn it into a career.

My love for *Supernatural* led me to write about it, which quickly spread to other pop cultural and legal subjects, professionally. And for the past few years, that's been my actual job. I went from a fan squeeing over Sam and Dean, and Cas on Tumblr, to a reporter interviewing actors at conventions and events, even covering the show's landmark 300th episode gala.

Now, that's what *Supernatural* did to me and my life, but that doesn't quite explain why. Why does this show have such a devoted fandom? What is it about *Supernatural* that inspires such obsession and love? Fans of the show travel all over the world to attend conventions and meet the stars. They create remarkable fiction, and fan art, and started a community that has done incredible work for charity, making the world a better and weirder place.

But why? Is it the cool car? The homo-eroticism? The great tunes? The meta madness? Maybe that's all part of it, but I think the answer is a little simpler.

When I describe *Supernatural* to people it's hard to get across what really makes it such addictive television. "It's about these two brothers that drive across the country, fighting ghosts and monsters." That sounds cool for sure, but it doesn't really capture what made this show so special that it ran for 15 seasons. It focuses too much on what the brothers are doing. But what drew me in, and what still draws new fans, is that first bit.

Supernatural is a show about family. It's a show about love, about how standing up for and holding onto what you love, and the people you love, can save the whole damn world. It's about the fight for free will and making the right choices, because of love.

In November of 2020, after Joe Biden won the presidency and while the Georgia Senate run-off election was about to decide the balance of the US Senate, the *Supernatural* cast had a reunion over zoom with some special fans: Stacy Abrams and Senator Cory Booker. Booker didn't want to talk politics. He and Abrams wanted to explain how this little show, about very hot men fighting monsters, had given them hope and still gave them hope in saving America.

Sam and Dean Winchester are hard men to keep down, but they're human. They've saved their world again and again, not because of their guns or their power, but because they believe in each other. And Castiel changed the course of the apocalypse because he believed in them too. Together, they stood up against incredible odds, even against (spoiler) God himself, for love. And that's powerful stuff.

As you'll see in this book, and as you'll know if you watch the show, there's so much great stuff about *Supernatural*. Jared Padalecki, Jensen Ackles, and Misha Collins are perfectly cast as the leads, and they do so with a kindness and warmth that showed through on screen. It's scary, funny, sexy, smart, weird, and often subversive. There are meta episodes that take the death of the author to new levels, and there's some deep philosophical stuff about the nature of God, free will and the universe too. And also, some good dick jokes.

And yes, I'm a shipper and the queer subtext between Dean and Castiel kept me coming back, even when the main story would go stale for a while. It's an incredibly romantic story if you want to see it that way. But whether you have shipper goggles on or not, the love at the heart of the show is what makes it so special to me and many others. Even when I get snarky about the bad episodes—and there are a few—I do it because I love this show. It changed my life and these characters will always be part of me.

So, without further ado, let's rev the engine.

We've got work to do.

How To Use This Book

The point of this book is to watch along and enrich the experience of *Supernatural*. But when we're talking about a series that has 327 episodes, things can get a little complex. So let's break this down.

Before we get into the seasons and episodes individually, we're going to look at the show as a whole. We'll talk about the genesis and feel of the show, give you some background on how it was made, received, and changed, and then dig into some of the bigger themes of the series. Then, when we're ready, we'll go season by season with an overview before getting into each and every episode.

Of course, this book isn't a substitute for the show. In fact, parts of it might not make much sense if you haven't watched the episode I'm talking about. But my goal isn't to replace it, but rather to make your viewing experience better, explaining deeper meanings of things and how various episodes tie in with season-long themes. I'll get into what the writers were trying to accomplish and if I believe they succeeded.

Throughout the episode guides, you'll also find all sorts of fun bits such as trivia, Easter eggs, musical moments, and even cast members who went on to bigger things including Oscars. When it's relevant, we'll also have separate sections about shipping stuff. For those that don't know, a "ship" refers to a romantic relationship—real or imaginary—between two characters. All ships are fair game here. I don't discriminate. But if you don't like shippy stuff, feel free to skip those.

Also, of course, there will be spoilers. This is a binge watch and we're looking at the entire series, so we'll often be discussing what happens next, or how a plot point might hit or fizzle later on. If you're reading and watching for the first time, be aware of that. I'll put spoiler warnings in front of the big stuff, but everything is fair game here.

Now, with regards to the cast, it can be complicated. The only actors who appear in every episode of the series are Jared Padalecki and Jensen Ackles. But that doesn't mean other actors aren't regulars. They just aren't always around, which can be confusing. So, even though Misha Collins and Mark Sheppard were series regular in Season Nine, for example, they'll still be listed as "guest cast." Also, for actors whose names have changed since their appearance on the show (such as if they, for instance, married a Winchester brother), I'm going to use their current names.

Finally, the last chapter will focus entirely on the series finale, "Carry On," which was controversial to say the least. But, once again, I'm going to try to help you understand why certain choices were made and how the episode fits into the big picture.

The Zeitgeist

A black car streaks down a lonely highway, as a pale figure flickers on the roadside. There's a sign flickering above a seedy motel, where a man is looking up into the blinding light of an angel. A prophet takes a swig from a fifth of vodka and fixes a sentence in his latest novel, while lightning illuminates Death himself taking a slice of Pizza. The son of Satan contemplates free will over pie and coffee.

The spirit of *Supernatural* lives in the liminal, in the back roads and forgotten lore of America itself. It's a story about the shadows, both in this country and in ourselves, and it's at its best when it leans into the weird, subversive, and arcane. What first sold *Supernatural* might have been a look at what lurks in the legends and lonely roads of America, but became a complex meditation on family and free will.

"Two brothers hunt urban legends" is pretty much the pitch that creator Eric Kripke sold when he began developing the series. "For me, the core notion behind *Supernatural* was to make a series about urban legends," Kripke told *Variety* in an oral history for the show's 200th episode. "I think there's this incredibly rich mythology about the United States, and no one had really tapped into that, so when I started as a writer, one of the first ideas I ever pitched was an urban legend show."

Kripke's initial idea was a show about a reporter investigating urban legends, but no one bought that. So, on the spot in a meeting, he scrapped it. "I said, 'forget the reporter, we should do this show as *Route 66*, two cool guys in a classic car cruising the country, chasing down these urban legends,' and literally right on the spot I said, 'and they're brothers,' because it popped in my head. 'And they're dealing with their family stuff and they're fighting evil.' You just start making it up as you go. They were like, 'Brothers, wow, that's a relationship we haven't seen on TV before.' And from there, *Supernatural* was born… out of a piece of improvisation."

But it would still take some time before *Supernatural* became the kind of show that would run for 327 episodes and inspire a cult fandom. After Warner Brothers bought the idea for their network, there was the pilot to be written and shot. This original pilot had Sam and Dean (inspired by characters in Jack Kerouac's *On the Road*) carrying the last name Harrison. Eventually however, they ended up with the name Winchester, inspired by the gun and the infamous haunted mystery house, which amazingly is never referenced in the show. And they also figured out something else essential—the car.

Now, if you're new here, I'd like you to meet the leading lady of *Supernatural*. For a while, fans called her the "metallicar," but Dean and the rest of us just call her Baby. Baby is a 1967 Chevy Impala and she's the totem of the show in all ways. She's big, mean, scary and can fit a body in the trunk. She's unwieldy, loud, and has been torn up more times than the boys can count. And she's the most important car in the world.

To understand and love *Supernatural* is to understand and love Baby. She's not just the Winchesters' home, but arguably a cast member herself. In real life, she was played by six different cars—two of which went home with Jensen Ackles and Jared Padalecki when the series wrapped. The creak of her doors, the roar of her engine, and the sound of classic rock from her tape deck are the sounds of *Supernatural*.

Now, Kripke sold the show, but since he was a newer writer at the time, he couldn't run the series alone. Enter Robert Singer, who would co-run the show with Kripke and every other showrunner after him. Singer brought his own stamp to the show, making the big ideas work. And as a showrunner and director, he would be one of the few constants throughout the entire run, along with the boys.

Ah yes. "The boys." Casting the show was what took *Supernatural* from a fun idea to a show that would become a cult hit. Both Jensen Ackles and Jared Padalecki had experience on The WB before getting their roles on *Supernatural*, with Ackles on *Smallville* and *Dawson's Creek,* and Padalecki on *Gilmore Girls* (ironically as a character named Dean). These two giant Texas boys had great chemistry and a lot of talent, but the thing that made them special were big hearts that didn't come with big heads.

Jared and Jensen aren't simply great actors, they are truly kind people who care about their jobs. That's more rare in Hollywood than it should be, but their decency, professionalism, and commitment to their crew and co-workers is something that's really legendary. I cannot tell you how many dozens of guest stars have talked about how good of a set *Supernatural* was, how they were treated with respect and kindness, and how that spirit came from the top of the call sheet down.

These guys, plus a cool car and a great hook of a story, made for a modest hit, but it took one more actor and element to elevate *Supernatural* to a show that would last a decade and a half. And he first appeared with shadowy wings and trench coat.

As much as I enjoy the first three seasons, in my mind *Supernatural* doesn't really get its wings until the introduction of Misha Collins as the angel Castiel. Not only did the introduction of angels give the show material for eleven mores seasons of celestial and biblical storytelling—and possibly launching the most popular ship in the history of the internet—it also added a third incredible human to the cast. Misha Collins, like his co-stars, cared about making the world better, and harnessed the *Supernatural* fandom to really help people and bring them joy.

Collins founded the charity Random Acts, based on the energy and devotion of *Supernatural* fans. He launched an international scavenger hunt GISHWHES (now just GISH) to make the world a weirder, better place. And his kindness and activism inspired fans and his cast-mates alike. Jared became an advocate for mental health and suicide prevention, launching his "Always Keep Fighting" campaign, with Jensen joining in as well. Other fan favorite actors have since joined, and now the whole cast works for worthy causes and to spread kindness.

And they couldn't do this without the fans—the *Supernatural* family as we're called is a seriously committed bunch of folks. And that fandom is still growing, because year after year *Supernatural* continued to be more interesting and more creative. It was so many things. Scary monsters yes, but as the angel story expanded, it became a show about faith, free will and about the fight against huge powers for what's right. And of course, it was still about family.

On the backs of creepy monsters, homoerotic tension, classic rock, and very self-referential meta, *Supernatural* goes deep. It deals with death, loss, trauma, and toxic masculinity. Abuse and the cycle of violence is a big deal on this show, as are issues of codependency, depression, suicide, and capitalism. Most of the time, these big ideas are explored in really interesting ways driven by character. But sometimes they aren't. That capitalism theme I mentioned? It sticks out for a reason, and the season where it takes the fore is one of the weakest.

There are bad episodes of *Supernatural* for sure. With 327 episodes, there are bound to be some lemons in there. But there are way more incredible ones—episodes I've watched a dozen times and will keep watching again and again. There's so much to this show and in some ways this book will just scratch the surface. But it stayed on the air because of its creativity, heart, and willingness to go big in terms of ideas and story. And I think they did a pretty good job.

Before You Watch

What is *Supernatural* about? I don't mean the plot, I mean the ideas the writers are trying to make work. That's what I want you to keep in mind as you use this book. There's the plot of the show of course, but also a moral to the story, and what we're interested in here is that second bit. These are what drive the story and make it interesting.

But before we get into that, let's talk about how to find them, because they're often in surprising places. Starting especially in Season Two, the monsters are often not just a monster. They're usually something more, whose story somehow relates to our main characters. We call this narrative mirroring and I'll be using that term a lot. And these narrative mirrors tell us a lot about what the episode, season, or even series is about, often echoing specific themes that define each season.

Now, these themes developed and changed over the years, so many from Season One won't make it through the whole run, but some will. The focus of the show changes as the characters evolve, after all. And that's a good thing. Naturally, we're interested in how these characters grow and their relationships change.

So, what are the themes that we'll see the most, that you should keep an eye out for? First and foremost, family. Loyalty to one's family, guilt for leaving one's family, found family and abusive families, family as a motivation for revenge and for change, and family as the thing that makes us who we are. Family is the thread that ties everything together, and it means love, but also conflict, resentment, codependency, and independence. And of course, that television favorite: Daddy issues!

The other big one is free will, which of course relates to family. How you're raised can affect your choices. Family can try to control you and tell you want to do, but growing up means finding your own path. That goes for Sam and Dean finding their own road without their father, all the way to them raising a kid who, well, we'll get there. No spoilers here. Not just yet.

Other stuff to watch out for is Americana, toxic masculinity, homoeroticism, duty, guilt, heroism, anger, and brotherly love. And it all gets summed up in one little phrase that comes up at the start and gets repeated until the very end: "We've got work to do."

There's just so much right there. It implies a mission, a destiny. It comes from a sense of duty and heroism wrapped in an all-American working-class ethos. It's a collective statement because the Winchesters are a team. There's hope in a higher purpose, but a higher purpose can also be a controlling trap. And how do you know when you're done with that work?

And it's a dangerous manipulation of fate—a subversion. See, *Supernatural* begins as a show about boys in a big car, listening to rock music and shooting scary ghosts in the face. It's hyper masculine and plays with lots of horror tropes and expectations. Until it doesn't.

These manly heroes are actually extremely sensitive, wounded characters. Early on we figure out that Dean is actually the more loving, soft character, while Sam turns out to be the dangerous one. The show constantly surprises the audience, taking wild left turns and big chances. Subversiveness is baked into the show, and that allows it to get really creative and weird, which leads to some of the most awesome and surprising episodes. And the most meta.

Meta is a word you'll see a lot in this book. It refers to when a work of art refers to itself, which *Supernatural* does more than almost any show out there. As a show and story, *Supernatural* is incredibly self-aware. Within the universe of the show, starting in Season Four, there are books about Sam and Dean. Through this, it both mocks and celebrates its own flaws and tropes, and that's cool. Later developments have all sorts of implications about who gets to write stories, and who gets to decide how they end. And yes, the very nature of life in terms of free will and divinity.

But these stories also have fans, some of whom write fanfic. Fanfic that includes the boys, you know, *that way* (yes, they know they're brothers). That brings us to another element of the show that wasn't intended, but comes up a lot: queerness. Homoeroticism is inevitable in hyper masculine stories staring two or more ridiculously hot men, but Sam and Dean aren't the only characters people shipped. When Castiel enters the story, his relationship with Dean immediately has subtext. The show actually leans into it in a way that's pretty surprising.

Which brings us all the way back to the beginning. This is a show about a lot of things, but at its heart is about a family, built on love. And it all starts and ends with that.

SUPERNATURAL

CHAPTER ONE

Dad's on a Hunting Trip

Season One is all about the monsters at the edge of the American dream. A family haunted by ghosts and demons, dark bars and creepy scarecrows—it sets an extremely specific tone for the series: Sam and Dean, side by side against the world.

Uniquely, it was the only season that aired on The WB and, unlike the rest of the series, was filmed on, well, film rather than digital. This would contribute to a literal darker look, along with a not-so-big budget for monsters. But that low budget forced the show to be more atmospheric, relying on suspense and production design to set the tone, rather than special effects.

As a whole, the premiere season is about a search. The boys are looking for their father, but also finding their own path along the way. Much like how the show is also trying to find itself, seeing what works and what doesn't. Of course, it stumbles as it does, but by the end manages to find a groove that stays for over a decade.

Make sure to watch for who seems to be the "hero" of the show. Initially, Sam was conceived as the lead, with Dean in a supporting role. In the early episodes, Sam is clearly our point of view, but around episode 12 things begin to shift in a significant way and we see Dean become a true co-lead. And this all happened because the writers believed that Jensen was just that good.

What wasn't always good though, was the writing. Eric Kripke and Bob Singer were running the writers' room, but it wasn't a consistent crew. There are several episodes from one-off writers we'll never hear from again, but other voices in the room like Sera Gamble, Raelle Tucker, John Shiban and Cathryn Humphris would go on to be significant creators on the show. Also here from the beginning are producer/directors Kim Manners and Phil Sgriccia who very much defined the tone of the show, along with cinematographer Serge Ladouceur and production designer Jerry Wanek.

A note on the music: if you're streaming (probably Netflix) then some of those iconic moments may not be there due to licensing issues. Because this series is so old and switched networks, the music rights for Season One are incredibly wonky, so just be aware that if I mention a song that you don't hear, blame the lawyers, not me.

Pilot

Episode 1.01. Airdate: September 13, 2005
Written by: Eric Kripke
Directed by: David Nutter
Guest Cast: Jeffrey Dean Morgan (John Winchester), Samantha Smith (Mary Winchester) Adrianne Palicki (Jess), Sarah Shahi (Constance Welch)
Synopsis: Dean and Sam Winchester go on a road trip.

There are good pilots and there are great pilots. Not only is the first episode of the series still one of the best, but it's also just one of the best pilots period. It sets everything up perfectly, delivering so many captivating and now iconic moments. Mary's death being repeated with Jessica's immediately hooks you, but more importantly it introduces us to the "the boys."

As far as Sam goes, his introduction is pretty standard, but I love that we know exactly who Dean is and how he and Sam relate from the iconic line "Dad's on a hunting trip and he hasn't been home in a few days." Everything that hooked me to the show is in that line, from Dean's delivery to Sam's reaction.

And they're both so good, right from the get-go. More than anything, it's what makes this episode work. Sam is our entry point, the semi-outsider who begins his hero's journey with the call to adventure. Dean is a typical macho, metal-loving bad boy. But there's a depth to them. There's an edge to Sam that's intriguing, and despite Dean's "no chick flick moments" talk and bravado, he clearly cares about his brother and father that hints at the big heart under all that bluster.

Despite huge swaths of exposition and clunky dialogue, it all somehow just works. The boys' first case is a great one and provides our first narrative mirror that I mentioned earlier. The ghost story of Constance Welch and her difficulties returning home echo Sam's own return to his family and dark past. And just like how things go bad for Constance, they almost immediately get dark for Sam too.

Driver Picks the music: AC/DC's "Back in Black" and "Highway to Hell" will show up again in the series. Interestingly, despite Sam's mention of Dean having Metallica tapes, the show never actually featured any Metallica songs.

Name Game: Dean calling himself "Ted Nugent" starts a gimmick we'll see frequently, of Dean and Sam using alias related to classic rock.

Ship Shape: Sam and Jess are pretty cute, but it's a pity we don't get to know who Jess was beyond being objectified and burning on the ceiling. She seems to support Sam, and that's nice for him. But it's too bad that it can't last.

Wendigo

Episode 1.02. Airdate: September 20, 2005
Written by: Eric Kripke (teleplay), Ron Milbauer & Terri Hughes Burton (story)
Directed by: David Nutter
Guest Cast: Callum Keith Rennie (Roy), Alden Ehrenreich (Ben Collins), Gina Holden (Haley Collins), Donnelly Rhodes (Mr. Shaw)
Synopsis: Sam and Dean follow John's clue to a wendigo, a monster created when a human resorts to cannibalism.

The second episode of a series is always tough, and "Wendigo" is no exception. The episode is very much written and shot like a miniature horror movie, and for a show still trying to find itself, it works. And it's something we'll see throughout the series, especially in this first season.

As for the monster, the wendigo is a good legend—one we all read as kids in Scary Stories to Tell in the Dark (and it won't be the last campfire tale that shows up)—but the actual effects are less than great. And as far as plot goes, their search for a lost family member echoes their own, which is important as we're still getting to know Sam and Dean and what they value.

One of the things I love about this episode is that we're already seeing that Dean is more than the person he projects. He's one of those guys that puts on a tough face, but he does also care about his brother and the people he's saving. Also, he looks damn good with an improvised blowtorch.

Future Famous Faces: It's episode two and already we have two cast members that went on to other big projects. The late Cory Monteith of *Glee* gets chomped in the cold open and yes, that's future Han Solo (in *Solo*) Alden Ehrenreich in his very first role.

Dead in the Water

Episode 1.03. Airdate: September 27, 2005
Written by: Sera Gamble and Raelle Rucker
Directed by: Kim Manners
Guest Cast: Amy Acker (Andrea Barr), Daniel Hugh Kelly (Jake Devins), Nico McEown (Lucas)
Synopsis: Sam and Dean investigate a series of mysterious drownings.

There's a lot here that's going to echo through the whole series, especially for Dean. His conversations with Lucas—the traumatized boy with a connection to this episode's ghost—are the highlight of the episode and shows us a smaller Dean who just wants to be brave after losing his mom.

Speaking of kids, this episode includes *Supernatural*'s very first creepy kid. And it certainly won't be the last. Given that the ghost is only soothed by the sheriff's death, it provides a lesson that the boys can't always save everyone, and that the conclusion to some of their hunts will be pretty tragic.

For a first season effort it's pretty solid and had some big scares at well. Personally, I find all the stuff with the drownings terrifying.

Famous Faces: Amy Acker was already well-known from her work on *Angel* when she guest starred, but in later years she would co-star on *Person of Interest* as Root. On that show she would share a screen and ship with Sarah Shahi, who played Constance Welch in the pilot.

Phantom Traveler

Episode 1.04. Airdate: October 4, 2005
Written by: Richard Hatem
Directed by: Robert Singer
Guest Cast: Brian Markinson (Jerry Panowski), Jaime Rae Newman (Amanda Walker).
Synopsis: The Winchesters investigate airplane crashes caused by a demon.

Now this episode has some great scares and supporting characters. We also get some more insight into Sam's torment over the loss of Jessica, and the search for his father John. But that's not the biggest thing here. What "Phantom Traveler" is most notable for is what it introduces to the *Supernatural* mythos—demons.

Speckles, as I like to call the plane crash demon, isn't very scary in hindsight. And the whole "someone needs to be in a compromised emotional state to be possessed" gets dropped pretty quickly. Further, it takes 15 entire seasons for the boys to try using "Christo" again to test if someone is possessed. But the introduction of demons, hell, and their role in predestination are a cornerstone of *Supernatural*.

There's also some other stuff that will come up a lot later, only to be subverted such as Sam and Dean's hesitance about impersonating feds. They do it all the time! Dean's hilarious fear of flying does also remain and will get revisited in the future.

Future Famous Face: Jaime Ray Newman may be familiar to you from her work on shows like *The Magicians* (which you must check out if you love *Supernatural*), but she's also technically an Oscar winner for her short film *Skin*.

Bloody Mary

Episode 1.05. Airdate: October 11, 2005
Written by: Eric Kripke (teleplay), Ron Milbauer & Terri Hughes Burton (story)
Directed by: Peter Ellis
Guest Cast: Adrianne Palicki (Jess), Marnette Patterson (Charlie)
Synopsis: Sam and Dean fight the terror of sleepovers everywhere: Blood Mary.

This is a decent episode, but not a great one. Most everyone has played "Bloody Mary" at some point, so it's a smart legend to use, but not necessarily mysterious. And talk about narrative mirrors, it serves to show that Sam is keeping a secret—his dreaming of Jess' death. This season asks who Sam and Dean really are, so the emphasis on dark family secrets is pretty apt.

But outside the obvious, there's nothing really remarkable about this one. And it doesn't help that it's sandwiched between two really good episodes, leaving it to sort of blur and fade into the background.

Plot Hole: Dean's eye starts bleeding at the climax, implying that he's hiding some sort of dark secret about someone's death, and it's just never addressed.

Future Famous Face: Adrianne Palicki would go on to star in all sorts of shows, like *Friday Night Lights*, *Agents of SHIELD* and *The Orville*.

Skin

Episode 1.06. Airdate: October 18, 2005
Written by: John Shiban
Directed by: Robert Duncan MacNeil
Guest Cast: Amy Grabow (Becky), Peter Shinkoda (Alex)
Synopsis: When you're not comfortable in your own skin, peel it off!

Now "Skin" is incredibly fun, as well as scary and gross, and one of my early favorites. There are a lot of thrills here and Jensen does a great job in his (first of many) non-Dean role (Jared will get many turns at this game too).

What I love about this episode is that it's the first real foray into subverting the audience's expectations. *Supernatural* has two very hot leading men, whom it would be easy to objectify and get shirtless all the time. But the first time we see Dean like that, it's an incredibly gory scene! It's very much "give people what they want, but do it in a way that they don't expect."

Something else of note is just how human the monster looks here. Because of their low-budget, they couldn't afford crazy make up and effects, leaving most creepy crawlies on *Supernatural* to look a lot like regular people. But just because it's cheaper doesn't make it bad—it means anyone could be a threat hiding in plain sight.

Legal Trouble: "Skin" is also our first hint of the boys being wanted by law enforcement and/or presumed dead. It's wild that they'll still be legally dead and/or wanted in various ways for the next 300 or so episodes.

Driver Picks the Music: "In-A-Gadda-Da-Vida" by Iron Butterfly plays when the shapeshifter is surrounded in the awesome opening. The boys will eventually meet several residents of the actual garden of Eden.

Hook Man

Episode 1.07. Airdate: October 25, 2005
Written by: John Shiban
Directed by: David Jackson
Guest Cast: Dan Butler (Reverend Sorenson), Jane McGregor (Lori)
Synopsis: A brutal murder in a college town leads the Winchesters to the source of the infamous "Hook Man" legend.

Episode seven is fine, and it does a really good job transforming one of those scary campfire stories into something adults can enjoy. There are some good twists here, like the fact that it's young Lori "controlling" the vengeful Hook Man ghost. Just more examples of people not being what we expect them to. You know, like Sam and Dean.

We get the sense that Sam misses college, and that Dean missed Sam while he was studying at Stanford, but Sam is also so committed to finding the "thing that killed Jess and Mom" that he can't go back to his normal life. Not just yet.

Spoiler Alert: There's also a fun pattern that ghosts don't go away when the body is burned. Sam and Dean dig a lot of graves throughout the show, and I swear more than half the time it's not actually useful.

Bugs

Episode 1.08. Airdate: November 8, 2005
Written by: Rachel Nave, Bill Coakley
Directed by: Kim Manners
Guest Cast: Andrew Arilie (Larry Pike), Tyler Johnston (Matt Pike), Carrie Genzel (Lynda Bloome), Anne Marie Deluise (Joanie Pike), A whole bunch of bees (themselves)
Synopsis: Sam and Dean deal with a suburb built on Indigenous land that's being tormented by, you guessed it, bugs!

Oh, "Bugs." This is what's generally seen as the first real clunker, with Eric Kripke going out of his way to call it one of the worst episodes both on and off screen. And I get that. It's not what you would call a good episode, and the whole plot about homes built on sacred Indian land was already hackneyed and racially insensitive in 2005, let alone now. And the bug effects are generally terrible.

But it's not horrible. Not really. I'd say it doesn't quite deserve the bad rap that it gets. I mean, there's thematic stuff here with Matt and Sam about not listening to your family that's really important for Sam's character. And Dean's reactions to that are telling as well. Plus, Dean is adorable in that steam shower. There are other much worse episodes in the future, but this one just, well, bugs people for some reason.

So, Get This: In the climactic attic scene, director and producer Kim Manners decided on using *actual live bees*, which was not fun at all for the actors, resulting in a lot of stings. Then, when the footage came in, the bees weren't visible and had to be replaced with digital bugs anyway. That's showbiz, I guess.

Home

Episode 1.09. Airdate: November 15, 2005
Written by: Eric Kripke
Directed by: Ken Girotti
Guest Cast: Jeffrey Dean Morgan (John), Samantha Smith, (Mary), Loretta Divine (Missouri Moseley), Kristin Richardson (Jenny)
Synopsis: The Winchesters face a haunting in their childhood home.

Ah yes, self-loathing and daddy issues, the building blocks of most great television. This one is stellar for giving us the boys, emotionally vulnerable. Sam, rattled by his abilities and longing to save people is moved to tears by seeing his mother, while Dean cries and reaches out to an absent father.

Dean's phone call to John and Sam's moment with Mary's spirit are great, but the big reveal here is that John has known where the boys were all along. And he knew that they were looking for him. It's starting to look like John may not be the best dad, even if he loves his kids. Hold onto that.

Not only is this episode emotional, but it's really scary. The garbage disposal scene is a moment that still makes me hold my breath and shriek. Even the refrigerator scene is terrifying. There are lots of references here to The Shining and Poltergeist, and they really work, but there's more emotion in these 43 minutes than either.

Fan Favorites: Missouri Moseley makes such an impression in her appearance here that she remains a fan favorite, often showing up in fanfic galore, thanks to Loretta Divine's wonderful performance.

Spoiler Alert: Missouri will return 12 years down the line. This also isn't the last we'll see of Mary Winchester. Given how many more times we'll see her, the writers obviously didn't know how long the show would run. It's almost funny that the series seems to "resolve" Mary's story in the ninth episode out of 327.

Asylum

Episode 1.10. Airdate: November 22, 2005
Written by: Richard Hatem
Directed by: Guy Norman Bee
Guest Cast: Brooke Nevin (Katherine), Nicholas D'Agosto (Gavin)
Synopsis: Sam and Dean work out some issues as they investigate a haunted mental asylum.

After the big emotions of "Home," reverting to a standard urban legend is a bit of a letdown. Though this episode is fine in terms of scares, the episodic stories relying on just urban legends are already feel old. What's really good in the episode, however, is the brother drama, a staple of the series.

Up until this point we haven't really seen Sam and Dean fight. Sure, they've bickered as siblings do, but this episode opens up some big wounds between them. The big confrontation while Sam is under the influence of the ghost of Dr. Ellicott is especially good. And Sam shoots Dean! That's dark! They went to the brother killing brother drama in episode ten.

I'm sure that's the end of that conflict, right?

Name Game: Dean uses the alias Nigel Tufnel, a reference to *This is Spinal Tap.*

Scarecrow

Episode 1.11. Airdate: January 10, 2006
Written by: John Shiban (Teleplay), Patrick Sean Smith
Directed by: Kim Manners
Guest Cast: Jeffrey Dean Morgan (John), Nicki Aycox (Meg), Tania Saulnier (Emily), Tom Butler (Harley Jorgenson), P. Lynn Johnson (Stacey Jorgenson)
Synopsis: The apple pie that requires human sacrifice is so not worth it. Sam meets a girl that seems nice.

This is it readers, the episode that hooked me and the one that will hook you. "Scarecrow" falls right in line with folk horror movies like The Wicker Man that delve into scary pagan cults practicing human sacrifice. As a pagan myself, I dislike this, but the way it's executed here is well done here and the "fugly" scarecrow is truly creepy. But it's also an episode about toxic family situations.

The meat of it is in how it digs into all of the Winchester family issues. We have John asking for unquestioning loyalty and sacrifice, which is echoed in the Burkitsville residents deciding to sacrifice their own niece for the "greater good." And then we have Meg and Sam's excellent discussion about obeying overbearing family (and wait until you meet Meg's "father").

Fan Favorite: Meg is a perfect foil for Sam in that she too has a complicated family relationship and some inner darkness. She's excellently played by Nicki Aycox. I love her and the shock of her pulling that knife out and making the call is one of the best moments of Season One. That's the kind of ending that blows you mind and makes you want to keep watching.

And spoiler: Meg will show up again in ways that are surprising until the end.

Faith

Episode 1.12. Airdate: January 17, 2006
Written by: Sera Gamble & Raelle Tucker
Directed by: Allan Kroecker
Guest Cast: Julie Benz (Layla Rourke), Rebecca Jenkins (Sue-Ann Le Grange), Kevin McNulty (Rev. Roy Le Grange)
Synopsis: When God seemingly spares Dean from death, the boys have to ask some big questions

"Faith" isn't just fantastic in terms of drama, surprises, and acting, but it sets up some of the big themes for the entire series. Between this and "Scarecrow," this is when *Supernatural* becomes *Supernatural*, with everything truly clicking into place.

This is where all the big ideas—the ones that have been hovering around the edges for some time, but haven't quite made it—come into full focus. And one of those core ideas is of faith itself. What makes these boys special? Is it who they are or were they chosen by God? Or both? How much damage and guilt can they endure, and how many lives will be lost for the greater good? Can fate be controlled, and at what cost?

And of course it's all tied in with love and family. Everything here starts, because Sam doesn't want to see Dean die. And from here until the bitter end, there's a cycle of one Winchester not letting the other go that's going to cause some big problems later.

Eric Kripke even acknowledged how important this episode is: "It's when I first realized what the show was capable of. Here's what this episode is about: Is there a god? What's meant to be? And is there free will? And is your life worth the cost of someone else's life? It's a metaphysical and moral study of the boys' universe. There's so many different places the show can go and so many tones."

Spoiler Alert: Dean makes a big deal about how they shouldn't kill people, and obviously can't kill a reaper or death. Three things they do *a lot* in later seasons. Also, it becomes clear later that Dean was probably legitimately saved by God. since reapers are retconned as a breed of angels. This is the first, but not the last by far, time that Dean is touched by an angel.

Death Notes: So, spoiler again, but this won't be the only time a Winchester dies. So, for fun, let's start a tally of those deaths and close to death moments. So far, it's Dean: 1, Sam: 0.

Driver Picks the Music: The reveal set to Blue Öyster Cult's "Don't Fear the Reaper" is absolutely the best Driver Picks the Music in Season One.

Route 666

Episode 1.13. Airdate: January 31, 2006
Written by: Brad Buckner and Eugenie Ross-Leming
Directed by: Paul Shapiro
Guest Cast: Megalyn Echikunwoke (Cassie), A Very Large Monster Truck
Synopsis: Racist truck ghost.

From the sublime to the ridiculous, while "Faith" is the best of Season One, "Route 666" is probably the worst. I'm not kidding. Along with "Bugs," "Route 666" most often gets cited as the low point of the early series. Yes, there's some thematic stuff here about family legacies, but we get that a lot and it doesn't really click here.

The stuff with Dean and Cassie is fine, and I really do like Cassie as a character, but a show starring, written, and directed by mostly white dudes trying to make a point about racism with a literal monster truck… just doesn't work. The final chase is fun, but the "racist truck" episode is one you can skip unless you're a completionist.

Ship Shape: Cassie is the first love interest we meet who survives an episode, and she's smart and cool, so she obviously never returns. However, in a bit of irony, a different "Cassie" is pretty important down the line.

Nightmare

Episode 1.14. Airdate: February 7, 2006
Written by: Sera Gamble & Raelle Tucker
Directed by: Phil Sgriccia
Guest Cast: Brendan Fletcher (Max Miller), Beth Broderick (Alice Miller)
Synopsis: A bad dream leads Sam to a troubled kid who also has powers.

This episode gets us back on track and it's really quite excellent, if not a bit disturbing. Max Miller's story is one of the saddest we've seen, and this is one of many times where the Winchesters hunt things, but don't necessarily save people. It happens a lot when the series leans more into horror, an inherently tragic genre.

And this certainly is a horror episode.

The moment with the knife poised over Alice Miller's eye still makes me squirm, and the human horror of what the Millers did to their son is even worse. But hey, it makes John Winchester—a character we've heard about in mostly negative ways—seem a bit nicer? Max and his family both mirror and contrast with Sam.

Of course, the standout from this episode is Sam. Not only does he finally start to move some of his hair out of his face, but we see how his power lies in his compassion for the other "freaks." Luckily, he has a brother who will always be on his side. Right?

Name Game: Fathers Simmons and Frehley are references to the band KISS.

So, Get This: The part at the wake where Dean starts eating cocktail sausages was improvised by Jensen Ackles, and he was told after that they weren't meant to be eaten and apparently tasted terrible. But this began a running gag throughout the show that Dean loves to eat, especially junk food.

The Benders

Episode 1.15. Airdate: February 14, 2006
Written by: Eric Kripke, John Shiban
Directed by: Peter Ellis
Guest Cast: Jessica Steen (Officer Kathleen), John Dennis Johnson (Pa Bender)
Synopsis: Some hillbillies hunting humans prove that people can be monsters too.

Supernatural, especially in the early seasons, owes *a lot* to *The X-Files* due in part to the fact that a lot of the people worked on both shows, including director and producer Kim Manners, and writer John Shiban, who wrote this and many other early ones.

Of all the early *Supernatural* episodes, "The Benders" is by far the most *X-Files*-esque. This episode, and its "evil redneck" villains, remind many folks of the infamous "inbred hillbillies" episode of *The X-Files* which was so gross that it wasn't aired in some places for a while. I don't think this episode is as successful, but it's still good and the whole "the worst monsters are people" ties in well with the tragedy of "Nightmare."

This episode is also a good companion to "Nightmare" in that we see the lengths Dean will go to for Sam here, just after seeing how far Sam went for him. The brothers are way closer now than at the beginning, and they are very much willing to kill and die for one another. Once again, I'm sure nothing can go wrong there.

Legal Trouble: This is the first time we see the boys work cooperatively with a member of law enforcement, and find out Dean is still "dead" and wanted for murder.

Shadow

Episode 1.16. Airdate: February 28, 2006
Written by: Eric Kripke
Directed by: Kim Manners
Guest Cast: Jeffrey Dean Morgan (John), Nicki Aycox (Meg)
Synopsis: Meg's back and she brought some really mean pets as part of a trap for John.

In an episode that's full of great moments, like Dean being a genius figuring out the pattern on the floor, and twists like Meg not dying after being thrown out of a building, the highlight is the long-awaited reunion between the boys and John.

And it's worth the wait.

This episode busts open the mythology, and the scenes with Meg are all excellent. The one with Meg trying to keep the deavas on a leash is a bit like John trying to keep Sam and Dean in control. So of course, they won't be together for long.

It's great to see all the Winchesters together, and the different ways that Sam and Dean relate to John are super interesting. Dean immediately reverts to an obedient soldier, while we see Sam's complicated combination of love and defiance. It's juicy and the sort of scene that works extra well with these excellent actors. We see how much they love their dad, but also get more hints that Sam has good reason to be angry at him.

Future Famous Face: Let's talk about Jeffrey Dean Morgan. At the same time he was smoldering as John Winchester, he was making other audiences and Izzie Stevens fall in love with him as Denny on *Grey's Anatomy*. The combination of both roles really put him on radars, and in the following years he rose to fame with roles in movies like *Watchmen* and then most famously, *The Walking Dead*. But we'll always think of him as Papa Winchester.

Hell House

Episode 1.17. Airdate: March 30, 2006
Written by: Trey Callaway
Directed by: Chris Long
Guest Cast: Travis Wester (Harry Spengler), A.J. Buckley (Ed Zeddmore)
Synopsis: The Winchesters learn that the internet is powerful and that some ghost hunters are idiots.

"Hell House" is notable for one big reason: it's the first time *Supernatural* really lets itself be funny. Sure, there have been quips and jokes from the get-go, but this is the first episode where parts of the plot, however dark, are pretty humorous. And it's mostly thanks to Ed and Harry.

Not only are Ed and Harry funny on their own, they allow *Supernatural* to make fun of itself, as well as the entire genre and the idea of ghost hunters in general. This is kind of meta and plays into the power of ideas, even the power of faith which the show continues to be interested in. Add in the lighter tone from the delightful prank war between Sam and Dean and some gratuitous shirtlessness, and we've got a great episode.

Spoiler Alert: Don't get too used to shirtlessness. We rarely see these guys in single layers, let alone naked.

Driver Picks the Music: In a nod to the Blue Öyster Cult logo being used throughout the episode, their song "Fire of Unknown Origin" plays while Dean pranks Sam at the beginning, as well as "Burnin' for You" which pops up later.

Fan Favorites: Ed and Harry are an annoying delight and the way they push all of Sam and Dean's buttons almost guaranteed that fans would love them… and that's why we'll see them again.

Name Game: Spengler and Zeddmore are references to Ghostbusters.
So, Get This: Richardson, Texas is Jensen Ackles' hometown.

Something Wicked

Episode 1.18. Airdate: April 6, 2006
Written by: Daniel Knauf
Directed by: Whitney Ransick
Guest Cast: Jeffrey Dean Morgan (John), Ridge Canipe (Young Dean), Alex Ferris (Young Sam), Adrian Hough (Dr. Hydeker)
Synopsis: A case from the past reveals John Winchester has always been a crappy parent and that Dean has always look out for Sammy.

Baby Winchesters! This episode has some truly scary monster (that hand!), but the best part by far is the insight it gives us into how Dean and Sam grew up. Getting to explore their relationship with each other, and with John, is a joy.

Once again, we see that the way Dean presents himself as a cocky Han Solo is just a cover for a very scared little boy, who doesn't want to disappoint his daddy or get his little brother hurt. I love seeing the way he relates to young Michael as another big brother, and how tortured Dean feels, believing that he failed long ago and now.

All season we've seen that Sam is angry at John, while Dean is loyal to him. But seeing what kind of parent John was, and what he put his sons through… it definitely makes you side with Sam. But you also have to feel bad for Dean. He's the one who raised Sam and, despite what Sam said in "Nightmare," it's because of Dean that Sam is the good person he is. Not John.

So, Get This: The previous towns Striga is said to have visited—Ogdenville, North Haverbrook, Brockway—are all fictional towns from *The Simpsons.*

Provenance

Episode 1.19. Airdate: April 13, 2006
Written by: David Ehrman
Directed by: Phil Sgriccia
Guest Cast: Taylor Cole (Sarah Blake)
Synopsis: The guys fight a haunted painting and Sam goes on a date.

I told you we weren't done with creepy children! By this point, the series has moved a bit beyond regular, specific urban myths, and is leaning more into ghosts and horror. This episode has some great ghost stuff, and see how good the Winchesters are at what they do, but the highlight is Sam finally making a love connection.

And Sarah is a great match for him. I love Dean encouraging his baby bro to go for it too. Sam and Sarah are so cute together, and I like to think they would have made a great couple if things had gone differently.

This episode is subversive in the sense that the ghost isn't who we thought, but it also nods to those bigger themes that family can be the real horror show.

Ship Shape: Sarah is great, but Sam isn't wrong that people he cares for die. Spoiler: Eventually, we will see her again and it will prove Sam entirely right.

Dead Man's Blood

Episode 1.20. Airdate: April 20, 2006
Written by: Cathryn Humphris, John Shiban
Directed by: Tony Wharmby
Guest Cast: Jeffrey Dean Morgan (John), Warren Christie (Luther), Anne Openshaw (Kate)
Synopsis: The boys reunite with John to take on a nest of vampires and recover a gun that can kill anything.

This episode takes us into the endgame of Season One, and in some unexpected ways. For one: vampires! I can understand why the show was reluctant to bring vampires in, given all the comparisons to Buffy that were made when *Supernatural* debuted, but their take on blood suckers is interesting, if not a little underwhelming at first. However, the whole idea of pulling someone into a "family" they don't want to be a part of resonates for John and Sam specifically.

Once again, the real highlight here is the family drama. John is a complicated character—just like his sons—but he's definitely not as lovable. Still, the amends scene between him and Sam does a lot of rehab for both the boys and the audience. And it's a good contrast to see Dean standing up to his old man for once as well.

And then there's The Colt.

Spoiler: we'll see a lot of this gun over the years as a plot device, but what I really love is how its existence—and Elkins' as well—points to a much larger world of hunters and mythos that we haven't seen thus far. The Winchesters aren't fighting monsters in a vacuum and that's just cool. The limits to the Colt in terms of limited bullets work well too, and John using one to save Sam is great drama.

Spoiler Alert: The victim-turned-vampire Kate shows up one more time in the series finale "Carry On," and that makes this episode a lot more emotional on rewatch.

Salvation

Episode 1.21. Airdate: April 27, 2006
Written by: Sera Gamble & Raelle Tucker
Directed by: Robert Singer
Guest Cast: Jeffrey Dean Morgan (John), Nicki Aycox (Meg), Sebastian Spence (Tom)
Synopsis: Just as the family gets back together, Meg returns to kill everyone they know to get the Colt.

Honestly, I see the final three episodes of the first season as one big, long episode, with Salvation right in the middle as the connective tissue. It's got a lot of plot, but not much deeper stuff than that.

But that doesn't mean it's not good. We see how the Winchesters work together and how it's not quite as fun with John around. And also, how the quest for revenge turns Sam into someone uncomfortably close to the worst version of his father. Much how John fell onto the path he did because of the death of Mary. This whole season isn't just about the Winchesters looking for their father and finding that they don't need him, but also that they are afraid of becoming him.

Despite that, John does okay in terms of not being a jerk, and I think his holy water trick is brilliant. But we also see how much hunting has cost—and will continue to cost—the Winchester family. When John says "this ends now" I have to laugh.

Drive Picks the Music: This is the first "Road So Far" recap set to Kansas's "Carry on Wayward Son." This song became *Supernatural*'s anthem throughout the show's run, playing at the start of every season finale, from here until Season Fourteen. In the series' finale of Season Fifteen, it was supposed to be sung by Kansas on screen, but that was cut due to the COVID-19 pandemic. Still, Kansas did sing it before the Season Thirteen panel at San Diego Comic Con in 2017. I was there and it was truly the coolest Comic Con moment ever.

Devil's Trap

Episode 1.22. Airdate: May 4, 2006
Written by: Eric Kripke
Directed by: Kim Manners
Guest Cast: Jeffrey Dean Morgan (John), Jim Beaver (Bobby Singer), Nicki Aycox (Meg), Sebastian Spence (Tom)
Synopsis: With the help of salty hunter Bobby Singer, Sam and Dean trap and exorcise Meg to find John, but the rescue doesn't go well thanks to a small case of possession.

What an ending! The idea of Sam and Dean confronting who their father is, and what they are willing to do for their family, comes full circle. Sam and Dean finally "find" their dad after a season of searching, only for the things to be even more dangerous. That's deep stuff that resonates with all of these dark family secret episodes, and it's also subversive as hell.

And that's what Season One was ultimately about: redefining family, loyalty and contemplating the cost of revenge. Dean is the one who truly needs his family, and loves them the most unconditionally and deeply. And that's beautiful. But we see in this finale where that kind of dependence leads him. It's a dark path he's going to be on for a while.

Sam is different though. He's much more like his father as we've been noticing, but he's trying to make different choices. And ultimately, that's Sam's journey for the rest of the series—navigating who he is "meant" to be, in opposition to who he wants to be.

Fan Favorite: Let's raise a glass because Bobby Singer is finally here, and *Supernatural* isn't really *Supernatural* until Bobby joins the party. The role of "helpful ally" was initially supposed to mean a return of Missouri Moseley, but she wasn't available, so Bobby Singer was created, named after co-showrunner/producer and frequent director Robert Singer. Jim Beaver was so great in this role that he ended up becoming a huge part of the world of hunters and demons.

Plot Hole/Spoiler Alert: The show doesn't seem to know what a demon really is at this point. They have "families" and some of them can teleport?

But they can also possess people? And how does John not have anything to prevent possession? It all gets clearer in the future, but it's a bit of a mess here.

So, Get This: While playing the Yellow-Eyed Demon, Jeffrey Dean Morgan could not see through the special contacts at all, so there were sandbags on the floors to guide him where to move.

Drive Picks the Music: The use of Creedence Clearwater Revival's "Bad Moon Rising" is an ominous and perfect soundtrack to the big cliffhanger.

SUPERNATURAL

CHAPTER TWO

Storm's Comin'

If Season One was about the Winchesters coming together as brothers and hunters, Season Two is about what it means to be a hunter and a Winchester. The season asks questions about sacrifice. Who gets to make it? Who's worthy of it? And how does sacrifice, and living our life for someone who has passed, affect who we are and the choices we make? What if that person wasn't a saint? With monsters of course.

The monsters are the point. But what is it that makes a monster? Is it destiny? Biology? Choice? How different are the hunters from the hunted? This is all great stuff and makes for a great season. By now, the show has truly found a rhythm and a tone, and it works so well. There's a complete writers' room this time around, with amazing additions like Ben Edlund, Sera Gamble, and Raelle Tucker striking out on their own. Everyone has clear voice that really resonates with the show.

For one, the show is literally lighter with fewer shadows, brighter lighting, and more funny episodes. And the Winchesters' world is bigger. We start developing a supporting cast of characters that don't really make an ensemble, but really expand on the interesting world of hunters.

In My Time of Dying

Episode 2.01. Airdate: September 28, 2006
Written by: Eric Kripke
Directed by: Kim Manners
Guest Cast: Jeffrey Dean Morgan (John), Jim Beaver (Bobby), Lindsey McKeon (Tessa), Frederic Lehne (Yellow Eyes)
Synopsis: Dean lingers between life and death trying to evade a reaper.

This is one of the strongest season openers of the series. I'm just going to spoil that for you now. It's super emotional for every character, and the shock of John's death is one of the biggest twists in the early series. After an entire season looking for dad, he's dead in the first episode and now the boys must reckon with his legacy.

Sam really starts growing up here, from a bratty younger brother and son, to a more confident adult. But this one is very much Dean's episode, and his scenes with Tessa the reaper are wonderfully haunting. Lindsey McKeon has such a great unearthly presence as Tessa, and Dean seems awfully close to letting go and going with her. The idea of Dean becoming a vengeful spirit introduces a "what's a monster anyway?" theme.

John's final moments are moving and the admission that he really messed up his boys is going to echo throughout the season and, really, the entire series. There's a lot of debate about whether or not John was a good father, but his sacrifice to save his son is pure Winchester and, well, starts a bit of a pattern.

Fan Favorite: Frederic Lehne as Yellow Eyes simply owns the role and brings so much fun and menace to the part.

Death Notes: We're up to Dean: 2 Sam: 0 for near death experiences. We'll also pour one out for the Impala. Poor Baby.

Spoiler Alert: The doctor says to Dean "you have some kind of angel watching over you" and hon, you have no idea.

Everybody Loves a Clown

Episode 2.02. Airdate: October 5, 2006
Written by: John Shiban
Directed by: Phil Sgriccia
Guest Cast: Samantha Ferris (Ellen Harvelle), Alona Tal (Jo Harvelle), Chad Lindberg (Ash)
Synopsis: Dean and Sam meet an old friend of John's and pick up a hunt for the scariest creature they've faced yet: A killer clown.

I love that after four episodes of vampires and demons, the writers asked themselves "what's scarier than that?" and came up with "killer clowns." While the clown plot is fun, and the reveal of Sam's clown-phobia is great, this episode is more about world building.

Ellen, Jo, Ash, and the roadhouse exist because Season Two is about really digging into, and opening, the world of hunters. And it's nice to get some women in the mix. I'm not crazy about Jo and Dean flirting, but I know people like the idea of them together, so I won't judge.

This episode is uneven, both tonally and scattered, with John's funeral juxtaposed against new characters and a hunt that's so separate from everything with an unexciting conclusion. We do see Dean's first signature "single perfect tear" and get that great breakdown at the end though. There's also Sam's own coping, trying to do what John would have wanted, but it doesn't quite mesh with the clown stuff.

Fan Favorites: Jo and Ellen are fanfic staples and hugely beloved. Ash is a capital C character and he's certainly the most fun of the Roadhouse crew. Chad Lindberg, who you may recognize from the first *Fast and the Furious* movie, has made a post-*Supernatural* career as an actual ghost hunter.

Bloodlust

Episode 2.03. Airdate: October 12, 2006
Written by: Sera Gamble
Directed by: Robert Singer
Guest Cast: Sterling K. Brown (Gordon Walker), Amber Benson (Lenore), Ty Olsson (Eli), Samantha Ferris (Ellen)
Synopsis: Sam and Dean cross paths with Gordon Walker, a brutal vampire hunter.

No more clowning around. This is a great episode that really brings the themes of grief, family, and what kind of monster those can turn you into. Gordon is meant to mirror both John, as well as the Winchesters, showing them what they might become if they give in to their own bloodlust. And it's not pretty.

After meeting nice hunters like Ellen and Bobby, it's fascinating to meet a human who's as dangerous as the monsters. Gordon is one of the best early antagonists, because he's so close to Sam and Dean. And it's nice to see Dean bond with someone, and equally sad to see him worrying about becoming a monster. And strangely it's the vamps, the so-called monsters, who are the sympathetic face here.

Also let's be superficial: Sam's hair is finally out of his face! And the shot of Dean at the end with the lens flare is absolutely gorgeous.

Familiar Faces: It's a fun bit of casting having Amber Benson, who most viewers know as Tara from *Buffy the Vampire Slayer* as an actual vampire. But of course, the standout performance here is from Sterling K. Brown as Gordon. He's incredible in the role and it's no surprise at all to *Supernatural* fans that Brown went on to win multiple Emmys for his way less murderous role on *This Is Us*.

Drive Picks the Music: The opening montage to "Wheel in the Sky" as well as the great driving sequence with the rebuilt Baby to AC/DC's "Back in Black" are great.

So, Get This: This is the first time Dean calls the Impala "Baby.

Children Shouldn't Play with Dead Things

Episode 2.04. Airdate: October 19, 2006
Written by: Raelle Tucker
Directed by: Kim Manners
Guest Cast: Amara Zaragoza (Angela Mason), Christopher Jacot (Neil)
Synopsis: What's dead should stay dead when it's a girlfriend.

We're still deep in the themes of grief, and this episode really digs into Dean's survivor's guilt over John dying for him. The zombie girlfriend monster of the week isn't the strongest, but it works well as a metaphor for the bigger emotions the boys are going through. And Angela and Neil are super creepy in a different way than we're used to.

Neil bringing back Angela to be his willing concubine is horrible, and his having sex with a zombie is so gross. And then there's the whole murder thing. Though I'm glad Sam and Dean tried to save him, I'm glad this human died!

But again, this episode is about how grief, and the refusal to let someone go, is not good. And Dean isn't dealing with John's death. He's going darker, wallowing in guilt and consumed with worry about the monsters inside the Winchester family.

Spoiler Alert: "What's dead should stay dead" becomes a theme for the rest of the series, with the Winchesters treating heaven, hell, and all other afterlife options like a revolving door. They end up an affront to Death herself and so, hearing Dean declare that in this episode is more than ironic. But it's also foreshadowing for how Dean will deal with someone he loves dying.

So, Get This: Sam says, "I think she broke my hand" because Jared Padalecki actually *did* break his hand during a stunt fight in the last episode. It wasn't discovered until filming had started for this episode, so he had to finish shooting with no cast. The line was added to explain the cast that's visible for the next few episodes.

Simon Said

Episode 2.05. Airdate: October 26, 2006
Written by: Ben Edlund
Directed by: Tim Iacofano
Guest Cast: Gabriel Tigerman (Andy Gallagher) Samantha Ferris (Ellen), Alona Tal (Jo), Chad Lindberg (Ash), Elias Toufexis (Ansem Weems)
Synopsis: Another of Sam's visions lead the boys to not one but two of the Yellow-Eyed Demon's "special children."

I love this episode for many reasons. For one, it's the first episode from Ben Edlund, who will be a fixture of the show for many years, writing some of the most out-of-the-box episodes. But it's also a quintessential *Supernatural* episode that balances the funny and absurd moments, like the painted van and Andy taking the Impala, with horrifying twists like Ansem driving people to horrific suicides.

We're once again in nature versus nurture territory here, which is very much like fate versus free will. Neither Sam, nor Dean, want Sam to be a monster, but it feels like it's something he's destined for. And Andy's goodness, and Ansem's evil, mean it could be a coin toss for Sam.

All in all, it's a great episode, though once again Jo, Ellen and Ash serve more as backdrop and convenient sources of information, rather than actual people and characters with their own story.

Driver Picks the Music: The needle drops are pretty great. I love the "Stonehenge" moment, but Dean singing "I Can't Fight This Feeling Anymore" is a great reminder that this tough hunter is a bit of a goober.

No Exit

Episode 2.06. Airdate: November 2, 2006
Written by: Matt Witten
Directed by: Kim Manners
Guest Cast: Samantha Ferris (Ellen), Alona Tal (Jo)
Synopsis: Jo stows away on a hunt with the boys that brings them face to face with the ghost of serial killer H. H. Holmes.

Supernatural rarely deals in actual history, because there's usually a disconnect between demons and real human evil. But this in one of the few places where they use a real historic figure as the monster of the week, and H. H. Holmes is a particularly good choice. He's so horrible and honestly even creepier than the show makes him!

And it works thematically because this is an episode about reckoning with history—even unknown history. Through Jo with her desire to be a hunter—despite her own dead dad—and the revelation that John got Bill Harvelle killed, Dean and Sam continue to reckon with the Winchester legacy. The sins of their father. Most of Season One was subtextually about how bad and toxic John was, and the boys can't ignore that.

But being a hunter is a dangerous, messed up life, and it's worth questioning if it's a good thing that Sam and Dean are "picking up where dad left off." He, and they, don't always save people when they hunt things. They can't. And so, it might be good that Jo is dissuaded from that life.

So, Get This: One of the pictures we see of the victims of H. H. Holmes is Elizabeth Stride, who was a victim of Jack the Ripper in London, not Holmes. However, there is a popular theory that Holmes was actually the Ripper, given that those murder coincide with a blank spot in his bloody history.

The Usual Suspects

Episode 2.07. Airdate: November 9, 2006
Written by: Cathryn Humphris
Directed by: Mike Rohl
Guest Cast: Linda Blair (Detective Diana Ballard), Jason Gerdrick (Det. Peter Sheridan)
Synopsis: Sam and Dean are arrested for two supernaturally connected murders that seem to have been committed by a ghost.

Linda Blair as Diana is the first "big guest star" episode *Supernatural* attempts, but they don't make a pattern of it. More interesting to me is how this is one of the first times we get an outsider point of view of Sam and Dean. Diana serves as our point of view for most of the episode, and we see how these guys can come across as terrifying.

This episode continues the idea of what a monster is. The ghost isn't the thing killing people—it's an officer of the law. Just like the hunters we've seen go dark side, we see a police officer break bad here, further muddying the waters of what's good and evil. The whole thing is resolved by our heroine cop Diana killing her partner. Is that foreshadowing for Sam and Dean's relationship? (And yeah, they're paralleled to a romantic couple here—it's not the first or last time that will happen).

This episode feels disconnected from the rest of the season. There's no mention of the Harvelles, or the demon, and so it stands on its own. Which is fine, but somewhat disconcerting given the episode's place in the season.

Legal Trouble: The Winchesters are both wanted men now, though Dean is extra-wanted for that murder he didn't commit. I'm glad the show remembered this aspect of their characters, because it plays out in interesting ways for a while.

Famous Faces: Linda Blair! It's a great bit of casting to get a horror legend on the show in a very human role (she played the possessed child Regan in *The Exorcist*). Dean's pea soup line is so dumb though.

Crossroad Blues

Episode 2.08. Airdate: November 16, 2006
Written by: Sera Gamble
Directed by: Steve Boyum
Guest Cast: La Monde Byrd (Robert Johnson), John Lafayette (George Darrow), Jeannette Sousa (Dean's Demon)
Synopsis: A series of violent deaths lead the Winchesters to a cluster of people who made deals with a crossroad demon.

This is one of my favorite episodes of the season for so many reasons: the use of music, the expansion of mythology, and the excellent face-off between Dean and the Crossroad Demon. It's all great and I recommend this episode to a lot of people.

Again, we're not really dealing with just monsters here. We're looking at people who made bad decisions and have condemned themselves, tying it right back into John and the boys. It tackles their sense of self-worth (or lack of that for Dean) and their hope that they can change fate.

Now we know that demons make deals and they're out there doing their demonic thing all over. And there's so much more going on in hell than we thought. We'll learn a lot more, but I love this part of the series when we're still discovering all of this.

Driver Picks the Music: Robert Johnson was a real person, and the myth of him selling his soul to the devil is legit. The music makes this episode and gives it such an incredible atmosphere, especially in the scenes with Johnson. The use of "Crossroad Blues" is particularly perfect.

Croatoan

Episode 2.10. Airdate: December 7, 2006
Written by: John Shiban
Directed by: Robert Singer
Guest Cast: Kate Jennings Grant (Dr. Amanda Lee), Bobby Hosea (Sarge), Diego Klattenhoff (Duane Tanner)
Synopsis: A vision leads Sam and Dean to a town infected by a mysterious demonic virus.

This episode is seriously dark, and tense, and like so many great episodes it plays out like a miniature movie. It's sort of thriller, where we have no idea who the monster is inside, like The Thing. And the result is a fantastic episode thanks to great performances from the guest cast and the boys.

The moment between Sam and Dean, when Sam seems to be infected and Dean is willing to die with him, is incredibly powerful, and it shows how much their relationship and lives have changed since the pilot. It's not that they weren't always ready to die together, but it's at the surface now that they have no one else. Is that healthy? Uh, no. But is it good TV? Yes.

The cinematography, and use of slow motion and weird camera stuff when the infected go berserk in this episode are not great, but on a show with no budget at all, I guess they did what they had to.

Name Game: The Winchesters use the aliases Billy Gibbons and Frank Beard, two of the members of ZZ Top.

Hunted

Episode 2.11. Airdate: January 11, 2007
Written by: Raelle Tucker
Directed by: Rachel Talalay
Guest Cast: Katharine Isabelle (Ava Wilson), Sterling K. Brown (Gordon Walker), Samantha Ferris (Ellen), Chad Lindberg (Ash)
Synopsis: Dean tells Sam that John warned Dean he might have to kill Sam. Sam takes this poorly, then meets Ava, another special child. Dean ends up held hostage by Gordon.

This one does all the things. We have a huge brother confrontation and confession, more about the Yellow Eyed demon, Gordon is back, and we meet a character who we love who is then promptly kidnapped by the demon. Whew!

The many threads going on here make this episode feel disjointed. We don't see Sam ditch Dean, or his reaction, which is extra confusing after their big confrontation. Also, I know that this episode aired in 2007, but Sam and Dean weaponizing the police against a Black man makes me uncomfortable, even though Gordon is a legitimate threat.

Once again, we're back to the big themes of what defines as monstrous and who decides who's a monster. That's about fate as well. Sam and Ava's visions are not always what happens. Sometimes, they're warnings that show fate and the future can be changed. Sam won't be a monster if he chooses not to, right? And Dean won't become Gordon if he sticks with his brother. We hope. But they've already changed. Sam doesn't want a normal life anymore, and doesn't think he can have it, and Dean is just tired of it all.

Fan Favorite: I love Katharine Isabelle as Ava, she's funny and brave, and when she disappears at the end it's genuinely scary and shocking. She's such a great mirror to Sam in that she also was once normal, and that won't work out for her.

Ship Shape: It's a shame Ava is engaged, because she and Sam would make a cute couple. Gordon and Dean… less so.

Playthings

Episode 2.12. Airdate: January 18, 2007
Written by: Matt Witten
Directed by: Charles Beeson
Guest Cast: Annie Wersching (Susan Thompson), Matreya Fedor (Tyler), Conchita Campbell (Maggie) John R. Taylor (Sherwin)
Synopsis: The Winchesters take a case at a haunted hotel where a young girl's ghost doesn't want her playmate to leave.

As Dean says, this episode is old school. It's full of references to *The Shining* and *Psycho*, and the resolution of the haunting is well, haunting. Thematically, at this point we're deep in the weeds of monsters we can understand, and the brothers struggling to keep their humanity, finding it in one another.

So, let's talk about the homoeroticism.

Yes, this episode has some very intense and emotional moments between two dudes, and honestly the whole series does. These guys have chemistry, with others and each other, and Dean in particular can find emotional or flirty moments anywhere. So, although this episode's running joke is Sam and Dean being mistaken for a couple, coupled with Dean's throwaway line in "Croatoan" that he doesn't "swing that way," it doesn't mean that it's not there.

In fact, the queer reading of these characters is perhaps the more interesting one, especially if we look at Dean's hetero façade and his constant performative masculinity. Usually that he takes to a toxic degree to cope with his with pain and insulate himself.

Ship Shape: I said I'd be fair so, to Wincest fans for whom this episode is special, I acknowledge you. This episode is a favorite among those that like to see Dean and Sam a certain way for all the reasons above.

Nightshifter

Episode 2.13. Airdate: January 25, 2007
Written by: Ben Edlund
Directed by: Phil Sgriccia
Guest Cast: Chris Gauthier (Ronald Resnick), Charles Malik Whitfield (Agent Victor Henriksen)
Synopsis: A shapeshifter who likes to rob people leads the boys to a tense hostage standoff.

What if we made Inside Man but with monsters? That's where we're at here, and whadaya know, it works! "Nightshifter" isn't just a tense cat and mouse with a monster that sees Dean and Sam outside of their comfort zone, but it also has a couple great guest characters, including one whose death hits hard.

Adorable Ronald's death at the hands of the police, rather than the monster shocking moment echoes what we've been talking about all season: how people can go off the rails and make bad choices that go very wrong. And it all ties back to Sam.

However, the shapeshifter is not an interesting monster, nor a well-developed character. It just wants money and that's all we know about it. This episode has so many other great moments though (Mandroid!) that I'll forgive it a boring monster.

Legal Trouble: "We are so screwed" Dean says and… yeah. Now the FBI is after the boys for some really good reasons. Victor Henriksen is not going away, and we certainly don't want him too. He's a great character!

Driver Picks the Music: Jensen and Jared have both cited the use of "Renegade" by Styx in the final scene as one of their favorite music cues on the show. And I agree. It's an epic needle drop and the final shot of the Impala driving off is perfect.

Houses of the Holy

Episode 2.13. Airdate: February 1, 2007
Written by: Sera Gamble
Directed by: Kim Manners
Guest Cast: Dennis Arndt (Father Reynolds), David Monahan (Father Gregory)
Synopsis: A series a murder seems to be touched by an angel.

After a season and a half of demons and the dark side, Sam spends this episode focused on a search for a higher power and some hope that he can be saved. Sam is so happy when he thinks he sees an angel mid-episode, that the look on his face when he realizes it's just a ghost hurts like hell.

Faith, like being a monster, is a choice we've seen discussed before. These boys see the worst in the world, so they of course might also look for the good. The contrast in how each brother see the world, and the possibility of a higher power, makes this a standout episode. Dean explaining his mother's last words and why he has no faith, while Sam confesses that he prays is all wonderful.

We have another "monster" that seems very justified and understandable too, adjusting our perspective. And the final scene where Dean tells Sam about how the wannabe rapist got *Final Destination*-ed, is both an act of love and a big step for Dean…

Spoiler Alert: Of course, a lot of this episode reads very differently and ironically knowing that in about 18 months an angel will pull Dean out of hell, and that angels, God and more will dominate the narrative of the show for the rest the run. In fact, we've already met angels if you count reapers (retconned into angels in Season Nine) and we'll meet another very soon.

Despite the irony, this episode still works because it sets up Dean and Sam's attitude towards heaven and God in ways that don't change, but it's still incredibly funny to see Sam talking up the archangel Michael—and angels in general—when we know that most angels in *Supernatural*… are kinda dicks.

Driver Picks the Music: "Knockin' on Heaven's Door" by Bob Dylan is used perfectly in the final scene and will be used again in another perfect brothers scene in Season Five's "Dark Side of the Moon."

Born Under a Bad Sign

Episode 2.14. Airdate: February 8, 2007
Written by: Cathryn Humphris
Directed by: J. Miller Tobin
Guest Cast: Jim Beaver (Bobby), Alona Tal (Jo)
Synopsis: Meg possesses Sam, who tries to provoke Dean into killing his brother.

This episode really goes hard on our season-long theme of the boys becoming monsters, and actually makes Sam the monster of the week this time. Or to be fair, at least a version of him. Jared does a great job as Meg, and as a not-quite-right version of Sam, and it's incredibly disturbing to see him try to assault Jo.

Poor Jo has a hard episode here. She has a sweet moment showcasing her unrequited crush on Dean, but I feel like we just leave her. And the fact that (spoiler) we don't see her again until Season Five is somewhat of a letdown. The treatment of Jo, and Dean's joke about Sam having a chick inside him, stink of sexism and misogyny, which is present a lot in early seasons and leaves a bad taste. At least Bobby's back!

Spoiler Alert: Also, looking forward, this episode isn't particularly consistent in how it characterizes Meg, especially if we take her at her word for why she's going after the Winchesters. In later seasons, she's defined by her loyalty to her cause, so her going rogue here doesn't quite click.

Ship Shape: It's unclear if the show wants us to see Jo and Dean as a romance that never found the right time, or as a brother and sister. I think it works better as the latter, but it's sadder as the former.

Tall Tales

Episode 2.15. Airdate: February 15, 2007
Written by: John Shiban
Directed by: Bradford May
Guest Cast: Jim Beaver (Bobby), Richard Speight Jr. (The Trickster),
Synopsis: Slow dancing aliens, an alligator in the sewer, and a bunch of dicks getting their just desserts.

"Tall Tales" is an all-time favorite of every *Supernatural* fan. It has everything: dogs, aliens, sewer alligators, cake, and is just so incredibly fun. But it's not just the wild urban legends that are great, it's an outside the box episode that shows us what the brothers think of each other. It also shows them just being brothers, with all the annoyance and teasing that goes along with that.

This episode is a break from all the sad and depressing, and we get Bobby stepping up to be the boy's surrogate dad after he sort of disappeared for the first half of the season, as Ellen had become the default helper character.

At first glance "Tall Tales" doesn't fit our pattern of monsters and plots with the black and white perspective of hunting. But The Trickster is an incredibly likable and fun bad guy if you can really even call him that. We, the audience, love this guy, and it's pretty sad for the minute or so that we think he's dead. Good thing we know he'll be back…

Fan Favorite: So, spoiler, Richard Speight Jr. does indeed return to the show many times, and I won't get into how until we get to his episodes, but here I want to talk about Speight as just a favorite human.

Richard Speight is the beating heart of the *Supernatural* fandom. He's our MC at conventions, which led to the indie, meta series Kings *of Con*. He's a huge presence for fans, and he's returned several times from Season Eleven onward as a director. He's absolutely wonderful, kind, and smart, and the show and fandom is so lucky to have him.

Roadkill

Episode 2.16. Airdate: March 15, 2007
Written by: Raelle Tucker
Directed by: Charles Beeson
Guest Cast: Tricia Helfer (Molly McNamara), Winston Rekert (Jonah Greely)
Synopsis: The Winchesters investigate a haunted highway with one of the ghosts that haunts it along for the ride.

What better way to continue examining our preconceptions about monsters than having one help on a hunt? I love Molly's story, especially that she doesn't know she's a monster for most of the episode. She has so much pathos, and her fate is tragic. As a character, Molly's a great narrative mirror. She's a nice monster like one brother could be, and didn't die right, like the other one.

How the boys treat her says a lot too: Sam wants to be truthful, while Dean is wary of anything not human. But that's because Sam wants to believe that monsters or ghosts can have hope. And Dean's afraid of the emotional vulnerability and accountability that comes from that line of thinking.

At this point, the boys truly don't know what happens to ghosts when they're sent off from this earth. We got a hint here and in "Houses of the Holy" that they can go into the light, and we know that hell is real, so there has to be a nice side of the afterlife too, right? One would hope.

Famous Face: Tricia Helfer is pretty much a genre legend at this point for her work on *Battlestar Galactica*, *Lucifer* and *Van Helsing*. She's one of many *Battlestar Galactica* alums we'll see on the show. Given that it also films in Vancouver, BC, that's not surprising.

Heart

Episode 2.17. Airdate: March 22, 2007
Written by: Sera Gamble
Directed by: Kim Manners
Guest Cast: Emmanuelle Vaugier (Madison)
Synopsis: A werewolf case leads Sam to a romantic connection with a potential victim who turns out to be the monster.

More like heartbreak, am I right? Madison's progression from victim, to monster, to dead by Sam's hand takes the whole season—and Sam's deep emotional connection to that—to a whole new level. He doesn't just want to save Madison because he wants to be saved himself, he falls in love with a monster. That scene is brutal, and even though Dean is a bit of a caricature for most of the episode, the final image of Dean flinching as the gunshot goes off is haunting.

We do maybe need to talk about how this is yet another woman who has died for Sam's story, but… a lot of people have died on *Supernatural*. Even people the boys were trying to save. It's not so much sexist at this point that a woman dies again, it's just that everyone dies in this show.

But let's talk about that love scene! It's one of the absolute sexiest scenes in the entire show, and when we compare it to Dean's love scene with Cassie in "Route 666" the contrast is fascinating. Dean puts himself out as all domineering and strong, while Sam seems like a puppy. But in bed, Dean is the tender, gentle lover, and Sam is Mr. Bitey McManhandling. This is a great reflection of their characters in general: Dean's actually a marshmallow and Sam is way scarier than he seems.

Ship Shape: Madison and Sam could have been so great together… alas, Sam's luck with partners is, shall we say, kind of terrible. He's got two dead lovers now and that'd give anyone a complex.

Name Game: Landis and Dante refer to John Landis, director of an *American Werewolf in London* and Joe Dante, director of *The Howling*.

So, Get This: One of the policemen is played by Rob Hayter, who would return to *Supernatural* as their stunt choreographer from Season Thirteen until the end.

Hollywood Babylon

Episode 2.18. Airdate: April 19, 2007
Written by: Ben Edlund
Directed by: Phil Sgriccia
Guest Cast: Gary Cole (Brad Redding), Elizabeth Whitmere (Tara Benchley), Regan Burns (McG), Benjamin Ratner (Walter Dixon)
Synopsis: Sam and Dean confront the horrors of a haunted film set

After the pain of "Heart," this episode is a welcome lighter hour… at least lighter for *Supernatural*. "Hollywood Babylon" continues digging at the thing behind the monster being just a person, and Dean seems to be more comfortable away from hunting. Something that will develop a lot by the end of the season. But the more important thing is that this is the first truly meta *Supernatural* episode, where the forth wall is broken so *Supernatural* can make fun of Hollywood and itself.

Here, the self-referential, self-aware humor and satire comes from the mind of Ben Edlund, who will bring us many more meta episodes in the years to come. Edlund and others will eventually crush that fourth wall to dust, and *Supernatural* will become one of the most meta shows of all time.

The episode makes fun of their own plot holes and tendencies, and many of the notes and questions from the studio/producer are actual notes that Eric Kripke and co. got from the WB or the CW. (Why is it so dark?) But it also allowed *Supernatural* to make fun of the business and set life. And it gave them an opening for so many in-jokes.

So, Get This: Yes, the episode starts with a sly reference to Jared Padalecki's time on *Gilmore* Girls (as a character named Dean no less). Also, most of the sets of "Hellhazers 2" are reused sets from recent episode, like Jonah Greeley's cabin from "Roadkill" and all the posters in the screenwriter's officer refer to previous episodes..

Folsom Prison Blues

Episode 2.19. Airdate: April 26, 2007
Written by: John Shiban
Directed by: Mike Rohl
Guest Cast: Charles Malik Whitfield (Agent Victor Henriksen), Bridget White (Mara Daniels), Jeff Kobler (Randall), Garwin Sanford (Deacon)
Synopsis: The boys get themselves arrested to investigate a haunting in a prison.

This episode is surprisingly fun for an hour mostly set in prison. It's nice to see the boys in a different setting, but just like in "Hollywood Babylon," Dean adjusts very well, very quickly. But this isn't surprising, really. Back in "Playthings" Dean talked about being tired of hunting, and we're seeing over and over again in these final episodes just how much he longs for a different sort of life. Even prison would be less of a burden for him than hunting and saving people thanks to his massive survivor's guilt, and that's really kind of sad.

And it's all kind of about empathy. All season we've been finding empathy for the monsters, and this episode is about empathy for incarcerated people. And here it's Dean exhibiting that compassion, more so than Sam actually. The deaths of the prisoners are horrifying and remind us that they don't deserve that.

So, Get This: The inmate "Tiny" is played by Cliff Kosterman, Jared and Jensen's long-time driver and bodyguard.

What Is and What Should Never Be

Episode 2.20. Airdate: May 3, 2007
Written by: Raelle Tucker
Directed by: Eric Kripke
Guest Cast: Samantha Smith (Mary), Adrianne Palicki (Jess), Melanie Scrofano (Djinn Victim), Michelle Borth (Carmen)
Synopsis: A Djinn sends Dean to a dream world where his mother never died, and he lives a normal life.

Just like "Heart" made our, um, hearts ache for Sam, this episode does that for Dean. This poor boy. The look on his face when he sees his mom and the utter happiness, he experiences for just a second is both painful and beautiful. And that's before we learn that it's all a lie and he has to give it all up.

This hour tells us so much about who Dean really is. He's a person who loves so deeply—maybe even more than Sam—and wants to have a home, to love and be loved. But he's also a man of conviction and honor who won't put his happiness ahead of his mission. His scene at John's grave is a wonderful performance by Ackles.

But there's also an element here that shows us that Dean doesn't think he deserves this. This is his fantasy world, and yet his guilt and feelings of worthlessness intrude to make it all fall apart. This desire to escape his life as a hunter and his feeling that he doesn't deserve good things will be crucial for decisions he makes in episodes to come.

Future Famous Face: Yes, that is indeed hard-drinking, demon hunter, Wynonna Earp herself, Melanie Scrofano, as the other Djinn victim in one of her earliest roles.

Spoiler Alert: We learn in Season Four that Mary was a hunter, so this version of her is an extra layer of unreal. This is also the first time we really get hints of Dean using alcohol as a coping mechanism, which will intensify in years to come.

All Hell Breaks Loose: Part 1

Episode 2.21. Airdate: May 10, 2007
Written by: Sera Gamble
Directed by: Robert Singer
Guest Cast: Samantha Smith (Mary), Jim Beaver (Bobby), Frederic Lehne (Yellow Eyes), Chad Lindberg (Ash), Gabriel Tigerman (Andy), Katharine Isabelle (Ava), Aldis Hodge (Jake Talley), Jessica Harmon (Lily)
Synopsis: Sam and other special children are tested to see who survives to lead the Yellow-Eyed demon's army.

This episode and "All Hell Breaks Loose: Part 2" can meld together as one very big finale, and I know for you bingers reading this that it's unlikely you stopped watching after seeing Sam die at the end of the episode. But I do think we owe it to the show to look at this episode alone, because it really does wrap up Sam's larger arc for the season. (We'll get to Dean next time).

Now this is the episode where Sam is truly tested. Not just as a hunter and a leader, which are natural for him, but as a compassionate person who doesn't want to be a monster. We find the origin of his powers was that he was fed demon blood as a baby. And we get to see him literally confront the best—and worst—case scenarios of what he might become: Jake, Andy, and Ava. These appear to be his options: go bad or get killed. Even Jake, who seemed so cool and kind, goes dark side.

Sam chooses compassion for Jake… and ends up dead. That's not great for him! But he died the person he wanted to be, the person Dean and everyone else admires. But after that kind of betrayal, will he stay that person? Overall this is a great episode and those final moments of Sam dying in his brother's arms are incredibly shocking and effective, even if you know what's coming next.

Death Notes: We lose many characters we love here, including Ash who suffers a rather ignominious off-screen death which feels like a waste. It's especially disappointing given how Andy's death is so sad, and Ava's is so shocking. Also, RIP to the Roadhouse, the idea and location that Eric Kripke hated.

And hey! Sam is finally on the board with a really sad and complete death, bringing our score to Dean: 2, Sam: 1.

Future Famous Face: Aldis Hodge would go onto many roles including a long run on the series *Leverage.*

Spoiler Alert: For those of you dying to know, Yellow Eyes (real name: Azazel) was looking for children with a bloodline to be Lucifer's angelic vessel, so he could release Lilith from hell and in turn could release Lucifer. It's not clear if the writers knew that at this point, but the later retcon works.

All Hell Breaks Loose: Part 2

Episode 2.22. Airdate: May 17, 2007
Written by: Eric Kripke
Directed by: Kim Manners
Guest Cast: Jeffrey Dean Morgan (John), Jim Beaver (Bobby), Frederic Lehne (Yellow Eyes), Samantha Ferris (Ellen), Aldis Hodge (Jake Talley), Ona Grauer (Crossroad Demon)
Synopsis: Dean sells his soul to bring Sam back to life. Reunited, the Winchesters, Ellen, and Bobby race to stop the Yellow-Eyed Demon's plans.

What a great finale, honestly. It ties together so much of the season and gives us both huge leaps forward in the mythology and plot, but it's also incredibly emotional with particular scenes with Jensen Ackles.

Part 1 was all about wrapping things up for Sam, so this hour brings everything we've been building up for Dean: his guilt, his self-destructiveness, his deep love for his family, and his Winchester willingness to throw himself into the pit for his loved ones.

The big emotions of this episode all rest on Ackles and he does a truly incredible job. His speaking to Sam's dead body is gutting, the tension of him making his deal is electric thanks to a great crossroad demon, and his confrontation with Bobby is so good. Add in his hero moment taking down Yellow Eyes and this episode is truly a gift for the Dean girls among us.

But what about Sam? This episode sets things up for him for next season, along with the question of if he came back "wrong." Thanks to that, we see a much darker side to him at times. How will he cope knowing his brother is going to die for him?

Ship Shape: Bobby and Ellen are a match made in heaven, let's be real. And Dean and that Crossroad Demon really have some great chemistry. Won't be the last red-eyed demon he makes bad decisions with.

Death Notes: I'll admit, seeing Sam brutally execute a Black man resonates differently now in 2021 than in 2007, but it's a moment that's *supposed* to be disturbing. The better death by far is Yellow Eyes, whose story started in the pilot and drove John to hunting. Seeing John help take him down and get a final moment with his boys is a truly great climax.

Driver Picks the Music: This is our first use of Kansas' "Carry on Wayward Son" in a season finale recap. We also have nice bookends to these two episodes with the use of Boston's "Foreplay/Long Time" at the top of part one and "Don't Look Back" at the very end.

SUPERNATURAL

CHAPTER THREE

Family Don't End in Blood

So, here we are with Dean staring down a year left to live and Sam back from the dead. *Supernatural* is coming off a consistently great second season that really deepened both the mythology, and Sam and Dean as characters. That's a hard act to follow and, sad to say, I don't think Season Three is as successful.

Season Three is not one of my favorites, and although it has some all-time great episodes, I don't think it holds together and the tone falters. This isn't necessarily the fault of Eric Kripke and the writers. In fact, the room was strong with new writers like future showrunner Jeremy Carver. Third seasons are just hard, and in the middle of this one the writers had to face down a huge challenge not of their choosing.

In late 2007 and early into 2008, the Writer's Guild of America—or the WGA—went on strike over television writers being cut out of profits from shows on digital platforms. This was extremely valid to strike about, and the results were ultimately good for writers, but it meant that production and writing shut down completely for months.

And this is why Season Three is only 16 episodes long. Production shut down after the filming of episode twelve, only to come back to finish up the season in four episodes rather than the ten planned. Thus, through no fault of the writers, the final run of episodes is incredibly rushed and messy, with major plot arcs seeded early that were either dropped or concluded in a perfunctory way.

We'll talk at the end of the chapter about why this was ultimately a good thing for the show, but as a viewer of Season Three it means this is a rough patch in our binge. The network also wanted more female characters on the show, so Katie Cassidy and Lauren Cohan were brought on as season regulars… and as two of the most unlikable characters in *Supernatural*'s history. Sigh.

This season does have some interesting themes though. It's all about legacy, about what we leave behind and how the people who love us cope when we're gone. And it's about how that trauma changes us. This plays perfectly to Dean's ticking clock and Sam staring down the barrel of a life without his brother. It's an interesting season to look at critically, and the great episodes make it worth watching for sure.

The Magnificent Seven

Episode 3.01. Airdate: October 4, 2007
Written by: Eric Kripke
Directed by: Kim Manners
Guest Cast: Katie Cassidy (Ruby), Jim Beaver (Bobby), Peter Macon (Isaac), Caroline Chikezie (Tamara)
Synopsis: The boys, Bobby and two hunters take on the seven deadly sins, but a mysterious chick saves the day.

This episode, I'll be honest, may be one of my least favorite season openers. We pick up after the events of Season Two, but don't really get much about how Sam and Dean are handling everything aside from Dean's gluttonous, lusty coping mechanisms.

Where are these guys and Bobby emotionally? Who's to say, but hey there's a girl with a knife that can kill demons. Ruby flies in like a superhero in a cool way, but her demon-killing knife takes the wind out of two seasons worth of plot tension. Spoiler: From here on out, demons are a lot less scary and more expendable monsters.

Isaac and Tamara are set up as sort of mirror for Sam and Dean, establishing the season's question of "what do we do when we lose someone, or when they become something else?" It's a good idea, but it comes at the expense of the characters we know. Isaac's introduction framed by Dean's incompetence makes Dean look dumb for a joke.

I don't like these demons at all, because they aren't frightening, and their resulting carnage is really disturbing in a not great way. I hate the way Isaac dies and its overall so sad, but not impactfully so.

Plot Holes: Where's Ellen? She was a big part of the last episode so she should get mentioned, right? No. And now that the boys know Palo Santo is toxic to demons, they're gonna use it again, right? No. And surely this thing about demons with powers they haven't seen or don't know about will be a big plot point for the season? NOPE.

The Kids Are Alright

Episode 3.02. Airdate: October 11, 2007
Written by: Sera Gamble
Directed by: Phil Sgriccia
Guest Cast: Katie Cassidy (Ruby), Cindy Sampson (Lisa Braeden), Nicholas Elia (Ben Braeden), Kathleen Munroe (Katie's Mom)
Synopsis: Dean seeks out an old flame and finds both an infestation of changelings preying on parents and a young boy who might be his son.

Now this one is a huge step up from the premiere. In terms of the hunt, the changelings keep up the show's tradition of creepy kids and are absolutely terrifying monsters. As a parent, the scenes with Katie and her mom are brutal and so disturbing for me, tapping into real fears that many of us have about not connecting with our children. About feeling alienated in our own home. And talk about dehumanizing parents and reducing them to their relationship to kids: Katie's mom doesn't even get a name!

This all does well in contrast to Dean connecting with Lisa and Ben, and how it shows him what a family and regular life could be. Knowing that he's bound for hell makes this all the more poignant, and I love his dynamic with Ben, although portraying Ben as a mini-Dean obsessed with "chicks" and calls others "bitches" is less than great.

What doesn't fit is the stuff with Sam and Ruby, which is like a whole different episode. Ruby as a character tries too hard to be a badass, but just comes off as a jerk leaving the scenes to feel very disconnected from the rest of the episode.

Future Famous Faces: Yes, that's Katie Cassidy who you may know from many seasons on *Arrow* as Laurel Lance. And yes, she's kind of terrible in this role, but she gets better by the time she's on *Arrow*.

Ship Shape: Dean and Lisa are a nice pair, even if the show doesn't do a great job defining who Lisa is as a person on her own. She's strong and loving, but that's all we can say. But that does sort of work, because going forward Dean is enamored not so much with Lisa, but the idea she represents. Which of course is terrible for a relationship.

And then there's Sam and Ruby and… ooof. We'll get there later. Just know this whole thing where Dean has a relationship that makes him want to be better, and Sam's relationship may be a corrupting influence is a dynamic, we'll see a lot.

Bad Day at Black Rock

Episode 3.03. Airdate: October 18, 2007
Written by: Ben Edlund
Directed by: Robert Singer
Guest Cast: Lauren Cohan (Bela Talbot), Jim Beaver (Bobby), Sterling K. Brown (Gordon),), Michael Massee (Kubrick), Jon Van Ness (Creedy)
Synopsis: Sam has some good luck and some bad luck.

"Bad Day at Black Rock" is the first episode of the season that I absolutely love and it's because it's a welcome change in tone after a long run of seriousness. The outing is pure fun, despite the serious violence. We get to see how good Jared and Jensen are at physical comedy, and there are some iconic scenes like Sam knocking himself out.

We continue with our themes of legacies and curses, and even discover something new about John! The curse also figures into fate and free will, and the plot talks about how good luck can turn out to be bad, and vice versa.

The less great thing? We meet Bela Talbot and… I think they were trying to make her a foil for Dean, much as Ruby was a foil for Sam. The problem is that she presents as, like Dean says, a truly awful person. She's just mean and petty and we have no real good reason to like her.

Famous Faces: Yes, that is Lauren Cohan who will go on to many seasons as Maggie on *The Walking Dead*, where she'll work with Jeffrey Dean Morgan as Negan! But interestingly, Cohan also worked with Morgan playing Martha to his Thomas Wayne in *Batman v. Superman: Dawn of Justice*. That's extra funny considering Dean says "I'm Batman" in this episode, and would go on to voice the caped crusader in the animated film *Batman: The Long Halloween.*

Sin City

Episode 3.04. Airdate: October 25, 2007
Written by: Jeremy Carver, Robert Singer
Directed by: Charles Beeson
Guest Cast Katie Cassidy (Ruby), Jim Beaver (Bobby Singer), Sasha Barrese (Casey), Robert Curtin Brown (Father Gil), Martin Papazian (Richie)
Synopsis: A town has fallen into sin. Dean has a long talk with a demon.

This episode would go into the mediocre pile were it not for the brilliant conversation between Dean and the demon Casey at its center. It's a wonderful, one-act play about good and evil, death and devotion. It's sort of like a delicious steak stuck between two slices of wonder bread.

The plot with the town gone to hell is odd, and the morality angle is a plot that we just never see again. And the stuff with Richie is just weird, because he's such an out of left field caricature unlike any hunter we've seen before. Also, Ruby continues to be too over the top rough and tough for her own good.

But everything between Dean and Casey is wonderful. The actors have such chemistry and the writing in those scenes is stellar. It's the first episode from Jeremy Carver, who will go on to be a huge part of the show and we can see his biggest strengths as a writer. We also get that this episode is all about how easy it is for people to go "bad" with just a little push, although it's a bit clumsy.

Spoiler Alert: This is our first ever mention of Lucifer, and it tags him as an angel no less. I wonder if Ruby's line about being a fallen angel on Sam's shoulder was to imply that she might be Lucifer, but that doesn't come to anything.

Driver Picks the Music: Love the use of "Run Through the Jungle" by Creedence Clearwater Revival. Nothing good seems to happen when that band shows up on the soundtrack…

Bedtime Stories

Episode 3.05. Airdate: November 1, 2007
Written by: Cathryn Humphris
Directed by: Mike Rohl
Guest Cast: Christopher Cousins (Dr. Garrison), Sandra McCoy (Crossroad Demon)
Synopsis: Fairytales come to life in violent ways. Like … really violent.

In "Bedtime Stories" the concept is kind of fun (fairy tales!), but the execution is not perfect (violence!). I think it's here that we really start to notice how different Season Three looks from the previous seasons. The colors are bright and saturated, and it's a far cry from the washed-out side roads of Season One Americana. Also, I really hate Dean calling Sam's knowledge of fairy tales "gay." It's dated, gross, and a low point.

The (bedtime) story here is an obvious parallel to Sam and Dean, with Sam refusing to "let Dean go." It's really hammered home how destructive not moving on is, because Dean couldn't move on from that loss and now, he's gone fully murderous.

I would say without a doubt that the best scene in the episode is Sam vs. The Crossroad Demon. His cold-hearted murder of the demon is seriously scary. Just a few episodes ago, he was upset at Ruby for doing the same, and now he kills a girl being possessed without remorse. But also having both the colt and the demon-killing knife on the show makes demons so much more disposable that it's honestly too easy.

Spoiler Alert/Plot Hole: The demon mentions she has a boss who is scarier than her and uses "he" pronouns. I have no idea who this was supposed to be, because eventually it's revealed that the feminine demon Lilith holds Dean's contract.

Name Game: Detectives Plant and Page is a reference to Led Zeppelin. For the amount that Zeppelin is reference on the show, it's a real shame the producers could never afford to actually use their music in an episode.

Red Sky at Morning

Episode 3.06. Airdate: November 8, 2007
Written by: Laurence Andries
Directed by: Cliff Bole
Guest Cast: Lauren Cohan (Bela Talbot), Ellen Greer (Gert Case)
Synopsis: It's the ghost ship one.

Along with "Bugs," and the racist truck, this episode is later cited as one of the worst and… yeah. It's pretty terrible! We don't get anything that resonates with the themes of the season. It's just… a weird ghost ship story. Not a shock that the episode's credited writer, Laurence Andries, never writes another episode after this.

There are fun moments though, like the water effect on the ghost brothers. And Dean wears a tux! But Bela is just so dang mean to the Winchesters, and such a horrible person that watching this hour is torture. And the running gag with an older woman having the hots for Sam is lazy too.

Like Ruby, Bela ends up overwritten, as the writers attempt to make her seem cool by constantly insulting Sam and Dean. But we viewers like Sam and Dean, so that's a terrible strategy. Her lines aren't banter or snark, they're just hostile. And we learn that she killed a family member! She's completely terrible, and not even Lauren Cohan's questionable accent or pretty underbite can save this character.

Spoiler/Irony Alert: One of the names in Sam's ritual to summon the sailor ghost's brother is "Castiel." We're so close, guys.

Ship Shape: I will say, the ship looks very cool.

Fresh Blood

Episode 3.07, Airdate: November 15, 2007
Written by: Sera Gamble
Directed by: Kim Manners
Guest Cast: Lauren Cohan (Bela), Sterling K. Brown (Gordon Walker), Michael Massee (Kubrick), Matthew Humphreys (Dixon), Mercedes McNab (Lucy)
Synopsis: Gordon becomes a vampire, which really bites.

This is a seriously good episode, and it marks an upswing for a season that's been rocky so far. But I guess anything seems good after the friggin' ghost ship. This hour digs into questions of who we leave behind, and if life is worth living without family. Gordon's losses, transformation, and commitment to his cause and legacy all mirror where Sam and Dean are at right now.

Gordon is terrifying, but complicated, and he's a really fascinating exploration of how a person can become a monster. Sterling K. Brown is, and always has been, amazing in the part (no surprise he went on to so many awards) but what's interesting is how much of himself he retains as a literal vampire.

He's a dark mirror for Sam here, foreshadowing what he could become with a mission and not family. And that makes Dean's resignation to his fate even more upsetting. Sam continues to get really dark in this episode and losing Dean won't change that. In other news, Bela is still terrible! So, it's not a perfect episode.

Familiar Faces: We've got two here! We have another *Buffy* alum as a vampire Mercedes McNab, who played Harmony. And then we've got Michael Massee back as Kubrick, who former goths like me will recognize as Funboy from *The Crow*.

Death Notes: Gordon's beheading is the most brutal kill we've seen so far. It's dramatic for what it means for Sam, satisfying because Gordon was so bad, and tragic because he died as the thing he hated most. Bravo.

A Very *Supernatural* Christmas

Episode 3.08. Airdate: December 13, 2007
Written by: Jeremy Carver
Directed by: Phil Sgriccia
Guest Cast: Ridge Canipe (Young Dean), Colin Ford (Young Sam), Spencer Garrett (Edward Carrigan), Merrilyn Gann (Madge Carrigan)
Synopsis: The boys hunt a bad Santa that turns out to be a pair of perky pagan gods.

I love Christmas and I love the Winchesters, so I obviously love this episode. It does what *Supernatural* does best, combining the absurd with the scary and emotional for a result that's a gift. It's a recipe that's subversive as heck and a holiday classic here.

We get a very poignant "final holiday" for the boys with a great flashback to the tiny Winchesters. Ridge Canipe and Colin Ford are great as young Sam and Dean, and finally getting the backstory on Dean's amulet is a great way of integrating a long-established prop into the story. And every scene between adult Sam and Dean, especially the final Christmas celebration, is brotherly perfection. There isn't much mirroring here. Just nostalgia and love, front and center.

I also love the Carrigans and their interactions with the Winchesters, even though I usually hate the whole "pagan gods are monsters" thing, because they're so darn fun as villains. Even if that's not how gods work. We know that in "real life," Dean especially would swear like a sailor, so I love the "I'll fudging kill you" bit.

So, Get This: When Sam gives Dean the eggnog, Jared had spiked it with a lot of real rum as a prank, and the face Jensen makes is his legitimate reaction to the sip. The show liked it so much they kept it in.

Malleus Maleficarum

Episode 3.09. Airdate: January 31, 2008
Written by: Ben Edlund
Directed by: Robert Singer
Guest Cast: Katie Cassidy (Ruby), Marisa Ramirez (Tammi), Erica Cahill (Elizabeth), Kristin Booth (Renee)
Synopsis: It's a witch hunt until it's a demon hunt.

Great episodes of *Supernatural* are the ones that start one way, and end up somewhere really unexpected. They subvert and play with our expectations as an audience. Going into an episode about witches, only to end up with an exploration of what makes people into pure evil, is a welcome surprise.

The whole transforming into a monster thing is something that has been explored a lot, but this time it's not about Sam, but rather Dean and his being contractually bound for a trip to the pit to become that which he hates. This changes the entire way we see demons on the show and makes his fate even scarier. It also makes you wonder if there's any chance at all for free will.

Ruby's spiel about remembering what it was like to be a human is pretty convincing, and it does help make her a little more likable. At the same time, Sam is getting scarier. And he's doing it to be more like Dean. The thing is, the brutal, hard person Sam sees as his big brother isn't accurate. Not completely. Dean has far more heart and humanity than that, and he doesn't want to lose those.

Name Game: "Detective Bachman" and "Detective Turner" are references to, shocker, Bachman Turner Overdrive.

Ship Shape: Are Ruby and Sam supposed to be having chemistry at this point?

Dream a Little Dream of Me

Episode 3.10. Airdate: February 7, 2008
Written by: Cathryn Humphris (teleplay), Sera Gamble (story)
Directed by: Steve Boyum
Guest Cast: Lauren Cohan (Bela), Jim Beaver (Bobby), Cindy Sampson (Lisa), G. Michael Gray (Jeremy Frost)
Synopsis: The boys (with an assist from Bela) take on a dream job to save Bobby.

This is a great episode that gets overlooked, because the next episode is one of the series' all-time best. We get so much here. For one, it's the nicest Bela ever gets, even though Sam's sex dream about her is incredibly weird and feels out of character. My theory is that she was using some dream root to mess with Sam, but who knows.

We also finally learn why Bobby started hunting, and it's heart-breaking. Jim Beaver is always incredible, but here he's exceptionally good at combining rough edges and gruffness with deep feelings and love. And we also get scarier Sam! Maybe the sex dream was some sort of hint at Sam getting "darker" that never came to anything.

But the best scene in the episode is Dean vs. Dean. We're literally seeing into his head here and his belief that he's a worthless, blunt weapon. And all this poor boy wants, and needs, is someone to have picnics with and say they love him. Sorry I have to go cry.

Ship Shape: Dean is very much in love with the idea of Lisa and the fantasy of a normal life that she and Ben represent.

Spoiler Alert: You know, one day, someone will tell Dean they love him because he's not just daddy's blunt instrument and… yeah, I need to go cry again.

Driver Picks the Music: The Doobie Brother's song "Long Train Running" used in this episode asks, "without love, where would you be now?" and that's sort of the central question of the series so far. It's also a popular song at *Supernatural* conventions.

Mystery Spot

Episode 3.11, Airdate: February 14, 2008
Written by: Jeremy Carver (Story, Teleplay), Emily McLaughlin (Story
Directed by: Kim Manner
Guest Cast: Jim Beaver (Bobby), Richard Speight Jr. (The Trickster)
Synopsis: Yesterday was Tuesday but today is Tuesday too!

This isn't just the high point of Season Three, it's one of the best episodes of the whole series. I love this episode, because it takes what's best about *Supernatural* and dials it up to 11. Once again, we have an episode that's kooky and funny, but in a seriously dark way, until it's suddenly pure angst and pain in that final third.

The time loop of Dean deaths is brilliant. My favorite has to be "do these tacos taste funny to you?" tied with maybe the golden retriever. And the brother moments of Dean annoying Sam are so fun and a great contrast to Sam's heartless life, post-Dean.

This episode really does riff on the season's themes of what makes us human, where that humanity comes from, and how we treat and love. And how losing them can take that all away. It's a hard lesson for Sam, especially after Dean just decided that he wants to live. The Trickster is there to make the point that it won't be that easy.

Death Notes: Welp. How do we score this given that Sam lost count of how many times Dean died? If we go with on-screen, or specifically mentioned, we have 11 deaths. So, we're at Dean: 13, Sam 1. Sammy's gotta step up his game!

Spoiler Alert: Knowing who the Trickster is makes this episode extra interesting, given that he might understand what Sam and Dean's fates are in the big picture. Just like he will try to in "Changing Channels," this episode keeps the boys on their fated course.

Driver Picks the Music: Try to listen to Asia's "Heat of the Moment" and not think of this episode. Just try.

Jus In Bello

Episode 3.12. Airdate: February 21, 2008
Written by: Sera Gamble
Directed by: Phil Sgriccia
Guest Cast: Katie Cassidy (Ruby), Lauren Cohan (Bela Talbot), Charles Malik Whitfield (Agent Victor Henriksen), Aimee Garcia (Ella Fitzgerald), Tyler McClendon (Phil Amici)
Synopsis: Caught by Henriksen, the boys are under siege in a small sheriff's department.

Another great episode, "Jus In Bello" deals with heroism, humanity, and how far the Winchesters are willing to go for their missions and for each other. Bela continues to be utterly horrible, but Ruby is at least interesting as a "devil on the shoulder." The stand-out interactions however are with Henriksen who goes easily from foe to ally. I love Dean's confession to him that he thinks the world is gonna end bloody, but he chooses to go down fighting. That's our Dean.

This is also a great action episode with an excellent spin on siege-based flicks and horror movies where the heroes are trapped. It's a common trope, because it's the kind of situation that creates new alliances and loyalties, while revealing who really care. In this case, it revealed that Sam and Dean are still good people who won't sacrifice innocents…usually. Which makes Lilith's introduction at the end all the more upsetting.

Ship Shape: Listen, I'm not saying it would be a healthy relationship, I'm just saying that Dean and Victor have a lot of fun moments. And Dean, sweetie, no one who actually "doesn't swing that way" mentions it that much.

Legal trouble: The Winchesters are legally dead now! Which is convenient but also, might not stick.

Future Famous Faces: That's Aimee Garcia as Nancy Fitzgerald. Garcia would go on to play Ella Lopez in another show about demons, angels, and God: *Lucifer*! And seriously if you love *Supernatural*, check out *Lucifer*.

So, Get This: This was the final episode that aired before the writers' strike forced the show into a months-long hiatus. It could have been the last ever episode of the series, which would have been quite the unsatisfying and dark conclusion. Interestingly, this episode was originally written to air before "Mystery Spot."

Ghostfacers

Episode 3.13. Airdate: April 24, 2008
Written by: Ben Edlund
Directed by: Phil Sgriccia
Guest Cast: Travis Wester (Harry), A.J. Buckley (Ed), Brittany Ishibashi (Maggie), Austin Basis (Spruce), Dustin Milligan (Adam J. Corbett), John DeSantis (Freeman Daggett)
Synopsis: Sam and Dean get trapped in a haunted house with idiot ghost hunters Ed and Harry, as well as their crew of "Ghostfacers."

This is the first of four episodes post writers' striker that rush to the end of the season, and it's by far the best of them. It's another meta, outside the box episode from Ben Edlund, and the reality show format is a tongue-in-cheek reference to how reality TV flourished when there were no scripted shows on the air.

It's funny, surprisingly dark (our favorite) and uses a unique format to give us a different perspective on the Winchesters' story. I love how "Ghostfacers" confirms that, were they not on a network show, Dean and Sam's language would be way saltier. And it's always great to be reminded of how terrifying the Winchesters are to outsiders.

The interesting part of the episode though is the gay storyline. I like that we get a surprisingly moving scene between Ed and Corbett, and when Ed confesses his love it does nod to how love doesn't just mean romance. But this is also the second explicitly gay character on the show, and the second one to die, which—while not bad on its own—plays into the larger "bury your gays" trope that many shows struggle with to this day.

Ship Shape: "Gay love can pierce through the veil of death and save the day" is a nice summation of the rest of the series to be honest.

Future Famous Faces: Dustin Milligan would go on to be adorable on many projects, most notably as Ted on *Schitt's Creek.* AJ Buckley has also done well for himself with a role on *SEAL Team 6* where he is absolutely ripped it.

Long Distance Call

Episode 3.14. Airdate: May 1, 2008
Written by: Jeremy Carver
Directed by: Robert Singer
Guest Cast: Jeffrey Dean Morgan (John - Voice), Tom O'Brien (Clark Adams), Anjul Nigam (Stewie), Cherilyn Wilson (Lanie)
Synopsis: Dead people keep calling the living.

This episode isn't bad, but it's also not good. It's rushed, and it's sloppy, but we can't blame anyone for that. Story-wise, it's very much on theme about how loss changes people and makes them to do terrible or tragic things. But it's also about hope and faith.

Hope is a curious thing in *Supernatural*, because it usually doesn't pan out in the ways anyone expects. Faith is tricky too. Sam and Dean literally know what goes bump in the night, but at this point they have no faith in a higher power or hold any hope that anyone else can save them or the world. For the brothers, the real source of their hope and faith is, and always will be, each other. Family is everything in this show.

The Winchesters have family, and the crocatta exploits that because it's the one thing they believe in. They also have daddy issues, which I'm sure are resolved, right?

Name Game: Detectives Campbell and Raimi are references to Bruce Campbell and Sam Raimi, star, and director of the *Evil Dead* movies.

Time Is on My Side

Episode 3.15. Airdate: May 8, 2008
Written by: Sera Gamble
Directed by: Charles Beeson
Guest Cast: Lauren Cohan (Bela), Jim Beaver (Bobby), Steven Williams (Rufus Turner), Billy Drago (Doc Benton)
Synopsis: Sam hunts down a creepy immortal doctor, Dean hunts down Bela.

This is another episode heavy on the theme of how we stay human, and how the people in and around the hunter life lose their humanity in different ways. Doc Benton (played to creepy perfection by Billy Drago) is a literal reminder of how someone can become a monster, just by trying to evade their fate.

Bela is also a good example of this as well, coming through at the last minute with some semblance of a character arc. Though she doesn't really redeem herself, we do end up with some empathy for her when we find out why she sold her soul. And then we have Rufus, who shows us what happens to hunters who do survive—bitter, broken, and cynical. None of it is great and all bodes ill for Dean whether he survives or not.

But this episode is definitely rushed. The two different hunts could have been two different episodes, and they probably would have been if the season hadn't been truncated. Now we're going into the finale with one big question: will Dean make it?

Death Notes: Bye Bela, have fun becoming a demon. It will suit you!

Fan Favorite: Steven Williams is so great as Rufus, and his scene just talking with Dean is the highlight of the episode. Williams is a great actor and Rufus is a character we'll see more of and learn to love.

Spoiler Alert: We learn in Season Five that Bela tried trading the Colt to Crowley to win back her soul. I like to think that the little English demon girl talking to Bela is Crowley too.

No Rest for The Wicked

Episode 3.16. Airdate: May 15, 2008
Written by: Eric Kripke
Directed by: Kim Manners
Guest Cast: Katie Cassidy (Ruby), Jim Beaver (Bobby), Sierra McCormick (Lilith)
Synopsis: The Winchesters race against time to find Lilith, kill her and save Dean. As usual, it goes terribly, and Dean is killed and dragged to hell.

Now *that* is a cliffhanger! While it wasn't the original intention at the top of the season, the writers made the bold move to end the finale with Dean literally in hell. It's so shocking, and sets up so much, that I can't imagine what it felt like to watch live! But we're binge watching, and as you might guess from 12 seasons remaining, things work out more or less okay. I mean, they suffer terribly, but they live. Mostly.

But what this unexpected ending does for an uneven season is make us want to know what happens next. Our beloved Dean is in hell and Sam isn't vulnerable to Lilith's powers! It's so much plot, with so many emotional moments and goodbyes, that it works pretty dang well. On top of this, we got seriously disturbing possessed kids and some great moments from Bobby and Ruby.

Spoiler Alert: Let's talk about Ruby. Dean is 100% correct about her when we're looking in hindsight. She's manipulating Sam so he'll start drinking demon blood to help bring back Lucifer. She gets out because she's working with Lilith and it would have been better if they had just killed her. But that wouldn't have been as fun.

Driver Picks the Music: Can anything equal the poignancy and brotherly emotion of the boys rocking out to Bon Jovi's "Wanted Dead or Alive?"

Death Notes: Yes! Dean's goodbye to Sam is so sad, and emotional, and good! Spoiler: we'll see other goodbyes like this, but most don't hurt like the first one. Until the last. More than others so far this death seems to stick. Our score is now: Dean: 14, Sam 1.

SUPERNATURAL

CHAPTER FOUR

Raised From Perdition

We've made it, my friends. After the dark Americana and uneven expansion of the first three seasons, we've reached the season where *Supernatural* transforms into what it's known for. No longer does it merely alludes to questions of free will, and the role of family and love in maintaining our humanity, it moves to directly addresses them. And stabs them in the face. This is where *Supernatural* goes from really good to truly great.

Season Four is one of my favorites, because the writers—including new addition Julie Siege, as well as Andrew Dabb and Daniel Loflin—come in firing on all cylinders. And that's thanks to the introduction of one plot device that was never part of Kripke's original plan: Angels. But the spin is that most of them are kind of dicks, and it keeps the tone of the show consistent.

Here's Kripke himself explaining:

"If you had asked me in Season One, were there going to be angels in *Supernatural*, I would have said "absolutely not, you're fired." Up to that point I always felt like I didn't want any supernatural good guys in the show. If there was any force of good, it was going to be Sam and Dean, and they were going to be overwhelmed and outgunned. And as we were kicking towards the end of Season Three and we were doing lots of demon stories, I was worried that we were overplaying the demon stuff. But the idea that angels could be dicks and that they didn't have to be this warm fuzzy helpful force, they could actually be a really interesting antagonist, once I kind of realized that, I said, "I've never seen that depiction of angels on television before." It wasn't just these two boys versus all these demons; it became Sam and Dean trapped in the middle of this massive war where you had two sides battling, and humanity, represented by the boys, were caught in the middle, so how do they play both sides against the other? It balanced the mythology in a way that I think made it much more satisfying."

The introduction of angels, and all the Biblical/apocalyptic story that come with them, provides the show with plot fuel that lasts 12 more seasons and expanded the core cast of the show with Misha Collin's Castiel. Over time, he would become an integral part of the Winchester dynamic in a way few other characters had or ever will.

Since Season Two, the writers tried—with varying degrees of success—to zoom out from just Sam and Dean. Ellen, Jo, Ash and the roadhouse were their first attempt to give the boys a sort of home base. But it turned out that Bobby was a better foil for them, so that quickly fizzled.

And as much as I love Bobby, he's the definition of a supporting character. He doesn't have divided loyalties and, while once a season or so he has an issue that the Winchesters need to help with, he doesn't challenge them or the audience. Bela and Ruby were supposed to do that, but Bela was, let's say too challenging. And Ruby sort of worked, but she was primarily attached to Sam. So where does that leave Dean?

This season we'll see how it's Castiel that steps into that role, as a dynamic, intriguing character with a definite arc. He's also someone who we immediately like, and whose relationship with the boys—especially Dean—makes things interesting.

We also continue with some series-long themes like, what makes a monster, related to Sam's season-long descent into darkness, and who gets saved and if that's a reason for faith as it relates to Dean. Both of these are ultimately about fate and free will as we consider: if there's a God, why is he letting an apocalypse happen?

Lazarus Rising

Episode 4.01. Airdate: September 18, 2008
Written by: Eric Kripke
Directed by: Kim Manners
Guest Cast: Jim Beaver (Bobby), Misha Collins (Castiel), Genevieve Padalecki — as Genevieve Cortese (Ruby), Thunderbird Dinwindle —as Traci Dinwindle (Pamela Barnes)
Synopsis: An angel in a trench coat named Castiel raises Dean from Hell.

This episode is straight up fantastic. For one, the opening as Dean gets his bearings in a deserted world reminds me of a zombie movie, and the slow build of mystery and dread as little bits are revealed is great. Just the handprint on his shoulder alone is an incredible image, and it's the stuff a million fanfics are made of.

The Winchester reunion is also terrific, and I love the little moment where Sam returns Dean's amulet to him. And everything with poor Pamela is great as well. Heck, the demon stuff, the reveal of Ruby in a new body, and the news that Sam can expel demons is huge and awesome too!

But nothing compares to Castiel's entrance. It's iconic. The lightning, the graffiti on the barn doors. The trench coat. And those awesome wings! Misha Collin's unearthly performance, and his instant connection with Dean, are perfection. No wonder Cas sticks around for so long; how could we let a character introduced in such a cool way, go?

So, Get This: Knowing that the dirt Dean crawls through in the opening is ground-up chocolate cookies is almost as great as knowing the holy water that gets splashed in his face is lube!

Fan Favorites: Yes, Cas. But also, we have to give some love to Thunderbird Dinwindle as Pamela, who is so much fun and such a great character. And we have a new Ruby in the person of Genevieve Cortese. She may not be everyone's favorite character or guest star, but she's certainly Jared Padalecki's given that, after meeting on the show, Gen and Jared were married in 2010.

Ship Shape: Sam and the new Ruby have a lot more chemistry than her last meat suit, and were obviously up to something which doesn't bode well for her life expectancy. And then there's Dean and Cas, and I don't think there's a better meeting than being raised from hell and stabbed at first sight.

Driver Picks the Music: The song that plays briefly from Sam's iPod in the Impala is by an artist named Jason Manns, a good friend of both Jared and Jensen, and who became a fixture at *Supernatural* conventions. He has also recorded several albums of covers with the *Supernatural* cast, including an excellent Christmas album.

Are You There, God? It's Me, Dean Winchester

Episode 4.02. Airdate: September 25, 2008
Written by: Sera Gamble (story, teleplay), Lou Bollo (story)
Directed by: Phil Sgriccia
Guest Cast: Nicki Aycox (Meg), Jim Beaver (Bobby), Chris Gauthier (Ronald Resnick), Charles Malik Whitfield (Victor Henriksen), Misha Collins (Castiel), Genevieve Padalecki (Ruby)
Synopsis: The ghosts of people that Dean and Sam failed to save rise to torment them.

We're in psychological territory here and I like that. Sera Gamble is always good at getting inside the Winchesters' heads, seeing how they tick and how they hurt. We see how deeply Dean and Bobby are burdened by their guilt, and how weirdly Sam isn't. But it makes sense. Sam's got his own (sometimes very literal!) demons to deal with.

There's a lot of foreshadowing, especially with Dean's big confrontation with the real Meg Masters. She talks about being ridden for months by evil, and Dean gives the slightest flinch that tells us that there's a lot about his time in hell he's not saying. This episode also asks extremely big questions about God and the existence of evil. Questions no one, not even an angel like Castiel, can answer.

But boy does that angel smolder when he meets with Dean. I loved Dean's "I just told an angel I would kick his ass" look, and really the entire Dean and Castiel scene. Especially as it sets up the rest of the season's structure with 66 seals needing to be broken to release Lucifer. It's notable that the first seal is a failure. This whole episode is about a hunter's failures and why they deserve to live and be saved.

So, Get This: This episode gives story credit to Lou Bollo, who was the series' long-time stunt coordinator.

Ship Shape: Did they expect to have a super intense scene with Dean and Castiel getting in one another's faces, and not have us ship them???

In The Beginning

Episode 4.03. Airdate: October 2, 2008
Written by: Jeremy Carver
Directed by: Steve Boyum
Guest Cast: Misha Collins (Castiel), Genevieve Padalecki (Ruby), Mitch Pileggi (Samuel Campbell), Matt Cohen (John Winchester), Amy Gumenick (Mary Campbell)
Synopsis: Castiel sends Dean back to 1973 to learn some family history.

Time travel! This episode is like a really sad, violent version of *Back to the Future*. Turns out Dean himself was involved in some of the events that altered his own life. It's kind of mind-bending, but the emotional moments between Dean and his family work so well that this is a stand-out.

For the first time we have an episode where one brother is almost completely absent. Normally it would be odd to have an episode without Sam, but we get other family in his place, along with Castiel to give Dean meaningful looks and generally be attractive and mysterious. Matt Cohen and Amy Gumenick are great as John and Mary, and we also learn a lot about Azazel.

Honestly I have no idea if this was always the plan for him. It seems like the show changes what happened to Sam, and why, a lot in the first few years. But from here on they settle on it. In general, this is an episode that keeps up the theme of fate and pushes the idea that nothing we do can change destiny. Not very encouraging.

Famous Faces: Mitch Pileggi is best known to audiences as Skinner from *The X-Files,* but he's just so great here both as Samuel and as Azazel. His demonic scenes with Dean are so creepy and uncomfortable, and the same goes for Mary. Pileggi has a huge resume, but interestingly he'll play Jared Padalecki's father after this in the series *Walker*.

So, Get This: This is the first time Castiel says "Hello, Dean."

Metamorphosis

Episode 4.04. Airdate: October 9, 2008
Written by: Cathryn Humphris
Directed by: Kim Manners
Guest Cast: Genevieve Padalecki (Ruby), Dameon Clark (Jack Montgomery), Ron Lea (Travis), Joanne Kelly (Michelle Montgomery)
Synopsis: Dean finds out about Sam's power then the boys hunt another guy turning into a monster called a Rougarou.

The first three episodes of this season were focused on Dean—and with good reason since he did just rise from hell—but this is a big time for Sam that really dives into him as a character.

Jack Montgomery, the man with a taste for raw meat and wife, is an obvious mirror for Sam, who Dean says is becoming a monster. Sam feels that he's tainted by demon blood, but thinks he can decide to be good. His pleas to Jack to choose not to give into his monster nature might as well be Sam giving himself a pep talk. "It's not who you are, it's what you do." It's a mantra for Sam and reminds us why we love the big guy. But it doesn't work out for Jack, and we're left wondering if things won't work out for Sam.

Now we're back to themes of sympathetic monsters trying to outrun their fate, and Jack is a really interesting monster (though I don't like how gross, and at times rape-y, his scenes are). But while Season Two was asking "what makes a monster?" Season Four wants to know "what happens after you become one?" And also, do some monsters, as Cas puts it, deserve to be saved?

So, Get This: This is the first time Dean refers to Castiel as "Cas." The scripts and subtitles add an S for some reason to spell it "Cass" which is weird and wrong. We're calling him Cas here.

Monster Movie

Episode 4.05. Airdate: October 16, 2008
Written by: Ben Edlund
Directed by: Robert Singer
Guest Cast: Todd Stashwick (Dracula/Shifter), Melinda Sward (Jamie), Michael Eklund (Ed Brewer)
Synopsis: It's a black and white double feature as Sam and Dean take on a shapeshifter that lives his life as classic movie monsters.

Supernatural can do outside-the-box episodes like no one else. After last season's foray into reality TV with "Ghostfacers," now Ben Edlund gives us a full-on salute to the silver screen monsters of old. This is an all-time great episode that manages to be creative and funny, honor the horror genre's history, and also be scary and sad. Perfect.

We're still on our theme of monsters we can feel for, but much like Jack last episode, "Dracula" ultimately chose violence because he was lonely. It's a very smart, subtle take on The Phantom of the Opera, and serves as a mirror for both Sam and Dean. Sam went pretty dark when he was alone while Dean was in hell, and Dean, well, there's a lot going on with him. A lot of darkness and violence that needs digging into. And that's why this episode is just so so good.

Dean's most interesting moment here may be when he tells Jamie he feels better about his life, now that he has a mission from God. And obviously that's going to go wrong. The idea that someone has some faith in Dean as a good person is really sweet.

Fan Favorite: I adore Todd Stashwick in this role. It's a one off but he's just so incredibly funny, sad, and scary in such a short span of time that he rates as one of my favorite monsters of the week.

Spoiler Alert: This is not the only time in the series Dean claims he's a virgin.

Name Game: Agents Angus and Young reference the guitarist for AC/DC.

Yellow Fever

Episode 4.06. Airdate: October 23, 2008
Written by: Andrew Dabb & Daniel Loflin
Directed by: Phil Sgriccia
Guest Cast: Jim Beaver (Bobby), Sierra McCormick (Lilith), Jack Conley (Sheriff Al Britton)
Synopsis: They could also have called this "Dean Winchester Scared Stupid."

This is the first episode from the writing team of Andrew Dabb and Daniel Loflin, names you'll see for the rest of the series. And they hit it out of the park with an all-time classic. Like so many *Supernatural* greats, this episode is funny and wacky, until it's suddenly dark and terrifying. One minute, Dean's afraid of snakes and screaming at cats, the next he's hallucinating about demons and going back to hell, while Bobby and Sam brutally scare a ghost into oblivion.

Jensen Ackles is simply incredible here. We know that he can tear our hearts out as Dean, but he's also just so funny. He's not self-conscious on screen, so he can do things like run from a yorkie or drunkenly flirt with a sheriff receptionist, and it works. His "we are insane!" speech to Sam is perfect, and so is his terror towards the end of the episode. Jared does a great job too as the straight man, giving Dean some patented Sam "bitch faces" throughout.

And once again, we have a riff on this idea of a monster who went bad for reasons we can understand. In this case, it was fear and loneliness that turned Luther and created the ghost sickness. And that was true of the husband who killed Luther too. It's something that keeps coming up this season: the horrible things we do when we think we're alone.

Spoiler Alert: This is where we start getting some big hints about what happened to Dean in hell. Or more specifically, what he did.

Driver Picks the Music: Jensen's lip-sync performance to Survivor's "Eye of the Tiger" happened when the cameras were rolling, and Jared decided not to walk into the shot and see what would happen. The rest is history…

So, Get This: Jim Beaver is fluent in Japanese, and responding to Sam in Japanese was his idea.

Name Game: As noted, Agents Tyler and Perry are a reference to Aerosmith.

It's The Great Pumpkin, Sam Winchester

Episode 4.07. Airdate: October 30, 2008
Written by: Julie Siege
Directed by: Charles Beeson
Guest Cast: Misha Collins (Castiel), Robert Wisdom (Uriel), Ashley Benson (Tracy), Don McManus (Don Harding/Samhain)
Synopsis: A witch raises an ancient demon called Samhain to break one of the 66 seals.

This is another one of those subversive episodes, starting one way before taking a big turn. Here, it goes from a fun Halloween episode to a meditation on the righteousness of angels, and a big step forward in the season-long story about said angels.

Sam finally gets to meet angels and, well, much as Halloween is much darker than it's advertised, angels are much more dickish than Sam had hoped. The introduction of Uriel as the bad cop to Castiel's slightly nicer, squinty cop, is a good move that makes heaven truly scary, putting the angels in opposition to Sam. That's something that's going to push Sam towards his powers, and drive a wedge between the brothers.

But in contrast to Uriel, we get a big humanizing moment for Cas where he expresses that he has doubts about his mission. In the final, fantastic scene in the park, Cas shows vulnerability by emotionally connecting with Dean for the first time. He's so ethereal and sincere that it sets up real conflict for us. Maybe we can trust Cas, just not the angels. And what the heck does Uriel know about Dean's time in hell? Does the fact that Castiel knows what Dean did, and still confides in him, make a difference for how much Dean trusts him?

Future Famous Faces: Ashley Benson would go on to over 160 episodes as Hanna on *Pretty Little Liars*.

Ship Shape: I mean, do you think Dean telling Cas he'd defy heaven to save innocent people is the moment Cas starts falling for him? I'd say so.

Wishful Thinking

Episode 4.08. Airdate: November 6, 2008
Written by: Ben Edlund (Teleplay and story), Lou Bollo (Story)
Directed by: Robert Singer
Guest Cast: Ted Raimi (Wesley Mondale), Anita Brown (Hope Lynn Casey), Michael Teigen (Teddy the Suicidal teddy bear).
Synopsis: Be careful what you wish for because sometimes you get a suicidal teddy bear.

After a black and white episode, a funny episode, and a holiday episode, it's starting to feel like the season is relying too heavily on gimmicks and big swings, rather than the more traditional stories we know. We also get a conversation along the lines of "well, the world may be ending but nothing's happening now so let's take a case," which highlights a general flaw of the show's structure. It's a conversation Dean and Sam have dozens of times, whenever the season dictates that they need a monster of the week.

But those quibbles aside, this is a fun episode because, well, giant suicidal teddy bear. As always, Ben Edlund goes for it with the weirdness and little moments like "kneel before Todd!" Everything with the Teddy is really quite fun. But the bigger picture is much darker. Especially when Dean says he does remember hell and that he's not talking.

Wesley's story isn't our usual sympathetic monster, either. He's kind of a creep and what he does with Hope is rapey and gross, yet he survives when he's faced with consequences. I don't know what that says about the rest of the show, or if he's supposed to be a mirror for either brother, but it's not successful.

Famous Faces: As a *Xena* fan, I do love seeing Joxer himself as a guest star.

So, Get This: "On Thursdays we're teddy bear doctors." The show was airing on Thursday at this point. Which is coincidentally why the name Castiel was chosen for the first angel—he's the angel of Thursday.

Death Notes: We'll give Sam a point here for a temporary death by lightning strike, leaving the score at: Dean: 14, Sam 2. Good job, Sam! But more interesting is the fact that there are no permanent deaths at all in this episode. A series first.

I Know What You Did Last Summer

Episode 4.09. Airdate: November 13, 2008
Written by: Sera Gamble
Directed by: Charles Beeson
Guest Cast: Misha Collins (Castiel), Genevieve Padalecki (Ruby), Robert Wisdom (Uriel), Julie McNiven (Anna Milton), Mark Rolston (Alastair)
Synopsis: A young woman can hear angels, so heaven and hell are both after her.

There are some episodes that are all about the monsters or just a fun idea, but this one and the next serve as a sort of two-part, mid-season finale kicking the myth arc into high gear. We meet important characters for the season in Anna and Alastair, but more importantly, we see a softer, nicer side to Ruby.

The Ruby and Sam flashbacks offer a contrast to the present-day adventure with Anna, and neither woman turns out to be what they seem. I'm not sure if the two stories mesh perfectly though. It's like two episodes smushed together. But through their choices we learn about how much freedom supernatural beings are allowed, and by the end trust Ruby as opposed to Uriel.

Ship Shape: Welp, Sam's for sure sleeping with a demon, keeping up his excellent track record with women. But at least Ruby didn't disappear or die the moment they got their clothes back on! And they found a way around the creepy consent stuff that happens when demons possess people. Does knowing Jared and Genevieve's chemistry was very real, make their steamy scene sexier or more awkward to watch? It sure will be a treat for their three kids one day!

Fan Favorites: Anna and Alastair are two vastly different characters that made a huge impact on the fandom and show up in fanfic quite regularly. Julie McNiven in particular has made a big impact on the show and fandom.

Heaven and Hell

Episode 4.09. Airdate: November 20, 2008
Written by: Eric Kripke (teleplay & story), Trevor Sands (story)
Directed by: J. Miller Tobin
Guest Cast: Misha Collins (Castiel), Genevieve Padalecki (Ruby), Thunderbird Dinwindle (Pamela Barnes), Julie McNiven (Anna Milton), Robert Wisdom (Uriel), Mark Rolston (Alastair)
Synopsis: Anna Milton is an angel who fell to Earth, and the Winchesters pit the forces of heaven and hell against one another in an attempt to save her.

This and "I Know What You Did Last Summer" really just make up one big episode, but I think this half is stronger simply for the big emotional moment at the end. It's where Dean finally confesses what happened in hell. It's an incredible performance and one of the all-time big moments for Dean.

The stuff in between suffers though, in comparison to that incredible confession. We do learn a lot of new information about angels, but Anna doesn't get to stick around long enough for it to matter. Her fall and connection to Dean rattle Cas, which helps him develop more as well.

I love seeing Pamela back, and both Alastair and Uriel are great antagonists, but the torture and nudity of Ruby is unnecessary and exploitative. Dean's confession of becoming a torturer in hell parallels Sam's own dark turns, though while Dean regrets is, Sam does not. It fits with the hit-you-over-the-head contrast between last week's rough Sammy sexy times with Ruby, and Dean's tender lovin' with Anna too.

Ship Shape: So, let's talk about Dean and Anna! It works on paper, because they bond over that whole absent father expecting obedience thing. And heck, it's way sexy to hook up with an angel in the back of Baby. The focus on Cas' handprint in the love scene is meant to emphasize that Anna's an angel, but given everything, uh, later, it weirdly inserts the idea of Castiel into a romantic scene. Which is… something.

Spoiler Alert: As this point, I think the plan was for Anna to be a longer-term love interest for Dean, and/or an ally for the boys, but gets dropped in favor of Castiel taking that spot. Which does make things more interesting.

Driver Picks the Music: Dean and Anna get it on to Bad Company's "Ready for Love." Interestingly, Dean and Cassie also had a sex scene set to a Bad Company song in "Route 666." In that case, it was "She Brings me Love."

Family Remains

Episode 4.11. Airdate: January 15, 2009
Written by: Jeremy Carver
Directed by: Phil Sgriccia
Guest Cast: Helen Slater (Susan Carter), David Newsom (Brian Carter), Bradley Stryker (Uncle Ted), Alexa Nokolas (Kate), Dylan Minette (Danny)
Synopsis: In attempting to save a family that's just moved into a haunted house, the Winchesters discover the "ghost" is a pair of abused children.

When *Supernatural* fully goes with the "humans are the scariest monster" bit, the show gets very dark and not in a fun way. This episode is seriously disturbing, from the reveal that Lizzie—the girl in the walls—was a product of incest and abuse, to the horrifying deaths. And it's all in service to say that horrible conditions and circumstance can make even innocent victims into rabid monsters.

This is all about Dean of course, building on his confession about torturing souls in hell and setting us up for the reveal that he liked it. Dean, even before he went to hell, was abused and neglected by a parent. But of course, the abuse he endured in hell was incomprehensible.

It's a hard thing to consider and Dean feels a lot of shame because of how he coped. And this is another theme of the season and show: how the abused become abusers, and how victims end up continuing a cycle of violence. Does that remove free will? Does that excuse monsters from accountability? Cheery stuff.

Famous faces: Hey, that's Helen Slater who played Supergirl in the 80s and Supergirl's adopted human mom on the CW series of the same name later!

Criss Angel is a Douche Bag

Episode 4.12. Airdate: January 22, 2009
Written by: Julie Siege
Directed by: Robert Singer
Guest Cast: Genevieve Padalecki (Ruby), Barry Bostwick (Jay), John Rubinstein (Charlie), Luke Camilleri (Jeb Dexter), Richard Libertini (Vernon), Michael Weston (Young Charlie)
Synopsis: A magician seems to cheat death by transferring deadly tricks to others.

This episode starts as a fun take on actual magicians, but ends up being a big, sad meditation on getting old. It doesn't quite jibe with the series as a whole, but it's still very compelling. The "monster" of the week is a real magician who wants to live forever, and in doing so, truly screws up the lives of the people he cares for.

The way all this mirrors Sam and Ruby's relationship should be a major red flag, reminding him how wanting to beat death leads to bad things. Instead, he takes the exact opposite lesson, motivated to do something bad so he won't grow old as a hunter. And Ruby is very much mirrored by Charlie, who saved Jay's life when he was suicidal.

Meanwhile, Dean ends up at a gay S&M dungeon and, well, it's part of a trend of gay panic jokes for Dean that only serve to highlight he's not so much grossed out by male attention, just uncomfortable with how much he likes it. But that's just my reading.

Spoiler Alert: This episode is seriously sad in retrospect, given how the entire series ends. Dean is completely correct about his ultimate fate and death. He *doesn't* get to grow old, but Sam does. And he does it alone. At least he gets a full life and family?

Famous Faces: Hey! That's Barry Bostwick aka Brad from *The Rocky Horror Picture Show*. I'm sure Dean tapping into his inner Brad and meeting a dominant, sexy man in black in the same episode is just a coincidence.

So, Get This: The actors who play old and young Charlie are father and son!

After School Special

Episode 4.13. Airdate: January 29, 2009
Written by: Andrew Dabb & Daniel Loflin
Directed by: Adam Kane
Guest Cast: Colin Ford (Young Sam), Brock Kelly (Young Dean), Candice King (Amanda Heckerling), Chad Willett (Mr. Wyatt)
Synopsis: Dean and Sam investigate a series of ghost possessions at a high school they once attended.

People who are bullied become bullies. People who are sad, lonely, and feel unloved make it so other people feel the same. Those are the big, neon sign messages of this episode. It's a variation on the season's exploration of how bad people—including Sam and Dean—can get before they're monsters, and if there's any forgiveness for that. But also: Dean in gym shorts.

I like this episode, but find it difficult to watch because of all the bullying, teen angst, and brutal violence. Teenage Dean in general is also an insufferable douchebag for most of the episode. Young Sam on the other hand is great, and the contrast between what Sam wanted to be and what he's become breaks my heart.

This episode reminds us who Sam and Dean were before the series. Sam just wanted a normal life and Dean puts on a macho façade to hide the pain inside. Now, Dean's façade is crumbling more and more (except when he has a whistle and a head band) and Sam has become a person that young him probably wouldn't like or trust.

Future Famous Faces: This episode has some serious young CW star power. Candice King would go on to over 160 episodes as Caroline on *The Vampire Diaries*. And the first victim, Taylor, was the first ever role for Marie Avgeropoulos, who would later play Octavia Butler on *The 100.*

Sex and Violence

Episode 4.14. Airdate: February 5, 2009
Written by: Cathryn Humphris
Directed by: Charles Beeson
Guest Cast: Jim Beaver (Bobby), Jim Parrack (Nick Monroe), Genevieve Padalecki (Ruby), Matie Schwartz (Dr. Cara Roberts)
Synopsis: A siren masquerades as a stripper to get men to kill their loved ones

So. Dean's siren is male. That's a thing we just saw. It's a completely brilliant twist that works on so many levels, and it gives us a lot to think about. In an episode where Dean is extremely excited about strippers, doing his best to project his macho BS, he connected most with another man. That's not nothing.

First, the obvious. The siren becomes "Nick" because what Dean wants is a brother, emphasizing the huge rift that's growing between them this season. Dean is tangled up with heaven, while Sam is dancing with hell. He is ashamed of his ruthlessness and violence, while Sam's leaning into his darkness. They each want something from the other they can't give, and they resent how their brother has changed.

Sam and Dean's big showdown gets that all out in the open, emphasizing how they can't trust one another anymore because they are so different. Their bonds of love and family are being seriously tested, and they don't get healed here, or any time soon.

But even though the twist that Nick is the siren taps into lots of brother stuff, we can't ignore that sirens are sexual and Dean's perfect partner is a dude. There have been hints, jokes and subtext about Dean for the whole series. For those who want to see Dean as bisexual, even if he's repressing it, this episode is strong evidence.

Famous Faces: TV fans may recognize Jim Parrack as Hoyt from *True Blood.*

Ship Shape: Congrats to Cara Roberts for going for it with the extremely hot not-FBI agent and living to tell the tale! And I guess Sam and Ruby aren't monogamous.

Death Takes a Holiday

Episode 4.15. Airdate: March 12, 2009
Written by: Jeremy Carver
Directed by: Steve Boyum
Guest Cast: Lindsay McKeon (Tessa), Misha Collins (Castiel), Thunderbird Dinwindle (Pamela), Christopher Heyerdahl (Alastair), Alexander Gould (Cole Griffith)
Synopsis: People stop dying in a small town, leading Sam, and Dean to enter the astral plane and discover that demons are capturing reapers to break one of the 66 seals.

This episode is about the natural order of things, but also about what happens when that order gets broken. Better known as survivor's guilt. For almost three full seasons now, Dean has been grappling with that, thinking he shouldn't be alive. And now, he's hanging on to the idea that Castiel and the angels saved him for a good reason. And he probably knows in his heart that it's not true.

An episode all about grief, and loss, and how the end of life is inevitable means that Dean and Sam must go through loss too. Poor Pamela dies and Cole isn't spared, but it reminds the Winchesters that heavenly purpose can't save everyone. Of course, Dean takes that to a place of guilt while Sam leans into his anger and worst impulses.

Tessa's return works perfectly here and Lindsay McKeon is wonderfully detached and unearthly. But the big guest star is Christopher Heyerdahl as nu-Alastair. Just his voice is so creepy, and he radiates menace. And honestly, Castiel's "guess again" line is possibly one of his top coolest moments in the series.

Death Notes: Do we count this as death or astral projection for Sam and Dean? I think not, but we do have a big loss here with Pamela, who joins Ash, Andy, and more in the "being in the vicinity of the Winchesters got us killed" club.

Behind the Scenes: This episode and season are dedicated to the late Kim Manners. If you've been paying attention, you'll have noticed Manners' name as director on some of the absolute best episodes of the series. He wasn't just a director, he was a producer who ran the production in Vancouver, and was an incredibly important part of the *Supernatural* set and family. He died of cancer very suddenly midway through the season and it was a devastating loss to everyone. His catch phrase "Kick it in the ass" became a rallying cry for the rest of the series.

On The Head of a Pin

Episode 4.16. Airdate: March 19, 2009
Written by: Ben Edlund
Directed by: Mike Rohl
Guest Cast: Misha Collins (Castiel), Genevieve Padalecki (Ruby), Robert Wisdom (Uriel), Julie McNiven (Anna), Christopher Heyerdahl (Alastair)
Synopsis: With angels being murdered, Castiel and Uriel demand that Dean use his skill from hell to torture Alastair for answers.

There are a lot of incredible episodes in Season Four, but this one rises to the top because it's pivotal for everyone! Let's start with our favorite angel in a trench coat.

Here, Cas truly starts to grow as a character. We know he has his doubts and that he's outside the angelic norm since he cares about people. Well, not people. Dean specifically. Dean is Cas' gateway to humanity, and it's rough to see him watch Dean torture Alastair. It's also painful for Cas to see Uriel turn, because he's not wrong that heaven is corrupt. Cas just doesn't want to end up on the lamb like Anna. Tough day!

Poor Dean though. He's terrifying when torturing Alastair, and then a few scenes later, he's just a scared, broken boy, with the weight of the world on his shoulders. He reverts to his worse self, gets his ass kicked, and learns that he started the apocalypse. I'd be crying too, Dean!

And then there's Sam who is way too far down a dark road. And if Ruby's smile is any indication, it's not going anywhere good. Sure, he kills Alastair, but it's brutal and scary (and Dean should have done it). Everything is sad, and bad, and scary! And we're still a ways from the end of the season! Eeep!

Ship Shape: It's so clear that Cas cares deeply for Dean, maybe even too deeply for heaven's liking. The two of them bickering like an old married couple is delicious, but the way Cas wants Dean to be good—which means defying his orders—is a big contrast to Ruby's continued corruption and seductions of Sam.

Spoiler Alert: Anna is so badass and cool in this episode you would think she was being set up as an important ally for the rest of the season or even the series. But you would be wrong! Her big "but there's still me" moment ends up sort of pointless!

Death notes/Fan Favorites: Christopher Heyerdahl kills it in this episode, as does Robert Wisdom. They have two of the greatest voices in *Supernatural*'s history and make such an incredible impression. It's amazing that the episode had room for them to both be so good and die so well with such impact!

It's a Terrible Life

Episode 4.17. Airdate: March 26, 2009
Written by: Sera Gamble
Directed by: James L. Conway
Guest Cast: Travis Wester (Harry Spengler), A.J. Buckley (Ed Zeddmore), Jack Plotnick (Ian), Kurt Fuller (Mr. Adler/Zachariah)
Synopsis: Sales director Dean Smith and IT drone Sam Wesson find out something unnatural is going on at their workplace.

How do you follow up an episode that left Dean at his emotional low point for the whole series? By making him and Sam different people of course, to remind them who they are. If the season has continuously asked "how does trauma push people to the place they are beyond saving?" then this one instead asks, "how do our heroes fare when their trauma and angst are removed?"

This episode is so fun because we get to see Sam and Dean as literally different people. Since this was an angelic lesson for Dean, it makes sense that his alternate life is much further from his regular persona than Sam's. Of the two brothers, Sam has always been the more authentic one—less prone to posturing and putting up walls. Dean Smith is still our Dean, just without the toxic masculinity BS in his way.

Dean Smith's metrosexual nature is played for laughs and he's clearly a take on characters from Office Space and Patrick Bateman in American Psycho. But he still tells us a lot about who Dean is at his core. He's just meant for more… and sure, that's his destiny and what heaven wants for him. But is it truly what he wants?

At their core, these two are heroes and hunters. At this point, that's who they are meant to be. At least in the sense that heaven and God want them to be those things. They aren't in control of their story and this exercise is a manipulation.

So, Get This: The Ghostfacers made several in-character YouTube videos during Seasons Four and Five.

Ship Shape: Smith and Wesson are quite a pair and it's super weird that Dean thinks Sam is hitting on him, but I'll give you this one, fans.

Driver Pick the Music: Is the use of The Kinks' "Well Respected Man" in the opening Dean Smith montage on the nose? Yes. Is it awesome? Also yes.

The Monster at the End of this Book

Episode 4.18. Airdate: April 2, 2009
Written by: Julie Siege (Story & Teleplay), Nancy Baird (story)
Directed by: Steve Boyum
Guest Cast: Misha Collins (Castiel), Kurt Fuller (Zachariah), Rob Benedict (Chuck Shurley), Katherine Boecher (Lilith)
Synopsis: The Winchesters discover a series of books called "*Supernatural*."

You know how I said earlier, that *Supernatural* would break the fourth wall in a way no other show ever has or could? Well, here we are. The characters on *Supernatural*, on screen talking about... *Supernatural*. Many shows make fun of themselves, but it's a new level of meta to have Sam and Dean calling Wincest shipping gross right there on screen, and having the "author" apologize for stories like "Bugs" and the ghost ship.

Aside from the fun meta aspects, this episode is great on its own! Sam and Dean's rift continues to grow, with Sam thinking he's the one who has to save the world. And he's literally getting in bed with demons to do it, despite Chuck telling him he's not doing the right thing. And Dean reaches out to heaven through faith and prayer! It's important that his faith is rewarded, not by the heavenly host, but by Castiel doing some slight rebellion because he doesn't want Dean mad at him. Character growth all around.

But what this episode really does is hammer the ideas of fate and predestination that have been building all season. Do Sam and Dean's choices matter if the world operates on a "so it is written, so shall it be" basis? Do they have an agency? And on a meta level, do these characters have agency beyond their creator's intention? Stay tuned.

Spoiler Alert: Watching this episode, knowing what's to come, is a hugely different experience than watching for the first time. Re-watchers know that Chuck isn't just a prophet, he's friggin' *God.* And at this point he's just a spectator enjoying a good story. But knowing the truth makes his line about how he's a "cruel capricious God" a lot less funny and a lot more foreshadowy.

Fan Favorites: Rob Benedict is so good as Chuck. He's funny, whiny, twitchy, empathetic, and so good at reacting to the Winchesters. I love him and fans love him.

Name Game: Agents DeYoung and Shaw refer to Dennis DeYoung and Tommy Shaw of Styx. "Carver Edlund" references two writers on *Supernatural*, Jeremy Carver and Ben Edlund. The published "Sera Siege" references Sera Gamble and Julie Siege.

Death Notes: This is the first episode that hits a rare record: no one dies at all!

Jump the Shark

Episode 4.19. Airdate: April 23, 2009
Written by: Andrew Dabb & Daniel Loflin
Directed by: Phil Sgriccia
Guest Cast: Jake Abel (Adam Milligan), Dedee Pfeiffer (Kate Milligan)
Synopsis: Sam and Dean meet Adam Milligan, John Winchester's third son

Adding another unknown brother to the Winchester family is a big move, so of course *Supernatural* does it in a way that's both shocking and sad. Adam really is their brother after all, but he's already dead, hammering home how hunting is a family curse. One Sam feels he has to break.

This episode is about family becoming someone you don't know. Adam is, or was, Sam and Dean's brother, but who they meet is a monster impersonating him. Sam is still Sam, but his obsession with revenge and demon blood are turning him into John. Heck, ghouls don't even kill people, these monsters became killers for revenge.

Revenge and redemption, and how they intersect, are a big takeaway from the season so far. As well as how that relates to family, because what we're getting here is how family can be at the root of both. How we want revenge for our family, how their love can turn us around, and how we become them. And how we depend on all of that too much. It's all about daddy issues and codependency—the true blood of *Supernatural*.

Fan Favorite/Spoiler Alert: Adam's untimely demise is made even worse by the fact that Jake Abel is legitimately great in the role. And so it's nice that the series will find ways to bring him back… and then forget him in hell for 10 years. Whoops.

So, Get This: The diner "Cousin Oliver's" references the character of Cousin Oliver on *The Brady Bunch*, a random relative who was introduced out of nowhere.

The Rapture

Episode 4.20. Airdate: April 30, 2009
Written by: Jeremy Carver
Directed by: Charles Beeson
Guest Cast: Jim Beaver (Bobby), Misha Collins (Jimmy Novak/Castiel), Julie McNiven (Anna), Wynn Everett (Amelia Novak), Sydney Imbeau (Claire Novak/Castiel)
Synopsis: Castiel gets dragged back to heaven, leaving his vessel, Jimmy Novak behind.

We follow up the last episode about family becoming disfigured, with a dive into the backstory of Castiel's vessel, who lost everything for the holy mission. This is a clear mirror for Sam, who ends the episode in a demon blood detox. Just as Amelia and Claire lost Jimmy as soon as Castiel called on him, Dean and Bobby seem to have lost Sam to Ruby and Sam's "mission."

This is a great episode for many reasons, the least of which is Misha Collins getting to truly stretch his acting muscles, swapping between Jimmy and Castiel. Jimmy is so different from Cas, and such a tragic figure. And the way he and his family are hurt really highlights the callousness of heaven. Even Castiel himself seems different, and might have been questioning heaven, but he was reeducated. Good thing it won't stick.

Spoiler Alert: This episode sets up *a lot* that gets revisited later. Though never confirmed, Castiel's reprogramming probably happened with Naomi, who we meet in Season Eight. Claire and Amelia both return in Season Ten, and we most importantly learn how especially important blood lines and consent are for angelic vessels.

Plot Hole: Reading minds and visiting dreams is a cool power that the show rarely remember Cas has in the future.

Ship Shape: Once again, Castiel isn't getting in trouble because he cares about humans, as we see how unattached he is to Claire and Amelia. He's attached to *Dean*.

When The Levee Breaks

Episode 4.21. Airdate: May 7, 2009
Written by: Sera Gamble
Directed by: Robert Singer
Guest Cast: Samantha Smith (Mary), Jim Beaver (Bobby), Misha Collins (Castiel), Genevieve Padalecki (Ruby), Julie McNiven (Anna), Christopher Heyerdahl (Alastair), Colin Ford (Young Sam)
Synopsis: The Winchester brothers' relationship finally shatters.

It's another deeply personal and emotional hour for the boys from Sera Gamble, who do this kind of episode very well. Everything has been building to the big fight between Sam and Dean at the end. Not necessarily the fists, but their words. Sam started the series wanting to be normal, but slowly his "destiny" and the desire for power has driven him to become the monster he was afraid of being all of Season Two.

He doesn't really want revenge though, he wants agency. Freedom from his family and destiny, he just wants to feel like he has a say in who he is and what happens to him. Sadly, he's just being manipulated in a different way, walking the exact path that heaven, hell, and fate set out for him. It's so painful to see into Sam's head as he's confronted and encouraged by faces from his past. He already feels like a monster, but if he chooses to be one, that somehow makes it better. He doesn't think he can be good, and doesn't even know how. And that's tragic.

Sam's entire self-worth at this point is tied up in what Dean thinks of him. And the fact that Dean is the chosen one to save the day makes him feel worthless. Dean's self-worth meanwhile is tied into whether he can protect Sam, so he feels like he's already failed that. Neither of those things are good! These beautiful morons need to realize that they, and others, love them for who they are not what they do! But that'll take a while.

We have other people making bad choices for good reasons here too. Cas is following orders that he knows are wrong, leading to Anna's unceremonious exit.

Ship Shape: It's not really anything, but the crane shot of Dean and Cas just staring at one another for a long time is certainly a choice! And here we get a parallel with Dean paired off with Cas, and Sam paired off with Ruby. That's indicative of how far apart the guys are.

Lucifer Rising

Episode 4.22. Airdate: May 19, 2009
Written by: Eric Kripke
Directed by: Eric Kripke
Guest Cast: Jim Beaver (Bobby), Misha Collins (Castiel), Genevieve Padalecki (Ruby), Kurt Fuller (Zachariah), Rob Benedict (Chuck), Katherine Boecher (Lilith), Ron LaBelle (Azazel)
Synopsis: Pop goes the devil.

Supernatural keeps upping the stakes on season-ending cliffhangers.

From "Dean's going to hell" to "whoops Dean's IN hell" and now "Uh oh, Sam released freakin' Lucifer." Every season ends with the question "how will the boys get out of this?" And the answer is inevitably "they will not, and somehow will make it worse."

But honestly, this is a tremendously good finale. Sam reaches his absolute darkest moment thanks to Ruby, when he kills Cindy the Nurse for her blood. It's so upsetting, and we can't even entirely blame Ruby because this was all about Sam's choices. And really, do we really have a choice in what we do and who we are?

Both Sam and Dean are a product of how they were raised and the traumas and losses they've experienced. Those things impact their choices and their free will. Sam follows the path set for him and the consequences are disastrous. But Dean… doesn't.

While Dean doesn't save the day here, he does show that everyone still has a choice. The most important moment is his confrontation with Castiel, where he convinces an angel—a being defined by obedience—to make a choice and help him. And that changes everything. Dean is able to make that case, influence Castiel, and exercise his own free will because he loves people, humanity, and even Sam as they are. That's huge.

There are so many great moments here: the return of Azazel, Zachariah's reveal that the angels want the apocalypse, and Ruby's big "I'm awesome!" speech. Dean was absolutely right about her from the get-go, and the extent to which she came between the brothers is a wound that will take years to heal. It's going to take all of next season and a few more past that to come back from this.

Spoiler Alert: The show is actually quite clever here. When Zachariah tells Dean that it's his destiny to kill Lucifer, they're standing in front of a painting of the Archangel Michael. Dean is Michael's true vessel and that's how he'll kill Lucifer, eventually.

More importantly though, what Dean does here by choosing not to fight Sam, and to instead love and protect his brother instead is one of the most important things he does to upset Chuck's story in the final episodes of the series.

Ship Shape: Do we think that Sam is going to reconsider his romantic failures? Let's hope. At least things worked out well for the actors playing them. On the other hand the whole thing where Cas defied the entirety of heaven for Dean is pretty dang romantic.

Death Notes: For the first time, we're ending a season with no Winchesters close to death! Good job? Except Castiel maybe is dead, which more than anything makes him an honorary Winchester. I'd say Lilith's death here is a bit disappointing since we never really got to know her, but the boys jointly killing Ruby is very satisfying.

SUPERNATURAL

CHAPTER FIVE

When God Is Gone, and the Devil Takes Hold

We're in the end days, with the season that was supposed to be the end of *Supernatural*. Understanding that Season Five was the culmination of Eric Kripke's five-year plan gives this season important context. It's the apocalypse—so the stakes could not be higher—and it's all barreling towards one big confrontation. But on *Supernatural*, the final battle is never really about the fight, it's about the people doing the fighting.

The writers' room this season is remarkably unchanged from last season, which contributes to the continuity and propulsive story coming off Season Four. The two seasons honestly really function as a two-part story, with Four being Sam and Dean's relationship falling to its lowest point, and Season Five healing it.

This season is all about fate and forgiveness. From the beginning, *Supernatural* has been defying expectations. The viewers, or parents, or society, it doesn't matter. They defy their trauma. They defy the cycles of violence and abandonment. And in its climax, they defy both heaven and hell. It's a lot and makes for an epic season.

It's also a change from previous years, because while the Winchesters remain central, other characters get real arcs that support and compliment the overall story. Misha Collins is upgraded to series regular, with Castiel essentially in the same place the boys were in Season One—looking for a lost father. And while Jim Beaver stays a guest star, Bobby becomes a very important reminder of the costs of hunting.

And then there's Lucifer and Michael, our actual villains. But do they work? Lucifer more so than Michael, but it's not about the villains. It's about family. And isn't that the point?

Sympathy For the Devil

Episode 5.01. Airdate: September 10, 2009
Written by: Eric Kripke
Directed by: Robert Singer
Guest Cast: Misha Collins (Castiel), Jim Beaver (Bobby), Kurt Fuller (Zachariah), Rob Benedict (Chuck), Mark Pellegrino (Nick), Emily Perkins (Beck Rosen), Rachel Miner (Meg), Bellamy Young (Lucifer)
Synopsis: The devil needs a vessel and so does Michael. Sam and Dean need some help.

So much happens in this episode. New characters! Old characters! Fanfic! Possession, stabbing, and resurrection! It's a lot, yet it feels like it puts the plot into a holding pattern, rather than moving forward. But for a season premiere that's fine.

Let's dig into the emotional parts first. Dean doesn't trust, or forgive Sam, and everyone is mad at the big guy. And they've got good reason to be. Sam's guilt, and Dean's lack of trust in him, will be huge this season. Meanwhile, Dean is lying to his family to get by, because he's lost faith in almost everything. As Zacharaiah calls him, he's a "wad of insecurity and self-loathing." And most painfully, he's lost faith in Sam.

And then there's Lucifer. There's a great contrast between heaven's attempt to force Dean to consent to being Michael's vessel, and Lucifer convincing Nick to let him with an emotional appeal and a promise of revenge. Just another poor slob out for revenge, who happens to turn into a monster. I think we've seen this before.

There are so many little great moments here. Chuck with the molar and plunger. New Meg and Bobby fighting possession. Cas saving the day! I love it, and I do think Becky is a really fun character to introduce, poking gentle fun at the fans.

Fan favorite/Familiar Faces: Our new Meg is Rachel Miner, who will stick around the show for a while, and the fandom for longer. In 2010, Misha Collins founded the charity Random Acts to promote random acts of kindness, and Rachel Miner eventually took over as director. She may be a demon, but she's a true angel of a human.

This episode also introduces us to another face we'll see a lot: Mark Pellegrino, a tremendous actor with a huge resume ranging from *Dexter* to *Lost,* and eventually Eric Kripke's first post-*Supernatural* series, *Revolution.*

So, Get This: In anticipation of this episode, fans made "#LuciferIs Coming" trend on Twitter which deeply alarmed… Puff Daddy.

Death Notes: Cas died and came back, so I think we need to add him to the leader board! We're at Dean: 14, Sam: 2, Castiel: 1.

Good God, Y'all!

Episode 5.02. Airdate: September 17, 2009
Written by: Sera Gamble
Directed by: Charles Beeson
Guest Cast: Misha Collins (Castiel), Jim Beaver (Bobby), Samantha Ferris (Ellen), Alona Tal (Jo), Steven Williams (Rufus), Titus Welliver (War)
Synopsis: Cas goes to look for God. Sam and Dean go to War.

We start strong, with an intense scene of Cas in Dean's face, but the hour winds into a meditation on trust and paranoia. Cas taking the amulet is highly symbolic, as it represents the brothers' love and connection. It's gone, lost in service to a false mission. It's going to take a lot to get that relationship and trust back, but will it be the same?

Seeing all the forgotten hunters is great, because we've missed everyone. And this episode grows to the scope of the Apocalypse, while expanding the mythology. It's fun to imagine what could have been with a bigger budget. But there's a lot of fighting, and not a lot of plot here. Not so great. War is great bad guy though, because he isn't about violence as much as he's about tapping into people's worst fears.

And that gives us our first major brother break up! Seeing Sam and Dean go separate ways is a shock, but it's space they need for sure.

Familiar Faces: In a bit of irony, Titus Welliver would end up opposite Lucifer as his character Jacob's brother "The Man in Black" in *Lost*. Jacob and the Man in Black share an extremely Michael vs. Lucifer relationship.

Drive Picks the Music: "Spirit in the Sky" by Norman Greenbaum plays from War's "red horse" and its associations with the Vietnam War turn out to be a big friggin' clue about who the bad guy is.

Behind the Scenes: Ditching Dean's necklace was somewhat of a functional decision: Jensen hated how it would hit him in the face during fights.

Free To Be You and Me

Episode 5.03. Airdate: September 25, 2009
Written by: Jeremy Carver
Directed by: J. Miller Tobin
Guest Cast: Misha Collins (Castiel), Adrianne Palicki (Jessica), Jim Beaver (Bobby), Mark Pellegrino (Lucifer), Demore Barnes (Raphael), Emma Bell (Lindsey)
Synopsis: Castiel enlists Dean's help tracking down the archangel Raphael.

This excellent episode is all about contrasts, call backs, and character. Sam and Dean are separated for the entire hour, and we get two vastly different stories about how they connect to the world without a brother by their side.

Let's start with Sam, because it's not good. He has baggage and guilt which we can't blame him for. He's with people sure, but still very much alone as he's hiding and running from who he is, and what he did. He's isolating himself and into that void steps the actual Devil. Sam needs people and, more than that, he needs people that accept him as he is. And that's not Dean right now, which leaves as opening for Satan.

Dean on the other hand is pretty good at connecting with others. And without worrying about Sam, he can thrive and lean into other relationships. In this case, a friendship with Cas. This is such a huge episode for Cas as a character. He gets to be badass, funny, awkward, and emotional. He's already grown so much, but he's letting Dean help him to grow even more. Also, the scene between Dean, Cas and Raphael is epic, and Demore Barnes is truly scary.

We're reminded again this episode of how far apart the boys are, and now we know that they are destined to be on opposing sides in a battle between heaven and hell. With Dean saying he's happy on his own, because he truly gets to be himself without pressure, and Sam rejecting his nature, how are they going to resolve that?

Name Game: Dean and Castiel's aliases "Alonzo Mosely" and "Eddie Moscone" are references to the movie *Midnight Run*. It's telling that Dean doesn't use rock aliases this episode, showing how much he's stepping away from the persona he had when around Sam.

Ship Shape: This is the episode that launched a thousand fics, and for good reason. Dean and Cas are great together, and Dean is way too obsessed with Castiel's virginity. Heck, the "last night on Earth" thing even harkens back to his night with Anna, where he made personally sure an angel got laid before dying. Who's to say what happened after the guys left that brothel? (A bazillion fanfic writers is who).

But seriously, everything in this episode from "Cas, we've talked about this: personal space," to how comfortable Dean is with his weirdo angel, is Destiel catnip.

Driver Picks the Music: Lynyrd Skynyrd's "Simple Man" plays in the opening montage. Jensen Ackles covered the same song on Jason Manns' *Covers with Friends* album, and it's great.

The End

Episode 5.04. Airdate: October 1, 2009
Written by: Ben Edlund
Directed by: Steve Boyum
Guest Cast: Misha Collins (Castiel), Kurt Fuller (Zachariah), Rob Benedict (Chuck), Lexa Doig (Risa)
Synopsis: Zachariah transports Dean five years ahead in time to an apocalyptic future.

This episode was great on its own, but *wild* when we look at it with 2020 hindsight. A worldwide pandemic cancels everything, a moron as president, and people hoarding toilet paper? Maybe these writers are prophets.

On its own, "The End" represents the endpoint if the Winchesters stay apart. Dean's a monster who will let his friends die, while Sam is literally the devil. It's not good. Like Dean says, the brothers need each other to keep one another human. After a very dark look at the future, we end on a hopeful note.

It's also not a great scenario for Cas, though he seems to be, uh, enjoying himself. And it's nice to see Misha in full-on weird mode as hippie Cas. We call this world the "Endverse," by the way, and this one episode has spawned a whole genre of fanfic.

"The End" is a major showcase for Jensen Ackles, who does a tremendous job as Dean and, uh, also Dean. His scenes with himself are great, especially considering he was acting against a stand in. Also, uh, Dean, you don't need to be ashamed of liking pink satiny panties. It's fine.

And then there's Jared as Lucifer. It's an eerie, chilling performance, but the fact that he's our fourth Lucifer in as many episodes is a hurdle. We've seen so many takes on the character, and he's generally a very *Paradise Lost*-esque sad bad boy at this point I'm sure the characterization will become more consistent as things go on…

Spoiler Alert: It will not. Lucifer comes back a lot, with many different actors and, well, it's a crap shoot as to whether he's brooding and scary, or just an obnoxious dickwad. There's no version of him that's anything like the way Jared plays him (We call that Samifer) though, except Jared.

And then there's everything of the Endverse. Chuck is there, which is weird considering he's, ya know, GOD, and in general it's so dark that it makes me personally think this was an illusion by Zachariah, and not real time travel.

Death Notes: Yes, Dean dies on screen AGAIN, but that's not our Dean so I'm not counting that. Boy's far enough ahead as it is.

Ship Shape: "Never Change." Yeah, well, Dean, Cas does change because of you. Also is it creepy to ship Dean with… Dean?

Fallen Idols

Episode 5.05. Airdate: October 8, 2009
Written by: Julie Siege
Directed by: James L. Conway
Guest Cast: Paris Hilton (Leshii), Daryl Shuttleworth (Sheriff Rick Carnegie)
Synopsis: Time for the Winchesters to kill … Paris Hilton?

Can't go wrong with an episode where Dean's scared of a car, and Gandhi tries to eat Sam. That all happened. We're through the dark repercussions now, and on the way to actual healing. But that does mean confronting that pain first.

Leshii survives by becoming someone people idolize and, in the past, there was a lot of idolizing going on between Sam and Dean. Sam looked up to his big brother, so he's afraid to call him out on his BS. And Dean has spent a while reckoning with the fact that his idealized version of Sam, the one he knew as a kid, is gone. In fact, Dean not looking at Sam as an adult was part of their issues.

That's actually pretty profound for an episode where Sam cuts Paris Hilton's head off. Again, that happened. But seeing people as they are is the first step towards forgiving and healing. I'd just leave the celebrity decapitation out of things.

Famous Face: Paris Hilton obviously had a fun time playing an evil version of herself. She had previously worked together with Jared Padalecki in *House of Wax*, which Dean mentions as an inside joke.

Name Game: In a way of showing that Sam and Dean still aren't on the same page, their aliases are musicians from different bands, John Bonham from Led Zeppelin and Stewart Copeland from The Police.

I Believe the Children Are Our Future

Episode 5.06. Airdate: October 15, 2009
Written by: Andrew Dabb & Daniel Loflin
Directed by: Charles Beeson
Guest Cast: Misha Collins (Castiel), Gattlin Griffith (Jesse Turner), Ever Carradine (Julia Wright/Demon)
Synopsis: Childhood fears become real. Turns out it's the antichrist, as usual.

This is a tough one. There are fun bits (Dean electrocuting, then eating the ham) and bad bits (Castiel's merciless characterization feels off). We're revisiting old themes, many which are *Supernatural* standards. More subversion with a classic switcheroo, pointing in one direction with funny kid fear deaths, before suddenly going the other. Surprise antichrist! We're also back to that classic *Supernatural* question of if someone can choose not to be a monster.

And in a nice twist, Jesse Turner sort of… does. It's refreshing that he chooses to hop off the wheel and disappear, and surprisingly hopeful! Though the choice loses some emotion, because we never meet his real parents. Our unnamed demon of the week is interesting too, though I can't think too much about how it works that Jesse is "half demon" or how "demon blood" even works, but let's no tug on those strings.

Spoiler Alert/Plot Hole: So, the antichrist with God-like powers will be revisited and matter, right? Heck no! We never hear from Jesse again and fans will obviously never stop complaining about it. If he's only activated when Lucifer walks the earth, what happens to him in Season Eleven, huh?

What we do get is the remarkably similar character of Jack, created in part by this episode's co-author Andrew Dabb. Jack, the son of a human and Lucifer, even realizes that dream of a "world with no lies" in Season Fourteen.

The Curious Case of Dean Winchester

Episode 5.07. Airdate: October
Written by: Sera Gamble (Teleplay & story), Jenny Klein (Story)
Directed by: Robert Singer
Guest Cast: Jim Beaver (Bobby), Chad Everett (Old Dean), Hal Ozsan (Patrick), Pascale Hutton (Lia)
Synopsis: The boys and Bobby hunt a witch who plays poker for years of life.

This episode ranks low for me, coming down to one problem: I miss Jensen's Dean and I don't think Chad Everett is good in the role. Sure, he gets some of Jensen's mannerisms, but it's all surface level and reduces Dean to a horny, boorish punchline.

Dean's final scene with Bobby, explaining why he can't give him up comes along and is great, just showing how much depth Jensen brings in contrast. I'll forever be mad that they didn't cast Jensen Ackles's actual father, Alan Ackles—who is also an actor—in the role. (He does show up in a bit part years down the line).

Add Patrick's terrible accent, bad makeup and special effects, along with having the show lean way too far into a gross running joke about Asian women sex workers as objects (I hate the Busty Asian Beauties jokes too) and the episode has a lot of terrible.

But there are good moments though. Despite his bad accent, Hal Ozsan is good as Patrick, and he's an interesting character (who survives!) The overarching plot of Sam proving himself trustworthy is also good. The stuff with Bobby being suicidal and dealing with disability is emotional too, where Jim Beaver shines as always.

Spoiler Alert: So, Patrick and Rowena have to have met at some point, right?

Changing Channels

Episode 5.08. Airdate: November 5, 2009
Written: Jeremy Carver
Directed by: Charles Beeson
Guest Cast: Misha Collins (Castiel), Richard Speight Jr. (The Trickster/ Gabriel)
Synopsis: The Trickster, aka Gabriel, traps Sam and Dean in TV land.

I could write an entire book on this episode. It's so good, and on so many levels. The first level of course are the parodies of various other television shows, mainly the ones that were competing with (and clobbering) *Supernatural* in the same time slot: *CSI* and *Grey's Anatomy*.

I think Dr. Sexy MD, the *Grey's Anatomy* parody, is my favorite. Not just because it's so on point, but I love the deep cut joke about a doctor seeing a ghost as it's referencing the character of Denny on *Grey's*. Also, Dean is a complete bisexual disaster when he's star struck by Dr. Sexy himself.

Every parody is spot on and funny, from Sam's nuts getting cracked to Sam in the herpes commercial. These are brilliant moments, and alone would make the episode legendary. But this is *Supernatural*, so it's more than just that.

"Changing Channels" works, because there's real drama and emotion under everything, and the reveal that the Trickster is Gabriel is just perfect. To go from Sam as the Impala—one of the weirdest things the show has done—to the incredibly raw confrontation between the boys and Gabriel is astonishing.

Richard Speight Jr. is perfect as Gabriel. He's funny, scary and mischievous, but beneath all that, he's hurt. He's a brother that had to watch his family tear itself apart. As he describes the apocalypse, it makes sense that he thinks it has to be this way. There's a reason Gabriel is one of the most popular characters in fanfiction and in the fandom: because he's so complex and so much fun.

So, Get This: The minibikes Sam and Dean ride in the credits to the *Supernatural* sitcom are bikes Jared and Jensen owned and rode around on set.

Driver Picks the Music: The lyrics to the *Supernatural* sitcom theme were written by Jeremy Carver with music by one of the show's two composers, Jay Gruska.

Spoiler Alert: This won't be the only time the guys go into a TV show. And when they get cartoon-ified into Scooby-Doo, Dean will finally be able to fit that sandwich in his mouth.

The Real Ghostbusters

Episode 5.09. Airdate: November 12, 2009
Written by: Sera Gamble
Directed by: Charles Beeson
Guest Cast: Rob Benedict (Chuck), Emily Perkins (Becky), Devin Ratray (Demian/"Dean"), Ernie Grunwald (Barnes/"Sam")
Synopsis: Becky invites Sam and Dean to a *Supernatural* convention that ends up having a real ghost problem.

Did you think we were done breaking the fourth wall? Oh no, the wall is in pieces and we have an entire episode about Sam and Dean as characters, how they're perceived, and maybe most importantly to them, how they perceive themselves.

Getting an outside perspective on our lives is important, and for Sam and Dean (especially Dean), encountering people who see them as heroes is a good reminder of why they do what they do. Saving people and hunting things is the family business. But the Winchesters forgot how important that first part is. Meeting their own mirror reflections in Demian and Barnes is a reminder of what their "story" is really about.

This episode pokes fun at the show and the fandom. What is with all the creepy children, Kripke? Why can't these guys hold onto their guns? There are *Supernatural* conventions, and they're really fun, but the big difference is that the real ones are probably 90% female. And they are very queer.

I do sort of love that Demian and Barnes are a couple, and the joke of the reveal is on Dean, not aimed at them. This episode was actually nominated for a GLAAD media award, and I also like that the gay characters LIVE. Chuck and Becky are also a delight this episode, and the ghosts are creepy. It's an overall joy.

Spoiler Alert: So, when Chuck talks about losing his virginity to a girl claiming it "didn't count," is he talking about the Virgin Mary??? Becky dated god. Good job.

So, Get This: The various Impalas we see at the start are some of the six Babies used on the show. Three were "hero" cars, and three were stunt cars, one with a metal plate on the bottom. There was a seventh Impala in pieces, and another wrecked one used at times. Jared and Jensen took home two of the hero cars when the series ended.

Abandon All Hope

Episode 5.10. Airdate: November 19, 2009
Written by: Ben Edlund
Directed by: Phil Sgriccia
Guest Cast: Misha Collins (Castiel), Jim Beaver (Bobby), Samantha Ferris (Ellen), Alona Tal (Jo), Mark Pellegrino (Lucifer), Rachel Miner (Meg), Mark Sheppard (Crowley)
Synopsis: After getting the Colt from a helpful demon, the team makes a run at killing Lucifer. And fail.

Here begins the big, emotional, downward slope. After some hope last week, everything is loss after loss and it's so painful. After we were so happy to see Jo and Ellen back at the top of the season, they die in the saddest way possible. And it's for nothing. In fact, most people around the Winchesters tend to end up dead, and that's not doing much for Sam and Dean's morale. It seems that every time these boys defy fate, they lose and people die. Which is another kind of terrible destiny.

Meanwhile, Cas is becoming more human, much like what Dean saw in "The End." This is in part a function of outside forces from the narrative: it's just not good TV to have a character around who can kill any demon, and heal people with a touch. That's why this is the third episode where Cas has shown up, only to be somehow disabled. But that makes the stakes higher and the drama bigger. It is a bummer to see Cas constantly benched though. And his confrontations with Lucifer and Meg are fascinating, revealing a lot about all three characters. Cas is motivated by caring about people, Meg by idealism and loyalty, and Lucifer by revenge.

It's not all sadness though: Crowley is here! Mark Sheppard steals every scene he's in, and in a few minutes the show introduces one of the most interesting and fun demons we've ever met. And his motivation and morality are just murky enough to make him really interesting.

Death Notes: Ellen and Jo's demise never fails to make me cry. There's something about a mother choosing to die, rather than live without her child that's utterly heartbreaking. There are a lot of sad deaths in this show, but this one may be the saddest.

Ship Shape: Dean's moments with Jo go from fun to sad extremely fast. Their final kiss is a uniquely beautiful moment, and I feel like it's Dean saying sorry, begging forgiveness for putting Jo here and mourning *all* his mistakes. So poignant. But also, the only person who really seems to buy into the "last night on Earth" thing is once again Cas? Interesting.

Plot Hole: Why are reapers old men again? Also, what are the other five things the Colt can't kill? We're not sure, but the gun will show up again in seven years after Sam and Dean just leave it on the ground.

So, Get This: "Kick it in the ass," was a phrase used by director and producer Kim Manners. It was Samantha Ferris' idea to have Ellen say it, as a tribute to the late Manners. Also, the explosion in the shop was far larger than planned, so the show had to pay $20,000 to rebuild the backlot.

Sam, Interrupted

Episode 5.11. Airdate: January 21, 2010
Written by: Andrew Dabb & Daniel Loflin
Directed by: James L. Conway
Guest Cast: Jon Gries (Martin Creaser), Lara Gilchrist (Nurse Foreman/Wraith), Michelle Harrison (Dr. Erica Cartwright)
Synopsis: To help an old hunter friend, Sam, and Dean check into a mental institution.

If anyone needs therapy, it's the Winchesters, and this episode cleverly digs into their psyches. Dean has a martyr complex the size of the Titanic, born of self-hatred and low self-esteem. He has to save the world and suffer while doing it, to even get close to be worthy of any sort of love. And Sam is full of rage at everything, because deep down he still just wants to be normal.

We've moved past a lot of monsters we can understand, (aside from Lucifer) to monsters that bring out the Winchesters deepest issues and fears. In this episode, the monster doesn't so much reflect a conflict between the boys, rather she amplifies their inner demons. The boys also get another peek at another possible future with Martin. Choosing your future is another expression of free will, do the boys get that?

One other issue that gets highlighted here is Dean's drinking. Through the seasons, we've seen Dean move from beers to hard liquor more often, but we get an indication of how much he drinks and uses alcohol as a coping mechanism. Just like Dean seems to have upped his womanizing since things started to get worse for the Winchesters, the drinking is also an indicator of some not-great mental health!

Name Game: "Alex" and "Eddie" are a reference to Alex and Eddie Van Halen.

Swap Meat

Episode 5.12. Airdate: January 28, 2010
Written by: Julie Siege (teleplay & story), Rebecca Dessertine & Harvey Fedor (story)
Directed by: Robert Singer
Guest Cast: Colton James (Gary/Sam), Sarah Drew (Nora), Alex Arsenault (Trevor)
Synopsis: A teen warlock swaps bodies with Sam. It goes poorly for him.

This episode is the low point of Season Five. It's not necessarily bad, as the idea of Sam stepping into another person's shoes to deal with having his life planned out for him is interesting. And the demon twist is surprising. But it's all wasted opportunities.

The conceit of having Gary look like Gary when he's Sam, and vice versa, is so disappointing! I want to see Jared Padalecki playing Gary and having fun the way he does in the first scene. Not have him looking all angry as a teenager! Colton James is great as Gary too and I think he could have handled playing Sam, so why not?

Apparently, there was a plan at one point to have Sam and Dean switch bodies that never came to be, and the fact that in 327 episodes we never get a Sam and Dean body swap is one of my biggest *Supernatural* regrets.

Overall, Gary's magic story of him choosing his future and trying to find his power works. As does Sam learning to appreciate the life he has, but his rejection of normalcy is also sad considering he used to want it.

Famous Faces: Hey, that's Sara Drew who audience knew at this point from *Everwood*, and who would go on to over 200 episodes on *Grey's Anatomy*.

The Song Remains the Same

Episode 5.13. Airdate: February 4, 2010
Written by: Sera Gamble, Nancy Baird
Directed by: Steve Boyum
Guest Cast: Misha Collins (Castiel), Matt Cohen (John/Michael), Amy Gumenick (Mary), Julie McNiven (Anna), Matt Ward (Uriel)
Synopsis: Anna travels back in time to kill Mary and John Winchester before Sam and Dean are born.

There are some incredibly emotional moments in this episode, and when you look at it in terms of a final season, Sam and Dean getting important closure with their parents fits. Sam tells his dad he loves him, and for the first time really meets his mother! My heart! Dean gets big moments too, with Mary and his first face-to-face with Michael, and that's awesome.

But other aspects of this episode confuse and disappoint me. For a character that started with so much significance and promise, this is an ignominious end for Anna. Thanks to heavenly brainwashing, we lose her integrity as a character, and then she's just dead! Matt Cohen is great as both Michael and John, but meeting Michael now (I think he was also time traveling from 2010, by the way? Maybe?) emphasizes that one of our primary antagonists this season has been completely unseen, which is weird.

Poor Cas is also pretty much a plot device in this episode. He gets some funny lines in, then he's once again nerfed for the rest of the episode, which is frustrating.

What this episode does do is continue to hammer on the theme of fate vs. free will, and how the plight of "Team Free Will" seems increasingly hopeless. They can't change the past, so how can they change the future?

Fan Favorites: Let's give a shoutout to Matt Cohen and Amy Gumenick for nailing young John and Mary. Cohen especially is a fixture at *Supernatural* conventions, and even directed an episode all the way in Season Fifteen.

Death notes: Anna, we hardly knew yee. But hey, someone who slept with Dean died for once. And it's another on the board for Sammy! Dean: 14, Sam: 3, Castiel: 1. He's catching up!

My Bloody Valentine

Episode 5.14. Airdate: February 11, 2010
Written by: Ben Edlund
Directed by: Mike Rohl
Guest Cast: Misha Collins (Castiel), James Otis (Famine), Lex Medlin (Cupid)
Synopsis: Famine comes to town and people starve themselves to death.

This is one of the, well, bloodiest episodes *of Supernatural*, but it's also really good. It starts off kind of fun, if yucky, but improves. Cas and Dean nose to nose, the naked Cupid stuff, it's all kind of silly… and then things get dark. Then really dark.

This episode is about hopelessness. Famine only works on people who want things, but Dean's deep in that phase of depression where his lust for life is gone. He keeps going through the motions, but right now, fighting fate seems impossible. Sam relapsing just confirms to him that ending bloody is inevitable. His heartfelt prayer to God is even more heartbreaking, because it goes unanswered. These guys are getting the message that free will is an illusion pretty loud.

I do like this episode for Cas. We see him be badass and competent, and he gets to stare at Dean some. Although it's naked, he at least gets a hug from cupid, which is nice.

Spoiler Alert: We meet other cupids later on in the series, and none of them are naked and overly hug-y, so was it just this one who was weird?

So, Get This: The name of this episode is a reference in part to the fact Jensen Ackles starred in the film remake of *My Bloody Valentine.*

Behind the Scenes: This episode is a favorite for behind-the-scenes stories from Misha. In the coroner's office scene, Jared was messing with him constantly, and then Jensen betrayed him by making him laugh. Misha also had to eat some truly disgusting prop "raw meat" that wasn't even visible much on camera.

Dead Men Don't Wear Plaid

Episode 5.15. Airdate: March 25, 2010
Written by: Jeremy Carver
Directed by: John F. Showalter
Guest Cast: Jim Beaver (Bobby), Kim Rhodes (Sheriff Jody Mills), Carrie Anne Fleming (Karen)
Synopsis: The dead rise in Sioux Falls, including Bobby's wife Karen.

Our string of really, really sad episodes continues as the boys face yet more horror and loss. This episode is extremely effective, taking advantage of *Supernatural*'s small scale. This is just a town of regular people, whose dead family start to come back and kill them all. They're touched and incredibly traumatized by the apocalypse, which does more for the season arc than any background newscast about crop failures or hurricanes.

Season Five has been hard for Bobby. First he was paralyzed, then suicidal, and now the love of his life is back and he has to lose her all over again. His suffering is a microcosm for everyone in the Winchester orbit: horrible things happen, then something hopeful, which turns out to be horrible. It makes the cycle of violence seem inevitable, and again calls into question whether we have a choice in our lives.

It's like Dean and his pie, which after five seasons he finally gets to actually eat. In *Supernatural*, pie always comes right before death and destruction. Dean finally got some, and it turned out to just bring on more death. But surely things can't get worse?

Fan Favorite: Jody Mills' first episode gives her one of the most tragic backstories on *Supernatural,* but it also establishes her as one of the strongest, most resilient women on the show. Welcome to the family!

Name Game: Dorfman and Niedermeyer are a reference to *Animal House*.

Death Notes: Karen's goodbye is an incredibly tragic moment in a season full of them, but it's some of Jim Beaver's best work.

Dark Side of the Moon

Episode 5.16. Airdate: April 1, 2010
Written by: Andrew Dabb & Daniel Loflin
Directed by: Jeff Woolnough
Guest Cast: Misha Collins (Castiel), Samantha Smith (Mary), Chad Lindberg (Ash), Thunderbird Dinwindle (Pamela), Kurt Fuller (Zachariah), Roger Allen Brown (Joshua)
Synopsis: Sam and Dean die. Again. But this time they go to heaven.

This episode is the epitome of the "Carry On Wayward Son" lyric "I was soaring ever higher, but I flew too high." By making it to heaven, the Winchesters reach one of their lowest emotional points of the series. It's as brutal as shotgun rounds to the chest.

Just like how in Episode 16 of Season One, we finally found John only to lose him, this episode sees the boys and Cas find the ultimate bad dad, God. And he doesn't care about taking care of his children. Cas is in the same place as Sam and Dean used to be—left entirely on his own, scared, and furious. At least Sam and Dean had each other.

But that's past tense in this episode. Like the amulet—that symbol of their brotherly bond—their relationship ends this episode in the trash. The entire point of Sam and Dean's journeys through their very separate heavens, is just how disconnected they are. I think we're meant to realize they're not soulmates. And hey, I know others see it the opposite way, but this is my book! Whether they are soulmates or not, Sam's heaven is away from Dean, and that hurts Dean even more than losing the hope of God's help.

This episode is eerie, painful, and beautiful, and it's a great showcase of some of our favorite dearly departed characters. Especially Ash. It's a great acting showcase for everyone, including Samantha Smith as Mary. I also think this concept of heaven is really brilliant in that it's both poignant and lonely.

Spoiler Alert: God is indeed on Earth, publishing paperbacks. And he'll show up again with the amulet in, oh, six years. What a jerk! We'll see Joshua again too… and it'll end badly. As these things tend to.

Death Notes: Like Ash says, these two die more than anyone. With one more in each Winchester column, we're at Dean: 15, Sam: 4, Castiel: 1. This one really sucked.

99 Problems

Episode 5.17. Airdate: April 8, 2010
Written by: Julie Siege
Directed by: Charles Beeson
Guest Cast: Misha Collins (Castiel), Cindy Sampson (Lisa), Larry Poindexter (Pastor David Gideon), Kayla Mae Maloney (Leah Gideon/The Whore)
Synopsis: The Whore of Babylon is in a town.

Emotional journeys have peaks, falls and valleys. And this is a flat section where Dean and Cas wallow in their pain, while poor Sam tries to keep some sort of faith. It's a bit of a lull after so much emotion with one of the weaker apocalyptic heralds.

The whore stuff is a heavy-handed look at how faith can drive people to do horrible things, and mirrors how Dean's misplaced faith in the angels is driving him to do something really stupid. I appreciate what it's doing, but it's just here to draw out that decision and give us a sad scene between Dean and Lisa at the end.

This is, however, a great Castiel episode. He's funny, and sad, and smiles at jokes in Enochian. He's learned from the Winchesters how to cope with disappointment—badly, with booze and violence.

Ship Shape: At this point, it's nice to see that Cas really has developed a friendship with Sam. Back in "Abandon All Hope," he was protective of Sam because he was his friend, not just because of the apocalypse. And that friendship is decidedly different from his relationship with Dean.

The scene between Dean and Cas, where they bond over their deadbeat dads, is more, shall we say, profound than Cas' funnier scenes with Sam. Just saying. Of course, Dean still has a fantasy relationship with the idea of Lisa, another dream he's letting go, so that's a fitting visit as well.

Point of No Return

Episode 5.18. Airdate: April 15, 2010 (Episode 100)
Written by: Jeremy Carver
Directed by: Phil Sgriccia
Guest Cast: Misha Collins (Castiel), Jim Beaver (Bobby), Kurt Fuller (Zachariah), Jake Abel (Adam Milligan)
Synopsis: Sam, Cas, and Bobby try to keep Dean from saying yes to Michael, just as the angels resurrect Adam.

Unlike the 200th or 300th episode, the 100th episode of *Supernatural* is extremely plot-heavy and it's a big turning point in the story. It's called "Point of No Return," not only because it's the point at which the show could go into syndication, but it's where Dean almost makes an irrevocable choice. Almost. Instead, he fully commits to saving the world the Winchester way.

This episode continues the depressed, hopeless phase that Dean has been in since "Dark Side of the Moon," and he pulls everyone down with him. Bobby and Cas, who looked to Dean as their source of hope, are understandably furious. But it's Sam who doesn't give up on Dean, and that's key here. His act of trust, his absolute faith that his big brother will do the right thing, is the turning point for Dean.

We're also back to the "family don't end in blood" as we explore how the Winchesters relate to their blood family, Adam, differently from their chosen family of Bobby and Cas. Poor Adam gets a pretty raw deal across the board here, though Sam and Dean really did try to save him.

I think losing Cas and Bobby's faith means something to Dean too, and Cas exploding himself rather than see Dean fail, and Bobby saying Dean was keeping him alive, weigh on him. These acts prime the pump, but the last straw is Sam's trust. The theme of trust and family just might be important for the final run on the Death Star.

Ship Shape: We have to talk about Dean and Cas this episode because, well, what *is* going on? Dean makes constant sexual jokes at Cas, and in a very pointed way that seems aimed at making Cas angrier at him. You don't do that unless you know that's a sore point. And even so, we get the emotionally charged fight (is it a fight if it's just Cas kicking Dean's ass?) in the alley. Cas fell *for* Dean, and even Dean knows that means a lot. There's something here. Good thing it will only take them (spoiler) 225 more episodes to figure it out!

Death Notes: Let's pause to appreciate how great Kurt Fuller was as Zachariah. He's so sleazy and scary, and truly the perfect embodiment of Angels as dicks. Which makes his death even more satisfying. And hey, Dean said he'd stab him in the face and kept his promise. This is also the first time a human kills an angel.

Spoiler Alert: So, it turns out that even though Dean jokes about it, the power of love *does* save the day. But let's just take a second here to whine about how, about 180 episodes from now, Dean says yes to Michael and fights Lucifer in the most underwhelming confrontation ever, thus invalidating the entire Season Five arc!

Hammer of the Gods

Episode 5.19. Airdate: April 22, 2010
Written by: Andrew Dabb & Daniel Loflin
Directed by: Rick Bota
Guest Cast: Richard Speight Jr. (Gabriel), Mark Pellegrino (Lucifer), Rekha Sharma (Kali), Adam Croasdel (Baldur), John Emmet Tracy (Mercury), Matt Frewer (Pestilence)
Synopsis: A dozen Gods in a hotel and an archangel with a newly discovered love for humanity isn't enough to beat Lucifer.

Let's talk about Neil Gaiman! Gaiman's work has a lot of influence on *Supernatural,* and it's most obvious in Season Five with a helpful demon named Crowley (partly a reference to *Good Omens*, which Gaiman wrote with Terry Pratchett.) This episode also has a lot in common with his 2001 novel *American Gods*. I'd even say that this version of gods meeting up to keep their place in the world is more successful than the television version of *American Gods*, which aired on Starz. It was kind of terrible, and got canceled after three seasons.

The gods stuff in this episode is fun, though, even if I do hate any show or movie that kills gods. That's just not how they work. But the real meat of the episode is the boys convincing Gabriel to care about people, and care about the world. It's big step for the character, so of course he gets skewered for it. I also think this is the scariest Lucifer ever is, and that his confrontation with Gabriel is an incredible emotional scene. Pellegrino and Speight are perfect, and it might be the most exciting moment so far that doesn't involve a Winchester or Cas.

While things go poorly this episode, it's really about stoking that little spark of hope from last week into a flame. Sam believed in Dean, and now thanks to that, Gabriel stands up for humanity. Humanity constantly screws up and tries to be better, and that's worth loving and saving. And that gets them Gabriel's porn message, with instructions to lock Lucifer back up, thus more hope that might just save the world.

Spoiler Alert: *Of course*, Gabriel isn't dead for good here, and he doesn't use the actual "archangel blade" in his fight with Lucifer. I do like

Gabriel's arc when he returns way down the road, but I think his death here means much more, and works better dramatically than his ultimate pointless demise in Season Thirteen.

Familiar Faces: Rekha Sharma is probably best known for her time on *Battlestar Galactica*, and she's excellent as Kali here. And we'll see more of iconic genre face and *Max Headroom* alum Matt Frewer as pestilence in just a bit.

The Devil You Know

Episode 5.20. Airdate: April 29, 2010
Written by: Ben Edlund
Directed by: Robert Singer
Guest Cast: Jim Beaver (Bobby), Mark Sheppard (Crowley), Eric Johnson (Brady)
Synopsis: Crowley is back with and to help Sam and Dean track down Pestilence.

After quite a few episodes focusing on Dean's emotional low points and journey, and Gabriel's big moment, we turn back to Sam in an episode all about one thing: trust.

Sam and Dean's relationship fell apart because Dean didn't trust Sam, and that culminated in Sam choosing to trust Ruby over Dean. And now the tables are turned, with Dean trusting Crowley. It doesn't really matter that it was a good decision in this case, it contrasts the different standards Dean holds himself and Sam to.

This episode is also about trust being tested. Sam manages to not kill Brady when he has the chance, even when he learns that someone he trusted was manipulating him. And that shows Dean he can be trusted to control his rage—the thing demons and Lucifer want to use against him. It's a big step for Sam, and it sets up another big step for Dean later down the line.

The other thing this episode sets up is Crowley. He's as a fantastically fun, queer, and unpredictable character, both as an ally and antagonist. He's not a friend, not now, but he's the first demon ally that isn't working for Lucifer and he owns this episode.

Famous Face/Fan Favorite: Mark Sheppard, who returns this episode, was already a well-known actor in all sorts of genre shows at this point, from *The X-Files*, to *Leverage*, to *Doctor Who* and *Firefly*. But Crowley may be his most iconic role.

Two Minutes to Midnight

Episode 5.21. Airdate: May 6, 2010
Written by: Sera Gamble
Directed by: Phil Sgriccia
Guest Cast: Misha Collins (Castiel), Jim Beaver (Bobby), Mark Sheppard (Crowley), Matt Frewer (Pestilence), Julian Richings (Death)
Synopsis: Cas is back and takes out Pestilence which leaves him, Sam and Bobby to stop the release of a plague. Dean looks Death in the eyes.

This penultimate episode feels a lot like two smaller episodes stitched together, and one is much better than the other. The opening bits with Pestilence are fine, and Matt Frewer is fantastic in the role, but it ultimately feels somewhat wasted.

But the rest of the episode has some truly stellar moments, including the team's heroics at Niveus and great snark from Crowley and Cas. The highlight, however, is Dean's sit down with Death. Death is a terrifying guy, who likes pizza. And it's brilliant. Richings and Ackles are incredible in the scene. In convention appearances, Richings gives Ackles credit for how he reacts to Death, which makes him that much scarier.

This episode isn't heavy on thematic stuff, though we do see Sam's heroism and Dean confronting his destiny. It sets the board for the final episode, and poses big questions that the finale will answer: Can the boys defy fate?

Fan Favorite: Don't you love watching a show where you can say, "Death is one of my favorite characters?" Julian Richings is perfect in this role.

Driver Picks the Music: The introduction of Death set to Jen Titus' plaintive version of "Oh, Death" is one of the greatest musical moments of the entire series. It's an incredible sequence that gives me goosebumps no matter how many times I watch it.

Ship Shape: Nice of Cas and Dean to revert to being an old married couple the moment Cas is back. And hey, Bobby and Crowley smooched! That's something.

Swan Song

Episode 5.22. Airdate: May 13, 2010
Written by: Eric Kripke
Directed by: Steve Boyum
Guest Cast: Misha Collins (Castiel), Jim Beaver (Bobby), Cindy Sampson (Lisa), Rob Benedict (Chuck), Jake Abel (Michael), Mark Pellegrino (Lucifer),
Synopsis: Sam says yes to Lucifer. Dean lets his brother go.

What is there to say about this episode? It's pretty dang perfect and a really excellent cap to the Kripke era of *Supernatural*. Saving the world doesn't come down to some big fight. It's just two boys, a car, some rock music, and a lot of love and trust. And isn't that everything we could want?

That trust comes in a lot of forms, and at first it doesn't seem to be rewarded. Cas and Bobby aren't optimistic, and they get killed momentarily for their trouble. I like that Cas' ultimate defiance of heaven comes down to him setting his brother on fire, and calling him an assbutt. Dean certainly rubbed off on him.

All season—and indeed for the whole series—we've asked if there was any real choice in Sam and Dean's lives, if they could outrun their fate. Could they make a new story? And in the end, as Chuck writes, they do. They chose family, and that's the whole point. After a lifetime of trying to protect him, Dean finally trusts Sam. And for Sam, it's love, not rage, that allows him to subdue Lucifer and jump into the cage.

This is a major contrast to the conversation between Michael and Lucifer. They weren't able to break the cycle, because they've forgotten that they care about each other. In themes that will echo until the end of the series, it's love and choosing a different path that always saves the day.

Spoiler Alert: But the day isn't fully saved yet. Sam's back already and looking mighty scary! It's gonna be a good long while before the brothers are able to properly be brothers again. This episode also ends with Chuck poofing away, which had fans theorizing for years that he was God. But that wasn't confirmed until Season Eleven.

Ship Shape: Pick your ship and there are juicy moments for it here. Cas and Dean continue to be poignant and repressed. Dean finds his way to Lisa, and that dream of normalcy. Sam and Dean have important stuff that you can read however you like. Sam even becomes one with Lucifer. It's all love and it's all there.

Driver Picks the Music: Yes, Def Leopard's "Rock of Ages" is fun here, but I want to talk for once about the actual score. The piano piece that plays throughout the climatic moments is called "Americana" and it contains that beautiful Winchester family theme. It's a piece of music that we've heard accompanying many big moments highlighting devotion to family, and we'll hear it many times again.

Death Notes: Welp, it wouldn't be a finale at this point without a few Winchesters, or adjacent folks, dying or close to death. Cas got exploded again, Bobby gets on the death board, and Sam is as good at dead so we're counting it for his score. Luckily, Dean's only dead in spirit. Dean: 15, Sam: 5, Castiel: 2.

SUPERNATURAL

CHAPTER SIX

Who Would Want to Watch Our Lives?

Season Six… imagine me saying that in the tired voice of "Bob Singer" from "The French Mistake." It's a tough one because it was so transitional. Creator and executive producer Eric Kripke stepped back to work on other projects at this time—the majority of which flamed out after promising starts—leaving the show in an awkward position. He wouldn't really strike gold on another show until he moved to premium streaming, with the raunchy and violent *The Boys*.

Kripke handed the reins of the show to long-time writer Sera Gamble who, at this point, was the second-most senior writer, having penned some of *Supernatural*'s most emotional and intimate episodes. It seemed like a perfect fit. But unfortunately, being a great episodic writer is different than being a great showrunner. And it shows in the unevenness of Seasons Six and Seven.

Jeremy Carver—who would later return—also departed at this time, as well as Julie Siege. New in the room was Adam Glass, who stuck around a while after this, and Brett Matthews, who did not. Also joining was the team of Eric Charmelo and Nicole Snyder. Jenny Klein, who was an assistant in Season Five, continued to contribute as well.

Season Six tries a lot of things, and honestly tries to do too much. Too many interesting plots, ideas, and characters just get dropped unceremoniously. And when the season finally lands on an over-arching big bad, it's one of our favorites—Castiel. I like that Cas has his own story here, rather than just supporting Sam and Dean's plot, but it's painful to see him as a bad guy, even if just misguided.

If there's a theme to Season Six, it's asking the question "how do we recover from massive trauma?" Trauma changes us. And we make bad decisions to cope. We see this in Sam's arc for the season, who has come back from the cage as a profoundly different person. The idea of missing a soul is a good metaphor for PTSD in general… but it means that for half the season, we're missing the real Sam.

And that's weird!

Sam and Dean's relationship is the foundation of the show, no matter what else, and so the first half of the season ends up feeling strange, despite Jared's great work. It also doesn't help that Dean's emotional arc doesn't drive the story.

In Seasons Four and Five, Sam and Dean weren't just the heroes, they drove the story. And their relationship—the loss of trust and regaining it—was what made the difference, driving discussions. That doesn't happen here. Instead, it's Cas pushing the plot, but we don't even know that until 20 episodes in, leaving the story to happen around our boys, not because of them.

There are some incredible episodes this season, as there are every season, but with no Sam, dropped stories, bad Cas, and more, it makes for a less than cohesive whole.

Exile on Main St.

Episode 6.01. Airdate: September 24, 2010
Written by: Sera Gamble
Directed by: Phil Sgriccia
Guest Cast: Jim Beaver (Bobby), Frederic Lehne (Azazel), Cindy Sampson (Lisa), Mitch Pileggi (Samuel), Nicolas Elia (Ben), Corin Nemec (Christian Campbell), Jessica Heafey (Gwen Campbell)
Synopsis: After a year with Lisa, Dean runs into a Djinn… as well as Sam and a resurrected Grandpa Campbell.

This is one of only two premieres that doesn't occur directly after a giant cliffhanger, which makes it strange in terms of pacing. Jumping forward a year puts us in a bizarro world with no bearings. "Exile on Main St" is all about Dean, with Sam as a character in Dean's life, rather than as a central figure. And while that's interesting, as Dean has often been the emotional center of the show, it very much feels like a whole new show with new mysteries.

The idea of Dean going through the motions, living the life everyone thinks he wanted, is thought-provoking. It's a response to trauma and grief, with Dean faking it until he makes it. We have some people—Bobby, pre-cage Sam, and Lisa—telling him how to live, while others—present Sam, Samuel—tell him who he's meant to be. And I don't think Dean is comfortable with either.

These two worlds tugging at Dean represent two extremes, neither of which fits him. The Campbells are interesting characters on paper, but aside from Samuel they're kind of jerks. And we can't trust Samuel in general. Lisa and Ben, on the other hand, stand for normal, and aren't quite people on their own.

Overall, this episode sets up a lot of mysteries and gives Dean an interesting choice. He finds himself in Sam's shoes, back at the very start of Season One. But does he have the heart to answer the call to adventure? And what the hell is wrong with Sam?!

Driver Picks the Music: While I'm not a huge fan of this episode, the opening montage "Beautiful Loser" by Bob Seger is perfect showing how out of place Dean feels.

Plot Hole: What year is it now after the time skip? Who knows! The show will forget that this happened quickly and will do so again after the next time jump. Whoops.

Two and a Half Men

Episode 6.02. Airdate: October 1, 2010
Written by: Adam Glass
Directed by: John F. Showalter
Guest Cast: Cindy Sampson (Lisa), Mitch Pileggi (Samuel), Nicolas Elia (Ben), Corin Nemec (Christian Campbell), Jessica Heafey (Gwen Campbell)
Synopsis: Sam enlists Dean for help with a shapeshifter … baby.

A monster of the week feels out of place for the second episode of a season, but it does build up the mystery of what's up with Sam and Samuel. And it's mainly about one of our favorite things: family legacy, via a story about parenting. Will Dean become John? Does family define who we are?

I like seeing how natural Dean is with Bobby John, and the questions of whether he's becoming his own father in how he treats Ben, and if it's ethical or healthy to raise kids as hunters, are interesting. Also, Bobby John is cute, and it's telling that Sam goes to biological family for a name, while Dean goes to chosen. It emphasizes that Dean's more comfortable with family that don't end in blood, rather than trusting genetics.

But there's no resolution to this episode. The shifter wins and gets the baby! And we still have no clue what's going on internally with Sam, other than the fact that he's not acting normal. And how does this family episode fit in to any sort of overall theme?

Ship Shape: Lisa is a saint, let's get that out there. She's beautiful and amazing to tolerate Dean's crap, moving her kid and life to live with the guy who saved the world. I wish she had more of a character, because she's more symbolic of "normalcy" than an entire person.

Alas for poor Cindy Sampson, she, like many women who "came between the boys" was treated terribly by the fandom at the time, much like Genevieve Padalecki and Jensen's wife, Danneel, who he married as Season Five finished airing, on May 15, 2010.

The Third Man

Episode 6.03. Airdate: October 8, 2010
Written by: Ben Edlund
Directed by: Robert Singer
Guest Cast: Misha Collins (Castiel), Demore Barnes (Raphael), Sebastian Roché (Balthazar), Cindy Sampson (Lisa)
Synopsis: Biblical plagues lead the boys to call on Castiel, who has been fighting Raphael in a heavenly civil war.

So far, two episodes have been weird Campbell stuff and monsters, and now none of that matters! We have an entirely new plotline with Raphael and the angel war! Yay? Well, Castiel is back, so yes. But Cas, like Sam and everyone else sans Dean, has changed. Dean has become more of himself—more family oriented and nurturing—while Cas and Sam are both… kind of dicks.

What happens after? After a win, after a war, after the end of something major? That's what the show wants to know. Everyone has emerged into this new world, changed, and it seems like freedom from heaven's story has cost a lot of people their humanity, or at least reorganized their priorities.

I think the fractured relationship between Castiel and Balthazar—where Cas' brother emerges from the war alive, doing decidedly non-angelic things—is a mirror for Dean and Sam. At the same time, a kid taking a revenge spree he's unequipped for and killing people, might be a mirror for Cas. Sam is also acting uncaring and unsavory, even though at this point he still has Dean's back. But it's not quite the Sam we know. Castiel's changed priorities at least seem to serve a noble purpose of bringing freedom and keeping the apocalypse of the table.

But we do need to take a moment to appreciate, whatever is wrong with Sammy, *how damn good he looks*.

Ship Shape: Cas admitting that he and Dean share a more profound bond is pretty huge, though obvious to anyone with eyes. This and the episode's mythology about claims being left on souls even gave rise to the theory that Cas' handprint in Season Four was the brand he left when he claimed Dean's soul from hell.

Fan Favorite: Balthazar! This character is instantly interesting and fun. Sebastian Roché's accent, suaveness and general awesomeness make an indelible impression.

Weekend at Bobby's

Episode 6.04. Airdate: October 15, 2010
Written by: Andrew Dabb & Daniel Loflin
Directed by: Jensen Ackles
Guest Cast: Jim Beaver (Bobby), Steven Williams (Rufus), Kim Rhodes (Jody Mills), Mark Sheppard (Crowley), Jennifer Aspen (Marcy)
Synopsis: Bobby helps everyone, it's time for them to help him for a change.

While I like "The Third Man," this is the first great episode of Season Six. It's quite different from anything we've seen before on *Supernatural*, and that's fun! It's not meta, but a new, focused perspective on a character we love, which is just as cool. It has almost no Sam and Dean, because Jensen was busy directing! And he did a great job!

This is Jim Beaver's episode, and every second he's on screen he reminds us why we love Bobby, and how great he is. Jim is an incredible actor, and an incredibly gracious, kind person which shines through on screen. It's also an awesome showcase for guest stars, with Kim Rhodes back as Jody and Steven Williams stealing scenes as Rufus. Crowley is also now King of Hell, which seems important and means we'll be seeing a lot more of our favorite crossroads demon.

Does this episode play into any larger themes? Maybe something with Bobby dealing with his trauma, but it inches the plot forward with Crowley and the monster.

Ship Shape: I feel like nearly everyone we've ever shipped with Bobby shows up here, and yes, I mean Jody, but also Rufus and Crowley. I like that Crowley was introduced with an ambiguous sexuality that he uses to get the best of everyone.

Plot Hole/Spoiler Alert: Thanks to retconning and time travel, the Gavin stuff makes no sense, but whatever! And we don't find out until Season Twelve how Crowley fell into the King of Hell role. It also seems he lied about relinquishing Bobby's soul, as he later condemns it to hell.

Live Free or Twihard

Episode 6.05. Airdate: October 22, 2010
Written by: Brett Matthews
Directed by: Rod Hardy
Guest Cast: Cindy Sampson (Lisa), Nicolas Elia (Ben), Mitch Pileggi (Samuel), Joseph D. Reitman (Boris)
Synopsis: Vampires use the teen bloodsucker craze to build an army, Dean gets turned.

This is one of those "starts one kind of fun way, goes another very dark way" episodes, and I appreciate that. Dean getting vamped is seriously dramatic, and Sam allowing it is even more terrifying. It's fun to go from mocking *Twilight*, to Dean struggling to keep his humanity, even if that switch is jarring.

Still in thematic territory of people becoming different people after trauma, Dean's been trying to be a normal boyfriend and dad, but with the vampire change, he's reminded that his life as a hunter inevitably makes him a monster. And speaking of monstrous, Sam let Dean get turned to test the cure. We can even argue that Samuel has somewhat changed from an honorable hunter to whatever he is now, thanks to trauma.

Spoiler Alert: I can't help but make some connections to Dean's ultimate, final death here, coming on a random vampire hunt. And it's only after that, that Sam can be the one to have a normal apple pie life.

Ship Shape: I don't think Dean nearly eating Lisa and Ben is going to be a good thing for their relationship. Which is sad, because Lisa is the only person keeping Dean human right now. Boris and Dean seem to have some… interesting moments.

You Can't Handle the Truth

Episode 6.06. Airdate: October 29, 2010
Written by: Eric Charmelo & Nicole Snyder (Teleplay & story), David Reed (Story)
Directed by: Jan Eliasberg
Guest Cast: Misha Collins (Castiel), Jim Beaver (Bobby), Cindy Sampson (Lisa), Serinda Swan (Veritas)
Synopsis: The goddess Veritas compels people to speak and hear truth. Except for Sam.

People being compelled to tell the truth is a fun idea, if executed well (that suicide and not sexy drilling — yikes!) but six episodes into the season, the emotional toll on Dean is really high. And seeing Dean increasingly alone is tough. It's good to see that Cas really does care, but he's distancing himself from Dean too. And Dean loses Lisa, so what has this boy got left?

Killing, I guess. It's a dark moment when Dean confesses that he does want a family, but doesn't think he can have it because he's a killer. He still thinks he's daddy's blunt instrument. And I think he also believes he deserves this flawed, scary version of Sam. Survivor's guilt—Dean's favorite. And even though the bodies of the people he loves are around him, he feels like he couldn't save them from himself.

Man, this season is a downer.

Also, we're already done with the plot of Dean and Lisa trying to make it work? That was fast. In previous seasons, things have taken a long time to resolve (think about the hunt for dad taking almost a whole season, or heaven's plans and the special kids being slowly revealed) but the pacing of this season is really different. This won't be the first plot that's resolved too fast.

Ship Shape: Lisa, you're dodging a bullet, honestly. Sorry about the breakup, Dean, but Cas and his soulful looks are right there. Also, I don't think the bromance with Sam is going very well either.

Family Matters

Episode 6.07. Airdate: November 5, 2010
Written by: Andrew Dabb & Daniel Loflin
Directed by: Guy Norman Bee
Guest Cast: Misha Collins (Castiel), Mitch Pileggi (Samuel), Mark Sheppard (Crowley), Corin Nemec (Christian Campbell), Jessica Heafey (Gwen Campbell), Rick Worthy (Alpha Vampire)
Synopsis: Sam has no soul, Samuel is Crowley's bitch, and its monster hunt time.

This one feels more like connective tissue than its own distinct story, despite good scenes. That's fine. Sometimes you need to advance the plot. And boy do we get a lot of plot. We finally know the big villain, and it's Crowley. Man is he fun to watch when he's the baddest and smartest guy in the room. Cas is here once again, but barely used or explored. At least we know that Sam's deal is. Soullessness as a metaphor for PTSD is a choice, but I miss the real Sam.

Samuel's motivation to save Mary makes sense, and it tracks that he's related to Sam and Dean who love not letting family stay dead, causing massive messes. However, Samuel is the only interesting Campbell. There's not much to Gwen, and Christian is a douchebag. But Mitch Pileggi commands the screen, balancing pragmatic and humane.

It's easy to forget that this episode has a monster, with all the Crowley reveals and family drama. The standout performance though is the confrontation with the Alpha Vampire. Not only is Rick Worthy terrifying in the role, but he delivers vital information in a really interesting way. Exposition is better when it's entertaining.

Familiar Faces: Rick Worthy would go on to work on another series with Sera Gamble, as Dean Fogg on *The Magicians*. Whereas Gamble's urge to tell lots of story is a bit too busy for the pace of *Supernatural*, it works great on *The Magicians,* and I recommend the show for any *Supernatural* fan.

Plot Hole/Spoiler Alert: So, this whole season is about finding a way to Purgatory... too bad there's an easily accessible back door that it takes them half an episode to find in Season Eight! AHHHHH.

All Dogs Go to Heaven

Episode 6.08. Airdate: November 12, 2010
Written by: Adam Glass
Directed by: Phil Sgriccia
Guest Cast: Mark Sheppard (Crowley), Janet Kidder (Mandy), Andrew Rothenberg (Lucky)
Synopsis: Crowley sends the boys hunting for an Alpha who turns out to be a skin walker posing as a family dog.

We're at a low point for Season Six, and not just because Lucky is creepy. Nor is it that for some reason the Winchesters just let him escape after he killed three people. It's a bummer of an episode, because we really get the full blast of Soulless Sam… and he's not a very nice guy.

As I mentioned earlier, I understand why the writers chose to make Sam soulless. It's good way of showing how people change in the aftermath of terrible things, but when your show is about two central characters, taking one of them away—or making him a dickwad for half a season—undermines the whole dynamic. I miss Sam! And while Jared is excellent as Soulless Sam, I want the real deal. And so does Dean.

There's also some mirroring between Dean and Lucky, which I guess implies that Dean only cared about Lisa and Ben, because they were the first people to care about him and take him in. And that's not a positive take on that relationship.

Spoiler Alert: At least it will be interesting to see the boys continue to work with Crowley, right? I mean, that won't also get dropped after this episode, right? And surely, all the armies of vampires, skin walkers, and shifters rising across the country will matter, *right*? Sigh…

So, Get This: If the actress Janet Kidder looks familiar, it might be because she looks a lot like her aunt, Margot Kidder.

Clap Your Hands If You Believe …

Episode 6.09. Airdate: November 19, 2010
Written by: Ben Edlund
Directed by: John Showalter
Guest Cast: Robert Picardo (Wayne Whittaker), Linden Bank (Mr. Brennan)
Synopsis: "UFOs" are actually fairies and Dean maybe service Oberon king of the fairies.

After a run of serious, and frankly depressing, episodes, we finally get some fun. And boy did we need it. I love this one! It's creative and weird (it's Ben Edlund so no surprise there) and it actually lets the boys make some silly jokes!

This episode, I think Soulless Sam works. Making Dean the "sensitive" one, while Sam is left to be smarmy and without empathy, is a great and new contrast. If this had been the norm for this plotline—and it had been shorter—I think it would have worked better. But as it is, this is a highlight of the arc. And seeing Dean fight a tinker bell is pretty awesome too. The idea that fairies are UFOs is a real one, and it's such a great twist even with a small budget.

My only regret associated with this episode is that we never hear from the fairy realm much again, which is a shame. There could have been a lot of story there. But I guess with heaven, hell, and now purgatory that was realms enough. Alas. Would have been cool to meet Oberon.

Driver Picks the Music: Absolutely perfect use of David Bowie's "Space Oddity" given the UFO theme, especially as Bowie ruled a fae realm in *Labyrinth*.

Famous Faces: Casting Robert Picardo is a nice touch. We all know him as The Doctor from *Star Trek: Voyager* and thus associate him with space, making the leprechaun reveal even better.

Caged Heat

Episode 6.10. Airdate: December 3, 2010
Written by: Brett Matthews (Teleplay & Story), Jenny Klein (Story)
Directed by: Robert Singer
Guest Cast: Misha Collins (Castiel), Mitch Pileggi (Samuel), Rachel Miner (Meg), Mark Sheppard (Crowley), Corin Nemec Christian
Synopsis: Sam, Dean and a reluctant Castiel work with Meg to take out Crowley. And a lot of other stuff with blood and torture and betrayal

This episode exemplifies everything I hate about Season Six. Plots, which in previous seasons would have simmered for many episodes, are summarily dropped and nearly everyone is a big giant jerk or out of character entirely. Did you think the boys working with Crowley would matter? Nope. Over. Would they learn from, or connect with Samuel in any meaningful way? Uh uh. He's bad now.

Soulless Sam is terrifying, and mean, and scary, which isn't really much fun, while Cas is over there watching porn and making out with a demon for no real reason. And said demon? Well, Meg is fun, but then she gets tortured naked for no reason at all, except to objectify her. She's doubly sexualized this episode and it's doubly bad!

The writer of this episode is Brett Matthews, who gave us the disappointing "Live Free or Twihard." We'll see him again for another terrible outing later in the season "And Then There Were None." All of his episodes are a pacing and characterization disaster, and it's not shocking that he was only on staff for this one season.

Is there anything thematic here? Sure. People doing bad things to save and protect people they love, such as Samuel's deal with Crowley mirroring Dean shoving Sam's flayed soul back into him. It's also foreshadowing, which is nice, I guess? But over all this episode is a lot of noisy stuff without much of a point to it.

Death Notes: Goodbye Christian! You sucked! And nice flame out, Crowley. Weird how you didn't keep track of those bones…

Spoiler Alert: The thing that sucks about this episode is none of it matters. The monsters don't matter. Crowley isn't dead. The Winchesters forget they were working with Crowley and Meg when they get mad at Cas for doing the same later. Nothing with Samuel is ever resolved. The only consequence from this episode is Megstiel.

Ship Shape: Look, I like the idea of an angel and a demon who like each other, and don't really know why. Cas is great, and I see why Meg is fascinated by him, but my main takeaway from this episode is how much Cas just wants to be back with Dean, but doing as much as he can to protect him.

Appointment in Samara

Episode 6.11. Airdate: December 10, 2010
Written by: Sera Gamble, Robert Singer
Directed by: Mike Rohl
Guest Cast: Jim Beaver (Bobby), Lindsay McKeon (Tessa), Julian Richings (Death), Sebastian Roché (Balthazar), Robert Englund (Doctor Robert)
Synopsis: It's take your Death to work day for Tessa as Dean gets a temp job.

Now this is a quality episode, and it's actually interesting. A good change from our last outing. It's thematic, scary, emotional, and dramatic, and it gives us a satisfying resolution to a plot arc. So it is possible!

The big point of this episode is about natural order, as we see in Dean learning the cost of upsetting fate. But Sam's story is about when it's acceptable to hurt other people, because of our own feelings. Dean's moral compass keeps him from ending a girl's life when it's time, and that has a cost. He's potentially doing the same thing to Sam—not killing him, but really screwing things up. Even if it's out of love, Dean's screwing with things again. These ideas all come down to free will and consent, with Dean going against his previous ideals, buying into fate and taking away Sam's free will.

Thankfully, this episode is the end of Soulless Sam and the apex of the particular plot. Sam is terrifying here, and not in a fun way. It's tragic to see him try to kill Bobby and ruin that relationship. Even though Cas, and everyone else has a point about Sam's soul's condition, I think Dean did the right thing here.

Death Notes: I appreciate that Death chides Dean for just killing himself like it's nothing! Too bad this beautiful moron will learn absolutely nothing from that chat. But we're upping the score again to Dean: 16, Sam: 5, Castiel: 2.

Famous Faces: Getting Robert Englund—Freddy Krueger himself!—as a guest star is so cool! And it's so weird that the show wastes him entirely as doctor for one scene? This is something Season Six does a lot with all sorts of cast members including Misha and here, Sebastian: uses them for one scene in an episode and nothing more. I don't know if it was budget or what, but it's disconcerting and disappointing.

Like A Virgin

Episode 6.12. Airdate: February 4, 2011
Written by: Adam Glass
Directed by: Phil Sgriccia
Guest Cast: Misha Collins (Castiel), Jim Beaver (Bobby), Kim Johnston Ulrich (Dr. Eleanor Visyak)
Synopsis: Real Sam! Dragons! Eve?

Sam is back! That alone elevates this episode. Plus, despite the absolute lack of a budget or effect, the dragons make for a fun case and it's emotional watching Sam discover what happened while he was soulless. The way Sam's innocence needs to be sacrificed for the greater good is a great mirror to the dragons' sacrifice to summon Eve.

But there are other aspects that continue some of Season Six's problems. As much as Cas has his own plot this time around, he's only in and out of a few scenes which feels wasted. We've gone from finding ways to handicap Cas in Season Five, to just… leaving. And we get another character whose life's work gets destroyed by the Winchesters? Poor Dr. Visyak.

Dean versus the sword, and all the hugs, are great though. But, uh, another problem is that the Winchesters leave the job unfinished. Again. This isn't the first time this has happened, and it won't be the last.

Spoiler Alert/Plot Hole: Once again we ask, will all these new monsters running around be mentioned again, or be important? And once again, the answer is sadly no. But at least Purgatory is gonna be cool… in Season Eight.

Unforgiven

Episode 6.13. Airdate: February 11, 2011
Written by: Andrew Dabb & Daniel Loflin
Directed by: David Barrett
Guest Cast: Mitch Pileggi (Samuel), Miranda Frigon (Brenna Dobbs), Joe Holt (Roy Dobbs)
Synopsis: Soulless flashbacks and spider monsters. Yikes.

Maybe I hate this episode because I hate spiders. Maybe I hate it because I don't like Soulless Sam. Maybe all the black and white, grainy flashbacks just take me out of it. Regardless, I'm just not crazy about it.

As we transition into the later half of the season, we focus less on people changed by trauma, to more how we cope with those changes. Sam spends this episode reckoning with what he did while soulless. He banged and murdered his way all over the US, and I don't blame him for wanting to atone for that. Nor Dean for not wanting to think about it.

But we've barely had time to recover from soulless Sam, and we know how bad he was. So it's not new information for us. We do get a slightly more human side to Samuel, who has been so far underused, but since he's only in flashbacks, there's no real character development. Again, the job isn't finished at the end, and Sam and Dean just ignore that there are a bunch of Arachnes out there! (Don't worry, the show will too!)

Name Game: Samuel and Sam's aliases Roark and Wynand are a reference to Ayn Rand's *The Fountainhead*, if you needed confirmation that these guys are jerks.

Ship Shape: Well, the "slept with Sam Winchester and died" club gets a lot bigger this week! Yikes!

Mannequin 3: The Reckoning

Episode 6.14. Airdate: February 18, 2011
Written by: Eric Charmelo & Nicole Snyder
Directed by: Jeannot Szwarc
Guest Cast: Cindy Sampson (Lisa), Nicholas Elia (Ben), Rosalie Ward (Isabel Brown), Jake Richardson (Johnny)
Synopsis: A vengeful spirit takes over mannequins. Not creepy at all.

What is this episode about? Sex dolls? Haunted kidneys? Ben not wanting Lisa to move on? Baby being possessed by a ghost? (How dare!) There's a lot, but it's about not letting go and how we can hurt people without meaning to.

Rose, our ghost, was killed as part of a prank gone wrong, and possibly killed her own sister in pursuit of vengeance. There's some bearing on Dean's now-resolved relationship with Ben and Lisa, as well as what's going on with Sam and his delicate soul-wall. He did hurt a lot of people while soulless.

But does this relate to the larger season? Maybe. As I mentioned earlier, the theme of doing what you think is best, and it going horribly wrong, happens a lot this season. That is sort of the Winchester way—solving one problem by creating five more. Dean regrets leaving the people he cares about, but he did it to keep them safe. And that is going to be relevant to another character in about five episodes.

It's sort of a bummer that Ben finally gets some personality as he exits Dean's life. Lisa and Ben were always more of ideas than characters, both within the narrative and in the show. Not letting people be people isn't the way to treat folks, or write them.

Ship Shape: Well, Dean and Lisa, the longest running romantic relationship on the show seems fully done-zo. Did it work? Well, it was never about the romance or the chemistry, it was about Dean finding "normal," and now we know that doesn't work so well for him, which is inherently tragic.

The French Mistake

Episode 6.15. Airdate: February 25, 2011
Written by: Ben Edlund
Directed by: Charles Beeson
Guest Cast: Misha Collins (Castiel/Misha Collins), Genevieve Padalecki (Genevieve Padalecki), Sebastian Roché (Balthazar), Brian Doyle-Murray (Bob Singer), Carlos Sanz (Virgil)
Synopsis: Balthazar sends Sam and Dean into another reality where they are actors named Jared Padalecki and Jensen Ackles on a TV show called *Supernatural*.

Supernatural obliterated the fourth wall many times before this, but this time, Sam and Dean bring their fictional lives into our reality. The result is an episode that's so bonkers and brilliant it ranks as many cast member's favorite (including Misha Collins, despite the fact that "Misha Collins" is brutally killed).

This episode pokes fun at the whole of *Supernatural* still chugging along after six seasons. No one is spared from the jokes, which are sharp, but loving. From spoiled stars, budgets, very specific jokes about filming in Canada, or the guys not knowing who the new showrunner Sera Gamble is, everything here is gold.

And we even get to a few thematic things, like how it's better to be yourself rather than trying to live another, fake life. As hunters, Sam and Dean matter. And while they may not get why anyone would want to watch their lives, it's a reminder that they matter to us. This episode also alludes to larger, series-long themes about who control destiny and who writes stories. Is it the author/god or the characters/people/fans? And, well, it takes the "death of the author" idea quite literally.

Behind the Scenes: The crew here is entirely based on real people like Serge Ladouceur—the show's long-time director of photography—first AD Kevin Parks, producer Jim Michaels, and director/producer Bob Singer. Stunt coordinator Lou Bollo and Jared and Jensen's stunt men played themselves.

Gen Padalecki was nervous about coming back to the show, given how much fans hated her and Ruby, but once she was assured it was to make fun of everything, she was on board. That's also her and Jared's actual wedding photo! But not their actual house. Misha Collins loved playing the douchiest version of himself possible, and during the airing or the episode, he tweeted all the tweets "Misha" made.

Spoiler Alert: Weirdly enough, the idea of alternate universes will be incredibly important six seasons later?

And Then There Were None

Episode 6.16. Airdate: March 4, 2011
Written by: Brett Matthews
Directed by: Mike Rohl
Guest Cast: Jim Beaver (Bobby), Steven Williams (Rufus), Mitch Pileggi (Samuel), Jessica Heafey (Gwen Campbell)
Synopsis: A new monster made by Eve incites a murder mystery and a blood bath.

From the sublime, to the utterly ridiculous and infuriating. As a story this episode is fine. It's a riff on an old-school, Agatha Christie murder mystery, where anyone could be the killer with hints of *The Thing* for good measure. It's also got some good themes about forgiveness for past sins… but it also murders three characters—Rufus, Samuel, and Gwen—for no reason, cutting off stories that could have been far more interesting.

Now, I'm not saying that characters shouldn't die, especially on a show with such a high body count, but I think character deaths should matter. Characters should be affected by them, and they should affect the plot. And that doesn't happen here. Gwen's death is an afterthought for an underdeveloped character, but Samuel's is downright offensive. To have a character that was so built up and had so much potential, just die in the middle of an episode and immediately forgotten is so bad!

And then to add insult to injury, we lose Rufus! At least with Rufus, we learn some lessons about letting go of grudges before you go… not that anyone one applies that to Sam and Dean's relationship with Samuel, since they forget he ever existed after he's dead. But even so, Rufus's death is pointless in the larger scheme of things, and I wish there had been more from him.

This episode represents so many dropped balls and wasted potential in Season Six, which is the real tragedy.

Death Notes: These aren't even good deaths!

My Heart Will Go On

Episode 6.17. Airdate: April 15, 2011
Written by: Eric Charmelo & Nicole Snyder
Directed by: Phil Sgriccia
Guest Cast: Misha Collins (Castiel), Jim Beaver (Bobby), Samantha Ferris (Ellen), Sebastian Roché (Balthazar), Katie Walder (Atropos)
Synopsis: Balthazar unsinks the Titanic, changes the world a little bit, and personally pisses off fate herself.

From a low to another high, I love this episode because it has everything: Destiel, Celine Dion jokes, Bobby being domestic, and some of the gnarliest deaths in the show's run. This episode is why I have a garage door phobia.

Seeing a world that's subtly different, such as small things like Cuba not being communist, is fun, but this episode shifts the focus of the season to what's going on with Cas and heaven. It's something that's been hinted at all year, but we haven't actually seen much of. We get to see the lengths Cas is willing to go to, to win this war, and the moral gray area that it takes him. But we also see where Cas' line is—the Winchesters. Just like Sam and Dean are each other's weak spot, they (and let's be honest here, Dean specifically) are Castiel's. He won't risk them being harmed.

One thing this episode, and the ones before and after it, are missing though is a focus on what's going on with Sam and Dean. And that's fine. They don't need to be directly moving the plot in every episode. But it is a change for the central story to really be about Castiel, having Sam and Dean sort of be incidental. But that would work better if the Cas stuff wasn't so mysterious.

That focus on Cas also means that the thematic thrust of this episode is about the natural order and fate, and whether that's just. It's also about the deep cost of screwing with that natural order, as we see with Ellen's resurrection and loss.

Ship Shape: How much do I love Bobby and Ellen together as a couple. They fit so perfectly and bring out such warmth in one another. I love seeing Bobby supported and taken care of, even for just an episode, and the sweetness of these two makes losing Ellen again hurt even more. This is also the first time we get a variation of "I need you" as code for "I love you." Although we've seen Sam and Dean use variations of this to express love (not that way! Unless that's your thing) it's very explicit here. You know what's also explicit here? Balthazar looking directly at Dean and telling him Cas is in love with him. That's a thing that happened, and sure it's a joke but it's not wrong!

Driver Picks the Music: The "One Way or Another" by Blondie sequence is so much fun. And for the record, I'm in agreement with Balthazar's pretext for saving the Titanic and would love a Universe where Celine Dion is a destitute lounge singer.

Frontierland

Episode 6.18. Airdate: April 22, 2011
Written by: Andrew Dabb & Daniel Loflin (Teleplay & story), Jackson Stewart (Story)
Directed by: Guy Norman Bee
Guest Cast: Misha Collins (Castiel), Jim Beaver (Bobby), Sam Henning (Samuel Colt), Matthew John Armstrong (Elias Finch), Sonya Salomaa (Rachel)
Synopsis: Dean and Sam get Castiel to send them back to 1861 Wyoming to retrieve Phoenix ash to kill Eve.

This episode is sort of a magic trick, in that the main story of Sam and Dean going back to the old west is a big hunk of misdirection, distracting the audience from the much more important stuff with Castiel. That's not to say the western stuff isn't fun—because every second of it is delightful—but in the bigger scheme, this episode is building on and setting up big stuff for Cas going forward.

While Rachel counts as one of those interesting characters who's introduced only to be killed, she's important because she highlights how the Winchesters only use Castiel when convenient and, in turn, how he only values himself in terms of what he can do for them. This even relates back to "Weekend at Bobby's," also written by Dabb and Loflin, with the boys being so far up their own asses they forget to help another person they love.

These boys are smart enough to think up a plan involving time travel, and yet too codependent and focused on their own stuff to notice issues with their other chosen family members. And as great as it is to see Dean cosplaying a sheriff and wining a classic western shootout, these boys are not necessarily heroes here.

Name Game: Dean saddles Sam with the Texas Ranger alias "Walker" in a clear homage to the show *Walker: Texas Ranger* starring Chuck Norris. Nine years after this episode, Jared Padalecki would actually take on the role of Cordell Walker in the reboot of that series, simply titled *Walker*. With Mitch Pileggi as his father!

Mommy Dearest

Episode 6.19. Airdate: April 29, 2011
Written by: Adam Glass
Directed by: John F. Showalter
Guest Cast: Misha Collins (Castiel), Samantha Smith (Eve), Jim Beaver (Bobby), Amber Benson (Lenore), Mark Sheppard (Crowley)
Synopsis: Sam, Dean, Cas, and Bobby hunt down Eve, who is beta testing a new breed of monster. Also, Crowley's alive and working with Cas. Whoops.

This episode is another one of those transitional, plot-heavy installments, but it works thanks to good pacing and emotional resonance, as well as one hell of a final twist. It's sort of like a companion to "Caged Heat" in that it resolves and re-frames a lot of the story from that episode, but it's actually, ya know, good. Not perfect, but good.

Eve is, disappointingly, defeated pretty easily here. But she's never really been the point of the season. She was another red herring, and the real story has always been Crowley and Cas… but that sort of makes a lot of this season rather pointless.

The point of this episode though is Cas, the Winchesters, and the little monster boy. Dean and Sam mistakenly rescue the two brothers Eve turned into, because they see things in a very human and compassionate way. But Cas is pragmatic, and on a larger scale is willing to make sacrifices. And he's proven right about the orphans, which should tell us something about why he's working with a demon. And they way Dean and Sam react says a lot about them.

Driver Picks the Music: Of course, the song, "Miracle," playing at the end is by Jefferson Starship. Nice compliment to the "I believe in miracles" refrain of "You Sexy Thing" by Hot Chocolate that plays in the opening.

Death Notes: Hi Lenore! Uh, bye Lenore. Another wasted guest star and pointless death. Sigh.

The Man Who Would Be King

Episode 6.20. Airdate: May 6, 2011
Written by: Ben Edlund
Directed by: Ben Edlund
Guest Cast: Misha Collins (Castiel), Jim Beaver (Bobby), Demore Barnes (Raphael), Mark Sheppard (Crowley), Sonya Salomaa (Rachel)
Synopsis: Castiel tells his side of the story.

This episode is so good that it almost makes the rest of this not-so-good season better. Almost. Learning Castiel's story is such a revelation and makes everything he's been doing make sense, including avoiding the Winchesters. Like he learned from the boys, he's doing what he thinks must be done. And after a whole season of Dean making big, maybe bad, decisions to protect others, that's understandable.

Cas cares about freedom. Not just for himself and the angels, but also for Dean who taught him about it. Yes, Sam too, but the focus here is Dean. He wants to keep the apocalypse on ice for Dean. He brought Sam back for Dean. He doesn't ask for help, because he doesn't want to ruin Dean's life. He just watches him rake leaves because he loves this bowlegged, denim-wrapped nightmare.

That's why Dean's trust hurts him, and why it's Dean's look of betrayal that will haunt Cas. I think Cas in some ways wants to be caught when he makes his "Superman" slip up, because he's tired of the lies. And now he's the one that doesn't think he deserves to be saved.

And really guys, is working with Crowley so bad? They did it in Season Five and he's really funny and smart? Why be hypocrites about this? Unless you're telling me the Winchesters have learned their lesson about working with "bad guys," because I have about nine more seasons of bad decisions to counter that.

Ship Shape/Spoiler Alert: It is totally possible and entirely valid to look at everything between Dean and Cas this episode in a platonic way, and heck, maybe it was intended that way at first. But in hindsight knowing, that Castiel canonically loves Dean *that way*, this episode hurts even more.

But everything Cas does makes a lot more sense. And Dean may not understand his own feelings, but you don't look at friends the way he looks at Cas.

The romantic angle even makes the declarations from Dean in this episode that he cares for Cas like a brother hurt, because that's not really what Cas feels or wants, so it's plausible that might break his heart a bit and push him away, towards the very very bad decisions he's going to make in the next three episodes!

Death Notes: Crowley isn't dead! What a shocker. It's fine though because at this point, he's too much fun and too good of a foil to stay dead.

Let It Bleed

Episode 6.21. Airdate: May 13, 2011
Written by: Sera Gamble
Directed by: John F. Showalter
Guest Cast: Misha Collins (Castiel), Jim Beaver (Bobby), Mark Sheppard (Crowley), Sebastian Roché (Balthazar), Cindy Sampson (Lisa), Nicholas Elia (Ben), Kim Johnston Ulrich (Dr. Eleanor Visyak)
Synopsis: Crowley's demons kidnap Lisa and Ben in an attempt to keep the Winchesters from interfering with the plan to pop Purgatory, which H.P Lovecraft already did.

This episode goes all in with Cas and Crowley as antagonists, and the result are seriously angsty. We're doubling down on "doing bad things to protect the people we love" for both Dean and Cas, and it's ironic that Dean doesn't see how his own actions mirror Castiel's. He tortures to saves someone he loves. Cas does the same.

Dean's relationship with Lisa was about finding a family and trying his best to protect them, but he couldn't do that as himself. He had to step away and they still got hurt. And their peril makes Dean into something he doesn't want again—a torturer. But he really thinks that's his true nature, so to resolve things, he removes himself from Lisa and Ben entirely.

And just like Dean turns to terrible things to protect Lisa and Ben, Cas has turned to his own worst instincts to protect his found family and, in his mind, his actual family in heaven too. Both Dean and Cas end up making some pretty shady decisions, as Sam says, to "save" people.

Everyone is trying their best under the worst possible circumstances here, and it's all a giant mess. Meanwhile, Sam and Bobby are doing their jobs as they ride out the drama. I love seeing Bobby hunting on his own, figuring out this mystery, and his relationship to Ellie is so sweet. Sam… doesn't have much to do this episode and hasn't had much to do for a while. This feels like more misdirection, or there just wasn't room. At least Balthazar has a change of heart!

Ship Shape: Poor Lisa. Her new, dead boyfriend aside, Dean having Cas erase her memories is not going to solve anything! People are going to ask her questions about her male model looking ex, and she'll think she's going insane! This is an incredibly painful resolution to a plot that seemed hopeful.

Dean's lesson here is that civilian relationships aren't going to work. If only there was a celestial creature willing to tear down the walls of reality to keep you safe Dean. The extent which this episode is about Dean and Cas' constipated feelings is maddening.

And, when you really look at it, the person that got the most loving attention in this season was Bobby. Jody, Marcy, Ellen, now Eleanor—good for him. Too bad he's reaching Sam-levels of dead exes.

The Man Who Knew Too Much

Episode 6.22. Airdate: May 20, 2011
Written by: Eric Kripke
Directed by: Robert Singer
Guest Cast: Misha Collins (Castiel), Jim Beaver (Bobby), Mark Sheppard (Crowley), Sebastian Roché (Balthazar), Kim Johnston Ulrich (Dr. Eleanor Visyak), Lanette Ware (Raphael), Erica Cerra (Robin)
Synopsis: Castiel breaks the wall in Sam's mind so he can open Purgatory without Winchester interference. It works and Cas ... becomes the new god? Uh oh.

Welp. This sure is an episode, and Cas being right and winning only to become a new cruel god, is a fitting end to Season Six. It really highlights everything wrong—and the few things right—with the whole thing.

Balthazar seemed important all season and was fun and interesting, even when he was just there to move the plot along. So his turn to Team Winchester seemed important. But it wasn't. He was just there to die to… make Cas sad? Or make him seem scarier? Same with Ellie, who was so built-up last episode. She's done in, in one scene here, and that's such a waste. Even Raphael, one of the main antagonists all year, is disposed of with a snap. That's cool but… weren't we supposed to care?

Then there's Crowley, who is so much fun to watch that we forget nothing he did all season makes sense. He wants purgatory because power? That makes no sense unless you really believe his position as king is precarious. Spoiler Alert: it's not. And even if it was, he never wanted the gig and doesn't like it that much. So, the whole plot falls apart. And the whole plan about going after monsters and alphas… wasn't the way to get into purgatory! It was all pointless!

The same thing goes for Sam's head trip. The idea is good, and well executed, but the whole soulless Sam thing should have been dealt with like this at the beginning. Jared's acting is stellar, but Sam's big moment where he accepts his hell trauma so he can help Dean is ultimately, you guessed it, pointless! Because he doesn't actually help at all.

And then there's Cas. He's isolated, regretful and alone, betrayed by friends and rejected by the people he loves most. And still, he manages to pull it all off and defeat Raphael. But in classic Winchester fashion, his attempt to make things better actually makes things worse. He's God now, and well, that can't be good.

Spoiler Alert: It will also be *pointless*. Like most of the stories of Season Six, Godstiel will barely matter for an episode, nor will the consequences of that for the world, much like all those monsters running around thanks to Eve will all be forgotten.

Death Notes: Raphael and Balthazar's deaths are such shocks and yet the definition of anticlimactic. But at least Cas got to explode Raphael the way he exploded Cas at the end of Season Four!

And now Season Seven. Oh boy.

SUPERNATURAL

CHAPTER SEVEN

It's All Dick

We're here. Within the *Supernatural* fandom, there's a pretty strong consensus that Season Seven is the low point of the series. But, surprise, I think that's wrong! I would argue (and I have for the entirety of the last chapter) that Season Six was the nadir of the show's transition. That's not to say Season Seven is particularly good… but I do think it's better than Season Six.

While Season Six was all over the place, with stories getting dropped, characters getting shortchanged, and a general feeling that too many cooks were in the kitchen, Season Seven is at least coherent with a much clearer over-arching plot. I think this was a factor of Eric Kripke finally really stepping away, letting others run things. We also have important additions to the writers' room: Robbie Thompson—one of the best in the series history—replaces Brett Matthews, and the return of Brad Buckner and Eugenie Ross-Leming. They took the team spot from Eric Charmelo and Nicole Snyder, who left to run another CW show, Ringer, where Misha would guest star. Ross-Leming is also Robert Singer's wife.

A coherent story is a good thing, and it's nice to see themes and emotional arcs develop over several episodes to a larger conclusion, but the problem with Season Seven is that those arcs aren't particularly good. Or more accurately, they don't work on this show. The themes and villains of Season Seven are smart, and interesting, but they're like tropical plants trying to grow in a northern garden. Deconstructing American consumerism just doesn't belong in a story about family and free will.

Season Seven is about taking Sam and Dean to their lowest and loneliest points, stripping away everything and everyone that supported them. That's fine in theory, but taking away everything from them that makes them who they are (including Baby!) isn't terribly fun to watch. But it is satisfying when things get put back together.

Amid all of this is a season-long big bad that… parodies corporate America and capitalism? Okay? Fine. That's an idea, but once again, it doesn't quite fit here. But first, we have to clean up the mess of Season Six. I'm sure it won't be terrible.

Meet the New Boss

Episode 7.01. Airdate: September 23, 2011
Written by: Sera Gamble
Directed by: Phil Sgriccia
Guest Cast: Misha Collins (Castiel), Jim Beaver (Bobby), Mark Pellegrino (Hallucifer), Mark Sheppard (Crowley), Julian Richings (Death),
Synopsis: Things are terrible as Cas plays God, loses, then unleashes something called Leviathan on Earth.

Yup. Terrible. This feels like a second Season Six finale, where everyone we love is sad, or bad, and that's not fun. Godstiel does some admirable things in the big job, but he's just not our Cas and that's tough to watch. It's also hard to watch Dean give up hope while Sam slowly slips into madness. Thank someone for Bobby, who is eternally the only one keeping his shit together.

Cas starts to redeem himself by the end of the episode, which is a relief because he just doesn't work as a villain. But everything happens so fast that we don't get much resonance from his "I was soaring ever higher, but I flew too high." The confrontation with Death is fun, but only really serves to deliver exposition and plot devices. And then Cas is dead. Then not dead. Then dead again.

I think this episode was meant to really be the end for Castiel, which would have sucked. Sera Gamble and/or other powers that be wanted focus on the Winchesters, and Cas was hard to write for, so they pushed him away. That was the wrong choice. Cas made the show better and more interesting, and making him a bad guy before killing him off was a real error.

We hit low points with Dean losing people and Sam losing his mind, their car and life's purpose in tatters. But that darkness does give way to forgiveness, which I think will be important.

Ship Shape: Not a high point for Dean and Castiel, let's be honest. But everyone has rough break ups when feelings are unresolved. There are some great moments for them though, because among all of this, it's Dean who Cas cares about the most.

Death Notes: Well, that's one in the books for Cas, who has really earned his Winchester stripes by dying again, breaking the world. Dean: 16, Sam: 5, Castiel: 3.

Hello, Cruel World

Episode 7.02. Airdate: September 30, 2011
Written by: Ben Edlund
Directed by: Guy Norman Bee
Guest Cast: Misha Collins (Castiel), Jim Beaver (Bobby), Mark Pellegrino (Hallucifer), Kim Rhodes (Jody), Benito Martinez (Edgar)
Synopsis: The Leviathans melt Cas, infect the water supply, and start eating people.

This feels like a second season premiere, but not a good one. While Leviathan!Cas seemed like he would be a big threat at the end of the last episode, that was all a lie and now Cas is dead again, leaving Dean sadly folding his trench coat like battle flag. Suddenly, we're in an entirely new sort of show. And we've lost both our home base and our grounding.

Jody versus the Leviathans sort of works, but why should we care when just one episode ago Cas was the new God, and every relationship on the show was in tatters? The season pacing in the Gamble era continues to be a mess.

The emotional heart of this episode is Sam and his struggles with Hallucifer (his hallucinations of Lucifer. That's a fandom term, not my own). Pellegrino is great at portraying a Lucifer that's just a bit different from the one we know, and Jared is awesome with Sam's turmoil. The moment where Dean reaches Sam also gives us something we haven't seen in a while—a major brother moment. When literally everything else is on fire and failing, these guys have one another. That's the heart of the show and it's been a while since we saw it.

Death Notes: Cas has had a really rough week, so we're giving him an extra point for dying again in as many episodes. Of course, Dean still has the lead with a score of Dean: 16, Sam: 5, Castiel: 4.

The Girl Next Door

Episode 7.03. Airdate: October 7, 2011
Written by: Andrew Dabb & Daniel Loflin
Directed by: Jensen Ackles
Guest Cast: Jim Beaver (Bobby), Colin Ford (Young Sam), Jewel Staite (Amy Pond), Emma Grabinsky (Young Amy), Sean Owen Roberts (Chet the Leviathan)
Synopsis: With Bobby on the run from Leviathan, Sam catches up with Amy, a kitsune and childhood crush. He lets her go, but Dean goes behind his back and kills her.

This is not, on its own, a bad episode. I'll start with that. It's disjointed, sure. The Leviathan stuff is completely disconnected from the Amy Pond case and in general it feels like an episode that should have been later in the season. The acting is great (Colin Ford is so good as young Sam!) and Jensen does a wonderful job directing.

The thematic stuff here is pretty great too. We've returned to a theme of trust, much like in Season Five. At this point, Dean is focusing his new trust issues on Sam, because he thinks Sam's madness compromises him. At least that's what he says. What's really going on, is that Dean's trust was betrayed a lot, so he's got issues. He sees himself as a monster who can't change and sees Amy that way too. So he kills her for it.

And that's all fine, but it just doesn't quite fit for a random wrench to be thrown into the brother relationship. One we just reaffirmed and started to fix last episode. These guys haven't even processed Cas dying, or a new global threat, and suddenly… this?

Famous Faces: Jewel Staite, who audiences know well as Kaylee Frye, joining fellow *Firefly* alum Mark Sheppard as a member of the *Supernatural* family.

Ship Shape: Now even Sam's childhood first kiss is dead? Man, this poor moose cannot catch a break in the romance department.

Spoiler Alert: I think Dean's ultimate death in "Carry On" would have been more satisfying had it been at the hands of Amy's son, but oh well.

Defending Your Life

Episode 7.04. Airdate: October 14, 2011
Written by: Adam Glass
Directed by: Robert Singer
Guest Cast: Jim Beaver (Bobby), Alon Tal (Jo), Faran Tahir (Osiris)
Synopsis: Osiris is hanging around Dearborn, Michigan putting people with guilt hearts on trial, and Dean ends up in the courtroom.

Once again, this one is fine on its own and an improvement on Season Six's disjointedness. It has big thematic moments about Dean's massive guilt complex and how his self-esteem is so low it's hanging out in hell with Crowley. Osiris is a really fun monster of the week, and I like that he's not killed, just disabled.

But the aspect of this episode that gets to me, is that Dean's guilt and his worsening depression are framed as being all about Sam and killing Amy Pond? In all of Dean's flashbacks, we don't get a single glimpse or mention of Cas? Or Lisa! Those were huge losses for Dean, but they're glossed over here in a callous way that makes no sense.

At least Sam is doing okay! I mean, it's sort of tragic that he thinks he deserves insanity, in addition to hundreds of years of hell torture to make up for his mistakes, but it's nice that he's feeling okay. I'm sure this will last.

Ship Shape: This episode seems determined to remind us that Dean likes women, and honestly in an episode that erases Cas' death, that's a weird thing to do. It even reduces Jo to something objectified.

Shut Up, Dr. Phil

Episode 7.05. Airdate: October 21, 2011
Written by: Brad Buckner & Eugenie Ross-Leming
Directed by: Phil Sgriccia
Guest Cast: Sean Owen Young (Chet the Leviathan), James Marsters (Don Stark), Charisma Carpenter (Maggie Stark)
Synopsis: The boys take on a married couple who happen to be witches trying to kill one another.

Okay, now we're getting somewhere. Despite the fact that this episode is the first regular by Brad Buckner and Eugenie Ross-Leming, who were contracted for a single episode in Season One ("Route 666"), this hour feels very distant from the early days. Gone are the dark, haunted houses with grainy film textures and the hopeful young men who we knew. Things are brighter on screen now, but much darker for these "boys."

Sam and Dean are narratively mirrored with a married couple, and in this case it's a couple that's been together for hundreds of years. Dean is Don, the guy obsessed with doing the right thing who's also kind of a lying jerk. And Sam is Maggie, the rightfully pissed one who just wants the guy she cares about to talk. And I love to see things resolved nonfatally, with Sam and Dean acting as couples counselors. But the Winchesters don't learn their lesson.

Dean's still consumed with guilt, and it's nice that we see he's having nightmares about Cas, but also… why still Amy? But fine. This is a fun, gory episode that shows how bad things are for Dean in contrast to them going okay for Sam. And there's some interesting foreshadowing going in this episode with how Bobby is now always part of the hunt. They really need him.

Famous Faces: Fun fact: this is the episode that got me interested in watching the show, because I was a huge *Buffy* fan and wanted to see Spike (James Marsters) and Cordelia (Charisma Carpenter) as guest stars. I just had to get through a lot of other episodes to get here.

Plot Hole/Spoiler Alert: Once again, the guys let the monster go which is fine, I guess, but Dean made a whole stink about killing Amy because she murdered four people. Don and Maggie have done way worse than that?! But since when did witches transition from humans getting power from a demon, to whatever Don and Maggie are? This will eventually get cleared up, but it's confusing they can't just shoot them.

Slash Fiction

Episode 7.06. Airdate: October 28, 2011
Written by: Robbie Thompson
Directed by: John F. Showalter
Guest Cast: Jim Beaver (Bobby/Leviathan), Kim Rhodes (Jody Mills), Mark Sheppard (Crowley), Sean Owen Young (Chet the Leviathan), Kevin McNally (Frank Deveraux), James Patrick Stuart (Dick Roman), Michael Hogan (Sherriff Osborne),
Synopsis: A pair of leviathans go on a killing spree wearing Sam and Dean's faces.

This episode is remarkable for how good it is. It does so much in terms of character and moving the plot that it shouldn't work, but it does. The boys lose almost everything, learn all about the monster and get insight into them as people, and the truth about Amy! That's thanks to Robbie Thompson who, like Ben Edlund, will deliver some of the most interesting and out of the box episodes on his tenure.

The hour is the definition of winkingly self-aware, with Leviathan Dean and Sam commenting on their own character flaws, not to mention the title. In fandom parlance, "Slash Fiction" is a kind of fanfic focused on a relationship between two dudes. Not only do we get the pun that the Leviathan are creating violent lies, but it's also a Wincest joke.

But Sam and Dean aren't the only characters that shine here. We have brilliant, insightful moments for Bobby, a fun new character introduction with Frank, *and* a hugely important confrontation between Crowley and Dick Roman, our new big bad! It's so much but Thompson manages to balance it all! Kudos!

And finally, the Amy crap hits the fan. It doesn't feel earned that this bit of nonsense breaks up the boys again, but at least Dean can stop stewing. I'm sure.

Legal Trouble: Love seeing the boys wanted and dead… again!

Ship Shape: Bobby continues to be the most romantically successful member of this family, which isn't saying much. But yay for that Bobby and Jody moment.

But ow, it's hard to see the longest and most successful relationship in the show hit the rocks. Of course, I'm talking about Dean and Baby. Come on, he just fixed her up and now he needs to hide her away! This break-up hurts more than Dean and Sam!

Fan Favorite: Dick Roman and Frank are both pretty fun characters, and brilliantly played by their respective actors. It's a bummer that we're adding more white men to this category, though they're only confined to one season.

Driver Picks the Music: Dean letting it all go for a second to groove to Air Supply's "All out of Love" is iconic.

The Mentalists

Episode 7.07. Airdate: November 4, 2011
Written by: Ben Acker and Ben Blacker
Directed by: Mike Rohl
Guest Cast: Dorian Brown Pham (Melanie Golden), Johnny Sneed (Jimmy Tomorrow)
Synopsis: Separately at first, Dean and Sam investigate a series of deaths in a town famous for psychics, then work together.

Welp, that brother break up didn't last long! "The Mentalists" is about trust and learning to work together again. It's not really reflected in Jimmy Tomorrow's evil plot to kill other mediums, but the story about the strained relationship between the Fox sisters sure does echo Sam and Dean's domestic issues.

We also clear up that Dean's depression isn't just about Amy. In fact, he maintains that killing her was the right choice. His funk right now is about trust—how he can't trust Sam, how he's punishing them both by making himself untrustworthy, and that all goes back to losing trust in Cas. So that's something, and I'm glad that's at the front. Sam needs to learn to trust Dean again and… he'd rather have his brother. But that's sort of it for Sam.

So, Get This: Lily Dale is a real place that was deeply tied in with the Spiritualist movement in the late 19th century, which is a fascinating era of history when people started chatting a lot with the dead. The Fox sisters were a big part of that movement, though their act was revealed to be a hoax.

Season Seven, Time for a Wedding!

Episode 7.08. Airdate: November 11, 2011
Written by: Andrew Dabb & Daniel Loflin
Directed by: Tim Andrew
Guest Cast: DJ Qualls (Garth Fitzgerald IV), Emily Perkins (Becky Rosen), Mark Sheppard (Crowley), Leslie Odom Jr. (Guy)
Synopsis: Becky enchants Sam into marrying her, but the friend who helped her do it turns out to be a demon. Dean enlists another hunter, Garth to take on the case.

Becky has always been a tricky character. She's an on-screen depiction not just of fans, but of *Supernatural* fans. Sure, she was cringey, but she usually helped, and we liked her. So *Supernatural* painting their fangirl posterchild as someone so silly and insecure that she'd happily force Sam into marriage is maybe not the best way to show love for the fandom. Season Seven just feels designed to hurt the fandom. Still, Becky is there to remind the brothers that they can function with different partners.

Working with Garth and seeing Sam on his own, further alienates Dean at this point, which isn't really something that makes sense other than taking Dean to a lower emotional point. But hey, he gets to hang with Garth, so that's not so bad! Garth is fun, and Sam for his part shows what a caring, heroic guy he is.

There are some awesome parts to this episode, and most of them come from our guest cast. Crowley pops in for some excellent exposition, and Perkins, Qualls, and Odom Jr. are all incredible. Overall a kind of cringey episode, but not bad.

Future Famous Faces: It's Aaron Burr, sir! Yes, before he created an iconic roll in *Hamilton*, Leslie Odom Jr. was stealing souls and scenes here! He's so good in this roll that it's not surprising at all that he'd go on to be nominated for Oscars, as well as win Tonys and Grammys. Not bad!

Fan Favorite: After being mentioned in "Weekend at Bobby's" Garth is here.

How To Win Friends and Influence Monsters

Episode 7.09. Airdate: November 18, 2011
Written by: Ben Edlund
Directed by: Guy Norman Bee
Guest Cast: Jim Beaver (Bobby), James Patrick Stuart (Dick Roman), Benito Martinez (Edgar), Cameron Bancroft (Dr. Gaines), Sean Rogerson (Ranger Rick)
Synopsis: A hunt for the Jersey Devil turns into a snack attack gone very wrong.

This is another one of those classic episodes that starts in an ostensibly kind of fun way, but ends up in a vastly different place. In this case, with Bobby shot in the head! It's one of the most stressful cliffhangers of the series and it's even more unsettling because 20 minutes before, Dean was sandwich-stoned.

What this episode does very subtly, amidst the dick jokes and shaming of American consumerism, is establish how important Bobby is to the boys. He's their only family left pretty much, and he's always been a constant in their life, teaching and supporting them. But that's not always good, and we're reminded that his brand of cantankerous support isn't always the best. Sam lies and maintains that he's fine for Bobby and Dean's sake, and Bobby reinforces the idea that he's not "a person" and has to suck it up. And Dean hears that as proof that he's not worthy of being anything else.

And then there's the Dick of it all. Though we met Dick Roman previously, this is our true introduction to the season's big bad, and he's formidably hate-able. That's a change. Since Season Four, our antagonists have been some level of understandable. We may not want them to win, but we understand why they are the way they are. Not Dick. He and the Leviathans are single-minded and the farthest from a sympathetic monster. And Dick's final move this episode may make him the most evil villain so far.

So, Get This: The voice over on the nature sounds tape is executive producer Bob Singer. Singer's voice pops up all over the show if you know what to listen for.

Death's Door

Episode 7.10. Airdate: December 2, 2011
Written by: Sera Gamble
Directed by: Robert Singer
Guest Cast: Jim Beaver (Bobby), Steven Williams (Rufus), James Patrick Stuart, Henri Lubatti (Bobby's Reaper)
Synopsis: Trapped in his own memories, Bobby races to escape his reaper and get a final message to Sam and Dean.

Death is something that's familiar on *Supernatural*. We've lost so many major characters, in ways that were both satisfying and disappointing. The main characters have even died a lot. But this episode is different, because it's not really about Bobby's death. It's about the relationship Bobby had with his boys and about his life coming full circle.

So much of what we see are characters we love unwittingly perpetuating toxic cycles, be it of violence, or abuse and dependency. Bobby was part of such a cycle, but manages to break it by being the kind of loving father Sam and Dean truly needed. They wouldn't be the men they are without him. Or the heroes. The breaking of cycles is important for the rest of this season, and really for the rest of the series. Fate is a cycle the boys have to break free from as much as abuse is.

Bobby's declaration "As fate would have it, I adopted two boys. And they grew up great. They grew up heroes," is one of my absolute favorite moments in the series, because it's exactly what *Supernatural* is about. Choosing family and love in the face of horror and making that your fate. It's perfect.

This episode is also amazing for Sam and Dean as they grapple with the possibly of losing Bobby, but we see more of Dean's interior struggle than Sam's which bugs me. But this hour is an incredible showcase for everyone, including Steven Williams.

Death Notes: I have to say that "Idjits" may be the best final words on the show.

Adventures in Babysitting

Episode 7.11. Airdate: January 6, 2012
Written by: Adam Glass
Directed by: Jeannot Szwarc
Guest Cast: Kevin McNally (Frank), Madison McLaughlin (Krissy Chambers), Ian Tracey (Lee Chambers), Meghan Ory (Sally)
Synopsis: As they mourn Bobby and try to figure out the numbers he left, Sam and Dean answer a call from a hunter's teen daughter in need of help.

How do you follow up an episode like "Death's Door" or cope with the loss of a character like Bobby? It's hard, and in line with Gamble's pacing problems, I'm not sure if this episode does a great job of it. There are two very divergent stories that don't really work together, nor as reflections of Bobby.

On the one hand we have Frank as a sort of new Bobby, who gives Dean some pretty brutal and honestly bad advice about faking it, to keep pretending it's okay until it is. Both of these guys have emphasized to Dean that he's not allowed to hurt.

Then we've got the story with Krissy, which represents a kind of change in roles for the boys. With Bobby gone, Sam and Dean step into the mentor role for a new hunter, Krissy. And contrary to how they're living their lives, they encourage Krissy to leave the life. They're trying to find some hope among all the grief, and that it comes in the form of family breaking another cycle.

But toxic cycles don't break in this episode however, they continue.

Familiar Faces: We're full up with actors you may know from other cult series. Madison McLaughlin was a hero in training on *Arrow*, Meghan Ory played Red on *Once Upon a Time,* and Ian Tracey went on to guest star again on *Supernatural* in Season Twelve.

Time After Time

Episode 7.12. Airdate: January 13, 2012
Written by: Robbie Thompson
Directed by: Phil Sgriccia
Guest Cast: Kim Rhodes (Jody), Jason Dohring (Chronos), Nicholas Lea (Eliot Ness)
Synopsis: The god Chronos drags Dean to 1944 to hunt him with Eliot Ness.

It's one of my favorite versions of Dean—giant nerd! Getting sent back in time is the most fun Dean's had in a long time, and it's nice to see him smile, rock some vintage duds, and in general be an adorable bisexual disaster.

And it's great to see Sam bonding with someone! Generally, Dean makes the big connections with others, but Sam and Jody make a great team, and I love seeing Jody both dipping her toe into hunting and mourning Bobby.

Sam feels Bobby's loss just as much as Dean, but keeps steady. Dean's just more openly emotional. For the third episode, an older hunter/mentor tells him he's soft and wrong for having feelings. Three is a pattern, and when we add that on top of the grief and loss it makes you think. Sam and Dean are going through different stages of grief. Sam is denial and bargaining, while Dean is anger and depression.

How does Chronos figure into this? Well, like Sam and Dean, he was unmoored, homeless, and a killer, but found something to hold onto. Like Krissy and her father, he tried to "get out." In the shadow of Bobby's death, we have another story about how it's very hard for anyone in this life to escape.

Familiar Faces: Jason Dohring will be familiar to fans of *Veronica Mars*. Though I think he's wasted here, he brings a lot of pathos to Chronos' scenes.

So, Get This: In Eric Kripke's time travel series, *Timeless*, Misha Collins showed up for a quick cameo as Eliot Ness.

The Slice Girls

Episode 7.13. Airdate: February 3, 2012
Written by: Brad Buckner & Eugenie Ross-Leming
Directed by: Jerry Wanek
Guest Cast: Harry Groener (Professor Morrison), Sara Canning (Lydia), Alexia Fast (Emma)
Synopsis: After a one-night stand with an amazon, Dean ends up with a monster daughter who wants to kill him.

As if Dean wasn't having a crappy enough year, he has to watch his own offspring be murdered in front of him! All to hammer home the big theme about cycles of violence, and how inevitable it is that Sam, Dean, and anyone around them will die bloody and brutal. That includes their family. Cheerful stuff.

We're at a real low point in the season right now. Not really in terms of quality (this episode is… fine), but in terms of how bad things are for our boys. Something has gotta give, but all these messages about how they and the world are doomed aren't helping. But I guess that's how depression work—it feels hopeless.

But hey, at least Dean got some and we got a rare shirtless Winchester scene! In fact, let's just take a moment to be superficial and appreciate that Jensen Ackles is peaking in attractiveness right about now. And Jared Padalecki is peaking in sideburns.

Spoiler Alert: "Next time they surface we'll be ready." Actually, you won't be because we'll never hear about Amazons or Emma again!

Familiar Faces: It's time for more *Buffy* alumni, with Harry Groening, best known as the evil mayor of Sunnydale.

Plucky Pennywhistle's Magical Menagerie

Episode 7.14. Airdate: February 10, 2012
Written by: Andrew Dabb & Daniel Loflin
Directed by: Mike Rohl
Guest Cast: Michael Blackman Beck (Howard), Jennifer Spence (Jean Holiday), A bunch of very scary clowns
Synopsis: Sam fights evil clowns, and a guy gets killed by a unicorn.

I have a weird love for this episode, mainly because it comes at a spot in our binge watch where we haven't had many kooky episodes for a while. Sure, a random wedding is fun, but you can't beat a murder unicorn. But the other thing this episode brings back that we've been missing most of the season is a focus on Sam.

Sam has been holding steady since the start of the season, which is honestly impressive, but that's sort of who Sam is right now—doing his job and saving people, despite his trauma. Put into a place called Plucky's, he faces one his greatest fears, clowns, and keeps going! And he does great! The problem remains though, that Sam grinding through his issues is not actually interesting for us as the audience. Sure, we love him as a hero, but we also need to see him struggle rather than just support Dean's showier emotions.

Speaking of, we get to see Dean and another kid, which is something else we've been seeing a lot of. And again, the whole episode feeds into this mini arc about parents, hunting, and other families pushing their BS onto another generation. What does that have to do with the greater Leviathan story of the season? I'll get back to you. Maybe it's something about facing your own fears and issues before they ruin someone else's life, and someone gets killed by a unicorn.

Death Notes: Seriously, "impaled by a unicorn farting rainbows" is an all-time best demise.

Repo Man

Episode 7.15. Airdate: February 17, 2012
Written by: Bed Edlund
Directed by: Thomas J. Wright
Guest Cast: Mark Pellegrino (Hallucifer), Russell Sams (Jeffrey), Nicole Oliver (Nora), Jeffrey Ballad (Demon/Nora's son)
Synopsis: The meatsuit of a demon Sam and Dan exorcised four years ago begins killing on his own. Sam breaks and lets Hallucifer help him.

This episode is incredible. It's a miniature serial killer mystery, with hints of *Silence of the Lamb*, with Hallucifer as Hannibal Lecter. Pellegrino is great here, as is Padalecki, and it's fun to see them shine. But this outing is also a great exploration of dependency, trauma, and in a weird way, love.

Jeffrey is a great one-off character, because his relationship to his demon works as a mirror for both Sam and Dean. In terms of Sam, this episode is all about an evil force as a missing piece. Sam, who has been faking 'til he makes it, gives in to Hallucifer, and it breaks him. Meanwhile, Jeffrey's demon returning in an unexpected, freshly traumatic way, is very much like Sam's reopened relationship with Lucifer and his escalating madness. I'm so happy we're getting back to Sam's story.

But Jeffrey also has some big discussions with Dean about depression and loss. Dean has lost people who saved him, who made him feel important, and who he in turn loved. This applies to Bobby, but to Cas as well.

"Repo Man" is interesting because it shows us the collateral damage the boys leave behind. We've moved past the days when the Winchesters cared about not killing humans, and it's worth asking how far off from serial killers they are. Once again, we're back to the cycle of violence, trauma and how that affects later generations.

Ship Shape: There are definitely people out there who shipped Sam and Lucifer, and I certainly see the connection but… not my thing. I'd rather focus on Jeffrey calling his demon the love of his life, and how that's kind of connected to Cas. I would posit that Dean having to live without Cas for this terrible time has taught him how much he needed and cared for the nerdy little guy with wings.

Out With the Old

Episode 7.16. Airdate: March 16, 2012
Written by: Robert Singer & Jenny Klein
Directed by: John F. Showalter
Guest Cast: Kevin McNally (Frank), Bryan Cuprill (George), Mary Page Keller (Joyce Bicklebee)
Synopsis: A cursed object hunt brings Sam and Dean back into contact with Leviathans.

This is a weird one, to be honest. The pieces are all actually pretty good. We have some very gross and gory deaths with cursed ballet shoes and evil tea pot, we get Sam and Dean being competent, funny, caring, and angsty at appropriate times, and the leviathans are really quite fun as surprise antagonists.

But I'm not sure it all fits together and that sort of applies to this whole season. Season Seven so far has been more consistent in terms of episode quality than Season Six—the pacing is better and there's been a better focus on story—but it doesn't quite come together. The grief arc for Dean and Sam's unraveling mental state is interesting, but that stuff is generally unrelated to the leviathans who continue to just be there to parody consumerism.

And then there's Frank. Kevin McNally is great in the role, but he's certainly kind of a poor man's Bobby and it makes Bobby's absence more glaring, which I very much think is the point.

Driver Picks the Music: The use of "Bad Moon Rising" is really well done and ominous, maybe intentionally harkening back to the Season One finale car crash.

Name Game: After months of no aliases, Sam uses the name "Bruce Hornsby" who was a songwriter and singer known for working with the Grateful Dead.

The Born-Again Identity

Episode 7.17. Airdate: March 23, 2012
Written by: Sera Gamble
Directed by: Robert Singer
Guest Cast: Misha Collins (Castiel/Emmanuel), Mark Pellegrino (Hallucifer), Rachel Miner (Meg), Kacey Rohl (Marin)
Synopsis: Sam ends up in a psych ward. Dean seeks out the help of a healer who turns out to be Castiel with no memory.

This is by far my favorite episode of Season Seven. It's simply great on every level, for every character, and perfectly balanced between Destiel goodness and Sam Winchester awesomeness.

I'll get to Dean and Cas in a second, but this is an amazing Sam episode in a way that's been missing from this season. Even at his very lowest, our Sammy keeps saving people. Crumbling from the weight of Lucifer's torture, Sam saves Marin and that's incredible. Especially with Lucifer at his most terrible, Sam keeps fighting. That's why Sam Winchester is a hero, and an inspiration, and I adore it.

And then there's Dean. All season he's been burdened by betrayal, guilt, and loss, and everyone has told him to suck it up and keep going. Then suddenly Cas is back and alive, right there telling him *his feeling matter*. Since Cas pulled Dean from hell, he's always represented hope. He's a rebel angel who chose another path, and so Cas coming back not only gives Dean hope, but inspires Dean to break a toxic cycle of anger and violence. He also spends the episode working with a demon, to save someone he loves, so maybe he gets what Cas was doing with Crowley now.

Dean forgiving Cas, leaning into hope and trust of the guy he knew, rather than what he became, is a huge moment for the season and it represent the first real step for Dean.

Familiar Faces: Kacey Rohl is fantastic as Marin. She went on from here to recurring roles on *Hannibal* and *The Magicians* (both shows any SPN fan will love.) And she has another *Supernatural* connection: her father Mike Rohl is a frequent director.

Plot Hole/Spoiler Alert: Surely someone will tell poor Daphne what happened to her husband, and the fact that Cas was married, however chastely, will be addressed again. Haha. *Nope*.

Ship Shape: I think this episode wants us to feel the Cas and Meg vibes, or set them up for later. While I love Meg, this episode is all about Dean and Cas. I mean just the way Dean *looks* at him! The tension! The utter focus on their relationship and how much they mean to each other! And Dean carried the trench coat around from car to car just in case??? Are you kidding me?!

Party On, Garth

Episode 7.18. Airdate: March 30, 2012
Written by: Adam Glass
Directed by: Phil Sgriccia
Guest Cast: Jim Beaver (Ghost Bobby), DJ Qualls (Garth), Terry David Mulligan (Randy Baxter), Mr. Fizzles (himself)
Synopsis: The boys and Garth fight a monster that only drunk people can see.

We get a pretty mediocre episode to follow up the greatness of last week, and to prime us for the big reveal that Bobby is a ghost. The shojo is a fun monster, but the big point of this episode—what with the family ambitions causing a curse and overindulgence in alcohol—is once again toxic cycles and how those hurt the next generation.

Bobby's refusal to move on is sort of the opposite of what we saw last week—he's hanging on and that's going to keep Sam and Dean from getting closure. This focus on moving on, ceding the reins to the next generation, makes more sense if you think of this season as another potential swan song for the show. The writers might have thought things were ending and wanted the fandom to move on too… whoops.

But like Garth, we stick around and we're awesome. And appreciate a good microbrew!

Drive Picks the Music: How great is Garth's opening montage to "Poison" by Bel Biv Devoe? Almost as great the beautiful use of the "Americana" theme on the Bobby reveal.

Of Grave Importance

Episode 7.19. Airdate: April 20, 2012
Written by: Brad Buckner & Eugenie Ross-Leming
Directed by: Tim Andrew
Guest Cast: Jim Beaver (Bobby), Jamie Luner (Annie), Antonio Cupo (Whitman Van Ness), Elysia Rotaru (Victoria)
Synopsis: Stuck as an unseen ghost, Bobby tries to help Sam and Dean with a haunted house full of trapped ghosts, including the ghost of a hunter named Annie.

This is one of those rare episodes that takes the focus off Sam and Dean, and puts it on another character. These episodes are often really good, because they allow us to go deep on non-Winchesters, and this one succeeds thanks to a ghost story that's like the creepiest, saddest version of the Haunted Mansion ever.

With its focus on Bobby not moving on, and how ghosts just perpetuate violence, this episode begins a really interesting arc for him that's very reflective vengeance and toxic cycles. Ghosts are the perfect way to explore this, and Bobby's refusal to let go of his vengeance getting him stuck in a spectral roach motel teaches a lesson he doesn't want to acknowledge.

Bobby is an incredible character, just like *Supernatural* is an incredible show, and I think there was definitely an effort here to make a point about how it's bad to hold onto something for too long. Even if you love it and feel there's work to do. Again, this makes more sense if you consider that the writers were looking at this as a possible final season. Considering the future… let's bask in the irony.

Ship Shape: I love Annie. She's strong and competent, and I respect the hell out of her being the only woman on the show to shag Dean, Sam, and Bobby. That's power right there. Sadly she's another member of the "sleep with Sam and die" club.

The Girl with the Dungeons and Dragons Tattoo

Episode 7.20. Airdate: April 27, 2012
Written by: Robbie Thompson
Directed by: John MacCarthy
Guest Cast: Jim Beaver (Bobby), James Patrick Stuart (Dick Roman), Felicia Day (Charlie Bradbury)
Synopsis: With the help of a nerdy, gay hacker named Charlie, Sam and Dean finally manage to score a win against the Leviathans.

Season Seven is a transition from the "traditional" version of *Supernatural,* to a newer, more enlightened show. Finally, we have a complex and awesome queer character who relates best… to Dean. There's no better example of this change than the contrast between Becky Rosen and Charlie Bradbury. These two portrayals of fangirls are worlds apart, with one being a (sometimes) mean parody of the desperate, creepy fans, and the other showing that nerdy girls are cool, powerful and, usually, kind of queer.

As a *Supernatural* fan—and a general fangirl—I see myself in both Charlie and Becky, to be honest. Maybe Becky represents a certain obsessive extreme we all go to when we really love a show. But we also need the contrast of Charlie, who finds affirmation and inspiration in her nerdiness without letting it take over her identity. And honestly, as a gay redhead who loves Sam and Dean a lot, Charlie is very much me.

This episode continues to take Sam and Dean out of their darkest days and into a place of hope, affirming that they need *people*. They can't do their job without friends, family, and allies like Cas, Bobby, and Charlie. After this season took everything away from them, they're slowly building a new coalition that's stronger and better… except maybe for Bobby, who's still stuck as a vengeful ghost.

Also, we now know the Leviathan's plan to turn the human race into an endless food supply, and maybe this metaphor of corporate greed literally eating America alive is a bit too on the nose?

Death Notes: Well, I guess Frank is dead and we never saw a body. I believe Kevin McNally was supposed to come back for a final episode, but scheduling prevented it. This won't be the last unsatisfying off-screen death we get.

Fan Favorite/Familiar Face: Felicia Day! The role of Charlie was written with Felicia Day in mind, best known at the time for her work on *Dr. Horrible's Sing-Along Blog* and *The Guild.* Charlie in turn became an iconic role for her, cementing her status as queen of the geeks.

Driver Picks the Music: There's no better theme song for a character who is pure sunshine than Katrina and the Waves' "Walking on Sunshine."

Reading Is Fundamental

Episode 7.21. Airdate: May 4, 2012
Written by: Bed Edlund
Directed by: Ben Edlund
Guest Cast: Misha Collins (Castiel), Rachel Miner (Meg), Benito Martinez (Edgar), Osric Chau (Kevin Tran), Emily Holmes (Hester)
Synopsis: The boys bust open the word of god to activate a prophet named Kevin. He's in advanced placement and not prepared to integrate the supernatural into his world view.

We're on a roll now, with another great episode that seriously expands the mythology and show's ensemble. It also explores all sorts of relationships and character developments. And it's just plain fun. Seriously, I love this episode. And yes, that's mainly because I love Castiel and Kevin but, can you blame me?

Poor Kevin, plucked from a nice life where he had his future all planned out, just to be activated as a prophet. He's not quite collateral damage, but he's certainly a cautionary tale about how what Sam, Dean, and Cas do, or have done, have serious consequences for real people. On the other hand, Cas is also coping with consequences and craziness, trying to avoid confronting what he did at the beginning of the season.

Crazy Cas is an interesting turn. His antics are funny, but also sad as heck. He views this madness as penance for what he did. And the scene where Cas and Sam connect is really lovely. But the crazy allows Cas to avoid any confrontation or conflict, especially with Dean. Like Dean might say, Cas needs more than sorry.

Ship Shape: And of course Cas is concerned with Dean, because Dean is his primary relationship and connection. Hearing Hester say that the moment Cas laid a hand on Dean in hell, he was lost, is hella romantic. But Dean doesn't hear that as Cas loving him—he hears that as making him responsible for everything Cas did and how broken he is right now. These two have lots of feelings but, shocker, aren't great at communicating them.

Cas and Meg on the other hand are pretty darn cute, and it's clear that Meg actually cares for the weirdo angel, and that he wants to take care of her. It's sweet!

Fan Favorite: Osric Chau is incredible as Kevin, and he almost steals this episode with perfect line deliveries of classics like "Is this a sex torture dungeon?" Sadly no, Kevin, you'll need to switch to fanfic for that.

So, Get This: This isn't a Sam heavy episode because it was right around when Gen and Jared's first child was due. According the Osric Chau, the crew was on high alert the whole time he was filming, getting ready for "operation moose drop" when Gen went into labor. Thomas Padalecki was born March 19th, 2012!

There Will Be Blood

Episode 7.22. Airdate: May 11, 2012
Written by: Andrew Dabb & Daniel Loflin
Directed by: Guy Norman Bee
Guest Cast: Jim Beaver (Bobby), Mark Sheppard (Crowley), Rick Worthy (Alpha Vampire), Benito Martinez (Edgar), James Patrick Stuart (Dick Roman), Osric Chau (Kevin Tran), Laci J. Mailey (Emily)
Synopsis: To bone Dick, Sam and Dean need alpha blood.

This episode isn't bad, it's just sort of boring. Again, the pacing of the season is off, because do we really need a side quest *now*? It's a bunch of place setting, and as great as Rick Worthy is as the Alpha Vampire, it feels like a waste of all the momentum we built up over the last two episodes. Sure, we have Bobby going full vengeance, and the alpha vamp and his "children" but let's talk about corn syrup.

In another horror show or movie, the Leviathan's plan to drug all of America with food additives would be scary, but not only does it not really work with the DNA of *Supernatural*, but in this episode it plays as lazy writing based on fat shaming and trite "America is terrible" tropes.

Supernatural is backroads and decrepit barns. It's gods and angels drinking brown liquor with two heroes in a muscle car. This story is so far from that, and it's something the boys are only reacting to rather than being involved. James Patrick Stuart is *great* as Dick, but he's so scary and inhuman it makes the show less complicated. And that's not *Supernatural* either.

So, Get This: The man looking at stuff in the aisle with a Gas-N-Sip clerk in the foreground, is Andrew Dabb, co-writer of the episode and future showrunner.

Spoiler Alert: The Alpha vamp does not, in fact see them next season, as his next and final appearance is in Season Twelve.

Survival of the Fittest

Episode 7.23. Airdate: May 18, 2012
Written by: Sera Gamble
Directed by: Robert Singer
Guest Cast: Misha Collins (Castiel), Jim Beaver (Bobby), Rachel Miner (Meg), Mark Sheppard (Crowley), James Patrick Stuart (Dick Roman), Osric Chau (Kevin Tran), Baby (Herself)
Synopsis: Time for the boys to finally get Dick.

This finale is short on action and twists, but big on the character moments, which is fine with me. It turns out that the key to boning Dick (yes, these jokes are fun, I get it now), isn't the magic, it's ending all those pesky toxic cycles we've been emphasizing since Bobby died.

First, Bobby lets go of his vengeance after seeing how bad it can get. It's a poignant goodbye that's only a little diminished by the fact that we already said goodbye. But it stops the merry-go-round and in part inspires Cas. But, as always, it takes Dean to push him all the way.

Dean not just forgiving Cas, but explaining that he'd rather have him, cursed or not, is kind of huge. He doesn't need Cas for what he can do—he needs him because he's Cas. And Dean has lost too many other people he loves. So, they move towards a different kind of penance in what, biblically, was all about cleansing sin—purgatory.

What about the rest of our team? Things aren't looking good for Meg and Kevin, and of course Crowley comes out on top, because he's Crowley. And Sam? He's *alone*. Unfortunately, there's extraordinarily little emotional story for Sam this finale, but Jared had just had a baby. It was fine to give him a break. There's more ahead.

Death Notes: Okay, do we count Dean and Cas getting sent to purgatory as dying? It's tricky since it is an afterlife but, since they just got zapped there (and it won't be their last time just hopping into another plane), I'm not gonna give it to them. But Dick's death was fittingly epic for such a big bad.

Ship Shape: Meg jokes that Cas is her boyfriend, but that he was Dean's first and ain't that just the whole show. But just look at the way Cas looks at Dean when he says he'd rather have him… that's a look that says "Oh. I love this idiot. I'd rather die by his side too." Which is a great transition to Season Eight—a season that raised the gay bar on Destiel in a way that's truly legendary.

SUPERNATURAL

CHAPTER EIGHT

Dean Went to Purgatory; Sam Hit a Dog

Supernatural Season Eight felt like a bit of a miracle just for existing. After the widely reviled Season Seven, audiences were only willing to give *Supernatural* one more chance. Sera Gamble's attempts to change the show into something else were admirable, but just didn't work out. Gamble departed *Supernatural* after "Survival of the Fittest" and to replace her, Jeremy Carver—who was a force on the writing staff in Seasons Three through Five—was brought back as showrunner.

The Carver era represents a return to form for the series, with the focus put back on the angels, demons, and most importantly, character relationships. Specifically, the whole of Carver's tenure is built around the brothers' relationship and the ways it's good and bad. The Winchester codependency is at the forefront here, as both Sam and Dean's biggest strength and greatest flaw. By the end, their relationship, while different, will be much healthier.

Season Eight transitions the show into a different form and formula that will pretty much stay there for the rest of the series, giving the boys something they never really had until now—a home base. But the season is also a reboot of sorts, starting off just like the pilot with Dean taking Sam out of a normal life and back on the road.

But what is it about? I think the fact that purgatory is such an important part of the season is a clue. There's so much in these runs of episodes about redemption, penance, and forgiveness. The boys (including Cas) have a lot to atone for, but there's also big themes about what we'll do for family—something we're familiar with that doesn't just apply to the Winchesters. And that's not always good, as codependency makes a big impact in the season as well with some seriously bad consequences.

We Need to Talk About Kevin

Episode 8.01. Airdate: October 3, 2012
Written by: Jeremey Carver
Directed by: Robert Singer
Guest Cast: Mark Sheppard (Crowley), Osric Chau (Kevin), Ty Olsson (Benny Lafitte) Liane Balaban (Amelia Richardson)
Synopsis: Dean escapes Purgatory after a year with the help of a vampire named Benny. He finds Sam, who didn't look for him because … he hit a dog. They track down Kevin who escaped from Crowley with the demon tablet.

And we're off with a lot of plot, and another big time jump the show will ignore in terms of continuity! Let's talk about the moose in the room first; Sam didn't look for Dean after Dick exploded. That's shocking to us, and to Dean, because these idiots always look for one another. Maybe Sam took all those messages about ending toxic cycles to heart but… really, man? You hit a dog and left your brother who knows where? It's baffling and represents a new kind of original sin that Sam will have to redeem himself from for a while.

Dean on the other hand, spent a year in his element—killing things and having insane chemistry with non-human men of uncertain moral compasses. He starts this season with new scars and a new, darker edge. He's been through a lot, and lost a lot as well, and Sam was all he had left to come back to. For Sam not to look for him just hurts.

The consequences of the boys' last year abroad are manifested in Kevin. Like Dean, he's become hardened, but like Sam, he still wants a normal life. But because Sam chose that, Kevin's totally screwed and Dean's not gentle about it. But hey, shutting the gates of hell sounds cool. I'm sure that will go well!

Plot Hole/Spoiler Alert: Where are the leviathans?! At the end of last season, Crowley implied Sam would need to deal with them, but he didn't. Just like no one dealt with the armies of monsters left over after Season Six. But they're gone now so… what? Well, the extradiegetic reason is the writers just didn't want to deal with those old plots. In Season Fifteen we actually do get a clue as to who keeps the monsters at bay—Chuck, the "author" of the story.

Ship Shape: Dean tears through purgatory looking for "The Angel," which I guess means he's forgiven Cas, but along the way he meets a new boyfriend, Benny. Benny and Dean are shipping catnip, and their bond—and the fact that being around Benny makes Dean/Jensen revert to more of a southern accent—is so hot. But we know Cas is still The One.

And then there's Sam and Amelia. The only interaction between them we see is pretty negative, and I don't know if it counts as chemistry, but I guess Sam eventually was into it? Maybe?

Driver Picks the Music: The season announces itself as a full return to form right off the bat with not one, but two great needle drops: first Jethro Tull's "Locomotive Breath" in the recap, and then a great sequence (peak bowlegs!) set to Styx's "Man in the Wilderness."

Familiar Face/Fan Favorite: From the very start, Ty Olsson is fantastic as Benny, and you may also recognize him with fangs; he played the vampire Eli all the way back in Season Two's "Bloodlust."

What's Up, Tiger Mommy?

Episode 8.02. Airdate: October 10, 2012
Written by: Andrew Dabb & Daniel Loflin
Directed by: John Showalter
Guest Cast: Mark Sheppard (Crowley), Osric Chau (Kevin), Ty Olson (Benny Lafitte), Lauren Tom (Linda Tran), Tyler Johnston (Samandriel)
Synopsis: Kevin and The Winchesters check up on Kevin's mom, Linda, and somehow end up at an auction of in an attempt to get the demon tablet back.

This episode is all about the lengths we go to be with and protect those we love. I'm not talking about any one type of love either, but just love in general for the people who make up our family.

I love Linda Tran. As a mom, I completely understand everything she does to protect and stay close to her child. Despite some slightly, ugh, Asian parent stereotypes (in a show with a bad track record on Asian racism, let's be honest), Linda is amazing and her relationship with Kevin is great.

Dean kills and maims into his darkest place to get to Cas, the person who (along with Sam) really brings out the best in him. And Cas, by fleeing when they hit purgatory, also did something incredibly painful to protect Dean. Not that it's any use trying to stop a Winchester on a mission. Once again, Cas represents hope and Dean won't give him up… and the fact that he lost Cas is the reason that Dean's so friggin' scary right now. Sam though, he's just trying to cope and we really don't get much on how he's doing. But hey, he gets to channel Thor for a hot second.

Ship Shape: When I say this season brings Destiel to a whole new level, *this is what I mean.* Not only does this episode give us our first Dean and Cas hug (it only took four years!) but Dean's speech to Cas, the praying, the devotion and how much losing Cas has messed Dean up… it's all huge. And again, looking at this knowing that Cas really loves Dean that way, makes Cas keeping himself away to save Dean that much more poignant.

So, Get This: This is the first time we see Crowley's demon eyes, which are crossroads demon red, and also the first time we see his very cool, true red form.

Name Game: Agents "Neil" and "Sixx" refer to Wince Neil and Nikki Sixx from Motley Crue.

Heartache

Episode 8.03. Airdate: October 17, 2012
Written by: Brad Buckner & Eugenie Ross-Leming
Directed by: Jensen Ackles
Guest Cast: Liane Balaban (Amelia), Kyra Zagorsky (Randa), Patty McCormack (Eleanor/Betsy)
Synopsis: The boys are back on the road for a case involving immortal athletes and lots of heart snatching.

So, here we are retreading themes *Supernatural* has addressed before, but in a different way. Sort of like an immortal athlete changing sports. Sam, who for many seasons convinced himself hunting was all he could do, is back to the Sam we knew in Season One. He just wants a normal life away from hunting, and once more Dean's come into his life to change that.

Sam and Dean are mirrored by Brick/Inyo and his blood devotion to Cacao. Dean is old Brick—the one who loved the game and who felt the bloody cost was worth it. But Sam is the Brick who fell in love with Betsy, who's tired of the violent, lonely life he leads. The persistence of Brick's sacrifice after his death implies that it's not so easy to walk away, especially when there are people who claim they need you. Dean has never wanted to do this alone, and so he's pulling Sam along for the ride.

Otherwise, this episode is an interesting mystery that doesn't go how you'd think. With more great directing from Jensen, whose hotness this season is only exceeded by Sam's hair, it's going much better than the last.

So, Get This: The detective speaking with the boys in the beginning is played by Alan Ackles, Jensen's dad!

Ship Shape: Did you know that there was a very vocal contingent of fans who decided Amelia was a hallucination? I can see why.

Bitten

Episode 8.04. Airdate: October 24, 2012
Written by: Robbie Thompson
Directed by: Thomas J. Wright
Guest Cast: Brit Sheridan (Kate), Leigh Parker (Brian), Brandon W. Jones (Michael), David Lewis (Professor Ludensky)
Synopsis: Footage from the lives of three college students reveals how insecurity and jealousy don't mix well with lycanthropy.

This episode was, for many years, one of the lowest-rated entries on IMDB ratings for *Supernatural*, and its unorthodox format made it less than beloved by fans. But I think that's unfair. The found footage conceit is really interesting, and I like that *Supernatural* went a little Paranormal Activity for one installment. It is disconcerting to see Sam and Dean as side characters, but I always enjoy how scary they seem to outsiders. Also, the "workplace romance" vibe jokes are fun.

This episode is heavy on insecurity and loneliness, and how those things—mixed with a little toxic masculinity—can lead to men pulling innocent people into bloody ends. That idea doesn't just apply to Kate, Michael, and Brian, but also to Dean who's pulled Sam back into the hunting life. This isn't to blame Dean for wanting his brother with him, but it's a way of examining the codependency the brothers have going—codependency which Sam is trying to escape but, which Dean is deepening.

Plot Hole: A new kind of werewolf that can change at will? It seems weirdly convenient, especially given that this type will show up more in the series.

Blood Brother

Episode 8.05. Airdate: October 31, 2012
Written by: Ben Edlund
Directed by: Guy Norman Bee
Guest Cast: Misha Collins (Castiel), Ty Olsson (Benny), Liane Balaban (Amelia), Athena Karkanis (Andrea)
Synopsis: Dean helps Benny take out his old nest of Vampirates.

This episode is a bit of a mess with one plot too many. Benny's back story is weird, but fine. But it's also too much info too quickly, and it's honestly weird to see him suddenly in this heterosexual romance with Andrea, when obviously he and Dean have more of a spark. However, the way Benny's story mirror's Castiel's (leaving the service of a distant father/god because he fell in love with a human) is interesting.

I think Benny's plotline with Andrea may also be meant to mirror Sam falling in love with Amelia. In which case, yikes. Not a good sign for that relationship. But neither is the fact that—in the very boring flashbacks—Amelia is sour and unlikable. And why would Sam leave hunting behind for a life in a dingy motel room with a sorta mean vet? At least this sets us up for some brother drama and we get to hear Dean say "Vampirates."

Ship Shape: As mentioned above, Samelia is now firmly into "woof" territory. She just doesn't work as a character, and Liana Balaban not a good actress for this role in terms of her performance and chemistry with Jared.

Do you know what is great though? The fact that Dean trusts Benny because he saved Castiel's life. That's the whole reason. Benny saved Dean's angel, and because of that they're brothers. Hope he can come to the wedding.

Southern Comfort

Episode 8.06. Airdate: November 7, 2012
Written by: Adam Glass
Directed by: Tim Andrew
Guest Cast: DJ Qualls (Garth), Liane Balaban (Amelia)
Synopsis: A bad penny haunted by a confederate soldier makes Dean and others go postal. Luckily, Garth is there and has become the "new Bobby."

After some stumbles in the last one, this episode really works. There's a good balance of humor from Garth, as well as genuine emotion. And the specter works thematically to accentuate Dean's anger. Right now, there's a focus on monsters that somehow pull others into their worlds. From Brian and Michael turning Kate, to Benny causing Andrea to be turned, and the specter's unlucky penny turning others into killers.

And yes, this is about Dean, but also to some extent Sam, and how their lives as hunters tend to cause a lot of collateral damage to others. But their anger is still at one another. Dean's mad at Sam for his many betrayals—real and imagined—and Sam is rightfully mad at Dean for not letting mistakes go. It's a complicated dynamic that will come to a head again soon, but it's explored well here.

Spoiler Alert: What doesn't pan out though is Garth as the "new Bobby." I like the idea, but Garth is too nice and a bit too funny to really replace Bobby, and I think the show knew that too. Later this season, the Men of Letters bunker becomes the new source of lore and down the line, Garth's story takes a big left turn.

Ship Shape: I'm still not sure how or why Sam and Amelia hooked up, or what they like about each other than they are both traumatized. The relationship continues to not work for me. But hey, the Purgatory in Miami is a famous gay bar, that's a thing.

Driver Picks the Music: Although Soundgarden's "Black Days" has been used on the show before, I think the penny montage is a really excellent moment.

A Little Slice of Kevin

Episode 8.07. Airdate: November 14, 2012
Written by: Brad Buckner & Eugenie Ross-Leming
Directed by: Charles Robert Carner
Guest Cast: Misha Collins (Castiel), Mark Sheppard (Crowley), Osric Chau (Kevin), Ty Olsson (Benny), Lauren Tom (Linda), Tyler Johnston (Samandriel), Amanda Tapping (Naomi)
Synopsis: Cas returns from purgatory just in time to help save Kevin from Crowley.

We're off to the races in this episode, with huge plot movement and incredible ship stuff. I'll get to that in a second, but let's talk about how this season continues to be about collateral damage and penance. Castiel wanted to stay in Purgatory to atone for his actions in Season Seven, while Sam is still atoning for checking out for a year. As for Kevin, he bailed and look what happened to poor Samandriel and the prophets. And Dean? Well, Dean feels like he has to atone for things he didn't even do, because that's the kind of guilt this poor, beautiful moron carries.

Of course he doesn't need to, but Dean feels responsible for everything. Ever since he grew up being responsible for Sam, he thinks that saving everyone is the only thing that makes him worthy of living. And even that's a maybe. That's also what make Crowley, Benny, and Kevin such good characters for this season. In various ways, Dean is responsible for them just being part of the world, and in turn the hurt they endure or cause.

But Cas being back matters a lot, because he's there to tell Dean he's wrong, that he doesn't—and in fact, can't—save everyone. What Cas forgets to say is that not saving everyone is okay. I'm sure he thinks that's implied, but it takes a lot to get through to Dean Winchester. Then again, Cas is going to have some issues of his own with Naomi controlling him.

Ship Shape: These two. I swear to Chuck. Before this episode, I think it was possible to think Dean and Cas were just friends, but holy moly, not after. Somewhere in purgatory, these pining, smoldering idiots must have gotten married, because they bicker like it. That is, when they aren't staring at each other like they're the only person in the universe. (Sorry, Sam, that's got to be awkward).

Everything about this episode is Dean and Cas—even the plot holes! How did Cas find Dean with that angelic warding on his ribs? Well, in Season Ten there's a throwaway line about how angels can sense longing just like a prayer, and Dean sure was pining for Cas. Throw in Dean getting flustered when Cas comes out of that bathroom looking all spiffed up and you have a perfect Destiel storm.

Hunteri Heroici

Episode 8.08. Airdate: November 28, 2012
Written by: Andrew Dabb
Directed by: Paul A. Edwards
Guest Cast: Misha Collins (Castiel), Liana Balaban (Amelia), Brian Markinson (Stan Thompson), Amanda Tapping (Naomi), Mike Farrell (Fred Jones)
Synopsis: The Winchesters and Cas take on a case that's all together loony.

Ignoring the Amelia flashbacks, I sort of wish every episode of the series was just like this—fun and poignant, with Sam, Dean, and Cas saving the day by bringing their different strengths and weaknesses to the table. I love the cartoon stuff. I love Team Free Will together. I love it all.

This episode drops the idea of how dangerous it is to live in a dream world, but it helps us to better understand Sam's decision to leave hunting. It was a trauma response and that's fair, because he has a lot of trauma! Like Fred, he feels better in his fantasy world. But the whole front half of this season is about the collateral damage caused by the supernatural, by the Winchesters hunting and not hunting. Every action has consequences, even if we don't understand them, and that includes living in a dream.

This transitions into Cas' story really well too. He's hiding, choosing not to go to heaven and see what he did. He'd rather be with his chosen family, but he can't stay there either… however, the consequences are already happening, with Naomi and her strange control over him.

Ship Shape: So, Sam and Amelia are… cute? Maybe. But basing a relationship on trauma and escaping something is never good, because reality will come back to bite you. Not looking good for these two which is fine honestly.

Dean and Cas continue to be completely married from the bickering to the 100% emotionally honest conversations that can only happen between people who love and trust one another.

Familiar Faces: Folks may recognize Amanda Tapping from her work on *Stargate: SG-1*. And you might recognize Amelia's dad from… *Supernatural*. He appeared way back in Season One in "Phantom Traveler."

Name Game: The boys and Cas are agents Crosby, Stills, and Nash, referencing the folk group of the same name. Pity they never got to add Jack as Young down the line.

Citizen Fang

Episode 8.09. Airdate: December 5, 2012
Written by: Daniel Loflin
Directed by: Nick Copus
Guest Cast: Jon Gries (Martin Creaser), Ty Olsson (Benny), Liana Balaban (Amelia), Kathleen Munroe (Elizabeth)
Synopsis: Thanks to Martin Creaser, Sam thinks Benny is killing again.

Let's pause after this underwhelming mid-season finale and reflect on what a great character Benny is. He has a really rough episode, with his own sins refusing to let him rest. Ty Olsson is great in the role, bringing both warmth and danger to Benny, but he's also great in what he represents for the brothers. He's the one person who has never let Dean down (Until he kills Martin maybe?) and that means a lot since almost everyone has lied to him. And the few people that didn't, like Bobby or Lisa, are dead or gone. Heck, even his father was a bastard sometimes, as Martin reminds us.

But for Sam, Benny is a big, living reminder of his failures. Dean trusted him, and Benny saved him. Not Sam. So yeah, he's mad at Benny, because he's mad at himself. Benny surviving and still being Dean's new brother also reminds Sam of how the new person he found in the year apart of is lost to him. So, it hurt doubly. But these are Sam's choices. He ran away from hunting, and from Amelia.

This final Amelia flashback is weird and strange though, because not only do we not get why Sam ever chose her, but his decision to leave doesn't make sense. And I think there's some metaphors or mirrors with Don coming back from war/death to parallel with Dean. But overall, I'm glad this is almost over.

Plot Hole: Seriously, what happened Sam? In the season premiere, we saw him leave Amelia in the middle of the night. Was he having an affair? Just hanging out? What happened? How did the writers forget that so quickly?

Torn and Frayed

Episode 8.10. Airdate: January 16, 2013
Written by: Jenny Klein
Directed by: Robert Singer
Guest Cast: Misha Collins (Castiel), Mark Sheppard (Crowley), Osric Chau (Kevin), Ty Olsson (Benny), Liana Balaban (Amelia), Tyler Johnston (Samandriel), Amanda Tapping (Naomi)
Synopsis: Castiel enlists Dean to help him save Samandriel from Crowley, but Cas is being controlled by Naomi.

There's not a lot of subtext or thematic content here. It's all just text. And I'm not talking about the ship stuff either, I'm talking about how this mid-season premiere put all the myth and character stuff right on the table. Sam and Dean both make the decision to commit to hunting, and each other, and that means cutting people out of their lives. Both Kevin and Cas do as well, though unwillingly.

For good or ill, everyone decides to commit to the greater good. Because they have work to do. But in a way, that's just another trauma response. And again, we this is reflected in a fun house mirror for Cas. Forced into service by actual, triggering, horrible trauma, choosing "the life" for the Winchesters leads to the brother codependency that comes with that.

And unlike the leviathans plot—which didn't mesh with the season—the concept of how trauma and loneliness lead to codependency works with the mythology here. The idea that, somehow, the boys can eliminate all demonic evil is absurd. Because in this show, there may be monsters, but humans are just as dangerous without fangs and magic. And what's to distinguish a hunter from a monster anyway?

How is Naomi enslaving Cas any different from the life enslaving Sam and Dean? These warriors for free will have all had their choice taken away from them by trauma.

Ship Shape: Goodbye, Amelia! The failure of this story shows how not suited the show is to a love story when it tries too hard to force it. The much better love story remains the one they didn't intend to tell—Dean and Cas. But it sucks for Dean that he loses *both* his boyfriends in one episode.

Death Notes: Poor, poor Samandriel. Crowley is really showing how bad he can be at this point, and Samandriel is the main victim who gets to die at the hands of a brother. So tragic. He'll live on forever in fanfic at least.

LARP and the Real Girl

Episode 8.11. Airdate: January 23, 2013
Written by: Robbie Thompson
Directed by: Jeannot Szwarc
Guest Cast: Felicia Day (Charlie), Hank Harris (Gerry), Mackenzie Dupont (Gilda)
Synopsis: Charlie is back to take the Winchesters on a magical adventure.

Good golly do I love this episode. It's so fun, so creative, and did I mention fun? Things got a little dark for a second back there, so it's nice to see the boys let loose. And especially to see Dean let his freak flag fly. Doesn't hurt that Jensen rocks his LARPing duds.

Charlie is always a great addition to the show, and here our favorite fangirl is used in a meta way to comment on…fans. Again, Charlie is a "good" fan, who takes comfort and inspiration from her chosen fandom. That's what fandom is for—to make us happy and give us a safe space to escape. But Gerry, the warlock fairy-enslaver, is a bad fan—the kind that takes things way too seriously, which *Supernatural* itself has its fair share of. To sum up: fandom is good, but hurting real human beings is bad! And it's not just the SPN family that needs (and completely missed!) this lesson.

Also, here we have a new theme we'll see a lot of that I want you to watch out for—enslavement. Gilda was summoned by Gerry and controlled, just like Cas was by Naomi. This is going to come up again and again.

So, Get This: It's high time I gave a shout out to the gag reels, which are available for every season of the show and just as delightful as the series. The Season Eight gag reel is a particular gem because of the blooper from the ending Moondoor charge where Jensen falls flat on his face.

As Time Goes By

Episode 8.12. Airdate: January 30, 2013
Written by: Adam Glass
Directed by: Serge Ladouceur
Guest Cast: Gil McKinney (Henry Winchester), Alaina Huffman (Abaddon)
Synopsis: Sam and Dean's grandfather Henry Winchester travels through time to escape the demon Abaddon and reveals his grandsons are descendants of an ancient order called the Men of Letters.

This episode isn't just really good, it's pivotal for the entire series and sets Sam, Dean, and *Supernatural* itself on a new course. The Men of Letters and Knights of Hell raise the stakes, expanding the world, and build on series-long ideas about fate, family, and free will.

The entire Kripke era was all about the boys fighting for free will, for the right to choose their destiny. But since Sam and Dean stopped the apocalypse, everything in their life—from violent cycles to family legacy and codependency—have taken away any choice they had. Introducing Henry and the idea that they are legacies of hunting. Despite everything, the Winchesters are fated to be hunters.

These boys will never be free it seems, because the authors and fans of the story can't let them go peacefully (and I mean that both within the narrative with God as their author and fan, and outside of it). So, we get new story, new tragedy, and new enemies because that's how it's gotta be.

Death Notes: Really impressive that Sam and Dean have watched both their grandfathers die in front of them, but at least Henry's death allowed them to make some peace with his and with the past.

Plot Hole: With time jumps of a full year after Seasons Five and Seven, the Winchesters wouldn't be in 2013, they'd be in 2015, but the show just sort of ignores that. Maybe they time traveled.

Fan Favorite: Abaddon as played by Alaina Huffman was an instant favorite, just thanks to her look. We may need to start a red head watch because between her, Anna, Charlie and one more character we'll meet in two years, gingers do have all the fun on this show. But Abaddon also inspired cosplay almost immediately, and Henry, and his actor, Gil McKinney became beloved as well, with both McKinney and Huffman becoming popular guests at *Supernatural* cons.

Everybody Hates Hitler

Episode 8.13. Airdate: February 6, 2013
Written by: Ben Edlund
Directed by: Phil Sgriccia
Guest Cast: Adam Rose (Aaron Bass), John DeSantis (Golem), Bernhard Forcher (Eckhart)
Synopsis: The boys open up the Men of Letters bunker and move in, then take on a case involving Nazi necromancers.

Another entry in a really solid run of episodes, and once again, a massive expansion of the world. I love the series reaching back into history and considering what hunters looked like back then. The Golem and Aaron are both really fun characters who could have honestly had their own spin-off, so that's great too. Though the resolution of the action here (just a few gunshots and trickery) is anti-climactic.

Once again, we have a story about stepping into a role set out by legacy and destiny, but mixed with a story about a supernatural being getting used as a tool It's kind of how that kind of enslavement can be used by bad guys and good guys. Does this imply Sam and Dean are tools, like Gilda and the Golem? Is Dean the one controlling Sam because he pulled him back into the life? It's worth considering.

Ship Shape: The brief scene where Aaron flirts with Dean is the stuff of legend, not just for how cute it is, but for how Dean reacts. He seems like he might have said yes to that drink on another day maybe. And this is why Aaron shows up in a lot of fanfic…

Trial and Error

Episode 8.14. Airdate: February 13, 2013
Written by: Andrew Dabb
Directed by: Kevin Parks
Guest Cast: Osric Chau (Kevin), Danay Garcia (Ellie)
Synopsis: Kevin figures out how to close the gates of hell: a series of trials that start with killing a hell hound.

This episode is fine in terms of quality; the Cassity family is corny and annoying, but Dean and Sam look hot in glasses. It's massively important both in mythology, and in understanding who the Winchesters are—how they see themselves, and what they want out of life.

Sam is defined by seeing the best in the world and people, and his faith that he and his family can make life better. He has to believe that because he still, despite everything, wants to be a part of that normal world one day. He wants to break free of fate, and legacy, and live his life. And he's willing to do anything to do that.

Meanwhile, Dean is very much the opposite. His core belief is that he's a tool, but that he can be used for good and that's fine with him. Because he wants the people he loves to have a good life. Despite how he's continued to pull Sam into hunting, Dean honestly wants Sam to go be normal once his work is done. But he can't do it alone. Sam reminds Dean that he's wrong about this, but he won't really listen to Sam over his guilt and savior complex. And it's also super tragic because Dean wants to be normal too! He finally has a home and a mattress! It remembers him.

Spoiler Alert: And because of the guilt and codependency, and all sorts of factors, the hell gate plan is going to go badly. But overall, what Dean tells Sam about going out swinging and letting Sam live a life happens. Notice that this episode is written by Andrew Dabb, who, half a series later, would end the Winchester's story *exactly* as Dean describes it here. In a way, Dean finally does get his wish. Sorta like making a demon deal, honestly. Happiness at a bloody cost.

Ship Shape: I love Ellie. She's a cool, strong woman and does the exact thing most of us would try to do if we had one night left on earth—bang Dean Winchester.

Man's Best Friend with Benefits

Episode 8.15. Airdate: February 20, 2013
Written by: Brad Buckner & Eugenie Ross-Leming
Directed by: John Showalter
Guest Cast: Christian Campbell (James), Mishael Morgan (Portia)
Synopsis: A witch who is also a cop has a dog familiar who is also a woman. It's worse than it sounds.

There are good episodes, there are mediocre episodes, and then there are episodes like this. Every decision here is terrible. There's a random friend who we've never heard of (seriously, when I first watched this, I thought I had just forgotten some previous episode) who takes center stage with a bunch of petty drama. And it's in a community that we know nothing about, that makes the entire world of the show make less sense . All bad, but fine. Everyone slips.

But having a Black woman wear a collar, calling a white police officer master? Holy crap that's horrifying! And there's the part where she's literally a pet, sleeping with her "master" because she chose to? Even worse!

There's some thematic stuff here about, once again, Sam and Dean being paralleled to creatures forced to serve, but neither that nor a few decent supportive brother moments are enough to redeem this pile of crap. Woof.

Remember the Titans

Episode 8.16. Airdate: February 27, 2013
Written by: Daniel Loflin
Directed by: Steve Boyum
Guest Cast: John Reardon (Shane/Prometheus), Brooke Langton (Hayley), Anna Van Hooft (Artemis), John Novak (Zeus)
Synopsis: A zombie turns out to be the Titan Prometheus.

This is a huge improvement from the previous dog of an episode, but it still commits one of my least favorite *Supernatural* sins—killing a God. And in this case, a really important one too. Zeus. And sure, I know Dean and Sam have gone up against big fish, but it's just annoying to see the king of Olympus killed off in a monster of the week episode. Whatever.

We're still in territory that's all about bondage, as well as the different ways family legacy affects characters. I think that Sam feels trapped right now by the trials, but also by what Dean wants from him. And Dean's messages are seriously mixed, by the way. He shamed Sam for months for leaving hunting, and now keeps going on about how he wants Sam to be normal one day.

But hey, we also just got our fifth human-supernatural creature love story this season, which certainly seems like an interesting pattern, considering things.

Ship Shape: I'm talking about Dean and Cas, again. Not for nothing, but both Artemis and Benny defied their godly fathers to protect the humans they love, which Cas has done too. And Dean's earning that love by showing Cas his most vulnerable, loving self in that wonderful prayer scene. If only Cas could reply…

Name Game: Aliases Bonham and Jones are, again, a Led Zeppelin reference.

Goodbye, Stranger

Episode 8.17. Airdate: March 20, 2013
Written by: Robbie Thompson
Directed by: Thomas J. Wright
Guest Cast: Misha Collins (Castiel), Rachel Miner (Meg), Mark Sheppard (Crowley), Amanda Tapping (Naomi)
Synopsis: Meg saves her unicorn. Dean saves Cas from heavenly mind control with the power of love.

Where to even begin with this incredible episode? Let's just dive in and talk about the power of love and hope to change lives. All season, we've been dealing with people the Winchesters are close to getting hurt. And many people—especially Cas and Sam—being controlled by their family. That was even Meg's story for a long time. So how do we break free of that control? How do we find the strength to not do as we were told? In the biggest picture on this show, how do we assert our free will? Love. Pure and simple.

Sam found love with Amelia, but he also found hope. Meg found a strange sort of love with Cas, and died in the most undemonic way possible. It's love for Sam and Cas that keeps Dean hoping. And it's love for Dean, that breaks Naomi's control on Cas.

And again, the show isn't confining love to just romance, but it's very much love that saves the day in this episode. But love without trust won't get you far, and the Winchesters have a long way to go in that area.

Let's also talk about how Crowley and Naomi as twin antagonists for the season work. They are both the personifications of power and control. Naomi uses literal mind control, while Crowley operates and gets his power from rules and ruling. Team Free Will is all about unending power structures so of course these two work well pitted against them. But are either of them the real threat or is it the violent, sad cycles that masquerade as "fate" that really are in control of things?

Death Notes: It hurts to lose Meg. Along with Bobby and the Ghostfacers, she was the only currently living character from Season One that we had, and her death here ends a long and glorious run for a great character.

Behind the scenes, actress Rachel Miner had requested a way for her to exit the role, due to her diagnosis of multiple sclerosis, which she had been managing privately at this point. After this episode, Miner stepped back from public appearances, thinking that fans might not want to see her unable to walk easily or visibly ill. But the SPN family isn't like that. Following high demand, Miner eventually returned to the spotlight at *Supernatural* conventions and the reception and support for her was incredible. She remains a visible and beloved feature of the fandom, running Random Acts and sharing inspiration and hope with everyone around her, which is why this isn't the last time we'll see her face.

Ship Shape: It would be easy to cynically guess that the flirting between Meg and Cas were added to this script to make it less gay… but if so, it didn't work. Meg and Cas' scenes are sweet, and I think the idea of a demon loving an angel in her way is great… but the Dean and Cas stuff blows it out of the water.

The crypt scene, as it's popularly called, is iconic thanks to Dean breaking through to Cas with "I need you." It's a beautiful line, but it was also written as "I love you," something Dean had never said to anyone on the show, not even Sam, so it was changed. But I think the "I need you" is even more romantic.

Driver Picks the Music: The use of Supertramp's "Goodbye, Stranger" in the closing scene marks one of the few times the song an episode is named for is featured in the same episode.

Freaks and Geeks

Episode 8.18. Airdate: March 27, 2013
Written by: Adam Glass
Directed by: John Showalter
Guest Cast: Madison McLaughlin (Krissy Chambers), Adam DiMarco (Aidan), Megan Danso (Josephine), Adrian Hough (Victor)
Synopsis: A hunted named Victor trains Krissy Chambers and other teens.

Following up the really good episodes is always tough. Adam Glass had to do it in Season Seven after "Death's Door," and has to repeat it again. So he's brought back the same character, Krissy. And she works really well here, This season really does tie in a lot of those themes from last season, Here though, we have yet another authority figure (much like Naomi) manipulating people to keep them in a cycle.

This serves to motivate Sam and Dean to break the cycle for good, shutting the gates of hell and thus allowing some hunters—like Sam—to be normal. There's foreshadowing here too, because this wasn't a demon case. There are still going to be monsters out there, so would that really change anything? And there will still be violent, broken, lonely people like Victor and Dean. I can't help but keep seeing parallels to Dean bringing Sam into hunting twice now, and how so many characters this season have been pressured into fights they didn't want, even good ones.

Spoiler Alert: I believe that a lot of the ideas about breaking the cycle were meant to be realized by the end of this season, or the next as part of an intended endgame for the series. Heck, it was Season Eight, but that fact that there are over 160 episodes *after* this means the guys very much stay until the endgame finally culminates in Season Fifteen. It works, but it makes things a lot darker in retrospect.

Taxi Driver

Episode 8.19. Airdate: April 3, 2013
Written by: Brad Buckner & Eugenie Ross-Leming
Directed by: Guy Norman Bee
Guest Cast: Jim Beaver (Bobby), Mark Sheppard (Crowley), Osric Chau (Kevin), Ty Olsson (Benny), Amanda Tapping (Naomi), Assaf Cohen (Ajay)
Synopsis: The second trial requires Sam to rescue a soul from hell, and it just so happens Bobby is there and the way in is through purgatory.

There's a lot of good in this episode—big drama in terms of a reunion with Bobby, Naomi trying to manipulate the boys, Kevin cracking, and a painful goodbye for Benny. It's also a beautifully shot episode, with incredible colors and images like the graffiti door, hell, and Bobby's soul ascending. Let's also note how cool purgatory looked as we say goodbye.

But oh my god the plot holes, and retcons, and continuity issues. Not just from this episode, but others around it. In one sense, this episode fills a hole in the mythology. We know what happens to ghosts now! They move on to either heaven or hell. Cool. And Bobby going to hell is fine, because Crowley. Why didn't the guys take Kevin to the Bunker right away, you know, the safest place on earth? And "Rogue Reapers" exist? And they have easy ways into Purgatory? And angels can get in there too, I guess? That completely invalidates the entire plotline of Season Six!

And then there's Crowley and Naomi, who seem to know each other. According to "Goodbye, Stranger" they may have been lovers in ancient times. And here, Crowley says he's "forever." But he's not! He's only like 400 years old! He was born in Scotland in the 1600s, a fact the writers just sort of… forgot?

But anyway, this is a big plot episode, and it does bring back issues of how Dean doesn't trust Sam, and what a crappy decision it was for him to not search for Dean. It's nice to see Bobby back to talk some sense into these idjits though. Too bad Crowley's pissed now, and Kevin is in the cross hairs!

Spoiler Alert: Some plot holes like where the hell Garth went, and what happened to poor Linda, will get resolved later with varying success.

Death Notes: Benny's death, and the terrible fact it has to come at the hands of his only true friend, is so sad and poignant. Jensen and Ty act the heck out of the moment. It's emotional and it actually matters in terms of the story, which is why it works so well and is a really good resolution to this story.

Ship Shape: Not only is Naomi lying through her teeth to Dean about Cas, but she's also using Dean's feelings for him to do so. Cas does want to come home, and she's sewing doubt that he doesn't. Not cool!

Pac-Man Fever

Episode 8.20. Airdate: April 24, 2013
Written by: Robbie Thompson
Directed by: Robert Singer
Guest Cast: Felicia Day (Charlie), Lynda Boyd (Dr. Jennifer O'Brien)
Synopsis: Charlie brings the Winchesters a Djinn case that makes Dean and Charlie confront fears of saying goodbye.

And it's time for some of my favorite *Supernatural* things: Charlie, Dean in a costume, Sam saving people when he can't even save himself, and crying. This episode is slightly meta in that it references the "*Supernatural*" books as a series, and it really gets the show and the Winchesters.

Charlie is fully our fangirl now. And like the many queer, female fans of the show—who found the series say, on Netflix around Seasons Seven and Eight—Charlie brings new energy to the hunt and the dynamic. That's why fans love her so much—she's us and like us. She knows Cas is dreamy, and loves and believes in these boys.

Despite all the bad and bloody consequences, the Winchesters together can save the world. And they're unstoppable. But that doesn't mean they'll be together forever, so this episode is about saying goodbye and letting go of guilt. It's about showing people we love them by being there *and* by letting them go. And it does this in a really beautiful, emotional way.

Future Famous Faces: The second body is Manny Jacinto, aka Jason Mendoza from *The Good Place*, my other favorite show about the afterlife.

The Great Escapist

Episode 8.21. Airdate: May 1, 2013
Written by: Ben Edlund
Directed by: Robert Duncan McNeil
Guest Cast: Misha Collins (Castiel), Mark Sheppard (Crowley), Osric Chau (Kevin), Amanda Tapping (Naomi), Curtis Armstrong (Metatron)
Synopsis: Stumped on finding Kevin (who's being imprisoned by Crowley), the boys seek out the scribe of God, Metatron. The angels catch up to Cas.

This is the final episode from one of my favorite writers, Ben Edlund. Edlund's work, along with Carver and Kripke, pushed the boundaries of meta narratives, so it's fitting that in his final work for *Supernatural*, he brings series-spanning ideas about free will, power and the author as god right to the forefront. This is an episode about choice.

When it comes to authorship and destiny, as well as our late-Season Eight themes of slavery, control, and manipulation, it all comes down to power and choice. Castiel has that crack in his chassis because he believes in choice. He won't go with the script written for him.

Do Sam and Dean even have choices though? They seemed to, but despite both of them choosing to leave hunting at different point, they're back. So, do their choices matter? Is it a real choice if God/their author is only giving them two crappy options? We see here that characters can still chose to be good and do good. But will it matter in the end? That's the final question Ben Edlund leaves us with, and it will take a long time for *Supernatural* to answer it.

Ship Shape/Spoiler Alert: Way down the line, we find out that it's this Cas in this universe that's the only one who's "broken" according to Chuck And that seems to be the main thing that distinguishes this universe from all the others that were more easily controlled. And the difference here? Cas loved Dean and fell for his sake. Seems important.

Famous Faces: It's Curtis Armstrong, famous nerd of cinema, as Metatron! You know him from *Moonlighting*, *Risky Business*, *Better Off*

Dead and more. He's perfect in this part, and I love him as Metatron. I also loved him in *Ray*, which interestingly also stars Robert Wisdom and Kurt Fuller making it the only three asshole angel movie to ever win Best Picture!

Plot Hole: Sam recalls a ride in the Grand Canyon, but in Season Two, Dean says they've never been there, so what's the truth?

Clip Show

Episode 8.22. Airdate: May 8, 2013
Written by: Andrew Dabb
Directed by: Thomas J. Wright
Guest Cast: Misha Collins (Castiel), Taylor Cole (Sarah), Mark Sheppard (Crowley), Alaina Huffman (Josie/Abaddon), Curtis Armstrong (Metatron)
Synopsis: The boys figure out how to cure a demon, but Crowley starts killing everyone they've saved. Metatron convinces Castiel to close the gates of heaven.

This is one of those penultimate episodes that has to do a lot of heavy lifting. And unlike some other seasons, it's more than up to the task. There's plot movement for Cas, based once again on his guilt over heaven. Abaddon also represents many sins of the past, and how trying to fix them. Also there's this idea that demons can become human again, which is also about cleansing, penance, and atonement. Appropriate for a season that started in Purgatory.

This episode is all about dealing with the past, and to tie into our Big Themes—the power the past has over us, good and bad. When we betray our family, we want to make up for that. When we do good, we hold onto that to justify the collateral damage. But at what point does the damage outweigh the good? That's the question all three of our heroes are left asking, and it's really sneaky how similar the stories for Cas and the boys are at this point.

And then there's Crowley, who's at his very worst, morally, this episode. Which is really his best. Crowley has always been a great antagonist, because he's smart, resourceful, and creative. He knows people and what they want, what they value. That's how he got to be the king of the crossroads. Sarah's death is so sad, but it and Crowley's whole plan is also brilliant, because he knows how the Winchesters work. Which is why the only person who'll ever truly beat Crowley… is Crowley.

Spoiler Alert: Crowley has a witch mother you say? And Nephilim are a thing? There's big foreshadowing here, though I don't think it was intentional at the time. Just fun expansions of the world that will end up being really important.

Ship Shape: Not a good episode for romance, I gotta say. Sarah falls prey to the "smooch Sam and die" curse eight years after they met, which honestly makes me think Amelia dodged a bullet. And Dean and Cas are arguing like a couple, leading to Cas nearly killing a guy to get apology pie. And it's not like Dean and Cas make each other think the other doesn't want or need them won't lead to horrible consequences—OH WAIT.

Sacrifice

Episode 8.23. Airdate: May 15, 2013
Written by: Jeremy Carver
Directed by: Phil Sgriccia
Guest Cast: Misha Collins (Castiel), Kim Rhodes (Jody), Mark Sheppard (Crowley), Osric Chau (Kevin), Amanda Tapping (Naomi), Alaina Huffman (Abaddon), Curtis Armstrong (Metatron)
Synopsis: Sam tries to shut the gates of hell by curing Crowley. Cas tries to shut the gates of heaven by helping Metatron. It goes badly for everyone, except for Metatron

Now that's a season finale! Drama! Twists! Smashing hetero-normativity! References to Girls! And the most visually beautiful final moment of any season, with the shocking fall of the angels from heaven. This is a truly great episode that serves all the stories in fascinating and surprising ways, and I love it.

Kevin's arc has been incredibly sad this season, as we've seen him fully traumatized, cynical, and lose everything. And it's not getting any better. The Winchesters pull him back in, and it's the Winchesters who also let out a new contender for the throne of hell. Negative consequences are piling up and that's just in the side plots.

To our main men, there's Cas who once again has the best of intentions. Dean and Cas both make more bad decisions this episode, because they feel shut out and left behind by the other. Cas wants to prove himself as well, so he's too trusting. And he's too driven by guilt, like Sam. Speaking of, Sam wants to please his dysfunctional family because of shame over his past. But they're not! This show is about forgiveness, but these morons can't forgive themselves and thus… apocalyptically bad discussions happen and how people like Metatron and Naomi can manipulate them. And thus—boom, Metatron baddie reveal, with angels falling all over the place.

Which brings us to Sam and Crowley. Let's take a minute here to appreciate the incredible performances from Jared and Mark in their scenes in the church. The vulnerability and rawness both actors bring to these moments is so amazing, and it's especially rewarding to see

Crowley's humanity come through, after he was just at his most demonic earlier. How does one begin to ask for forgiveness? Well, forgiveness comes from love, so if Crowley deserves to be loved… we'll have to see.

Sam too earns forgiveness at last from Dean, which has been a long time coming. And that convinces him not to complete the trials or seal the gates. That's because Dean wants him to live. They both chose each other over the world, and that's actually really bad. All their emotional eggs are in the brotherly co-dependent basket, at the expense of humanity.

Spoiler Alert: When I say Sam and Dean's decision to fully commit to each other is bad, I think the rest of the series bears that out, or at least the rest of the Carver era. It's more toxic cycles and more stories at the whims of capricious gods that can't end. Because it's just one Winchester refusing to let the other go after another, once again, that leads to the mark of Cain (literal eternal punishment for harming a brother!) demon Dean, and the release of God's actual dark sibling. The only way this gets resolved is one brother letting the other make an ultimate sacrifice to save the world. This isn't a triumphant moment—it's a huge, selfish, insecure mistake.

But in the even longer context, it leads to more fodder for Chuck's chosen story, an endless wheel of sacrifice that always ends with one brother killing someone they love or causing their death.

Ship Shape: This episode has stuff for all the shippers. For you Sam/Crowley folks there's some real connection there. If you're a Wincest fan, yeah. The guys sorta got married in a church? That's… something. Though as I said above, I'm fairly sure it's not actually a good thing?

And it's good for Destiel trash like me. Dean and Cas are confronted with two men getting set up by cupid, undermining the heterosexual expectations of everyone. This includes Metatron, who at this point does not get how in love Cas is with Dean. Neither do they. In fact, you could read Dean's U-Turn to stopping the trials and saving Sam, inspired by the fact he's losing Cas and he can't lose his whole family.

Also, let's take a minute to bask in this ending, because on its own it was the greatest fanfic prompt of all time. The hiatus between Seasons Eight and nine was a true golden age for the fandom. The ideas that folks came up with there were incredible and a lot better than some of what we got in the actual Season Nine. And speaking of.

SUPERNATURAL

CHAPTER NINE

There Ain't No Me If There Ain't No You

After Season Eight did better than anyone had expected, things looked good going into Season Nine. After all, that was an incredible cliffhanger that might have made things look a bit too good. I think Season Nine may work better in a binge, than it did live, because it's a season that messes with expectations in ways that are honestly disappointing. Jeremy Carver may have had a clear idea going in, with new staff member Robert Berens and the return of Charmelo and Snyder, but they can only do so much.

While many fans were hoping the season would be about Team Free Will regrouping with Cas, and threats from both heaven and hell on the horizon, it's… not really that at all. Instead of a team, we get stories we're not expecting, like Sam possessed by an angel without his consent. There's a lot this season about faith, even religion, and how it can be misplaced. In this case, there's faith misplaced with various angels, demons, and even between Sam and Dean.

This season is also about consequences and owning your mistakes… which is not a strong suit for the Winchesters! It's about identity, about becoming our best or worst selves, and if we have any choice in those changes. In a way, the season is also about consent and how bad an idea it is to take that away from people. Overall, we'll see the codependency that was fully embraced at the end of Season Eight get even more toxic.

What Dean did, and what Sam went along with last finale was bad, and selfish. And Dean keeps making selfish decisions, until it turns him into a person we as an audience may not like very much. That's tough, but if we see Season Nine as the second act in a three-part story (as it was intended to be then, wasn't), this where the heroes falter and reach their darkest points. Things are about to get morally ambiguous!

I Think I'm Gonna Like It Here

Episode 9.01. Airdate: October 8, 2013
Written by: Jeremy Carver
Directed by: John Showalter
Guest Cast: Misha Collins (Castiel), Jim Beaver (Bobby), Julian Richings (Death), Tahmoh Penikett (Ezekiel), Grace Gillam (Hael)
Synopsis: In order to save a dying Sam, Dean allows a newly fallen angel to possess Sam. Cas finds out that being human isn't so easy.

Let's just get to Dean's choice letting Ezekiel possess Sam. Sure, Dean wants his brother to survive because he can't bear the thought of living without him, but at this point that's not a good thing. It's not heroic or romantic—it's manipulative and comes from a place of insecurity and loneliness. Sam was ready to save the world and die, but Dean stops him in a gross violation of Sam's free will and his very personhood. That goes against everything they stand for! Bad Dean! Bad!

Yes, Ezekiel seems nice, and it's really cool to see how good Jared is at playing him, but… this is a huge screw up for Dean. And that's saying nothing about the choice not to shut the gates of hell. It makes sense from a writer's point of view, because Dean and Sam letting the world down is hard to show, but Dean betraying his brother is much easier. And it's going to be really complicated.

Cas, on the other hand, is trying to make the right decisions. He's learning the struggle of being human, and in a really big visual metaphor, he strips off the person he was as an angel, leaving his iconic trench behind.

Death Notes: Sam was literally talking to Death, so we're giving him a point here: Dean: 16, Sam: 6, Castiel: 3. But the biggest loss in this episode is clearly the original Cas trench coat.

Ship Shape: Dean praying to Cas will always be romantic, let's be real. Also, what are the implications of shipping Ezekiel with either brother? You know what, I'll just leave that to the fanfic authors for now.

Familiar Faces: It's yet another *Battlestar Galactica* alum! Tahmoh Penikett played Helo on the show's entire run, and he's great here as Ezekiel. As this episode was filmed third in the season, not first, Jared had already been playing Ezekiel, so he had to match his performance.

Devil May Care

Episode 9.02. Airdate: October 15, 2013
Written by: Andrew Dabb
Directed by: Guy Norma Bee
Guest Cast: Mark Sheppard (Crowley), Osric Chau (Kevin), Alaina Huffman (Abaddon)
Synopsis: Abaddon goes on the offensive. Crowley plays Hannibal Lecter with Kevin.

"Devil May Care" works in some ways, but fails in others. The main failure is Abaddon. This hour is supposed to establish her as some big threat, but it honestly makes her seem less scary—anything really frightening would have to be way beyond the budget of the show. But a few soldier demons and scary speeches about eating babes that we've heard before? Meh.

What does succeed is that we learn about Ezekiel and get a truly incredible visual of him powering up his broken, burnt wings. He seems to be trustworthy. Dean feels (rightly!) responsible for not closing the gates, but maybe family is worth it. And hey, Sam's happy and Kevin is okay. This is a great episode for Kevin being truly welcomed as part of the family. That's all good. So, yay?

Spoiler alert: Not yay. This episode works best on a rewatch, because it's all about that foreshadowing. Everything Crowley says to Kevin is true: Kevin will get thrown into the Winchester meat grinder. Dean *is* manipulating Kevin, just as much as Sam, because Linda is alive and she's okay! So, Dean's lies in the name of family are indeed going to screw over everyone. And all the things he cares about, that Sam lists as making him happy, those are all going away because they exist on a foundation of lies and manipulation.

And where is that going to lead? To exactly what Abaddon threatened—Dean as a demon, the worst and scariest version of himself. Yikes!

I'm No Angel

Episode 9.03. Airdate: October 22, 2013
Written by: Brad Buckner & Eugenie Ross-Leming
Directed by: Kevin Hooks
Guest Cast: Misha Collins (Castiel), Adam J. Harrington (Bartholomew), Shannon Lucio (April Kelly), Kevin Brief (Buddy Boyle)
Synopsis: Cas runs into trouble and a rogue reaper who takes all sorts of advantage.

There are some interesting pieces here—that talk Cas has with the nice lady in church is a great discussion of faith—but there are also a lot of "scream at the television" bad parts as well.

Seeing Cas as a human is fascinating, and I love that he's learning to be kinder and more compassionate than he already was. But there's also so much that makes no sense, like him not calling the Winchesters and everything with, um, the hedonism. From the weird shot of him looking at a woman's breasts, to him having sex with an admittedly evil and manipulative woman he just met, these plot points are not just gross, they're stupid and annoying.

April in her aid, then betrayal, of Cas is a mirror for Ezekiel who seems cool until he forces Dean to kick Cas out of the bunker. It's the worst thing he can ask Dean to do at this point, and is our big clue that trusting Zeke is going to work out just as well as trusting April.

There's a lot of other things going on here, with Bartholomew and the revered, but it's all silly despite how it mirrors the idea that putting your trust and faith into the wrong thing is bad. But people still need faith, and Cas certainly will now.

Plot Holes: Rogue reapers who anyone can see now, and who are also angels with vessels, is just confusing and dumb. And seriously, *why didn't Cas just call the boys???*

Ship Shape: Oh boy is everything that happens with Cas and April unnecessary and kinda rapey. Not good at all, but I think the writers knew that so they made sure to kill her. So… uh, win? And as heartbreaking as this episode is, seeing how broken Dean is by Cas being dead and having to leave, is pretty romantic.

Death Notes: And Cas is on the board again! This guy really is a Winchester. The score is now: Dean: 16, Sam: 6, Castiel: 4.

Behind the Scenes: You may be thinking "Hey doesn't Jensen direct the third episode in a season?" And yes, he does, but this year he skipped because he didn't want to spend two extra weeks in Vancouver due to the birth of his daughter, JJ!

Slumber Party

Episode 9.04. Airdate: October 29, 2013
Written by: Robbie Thompson
Directed by: Robert Singer
Guest Cast: Mark Sheppard (Crowley), Felicia Day (Charlie), Kaniehtiio Horn (Dorothy Gale)
Synopsis: We're off to see the wizard… er, witch?

This is a "big swing" episode, and I think it only works because of where it happens in the season. The whole "Oz is real!" stuff just doesn't fit into this world. Crowley and his musical theater reference and hissing are great though.

The plot mirrors the larger story, with people losing control of their lives and bodies, with Dorothy being controlled both by her family and literal possession. It's the same that's going on with Zeke and Sam. But we also have some lovely things about the bunker finally being a home, and affirmation that people like Dorothy and Sam are okay with their lives as long as they can write their own story. Except Sam isn't doing that. Unbeknownst to him there's an intruder in his home. Irony!

This seeming resolution of Charlie's story is fitting. She gets a big, beautiful send-off to a world of magic, where she can be a hero and that's great. A lot of this season is about if we can be who we say we are, or chose to be, and I think this is one of those story beats that show Carver was looking towards winding down the show… but that's not how it worked out.

Spoiler Alert: In fact, much like Season Six, nothing works out. The different angel factions, Crowley's list of demons, Charlie's journey—none of it ends up mattering and that's frustrating. Especially considering how badly Charlie's story ends when she does come back. It sort of makes me wish this had been her final episode.

Dog Dean Afternoon

Episode 9.05. Airdate: November 5, 2013
Written by: Eric Charmelo & Nicole Snyder
Directed by: Tim Andrew
Guest Cast: Steve Valentine (Chef Leo), Al Rodrigo (The Colonel-voice), Slater the German Shepperd (The Colonel-dog), Leslie Jordan (Yorkie-voice),
Synopsis: Dean takes his "Son of a bitch" catch phrase very literally.

Is this episode silly? Yes. Just the sharktopus nonsense is ridiculous.

But is it still fun? Absolutely. Jensen Ackles commits to dog Dean Dean, whether he's threatening to shoot a pigeon or making eyes at a poodle, and just goes for it. And just for that I'll say that this episode breaks the "episodes with dogs suck" curse.

The monster also has a lot to say about our subtext and themes. In trying to save himself, chef Leo became a monster—something that will inevitably happen with Sam and Zeke. Indeed, as another dark mirror, Dean loses his humanity trying to solve the case.

And really, what does human mean? The Winchesters no longer care about not hurting humans. And really, every monster they face at some point was human, so where even is the line now? Wait, sorry. That's too deep for commentary on an episode where Dean has the urge to sniff butts and Sam is forced to give a gay Yorkie a belly rub.

Name Game: The boys' aliases are based on Bret Michaels and C.C. Deville of the band Poison.

Heaven Can't Wait

Episode 9.06. Airdate: November 12, 2013
Written by: Robert Berens
Directed by: Rob Spera
Guest Cast: Misha Collins (Castiel), Mark Sheppard (Crowley), Osric Chau (Kevin), Alaina Huffman (Abaddon), Tanya Clarke (Nora), Ashton Holmes (Ephraim)
Synopsis: Cas (aka Steve the sales associate) calls in Dean for a case. Crowley helps with some translations in exchange for a call with Abaddon.

This entire series is about choices and free will, about if we can choose who we are and how that affects every other choice in our lives. Cas and Crowley are both faced with a choice between their old life and humanity. This episode doesn't give us their answers, but that's fine. It's all about asking the question in the first place.

The choice these two have is in heavy contrast to the choices that have been taken from Sam and Dean. I think Sam would like to not be an angel meat suit and Dean would prefer to spend his days lovingly smiling at Castiel. Just saying.

Listen, I can't even keep all the ship stuff in its section because in the long arc of Dean and Cas, this episode really matters. It's the first episode by the brilliant Robert Berens (spoiler: who will also write Cas' final episode where he confesses his love to Dean). There's so much love in this episode, amidst all the pain and longing. We have two guys considering how they keep fighting and screwing up, because they can't have the one thing they really want.

Ship Shape: I mean… what do we talk about? Dean helping Cas get ready for a date, looking at him like he's the cutest thing he's ever seen? The fact that when Cas leaves Nora's, it's like nine at night, but Dean drops him off in the morning?

Driver Picks the Music: Cas crooning the theme to *The Greatest American Hero* to a baby is the cutest thing ever. Originally, he was supposed to sing "Highway to Hell."

Bad Boys

Episode 9.07. Airdate: November 19, 2013
Written by: Adam Glass
Directed by: Kevin Parks
Guest Cast: Blake Gibbons (Sonny), Dylan Everett (Young Dean), Sean Michael Kyer (Timmy)
Synopsis: Dean heads back to deal with a haunting at a boy's home where he spent two months as a teen.

"Bad Boys" is a really good episode for many reasons, mainly Dylan Everett. We've had other actors play young Dean, but Dylan is by far our best. He's so sincere and does an incredible job channeling Jensen. These flashbacks are so heartbreaking, because he masters that mix of bravado, vulnerability and charm that makes Dean so special.

And we needed to be reminded why we love Dean, and why he is the way he is. Dean chooses family above his own wellbeing 100% of the time. And in many ways, it's inspiring and heroic like Timmy's mom. But when you don't let go—like she and Dean refuse to—people start dying. It's all a neon sign that Dean's attempts to protect Sam are leading him to a bad place!

What we see here we've seen many times. Dean is a sweet, smart, and tender guy who believes he has no choice but to live a life of violence. Sam is the reason for that, and he can't let that go. Maybe he believes he doesn't deserve nice things, but it's still really sad when you look at it overall.

Rock and a Hard Place

Episode 9.08. Airdate: November 26, 2013
Written by: Jenny Klein
Directed by: John MacCarthy
Guest Cast: Kim Rhodes (Jody), Lindy Booth (Bonnie/Vesta), Susie Abromeit (Suzy Lee)
Synopsis: Sam and Dean become… born-again virgins?

This episode isn't really bad, but it's not good either. The "Casa Erotica" joke suddenly being about Latinx stereotypes involving two white actors speaking Spanish is unbelievably bad. But there's still some stuff here that sets up for bigger moves and ideas of the upcoming mid-season finale.

Both "Rock and a Hard Place" and "I'm no Angel" contrast different kinds of faith and religion. There's misplaced faith that's repressive and exploitative, and then there's faith like Jody's that is comforting and built on love and community. Faith, like love, can be good or bad, and people can do terrible things in the name of both. Same goes for lust, apparently, leading to getting kidnapped by an angry virgin goddess.

This episode emphasizes how bad it was for Dean to let Zeke possess Sam, because it taps into all of Sam's issues about being impure and being controlled. He's got faith in Dean, and their life, and it's about to be destroyed!

The best thing about this episode is Jody, who is a rare side character who continues to grow. She's been through so much trauma, but she's still stalwart and kind, and she's a perfect ally for the boys. And she's becoming a pretty badass hunter herself!

Ship Shape: Do I buy that Dean is so stressed out and sad that he ignores Sam to sleep with a porn star? Kind of. It's out of character, but hey, they're consenting adults. Would have been more fun if Jody had been the one to get some action though, because the woman deserves it! Maybe with Sam!

Holy Terror

Episode 9.09. Airdate: December 3, 2013
Written by: Brad Buckner & Eugenie Ross-Leming
Directed by: Thomas Wright
Guest Cast: Misha Collins (Castiel), Osric Chau (Kevin), Curtis Armstrong (Metatron), Stephen Monroe Taylor (Malachi)
Synopsis: Angel war, blah blah blah, Cas gets more grace and Kevin gets killed.

Mid-season finales are supposed to blow things up, and move the story along—this episode does that and more. Dean's lies finally come crashing down on him with deadly consequences: Kevin is dead, Cas loses his humanity, and Sam loses his autonomy. But that's what happens when you betray people for selfish reasons!

The angel battling this episode is tiresome, but it does give us a lot of interesting stuff for Cas, leading him to take on the mantle of heaven again. In some ways, it's really disappointing, because I wanted more human Cas.

The sudden resolution of Kevin's story works better, though it is tragic. It comes out of nowhere, so it's shocking in a few ways, but this is exactly what Crowley said would happen. And it represents a big moment for Gadreel, who's been inside a Winchester long enough that he's doing exactly what they would do—trusting someone who says they can get redemption.

And that's what Dean, Cas, and Sam want—to make things right and fix their mistakes. But that just leads to more mistakes and cycles of violence. More revenge instead of redemption. And people like Kevin get lost in the process.

Death Notes: RIP Kevin Tran. This death hurts a lot, because Kevin was part of the family and his life had already been destroyed by proximity to the supernatural. It was inevitable that he'd end up dead, but that doesn't make it any less shocking or any less heartbreaking.

Road Trip

Episode 9.10. Airdate: January 14, 2014
Written by: Andrew Dabb
Directed by: Robert Singer
Guest Cast: Misha Collins (Castiel), Mark Sheppard (Crowley), Alaina Huffman (Abaddon), Curtis Armstrong (Metatron), Tahmoh Penikett (Gadreel), Dan Payne (Abner)
Synopsis: An angel and a demon walk into a hunter. Or: Castiel and Dean work with Crowley to save Sam from Gadreel.

This episode is terrific. It's as tense and surprising as it is sad and dramatic, and it's well balanced. We get big moments for everyone, making all the character journeys here interesting. For instance, Gadreel—who we should hate after he killed Kevin—is far more complex than that. He's just like the Winchesters, because he's been twisted by a lifetime of trauma and trying to make up for his mistakes. We get this guy and it's so sad that he has to give up someone he loves for what he thinks is the greater good.

Crowley, on the other hand, has become extraordinarily complex. He's no longer a big bad representing the evilest evil. Thanks to some human blood and a few months of imprisonment, he has a soft spot for the Winchesters. His turn to ambiguous ally shows that bad guys like Gadreel can still be good. Maybe? Abaddon, potential wasted, has turned into boring, brutish big bad, so I'm definitely team Crowley.

I don't think Dean is getting any of these messages though. Instead of grokking that his trying to control people that got him into this mess, he simply thinks he's "poison" and walks away. Sam's right for calling him out and for being pissed. Self-esteem issues can be so destructive.

Ship Shape: So, Abner and Gadreel were a thing, right? I mean, there was some love going on there that ended tragically. And hey, Crowley was in Sam, so the Mooseley ship is sailing as well. I kind of love Sam and Crowley's dynamic, and it's a fun contrast to Dean and Cas.

And oh boy, the Dean and Cas stuff in this episode is so good. These two support one another so completely, yet they don't actually see that they have someone in their corner willing to love them completely? Idjits. Heck, Dean and Sam are broken up too!

Familiar Faces: If you are young, or have a kid, you may recognize Abner's actor, Dan Payne, as the Beast from Disney's *Descendants* films. And to add to the *Supernatural* connection there, his queen Belle is played by Keegan Conor Tracey, who appeared in the "The Monster at the End of This Book" as the publisher of the *Supernatural* books, as well as a victim in "The Usual Suspects." She'll be back in Season Fifteen in "Golden Time."

First Born

Episode 9.11. Airdate: January 21, 2014
Written by: Robbie Thompson
Directed by: John Badham
Guest Cast: Misha Collins (Castiel), Mark Sheppard (Crowley), Timothy Omundson (Cain), Rachel Hayward (Tara)
Synopsis: Crowley convinces Dean to go searching for the first blade, which leads them to the demon who used it—Cain.

This episode is incredibly pivotal in showing exactly who Dean and Sam think they are. Sam's ready to die to make up for his sins, and Dean throws himself into darkness because that's what he thinks he's worth. Luckily, Sam has Cas telling him that his life has value, but Dean's stuck with Crowley as a devil on his shoulder. And so Dean finds a kindred spirit in Cain, the guy that killed his brother to save him. Ruh roh.

Cain is a fantastic addition to the mythology of the show, since Sam and Dean have been compared to Cain and Abel for years. By taking on the mark of Cain, Dean buys into that story and surrenders his free will, letting himself become the thing everyone has said he is. It's sad and represents Dean at the lowest point we've ever seen him. Worse even than Season Five. When he was ready to say yes to Michael, he was at least trying to help.

Also, let's take a moment to appreciate the epic fight scene which might be the best fight of the series. And Jensen did almost all of it on his own. Between that and the scruff of angst, Dean may be in a bad place, but it sure is a sexy one.

Spoiler Alert: The mark of Cain propels the story for the rest of the series, since it leads directly to the Darkness, back to Lucifer, and finally to Jack, so this may be the most important episode in the latter half of the series. Too bad the mark stuff takes way too long to resolve.

Ship Shape: You know, I talk a lot about Destiel, because it's the big love story of the show, but I'm not blind either so let's give a big Sastiel shout

out here. It's so nice to see Sam and Cas get to bond and support each other, so good for them.

But let's talk about the Cain and Colette thing. If Cain's story was about a person he loved asking him to stop, will it come to bear in some way on Dean's story? Not really, since the mark stuff gets bungled.

Familiar Face/Fan Favorite: Timothy Omundson is someone you might recognize from *Xena*, *Gallivant* or *Psych*. He's incredible as Cain and just owns this episode. We only see him once more in the series, but he's still on of the most popular characters on the demonic side.

Sharp Teeth

Episode 9.12. Airdate: January 28, 2014
Written by: Adam Glass
Directed by: John Showalter
Guest Cast: DJ Qualls (Garth), Sarah Smyth (Bess), Tom Butler (Jim Meyers)
Synopsis: Surprise! Garth is married, and a werewolf. And his werewolf wife is mixed up in a werewolf cult.

This episode is about two things we've seen a lot, especially during the Carver era: monsters that aren't so bad, and misplaced faith and family love. Much like other episodes this season, the werewolf family and cult demonstrate that good relationships with a healthy dose of faith in a higher purpose can make life better. But mix it up just a bit and you have an abusive, toxic cult that causes death and destruction.

Sam and Dean aren't broken up anymore, but Sam rightly calls him out when it comes to "family" as his catch all excuse for everything that he's ever done wrong. That's how cults talk, and it's the kind of thing that leads to the cycle of revenge that Jim, Bess, and Garth walk away from. Dean sees that and supports it, but doesn't see it for himself, remaining in his dank dark place. And Sam calling him out certainly doesn't get through to him either!

But hey, at least Garth found some happiness, even if it's weird. We don't see that a lot and it's nice for once that someone gets somewhat of a happy ending.. Garth is about an open heart and forgiveness, which the Winchesters are not into right now. That's why he can walk away and, at the moment, they can't.

The Purge

Episode 9.13. Airdate: February 4, 2014
Written by: Eric Charmelo & Nicole Snyder
Directed by: Phil Sgriccia
Guest Cast: Briana Buckmaster (Sheriff Donna Hanscum), Anabelle Acosta (Maritza), Joseph Julian Soria (Alonzo), Corey Sevier (Larry)
Synopsis: The boys hunt a Peruvian fat sucker, meet a perky sheriff, and have an emotionally devastating conversation.

The bulk of this episode is a fun monster of the week. Here, the sorta fat shaming plot leads to a story that's actually about a sibling who couldn't control her brother to make him be good. Dean can't help the violent tendencies that he's sliding towards (thanks to the mark) and his attempt to control Sam ends with people dead. We also meet Donna, who is delightful and makes a big impression! Love her!

But the big moment of the episode—and perhaps one of the biggest moments in the brother's relationship—is the extremely painful conversation between Sam and Dean at the end. And it gets at everything we've been talking about. Dean makes bad decisions because he's lonely. Sam's not wrong, and he's making a positive step when he says he wouldn't do the same, but he's also super insecure. So this momentary exertion of independence is probably not going to last.

Spoiler Alert: Dean will take this the absolute worst way of course. In fact, the red shirt he wears in this episode is one I like to call the Red Shirt of Bad Decisions. And that will go bad for Sam too. Sam will feel so bad about telling Dean he wouldn't save it, that he'll make his own terrible decision next season to save Dean which will start another apocalypse. Yeesh, guys.

Fan Favorite: Briana Buckmaster nearly steals this whole episode as Donna, so it's no wonder she returns to become such a beloved recurring character.

Captives

Episode 9.14. Airdate: February 25, 2014
Written by: Robert Berens
Directed by: Jerry Wanek
Guest Cast: Misha Collins (Castiel), Osric Chau (Kevin), Lauren Tom (Linda), Adam J. Harrington (Bartholomew), James Immekus (Del)
Synopsis: Kevin haunts the bunker and leads the boys to rescuing his mother. Castiel stands up to a heavenly faction.

This is where Season Nine really starts to get dark and honestly, sloppy. It's a thoughtful episode that resolves Kevin and Mrs. Tran's stories in a gut wrenching way that ultimately doesn't mean much. And the haunting, hunt and storage wars is… kind of boring. And then we have Cas resolving the Bartholomew stuff, which was also sort of boring. So we have two stories where not much happens and an episode that's just generally empty.

The good moments mainly come from Kevin, and Linda who breaks my heart as a mom. It's great that Kevin calls the boys out on their crap, but they are way too far gone down the road of bitterness for that to work. And Dean in particular is just getting darker. Everyone is a "captive" of their fate and decisions. As for Cas, he's still trying to make a third, different choice, to not be a soldier or a leader, which is why we love him. Even if this will probably go terribly as well.

Spoiler Alert: This episode highlights a problem with the latter half of Season Nine. The theme is *suffering* and what turns people bad, so we get lots of Dean being super angsty and mean, without any of the warmth and tenderness that usually makes it bearable. Jensen does an incredible job acting, but it's draining for viewers.

Also: Kevin. I wish this had been the end for this poor dude, and we'd just let him get to heaven when the whole ghost world thing gets fixed. Also, that veil thing… never gets truly resolved.

Plot Holes: What are Cas and Bart talking about? They mention Raphael, and orders from higher up, but Cas was leading that war. There were no superiors.

Name Game: The boys use the names Nicks and McVie, members of Fleetwood Mac who had a notoriously tense relationship at times.

#THINMAN

Episode 9.15. Airdate: March 4, 2014
Written by: Jenny Klein
Directed by: Jeannot Szwarc
Guest Cast: Travis Wester (Harry), A.J. Buckley (Ed), Nicholas Corella (Deputy Tom Norwood), Giovanni Mocibob (Roger)
Synopsis: The guys encounter the Ghostfacers on a case which is based on a fake urban legend.

Sometimes mirroring the monster plot with the brother plot is hard to see, but in this case, the Ghostfacers are the Winchesters. We have Ed lying to Harry, ruining his life, and getting people killed because of it. And they end the episode broken up, never to get back together again.

We're lucky to have Dean's speech about Sam jumping off the roof to remind us of the good times Sam and Dean have had, because this case overall doesn't bode well for anyone. There's actually another mirror here with Tom, the visionary, controlling Roger, the killer, echoing the way Crowley is controlling—and will control—Dean.

This episode is often cited as one of the few where the monster is human, but I think that's a misstatement as *Supernatural* is full of human monsters. And we see how they are made—alienation and anger. We see another monster developing in Dean, which is hard to watch, but his descent seems inevitable.

So, Get This: The Ghostfacers at this point set the record for the longest running characters, since they were introduced before Bobby and technically lived here. The only recurring character who appeared before them at this point was Meg, but, they won't live so… go Ghostfacers, you survived!

Blade Runners

Episode 9.16. Airdate: March 18, 2014
Written by: Brad Buckner & Eugenie Ross-Leming
Directed by: Serge Ladouceur
Guest Cast: Mark Sheppard (Crowley), Snooki (Herself), Kavan Smith (Cuthbert Sinclair), Rebecca Marshall (Lola)
Synopsis: The boys and Crowley navigate Crowley's human blood addiction and a disgraced Man of Letters to find the First Blade.

It's an interesting, if not perfectly executed, contrast to see Dean edging away from humanity as Crowley dives into it. The King of Hell is front and center here, and it's interesting to have a bit of sympathy considering how bad he was, but Mark Sheppard is such a compelling and multidimensional actor that this turn for Crowley really does work. Especially because we still can't quite trust the limey bastard.

Sam doesn't have much to do this episode besides snark at Crowley and Dean, and that seems to be a pattern post Gadreel. He's mainly reacting to the drama around him, and that's fine. The guy needs a break. Dean on the other hand is at the center of the mythology right now, and it's not a good place to be, emotionally or psychologically.

Dean's feral, kinda turned on, reaction to holding the first blade is… a choice. Just like Crowley crying over Casablanca is a choice. Maybe not the best way to show where these guys are at, but it works. The more interesting thing is that in a big reversal, Dean is the one being controlled and held captive. He doesn't like it, but he doesn't see what a prisoner he is already.

Just look at the Impala, which is as close as we have to a physical symbol of Dean's soul. It's been marked and maimed by demons. The mark and the blade, and Crowley's manipulations are working on a vulnerable Dean in the worst way. And Crowley's story about being forced into addiction is a lot like what's happening to Dean.

Spoiler Alert: In fact, this episode makes more sense when we think of what Crowley wants. He decides that he doesn't want to be human and weak, but he still wants a partner and thinks he deserves some kind of twisted version of love. So, since Sam isn't biting, he'll go for the more corrupted Winchester. He's Dean's dealer and seducer.

Famous Faces: Yes, that's Snooki from the *Jersey Shore*. Her casting is a fun bit of meta, but if you don't know who she is (bless you if that's so), it doesn't make much sense at all. Still, it's a fun cameo.

Mother's Little Helper

Episode 9.17. Airdate: March 25, 2014
Written by: Adam Glass
Directed by: Misha Collins
Guest Cast: Mark Sheppard (Crowley), Gil McKinney (Henry), Alaina Huffman (Josie), Jenny O'Hara (Julia Wilkinson)
Synopsis: Sam investigates a case that relates to Henry Winchester and Josie Sands, and ends up freeing harvested human souls. Dean has a date with Crowley.

Notably, this episode was directed by Misha Collins, which is why we haven't seen much Cas for a while. He does a great job with a contemplative script, giving us some great visuals. The scene of Sam freeing the souls is really beautiful and my favorite moment of the episode.

But not much else really happens here. Dean is doing terribly—lying, drinking, and fixating on the blade as Crowley further tries to seduce him. Not good. And Sam is just being Sam, keeping up the good fight. But that's it. We learn some things about Jose and Henry, and Abaddon, but it doesn't really add much to the overall story.

Josie and Henry's story mirrors Sam and Dean, with one taking on something demonic due to caring about someone else. And Abaddon's experiments are all about turning good people into monsters, like what's happening with Dean. But again, that's just sort of a place setting for what's to come.

Spoiler Alert: This Abaddon thing with her harvesting souls seems like a big deal that we should fix at some point in the future. Nope, the show totally forgets about this.

Ship Shape: We gotta talk about it, friends. Dean and Crowley. Crowley obviously wants Dean, and he's manipulated him into needing him. It's very messed up and kind of sad because Crowley is never going to matter to anyone the way Cas or Sam matter to Dean. Won't stop him from trying though and flirting with Dean.

Meta Fiction

Episode 9.18. Airdate: April 15, 2014
Written by: Robbie Thompson
Directed by: Thomas Wright
Guest Cast: Misha Collins (Castiel), Richard Speight Jr. (Gabriel), Curtis Armstrong (Metatron), Erica Carrol (Hannah)
Synopsis: Metatron tries writes his own story with Cas as the villain.

After a few stumbles, we get one of my favorite kinds of *Supernatural* episodes—meta. And it's so meta that it's in the name. So it's like meta on meta. It's a great, chewy rumination on stories and how much an author can control their subjects, which is something that the writers of *Supernatural* have confronted many times.

Yes, there's naked Dean in this episode, and the mark is making him go real dark. And Gadreel isn't wrong when he calls out all the boys' issues and insecurities. But the best part is that this episode is a commentary on writing—on the show and fandom itself.

There's only so much an author can do before characters run off on their own, especially when there are fans involved who can decide what the story means and how it should go. Metatron is writing fanfic, but pretending to be the author of canon. So the mirroring of this episode isn't actually about Sam, Dean, or Cas. It's about us, the audience, as much as it's about the writers. This episode is a direct admission that there's subtext in these stories, and that it's really the reader or viewer who decides what they "mean."

And our godly author gets the story wrong. He thinks he can force a story where he's the hero, but he can't. Cas, Dean and Sam will make unexpected choices every time. And Metatron can't control that. Even with the most heteronormative ideas about happy endings, or calling in fan favorites like Gabriel. Trying to manipulate these guys will always fail, because they'll always chose each other.

Spoiler Alert: So, the big question here is: is this the real Gabriel? We know Gabe really is alive, since we see him again in Season Thirteen. So, was he for real helping out Metatron for kicks, before getting nabbed by

Asmodeus? Maybe! We don't get a definitive answer, but I like to think this was him. And wow is it great to have him back!

Ship Shape: The tender way Dean and Cas smile when they speak on the phone? Perfection. But I also love the concern Cas has about the mark. The big ship thing in this episode isn't in the text. It's in the subtext, because at this point the queer elements of the show—especially when it came to Dean and Cas—were ambiguous. This episode is a neon sign telling viewers they're not crazy. Because sometimes characters do unexpected things, like remain heroes when they're supposed to be villains. Or fall in love.

Fan Favorite/Familiar Face: Hannah is one of my, and fandom's, favorite angels of the series. She's devoted, upstanding, and just generally interesting. And if Erica Carroll looks familiar it might be because she played two small roles in Season One!

Alex Annie Alexis Ann

Episode 9.19. Airdate: April 22, 2014
Written by: Robert Berens
Directed by: Stefan Pleszczynski
Guest Cast: Kim Rhodes (Jody), Katherine Ramdeen (Alex), Ashley Crow (Mama)
Synopsis: Sam and Dean help Jody save a young woman who was raised by vampires.

Gosh I love Jody Mills! After stopping by the series consistently since Season Five, she's really come into her own this season. Enough to carry a moving story of her own, about a different way of dealing with trauma and tragedy other than the Winchester method of violence and denial. Jody's commitment to kindness, and empathy, and hope is a big contrast to Dean getting scarier or Sam just shutting down and staying in "work" mode.

This episode is light on the Winchesters, but not light on themes: families that use a twisted kind of love to keep someone close out of fear of losing them, loss of humanity and becoming a monster, and the idea of choice. Jody gives Alex a choice at every juncture, while Mama forces her into being a monster. That's a big deal and the fact that Alex and Jody end the episode on a somewhat hopeful note is a big clue that maybe letting people make their own choices is the way to go.

Wish someone had told Sam and Dean this!

Spoiler Alert: Alex and Jody are such an interesting pair that they eventually attract other wayward women, forming the basis for an attempted spin-off that fans were all for. It's ironic considering the next episode, "Bloodlines," is a terrible attempt at a spin-off that no fans really supported or liked. I'm telling you this now because "Bloodlines" is really bad, and you can skip it.

Bloodlines

Episode 9.20. Airdate: April 29, 2014
Written by: Andrew Dabb
Directed by: Robert Singer
Guest Cast: random people who go on to be in much better shows.
Synopsis: Something something, monster families, something something, Chicago. This was a failed backdoor pilot for a spinoff that never happened.

Ugh.

Ship Shape: The fact that they used dialogue between a heterosexual romantic pair that was almost an exact copy of dialogue between Dean and Cas *while one of them was in a trench coat* is crazy-making.

Plot Hole: Because they didn't pick up this show, we have no idea what happens with the fact that *Chicago is run entirely by monsters*.

King of the Damned

Episode 9.21. Airdate: May 6, 2014
Written by: brad Buckner & Eugenie Ross-Leming
Directed by: P.J. Pesce
Guest Cast: Misha Collins (Castiel), Mark Sheppard (Crowley), Alaina Huffman (Abaddon), Tahmoh Penikett (Gadreel), Theo DeVaney (Gavin)
Synopsis: Abaddon plucks Crowley's son out of the past to trap him.

Like many episodes by Bruckner and Ross-Leming, this episode is doing a lot.. Abaddon is dead! Crowley broke time! Cas might have double agents! And Dean has reached a new level of murder horny. At least Sam is kinda okay? Wait, no, that's not okay because he's been forgotten again.

There's a big contrast here between Dean—who lies to his brother and brutally kills Abaddon—and Crowley, who actually is very human in the way he seems to actually care about Gavin. (He also has, as usual, some of the best lines of the episode). He's headed upwards, while Dean's headed down. And he's the undisputed King of Hell now, which is nice for him. Abaddon ended up not being as scary as we might have hoped, but she was never the final boss of the season anyway.

That would be Metatron, who seems to be squared off against Cas. Poor Cas doesn't have much to do here, as this episode is mostly set up for the end of the season, but I do like that he and Gadreel sort of bond over their character flaws of being too trusting and honorable.

Plot Hole: Gavin leaving the timeline kind of breaks the show? We need Gavin to die, because his ghost told Bobby about Crowley. That happened, even if the part was recast. So, Crowley undoing that has consequences!

Spoiler Alert: Maybe Gavin breaking time is why there's a different President in Season Twelve, but by Season Thirteen we're back to our Obama and Trump jokes? Eh?

Stairway to Heaven

Episode 9.22. Airdate: May 13, 2014
Written by: Robert Berens
Directed by: Guy Norman Bee
Guest Cast: Misha Collins (Castiel), Lindsay McKeon (Tessa), Curtis Armstrong (Metatron), Tahmoh Penikett (Gadreel), Erica Carroll (Hannah)
Synopsis: Metatron uses suicide bombers to manipulate the angels and beat Cas, while the First Blade and the mark continue to change Dean.

This is another episode doing a lot of heavy lifting, but in this case it's not about plot so much as it's bringing together a lot of the elements that have been floating around like angels waiting for vessels—ideas of misplaced faith and fanaticism, addiction and violence, and manipulation and choice. Those all work together, because Metatron is manipulating all the things that motivate our characters and people in general—their faith and love. He's a smart writer who knows how to tell a story with an inevitable ending.

Castiel's story culminates in this episode. Despite getting his grace back, the angels can tell he'll always be a bit human now, just like Crowley will remain tainted with feelings. But the humanity for Cas (and honestly, for Crowley too) doesn't come from weak grace or human blood. It comes from caring about people. Cas has always been different because he loved humanity.

Too bad humanity is being a little less than lovable this episode! Dean is off the deep end, and addiction is a good metaphor for what's going on. But his loss of himself is a good analog for depression, or anything that makes us feel less human and connected to the world. And he's there because of his own bad choices.

Sam is once again left behind in terms of story, aside from reacting to something about Dean or Cas. He's supportive, smart, and great, yeah, but he's riding backseat right now. Even Gadreel and Metatron get more interesting moments than Sam does, and while I really like angelic bowling, where's the other Winchester's story? Maybe next week.

Ship Shape: "He's in love… with humanity." The world's longest (unscripted, according to Curtis Armstrong) pause pretty much sums up Castiel's whole story. Sure, you can read this as about humans in general. But this was about Dean. He chose Dean and made up for some of the times he chose heaven in the past. Cas is admitting, just a bit, where his heart lies, and it's always going to be with Dean.

And Dean sees that, kind of, but it's not enough to keep him from going feral. He still only thinks he's a monster and weapon, so why would Cas ever really want to be with him? Sam doesn't want him as a brother so, Cas' big moment doesn't get through to Dean. Yet.

Do You Believe in Miracles?

Episode 9.23. Airdate: May 20, 2014
Written by: Jeremy Carver
Directed by: Thomas Wright
Guest Cast: Misha Collins (Castiel), Mark Sheppard (Crowley), Curtis Armstrong (Metatron), Tahmoh Penikett (Gadreel), Erica Carroll (Hannah)
Synopsis: Dean lusts for blood, Metatron makes a move to have humans worship him.

This episode highlights many of the best and worst things about Season Nine. In one sense, this whole season has been about faith and how easily that can be manipulated. It can be twisted and used by anyone. And you don't have to lie to do it—like how Crowley never lied to Dean—you just have to offer something people want and promise that it will make things better. Faith works best when it's in something bigger than yourself, but that's a hard path. That's what we see with Gadreel, who redeems himself in a violent act of faith. And it pays off. Dean lost his faith in Sam, and Crowley stepped in.

The demon Dean cliffhanger is very well done. It's foreshadowed enough that it doesn't come out of nowhere, but it's still shocking thanks to great filmmaking and an excellent speech from Crowley. Metatron's fall is satisfying as well, especially because it's nice to finally see Cas get a win. What works a little less well is the overarching idea about why Metatron needs to be God, and the mushy stuff about faith, cults, and religious extremism in general. Maybe this is saying something about contemporary America. The last time the show really tried to make a commentary on American culture, we got leviathans, so maybe it's fine that stuff stayed in the background.

But once again, we don't get much Sam aside from him grieving and saying he lied about being okay with Dean dying. Which is something I don't entirely buy, because he's just continuing the terrible cycle. Sigh.

Spoiler Alert: Ultimately, that will be the crux and the downfall of Season Ten—Sam trying to make up for saying he didn't care, by trying *too* hard to save Dean. So not only is that kind of disappointing, but demon Dean is both too short lived and too drawn out, yet somehow disappointing. So enjoy that final moment because it's actually where demon Dean and Crowley peak!

Driver Picks the Music: The song playing over Sam laying out Dean's body is "Can't Find My Way Home" by Blind Faith and the lyrics fit perfectly with the scene.

Ship Shape: So, the love in the episode is all in the Cas stuff, with Metatron directly calling him out that all he's done was to save one human. Note that he doesn't mention Sam at all, just Dean. But terrifyingly, the relationship that seems to be going to another level in this episode is Dean and Crowley, which will sure be… something.

Death Notes: Like Season Two, we're bookending the season with Winchester deaths! This one is really great, honestly, and I love Dean having enough of himself left to say, "I'm proud of us." And there's definite symmetry in Sam being saved by becoming an angel, with Dean returning as a demon. That takes us to Dean: 17, Sam: 6, Castiel: 4. Dean really is the best at some things.

SUPERNATURAL

CHAPTER TEN

You Have Your Version

Tenth seasons are a big deal in TV. They're rare, but in the case of *Supernatural* it wasn't surprising. The show wasn't going anywhere, which meant that whatever three-season-wrap-up plan Jeremy Carver may have had when he started had to be stretched out. No one went into this season thinking it was the end of everything. Season Ten is a stasis season—no writers left or joined, and the regular cast was the same.

In some ways, that's refreshing. The stakes of this season are the lowest and least apocalyptic we've seen since Season Three. The focus of the stories is more personal and intimate, but that also means the over-arching myths get lost and the season-long arc, when it shows up, meanders.

It isn't bad, but it's also not particularly good. Like the main story of the season—which comes down to the mark of Cain—season Ten extends small ideas a bit beyond their power. The result is an emotional and myth arc focused on Dean, which leaves Sam behind. Sure, he has his own descent into darkness, but the season is motivated by Dean.

But the intimate focus also brought some interesting stuff for Crowley and Cas. Part of this was practical; Jared and Jensen had been doing this for ten years and wanted a less grueling schedule, which meant more Crowley and Cas on their own. I like that in theory, but it turns out these characters are both more interesting when they're around Winchesters. Go figure.

Still, the season introduces at least one iconic character, has some great episodes, and does fine. Until it crashes with maybe the worst death ever on the show and a weird finale. But we'll get there. We have a demon Dean to deal with first.

Black

Episode 10.01. Airdate: October 7, 2014
Written by: Jeremy Carver
Directed by: Robert Singer
Guest Cast: Misha Collins (Castiel), Mark Sheppard (Crowley), Erica Carroll (Hannah), Travis Aaron Wade (Cole Trenton), Jud Tylor (Andina), Emily Fonda (Ann Marie)
Synopsis: Dean and Crowley howl at the moon while Sam searches for his brother. Cas and Hannah try to convince angels to come back to heaven.

If there's one thing we've learned in the nine previous seasons, it's that premieres are hard. Good ones set up the entire season, while others spin wheels or drop balls. "Black" is one of the latter. This episode is disappointing because not much happens, and nothing that does happen is interesting or what fans are hoping for. At least we get shirtless Cas and Dean!

First, there's Sam, who is set up to be going down his own dark path. But… he's not. He's just Sam, only alone and obsessed with getting Dean back. His quest to bring back Dean is paralleled with Castiel's mission to bring home some angels, but no one wants to listen neither are making particularly good pitches! Their way is just rules and restrictions—no wonder they strike out. Then Sam gets nabbed by Cole? Who is just some weird guy? With a freaking fax machine?

And then we have Crowley and Dean, which is somehow also disappointing. Instead of Dean going full demon and maybe killing all the monster families in Chicago, he's just a douche. His entire personality is a boorish façade of toxic masculinity, and even Crowley finds it tiresome. All Crowley has ever wanted to do was rule, but he's too besotted with this idiot to accomplish anything. Even a woman who's supposed to remind Dean of his mother can't get through to him.

So, Get This: Throughout this, and the next few episodes, Jared is wearing a shoulder brace. The reason? Backstage at a convention in Italy, Jared thought it would be a good idea to wrestle Osric Chau—a trained martial artist—and the match led to Jared's shoulder being dislocated. Don't mess with Kevin Tran, I guess.

Ship Shape: So, Crowley and Dean had a fivesome with triplets of unspecified gender? Are they related to the twins they face off against in foosball? Who knows but these two are kind of a thing, and it's very weird, but hey, we're open to it? They're a better match than Dean and Anne Marie, who deserves better.

I think there's also some attempt here to set up Castiel and Hannah, but all I see is Cas and Dean both forgetting to wear pants and Cas talking about how Earth is nice because of love.

Reichenbach

Episode 10.02. Airdate: October 14, 2014
Written by: Andrew Dabb
Directed by: Thomas Wright
Guest Cast: Misha Collins (Castiel), Mark Sheppard (Crowley), Curtis Armstrong (Metatron), Erica Carroll (Hannah), Travis Aaron Wade (Cole)
Synopsis: Cole hunts Sam. Sam hunts Dean. Dean hunts for thrills. Cas and Hannah get sidetracked.

This episode is fine, but it leaves me asking "what's the point of this?" Like, what's the point of Cas and Hannah, with the focus on him losing his grace? I think meant to contrast how Cas has decided to be an angel and die, rather than compromise his morals, while Dean wants to ignore his humanity. Maybe? There's no parallel to Sam, who just wants his brother. His motivation for that isn't really explored in this episode.

There's no monster in this episode, but the antagonist comes in the form of Cole—another character that leaves me asking both "why?" and "how can one dude suck so much?" And boy does he suck, especially not finding Dean until now, given that Dean's been a wanted criminal with his face on the news! Cole is just sort of pathetic, and maybe we're supposed to enjoy seeing Dean kick his ass, but I'm not sure. Metatron is better at being a bad guy, but he's also wasted.

Perhaps the most interesting element here is that it's Crowley who betrays Dean. It's not, as Crowley says, that Dean can't let go of being human, it's that the person Crowley wanted beside him after all of Season Nine is gone. Call it what you want, but last season Crowley got in touch with his humanity and wanted to stoke that fire. But demon Dean lacks the humanity and love that makes him Dean, so he's not what Crowley wanted. Ergo: break up.

Driver Picks the Music: The song playing behind Crowley is "Hey There Lonely Girl" by Eddie Holoman. The opener for the season was "Heartbreaker" by Pat Benatar. This this a love story!

Ship Shape: Seriously! Dean and Crowley use break up clichés and, despite Crowley's bluster, he's hurt that he could never get Dean's human affection. Or even his demonic affection!

Then there's Cas and Hannah. Cas and the little girl at the house where they stay is the cutest thing ever, so I can't blame Hannah for falling for him, but like Crowley it seems one-sided. Or Hannah is just more attracted to human life than Cas. Honestly, it's cruel that we haven't had much Cas and Dean interaction at all.

Spoiler Alert: The thing that bugs me about this episode is that there's so much hinted at that's not paid off, ever. Dean needs to kill? Okay… except he doesn't after this. And the Metatron threats? All hot air. Cole? Useless. It's just a mess.

Soul Survivor

Episode 10.03. Airdate: October 21, 2014
Written by: Brad Buckner & Eugenie Ross Leming
Directed by: Jensen Ackles
Guest Cast: Misha Collins (Castiel), Mark Sheppard (Crowley), Erica Carroll (Hannah), Jud Tylor (Adina), Ruth Connell (Rowena)
Synopsis: The cure for a Deanmon is blessed blood and good hug.

No disrespect to the last two episodes, but this would have been a better season premiere. It's certainly the strongest episode so far and unquestionably the best of demon Dean. He's actually scary here, and it's truly awful to see the Dean we love stripped of humanity. While this episode ending that storyline is a letdown, I also get it. Much like how the show wasn't the same when Sam was soulless, it's not the same without Dean. Dean is the heart of *Supernatural*, and without his emotional journey anchoring the series, it's not the same.

This episode also gets extra kudos for Jensen not only acting, but directing the heck out of it. Being handed the reins of the most important episode in the season, for your own character's big arc, is a huge responsibility and he more than met it. Awesome work.

We also begin to see a few themes emerge, mainly confronting the past, good and bad, and also specifically confronting family. Will these ideas pan out in a coherent way? I'm not sure. But they're there and they continue through the season so, points for effort. There's an attempt here to apply that to Sam as well, by having Sam trick Lester into selling his soul, but honestly both of these guys have done much worse things, like start the apocalypse. So that doesn't land at all. But hey, it's interesting to hear Dean's darkest opinions of Sam, and see Sam power through it.

Ship Shape: Cas gently telling Hannah not to get distracted, puts another nail in the coffin for any romance between them, so no progress there. Crowley seems determined to save Dean and, remarkably, he turns to Cas to do it. Which is I guess him being a supportive ex. I'm really frustrated we didn't get any scenes between demon Dean and Cas. Wish Cas hadn't had to say that "it's quiet out there" line then leave.

Fan Favorite/Spoiler Alert: Though we only glimpse her for a second here, it's Rowena! She's made out to be a big bad, which really isn't what she turns out to be in the series, but it's a great introduction to one of the best characters of the later seasons!

Paper Moon

Episode 10.04. Airdate: October 28, 2014
Written by: Adam Glass
Directed by: Jeannot Szwarc
Guest Cast: Brit Marling (Kate), Emily Tennant (Tasha)
Synopsis: A werewolf hunt brings back Kate from "Bitten."

This episode is simple—the boys can't stop hunting, even though they have reservations about themselves and each other. But since it's a case with siblings, there's also a lot of deeper stuff going on that's trying to be profound and thoughtful. I'm not sure it works.

Kate and Tasha clearly mirror Sam and Dean. Both siblings, both monstrous killers in different ways. And Kate made Tasha into a monster, which fits with Dean letting Gadreel possess Sam. But I think this episode would rather us see Kate as a parallel to Dean, in that both have monstrous natures they are keeping under control and siblings going dark.

In this episode we, once again, weirdly hammer home that Sam tricked Lester into selling his soul, which is bad, sure, but not the worst thing Sam has done. But it's meant to put Sam on this dark trajectory that just doesn't work. Otherwise, it's an okay episode about family and bad decisions (like most episodes of *Supernatural*).

Spoiler Alert: Knowing that Sam will make an apocalyptically bad decision to "save" Dean at the end of the season, makes all this "Sam is going dark in his desperation to save Dean" stuff make a bit more sense. But it's not a plotline the season emphasizes enough for this to work particularly well.

Driver Picks the Music: The opening set to "Werewolves of London" by Warren Zevon may be my favorite part. It's amazing it took the series ten years to use the song.

Fan Fiction

Episode 10.05. Airdate: November 11, 2014 (Episode 200)
Written by: Robbie Thompson
Directed by: Phil Sgriccia
Guest Cast: Rob Benedict (Chuck), Katie Sarife (Marie/Sam), Joy Regullano (Maeve), Alyssa Lynch (Siobhan/Dean), Nina Winkler (Kristen/Castiel), Hannah Levin (Calliope)
Synopsis: For the show's 200th episode, the boys walk into a case involving a high school musical based on the *Supernatural* books.

There are lots of shows that make episodes as a love letters to fans, but no one has ever done something quite like this. The uniqueness of this episode is fitting, since it's so rare for any series to reach 200 episodes, and this musical extravaganza is just so good and special, it's definitely one of the greatest episodes of the series.

Sure, this episode nods to some seasonally thematic stuff, but it's really about *Supernatural* and the fandom of the show. Like "Meta Fiction" (also by Robbie Thompson), there's always tension between authorial intent and fan interpretation. And this episode goes much further by not just acknowledging subtext, but blessing every fan's interpretation of the show.

This is the show itself saying "ship whatever you want, see whatever you want. This world is yours as much as it's ours, and that's incredible." It's all about love, because when we love stories enough to create our own versions, that's inspired and passionate. The most important moment may be where Chuck—the author/God himself—comes in to say "not bad."

There are too many great moments here to elaborate, from the songs to Dean looking at the camera. I love how, over the course of the episode, Dean loses his bluster and gets into things, which is typical for him. But I especially love that Marie is such a perfect fangirl, inspired by *Supernatural* both to create and to be brave. Because that's what great art does. It inspires us.

Driver Picks the Music: I mean, I can't pick a favorite number here. "A Single Man Tear" is so on the nose and funny, and it's delivered so sincerely, and "I'll Just Wait Here Then" is such a sweet little love song. But it's the cover of "Carry on Wayward Son" and seeing Sam and Dean really listen to it that gets me crying every time.

Ship Shape: Seriously, why *isn't* it Deastiel? The ship reactions here are fun, because yes, the fandom knows they're brothers but… subtext. Also, the relationship off-stage between "Castiel" and "Dean" is maybe the only reference in the show to the practice of "real person shipping," where fans imagine actors having love affairs rather than their characters. It's pretty popular in the *Supernatural* fandom, which may be why Dean's look to the camera was an unscripted ad lib by Jensen.

Ask Jeeves

Episode 10.06. Airdate: November 18, 2014
Written by: Eric Charmelo & Nicole Snyder
Directed by: John MacCarthy
Guest Cast: Izabella Miko (Olivia), Kevin McNulty (Phillip), Gillian Vigman (Heddy), Debra McCabe (Beverley), Marcus Rosner (Dash)
Synopsis: A message for Bobby leads Sam and Dean to a murder mystery.

This episode feels a lot like *Knives Out*, but came out five years before that film. It's inspired by Agatha Christie mysteries, as well as the game *Clue*—and for that, it's an incredibly fun little episode. The guest cast are all genuinely into it, and the underlying story about a family member trying to protect another in an abusive way is very on point for Sam and Dean's toxic relationship.

It's fun to see the Winchesters encounter different sorts of people, though in a binge this episode does come off as remarkably similar to "Trial and Error." At least this time Sam was the one who's the subject of advances.

But things aren't all that great. We're getting hints that Dean's still got some dark, murderous instincts in him from the mark, because of course he does! Good thing there's no new big bad on the horizon. For now.

Ship Shape: Sam being cougar catnip is a joke that will always be funny.

Girls, Girls, Girls

Episode 10.07. Airdate: November 25, 2014
Written by: Robert Berens
Directed by: Robert Singer
Guest Cast: Misha Collins (Castiel), Mark Sheppard (Crowley), Erica Carroll (Hannah), Travis Aaron Wade (Cole), Ruth Connell (Rowena MacLeod)
Synopsis: Dean and Sam deal with hookers snagging souls, a powerful witch, and Cole's return. Cas and Hannah deal with Hannah's vessel's past.

This episode embodies Season Ten as a whole. There are a lot of disparate parts—ranging from meh to good—and nothing quite meshes together. Cas and Hannah reckoning with their past and the consequences of their actions? Good! Demons stealing souls with hookers? Original! Cole? Ugh, fine. Rowena, a powerful rebel witch, who's ruthless and incredibly fun? Fantastic! And she's Crowley's mom! That's something.

Even the scene with Cole—who remains useless—is very moving and gives us a valuable lesson in Dean's view of himself and the world. I like all of it. And there's a bigger message there—you can't outrun the past, even after hundreds of years, and you shouldn't let it make you a monster. Still, this is a fun episode and works great in a binge because you don't have to wait weeks for more Rowena!

I also enjoy that this episode gets back to an old pattern we haven't seen for a little while. It starts as one thing and becomes another. Kind of like Season Ten tries to do.

Ship Shape: A dating app Dean, really? Well, he's trying to pretend to be human and normal in this episode so, that goes well.

Hibbing 911

Episode 10.08. Airdate: December 2, 2014
Written by: Jenny Klein (teleplay), Phil Sgriccia (story)
Directed by: John MacCarthy
Guest Cast: Kim Rhodes (Jody), Briana Buckmaster (Donna), Morgan Taylor Campbell (Starr), Fred Ewanuick (Sherriff Len Cuse)
Synopsis: At a sheriff's conference Jody meets Donna and they bond over the vampires that also happen to be around.

What a delight this episode is—a hard feat to accomplish with the focus not on Sam and Dean. It makes perfect sense to match world-weary Jody with perky Donna, and seeing them bond and support one another is so much fun. They're both capable, but also complex with lots of baggage. And it's always nice to have someone help carry that load.

And dealing with baggage is something that Sam and Dean have to do. Vampire sheriff Cuse is trying to go straight, and Dean is trying to not become a murder monster again. But the past and your nature tend to catch up with you. We also have a contrast between how open and supportive Jody and Donna can be, and how that allows them to grow and survive, with Dean not being honest with Sam about the mark.

Spoiler alert: And there is darkness aplenty. Though the episode leaves it ambiguous, we know by next week that Dean's whole line about feeling good is, as Donna might put it, a big ol' pile of cow crud.

Name Game: Donna knows Dean and Sam as Agents Criss and Frehley, referencing the lead singer and guitarists of KISS.

The Things We Left Behind

Episode 10.09. Airdate: December 9, 2014
Written by: Andrew Dabb
Directed by: Guy Norman Bee
Guest Cast: Misha Collins (Castiel), Mark Sheppard (Crowley), Ruth Connell (Rowena), Kathryn Newton (Claire), Roark Critchlow (Randy)
Synopsis: Cas seeks out Claire Novak to make amends.

Well, that whole "Dean surrounded by bodies of the humans he brutally killed" cliffhanger can't mean anything good. The mark is still making Dean his worst, and it's going to take more than family support to get him back. This episode seems to say that if you've got trauma, you can't just wish away. That's why Dean ends up covered in blood.

This is an interesting episode. Claire's trauma, struggles and rebellion make for a small, human story. For once, it's a Cas story that's not about heaven, but other people—the ones that were left in the wake of him and the Winchesters. It's about how hard it is to make amends. And Claire's anger is mirrored nicely by Crowley's fury, finding the mother who left him behind all those years ago.

Parenting is hard, and it's clear from Dean, Cas and Sam's excellent scene discussing John Winchester, that these guys get that. Just wait until they raise a kid.

Ship Shape: Dean and Castiel's burger date is one of the most wonderful and tender scenes between them, from the admiration Cas has for Dean to the easy trust and intimacy. It's incredible that Dean only trusts Cas with his fears, because he always needs to be strong for Sam. With Cas things are different and that's kind of romantic.

Future Famous Faces: Of the many actors who have gone on to big things from *Supernatural*, Kathryn Newton may be the one who owes the most to it. Claire was one of Newton's big roles, and she's great, so it's no surprise she went on to prestige with *Big Little Lies, Detective Pikachu, Freaky,* and the Marvel Cinematic Universe.

The Hunter Games

Episode 10.10. Airdate: January 20, 2015
Written by: Brad Buckner & Eugenie Ross-Leming
Directed by: John Badham
Guest Cast: Misha Collins (Castiel), Mark Sheppard (Crowley), Curtis Armstrong (Metatron), Ruth Connell (Rowena), Kathryn Newton (Claire)
Synopsis: The Winchesters turn to Metatron for clues to removing the mark of Cain, as Cas struggles to get through to Claire and Rowena continue to manipulate Crowley.

Much how the last episode was a subdued mid-season finale, this follow up is more intimate and character driven than what we're used to. The three stories going on—with Rowena, Metatron, and Claire—all work together, because they're about the same things: emotional manipulation and how people with bad intent can twist someone's bad feelings into bad actions.

In a series that's all about family, the emphasis is how manipulation can come from inside, with people like Rowena relying on blood connections to justify them. Or we have Metatron using Sam, Dean and Castiel's connections to their family to get under their skin.

But it's also family that can save the day. As Sam references, Cain was able to be strong against the mark because of love, and Dean can do that too.

Let's also take a minute to praise some great performances: Ruth Connell, Kathryn Newton and Curtis Armstrong are all great, as well as our three leading men. Armstrong in particular shows why he's one of my favorite villains, not just because he's such an opposing force to the Winchesters, but so fun and interesting to watch.

Spoiler Alert: Did the writers know at this point what they would reveal the mark to really be? I'm not sure, but I definitely think they knew Metatron was lying about knowing how to remove it.

There's No Place Like Home

Episode 10.11. Airdate: January 27, 2015
Written by: Robbie Thompson
Directed by: Phil Sgriccia
Guest Cast: Felicia Day (Charlies), Duncan Fraser (Clive Dillon), Barclay Hope (Russell Wellington)
Synopsis: Charlie returns from Oz split into a good Charlie and a dark Charlie.

There's nothing subtle here, as this hour is thematically on the nose. Charlie is confronted with the terrible actions of her darkest self, just as Dean is fighting against the mark. And the big lesson, of course, is that you can't ignore or lock away your darkness. You have to live with it.

It also emphasizes that revenge doesn't make anything better, which is an evolved view for a show that began as a revenge story. Then again, it was revenge that made John Winchester who he was and scarred his boys for life.

As with "Slumber Party," I don't think that the Oz stuff really fits with the tone of *Supernatural*, but this is a great acting showcase for Felicia Day. And we really get deeper into Charlie as a person, which is great unless you know why they're building her up as a character.

Spoiler Alert: Making Charlie more complex and fully integrating her into the larger myth should really be a red flag at this point, because aside from Cas, this makes her the person closest to the boys and thus… in the crosshairs.

Name Game: Agents Collins and Gabriel references Phil Collins and Peter Gabriel of Genesis, a band that eventually broke up. Foreshadowing for a rift?

About A Boy

Episode 10.12. Airdate: February 3, 2015
Written by: Adam Glass
Directed by: Serge Ladouceur
Guest Cast: Dylan Everett (Dean), Lesley Nichol (Katja), Mark Acheson (Hansel), Madeline Arthur (Tina)
Synopsis: Dean gets turned into a teenager by a witch with a taste for kids.

This is a mighty fun episode for one reason: Dylan Everett is absolutely perfect as kid Dean. This episode wouldn't work without his performance, and we've seen in the past how episodes where the Winchesters aren't themselves feel off. Everett is so good at channeling Jensen that at point I forgot he was a different actor.

This is a simple witch hunt solved with fisticuffs, so the story is thin, but it's fun. And it's about second chances, whether you can undo your past or be a new person. That's something we continue to see a lot of this season, and this episode leans towards a hopeful answer. Maybe Dean can imagine a new life where he tries cake instead of pie.

Driver Picks the Music: Dean grooving to Taylor Swift's "Shake it Off" is a great moment and shows Dean actually trying to learn from being a tween, shaking off a little bit of that toxic masculinity for now. But I don't know if it's gonna stick. "Shake it Off" was also the basis for the *Supernatural* parody music video made by the sister duo Hillywood, which co-starred Osric Chau and Rob Benedict with appearances by most of the cast.

Halt and Catch Fire

Episode 10.13. Airdate: February 10, 2015
Written by: Eric Charmelo & Nicole Snyder
Directed by: Serge Ladouceur
Guest Cast: Willa Milner (Delilah Martin), Barbara Kottmeier (Corey Silver)
Synopsis: The internet is haunted.

The premise of this episode—a ghost that can travel through Wi-Fi—is kind of clever, but poorly executed, leading to one of the silliest death's in the show's history. Plus, it's not a very scary ghost.

The only really good thing about this episode are the parallels between Dean and Andrew—the Wi-Fi ghost—about revenge turning you into a monster. It's good that Dean wants to choose peace. That's our Dean. But there's a parallel here with Andrew's wife, who didn't want to let the person she loved go, and also with Delilah who was driven by guilt, like Sam. It bodes badly for Sam that this is an imperfect mirror, because he's not going to give up on his brother. Winchesters don't do that.

Spoiler Alert: But let's also look at the reason Andrew became a monster, which was the same as Charlie a few episodes ago—revenge. It seems out of the blue, because Dean got the mark of Cain to clean up a mess after Crowley manipulated him. But this is actually a big ol' hunk of foreshadowing that may turn Dean dark again. Will he be able to step back from that and choose peace, and will Sam let him go? (Friggin' of course not).

Name Game: Keeping with Dean and Sam being "Gen X" their aliases are based on Kurt Cobain and Dave Grohl of Nirvana.

The Executioner's Song

Episode 10.14. Airdate: February 17, 2015
Written by: Robert Berens
Directed by: Phil Sgriccia
Guest Cast: Misha Collins (Castiel), Mark Sheppard (Crowley), Timothy Omundson (Cain), Ruth Connell (Rowena)
Synopsis: Dean kills Cain but learns there's no cure for the mark.

Alongside "Fan Fiction," I place this as the top episode of Season Ten. It's tense, emotional, beautifully shot and acted, and pivotal for both the season and series. Dean confronts his dark mirror, and Cain calls that out as Dean living his life backwards. And while Dean defeats Cain, retaining his humanity, he can't escape the mark.

The mark of Cain is interesting as a plot device. While it feels like it goes on for a bit too long, it does work better in a binge. As a metaphor for moral corruption—original sin even—it thus represents how we can't escape the past. It's how that past marks us, how it changes our nature. And in that echoes all the ideas of free will the show has played with for so long.

Does Dean have free will now? Is the mark "making" him do things, or just turning him into someone who makes the wrong choices? Does he have a choice in what he is or who he becomes? Sam, Cas, and Crowley certainly make choices in how they deal with this, and how they respond to Dean. They all care about him in some way, though as Rowena points out, Team Free Will doesn't seem to care much for Crowley. But Sam isn't letting the family go down without a fight.

Spoiler Alert: At this point it's possible that the writers knew what the mark really was, which is a seal to keep The Darkness imprisoned. So in a sense, the mark is destruction and chaos itself, as well as the opposite of God. And yet, it's another thing that points towards the end of the story that Chuck wants—brother killing brother. Narrative symmetry and all that.

Ship Shape: At this point in the series, Dean and Cas have a stable, trusting relationship that's pretty functional by their standards. Cas doesn't draw his blade until Cain threatens Dean, and Dean trusts Cas above Crowley with the First Blade. There's a lot of love there, and also a lot of heartbreak and rejection for Crowley.

So, Get This: When Dean falls into Sam's arms towards the end of the episode, Jensen accidentally stabbed Jared's leg with the knife he was still holding.

Name Game: Agents Moore and Ronaldo reference the band Sonic Youth.

The Things They Carried

Episode 10.15. Airdate: March 18, 2015
Written by: Jenny Klein
Directed by: John Badham
Guest Cast: Travis Aaron Wade (Cole), Michelle Morgan (Jemma Verson)
Synopsis: Cole ends up with a bad case of the khan worm.

Supernatural is a series about Americana, its back roads and their dark legends. And that works. But the show doesn't work when it's making commentary on America. The Leviathans attempted to parody American consumer culture and failed, and this episode tried to make a point about veterans, war, and PTSD; it just ends up being boring.

Cole's overly familiar tone with the boys after he tried to kill them is annoying, and honestly, we were at our limit of snarky white guys a few seasons ago. Cole and Dean trying to out-macho one another is just a hat on a hat, and it's not interesting to watch.

I will give the episode credit for some great direction, and some very gross and scary moments reminiscent of the scariest episodes of the past. This is still a horror show and there's a lot of horror here. But not a lot of thematic stuff, unless you count the mirror of Sam having to kill a soldier who became a monster, because of something evil inside him.

Behind the Scenes: Before the airing of this episode, Jared Padalecki launched a charity T-shirt campaign to raise money and awareness for mental health. While it wasn't the first charity project or T-shirt campaign from the cast, Jared's frank discussion of his own struggles with mental health, depression and thoughts of self-harm struck an incredible chord with the public. His "Always Keep Fighting" campaign embodied the spirit of the Winchesters, and influenced the show which continues to this day.

Paint It Black

Episode 10.16. Airdate: March 25, 2015
Written by: Brad Buckner & Eugenie Ross-Leming
Directed by: John Showalter
Guest Cast: Mark Sheppard (Crowley), Ruth Connell (Rowena), Steve Curtis (Father Delaney), Catherine Michaud (Isabella), Teryl Rothery (Olivette), Rachel Keller (Sister Mathias)
Synopsis: A nun's ghost kills untrue men. Rowena confronts her tormentor.

A haunted painting and a ghost talking to a friend are an interesting story idea—a lot like "Halt and Catch Fire" but better done. The flashbacks to renaissance Italy make this episode seem out of place, but overall it's not a bad outing. It's just not a particularly thrilling case for the Winchesters. In the final BM scene, Sam makes the parallels really clear—he won't let Dean go easy into that good night.

But let's talk about Dean's confession, which is the most interesting part of the episode. I love seeing Dean admit there's a way of living he wishes he could try. I could talk about Dean saying there are "people, feelings that I want to experience differently than I did before, or maybe even the first time," in the ship section, but I think there's more to this than subtext. Dean would like to experience freedom from guilt, acceptance, and transformation from the monster he thinks he is.

The confession is great, but real fun stuff here is with Rowena and Olivette. Crowley is trying to connect with his mom the way he connects to Dean and Sam—in a transactional way. But Rowena is more interested in power and revenge, than connecting with her son. She's willing to do scary things for revenge and power which is never good.

Spoiler Alert: This episode is frustrating somewhat in retrospect, because that confession scene never really gets paid off. And it takes until Season Thirteen for Rowena to finally unbind her power after the grand coven cursed her.

Inside Man

Episode 10.17. Airdate: April 1, 2015
Written by: Andrew Dabb
Directed by: Rashaad Ernesto Green
Guest Cast: Misha Collins (Castiel), Mark Sheppard (Crowley), Jim Beaver (Bobby), Curtis Armstrong (Metatron), Ruth Connell (Rowena), Lee Majdoub (Hannah), Richard Newman (Oliver Price)
Synopsis: Sam and Cas enlist Bobby to break Metatron out of heaven to help with the mark. Dean counsels Crowley on family.

"Inside Man" is excellent and well-balanced in a satisfying way. The intimate, family focus of this season doesn't always work, but it succeeds here with an episode that's surprising, emotional, action-packed, and poignant.

Let's talk about Sam and Cas first. They're going behind Dean's back, and even Bobby knows that's no good, warning them about trying to do good and causing bad. Which is honestly most of Sam, Dean, and Cas' lives. Even in this episode, all their efforts to save Dean end with a net loss—Metatron is free, and Bobby may be taking his place in heaven's jail.

But that's what you do for family. You protect them and want the best for them. That's in contrast to Rowena of course, who wants the best for herself. Though I do think Rowena cares for Crowley on some level, at this point she represents the most selfish and toxic family dynamics. She wants to kill Dean to kill Crowley's humanity, not help him.

This episode is also great, because it puts focus back onto Sam, which we've been lacking. Cas and Crowley are both in love with Dean, and want to help him, but they also have their own stuff going on. Sam really doesn't, and while the idea that he's going to go to dangerous extremes to save Dean is interesting, it's also informed by the fact that Sam has nothing outside of Dean. Everyone in the show seems to have a deeper emotional connection with Dean than with Sam, so that forces Sam into more co-dependence. And that's bad for the show, Sam, and the world.

Ship Shape: Take your pick here: Dean flirting with the bartender, Dean and Crowley talking openly and emotionally about family, Cas unquestionably helping Dean—there's lots to choose from. This episode is very queer. Especially the angels! Cas is all colors, and then there's Hannah who we see in a male vessel, again reminding us that angels don't have gender!

Book of the Damned

Episode 10.18. Airdate: April 15, 2015
Written by: Robbie Thompson
Directed by: P.J. Pesce
Guest Cast: Misha Collins (Castiel), Felicia Day (Charlie), Curtis Armstrong (Metatron), Ruth Connell (Rowena), Jeff Brandon (Jacob Styne)
Synopsis: Charlie brings the Book of the Damned to the boys. Metatron leads Cas to his remaining grace.

This is an important episode for Season Ten, but it's also the true end to a bunch of stuff that kicked up in Season Eight, simmering through Season Nine. Cas is an angel again, but his heart clearly isn't in the heavenly fight. Sam admits that like Dean, he can't go on without his brother. Hunting is the only life he knows, and he needs Dean for that.

Cas powering back up because he feels he has no other option, and Sam tricking everyone and going to work with Rowena are alike. Both of these men are refusing a normal human life, even if it would make them happier. Metatron reminds Cas about the joys of humanity, and Charlie reminds Sam of how much hunting can cost someone. But they both make the decision to sacrifice, to stay in the fight. This isn't to say either choice is good or bad, but it's complex and interesting to think if they even had a real choice, given their circumstances.

Despite the mark, Dean turns out to be the only one making good choices right now. Maybe that's because he's trying so hard to be good and, in the last ten years, he actually learned something about how "doing what you have to do" always ends badly. Too bad his whole family is lying to him! That will end well!

Ship Shape: Finally, Dean and Cas get to be in a room together, and hey, Dean's carrying pizza so does that make him the pizza man? Oh, and I think at this point Metatron should know exactly what Cas cares about and wants to fight for. But let's not forget that this episode sets up one of my favorite dynamics in the later seasons—Sam and Rowena! Aka: Samwitch!

Driver Picks the Music: The final montage to "Behind Blue Eyes" is super-haunting and gives off really strong last supper vibes.

Spoiler Alert: The nutso nun had "visions of Darkness" and her book ultimately leads to the unleashing of *The* Darkness, so, was it Amara talking to her?

The Werther Project

Episode 10.19. Airdate: April 22, 2015
Written by: Robert Berens
Directed by: Stefan Pleszczynski
Guest Cast: Ty Olsson (Benny), Kevan Smith (Cuthbert Sinclair) Ruth Connell (Rowena)
Synopsis: At Rowena's request, Sam seeks out a codex locked in a Men of Letters box that makes people kill themselves with hallucinations.

This is a very dark episode, not just in terms of the horror, but the content and examination of suicide, depression, and self-destruction. The contrast between Dean and Sam being pressured into killing themselves and how they respond says a lot about their characters, and puts up some big red flags for their relationship.

Sam's always felt guilty, but not in a way where he wanted to die. In Season Five, he did die to save the world, but also to prove to his brother that he was good. But since Season Eight, he's needed to prove himself to Dean over and over, and it's led to many bad things. And in his hallucination, it happens again. Sam's desire to be the hero for once, to make up for past sins, means he's willing to give his blood, to die for it. It's not depression—it's toxic dependency and lack of self-worth.

Amazingly, Dean is in a better head space. He understands he has to protect people, and that might mean dying, but he won't go through with it. It's thanks in part to the mark, but also his belief that it's not his time yet. And that Sam needs him.

The big lesson here is, of course, that the bros do better when they're together, but it also might be nice if they'd stop killing and dying for one another. Again, there's some major foreshadowing here that Sam's quest is going to have a cost in blood.

So, Get This: The title of the episode comes from the so-called "Werther effect" which has its origin in supposed copycat suicides that followed the publication of Goethe's *Sorrow of Young Werther*, where a lovesick poet commits suicide.

Angel Heart

Episode 10.20. Airdate: April 29, 2015
Written by: Robbie Thompson
Directed by: Steve Boyum
Guest Cast: Misha Collins (Castiel), Kathryn Newton (Claire), Leisha Hailey (Amelia), Treva Etienne (Tamiel)
Synopsis: The Winchesters and Cas help Claire search for her mother.

Despite Amelia Novak's incredibly sad fate, this is a surprisingly hopeful episode. It's about moving past the bad stuff, letting people grow, and forgiveness. Claire has a lot of justified anger towards Cas and Dean, but she manages to move past it to find her own strength and power.

There's hope here, because Claire realizes her family is part of her, and that she has other people watching her back. And there's even hope for Amelia who gets to heaven with her husband. Maybe there's even hope for Dean, Cas, and Sam as long as they watch out for one another, and let go of their anger and need for revenge (and don't lie about stuff, SAM).

This episode also unintentionally sowed the seeds for a spin-off that fans really wanted. With Claire's line about a home for "Wayward girls," the fandom latched onto the idea of Jody, Claire, Alex, and Donna all coming together to hunt and fight evil. Thus the fan-sourced title of "Wayward Daughters" was born. That was a hopeful and joyous moment of fandom.

Spoiler Alert: Which would be short lived considering what happens next.

Ship Shape: Cas and Dean being an old married couple is always great, but an old married couple parenting a teen? Chef's kiss.

Dark Dynasty

Episode 10.21. Airdate: May 6, 2015
Written by: Brad Buchner & Eugenie Ross-Leming
Directed by: Robert Singer
Guest Cast: Misha Collins (Castiel), Mark Sheppard (Crowley), Felicia Day (Charlie), Ruth Connell (Rowena), David Hoflin (Eldon Styne)
Synopsis: Sam enlists Charlie to help Rowena decode the codex that will crack the Book of the Damned, and in the process the Stynes find Charlie and kill her.

And here we are, the most controversial episode of *Supernatural*, barring maybe the series finale. I won't lie, there are good things in this episode. Cas versus the redheads. Crowley playing demon darts. Even the Frankenstein stuff, while ridiculous, is sorta fun and campy. And heck, I love the image of the Styne arm just hanging there by a chain for its sheer ridiculousness. But the decision to kill Charlie is all kinds of not good.

From a story perspective, killing Charlie makes a lot of sense. It's a terrible, horrible loss that's going to break Dean, and maybe even destroy the trust between the brothers. We've had so many revenge and trauma stories this season setting that this might make Dean go full dark side. Charlie dying on his watch is, I guess, supposed to show that Sam is just as bad or broken as Dean. But, as interesting as Winchester man pain is, I'd like my heroes to actually be heroes. Though it can be argued that Charlie had agency here… it just sucks that she has to die.

Characters dying to motivate the Winchesters are standard on this show, and in fact secondary characters dying to motivate main characters is just a common trope. But for fans, this one hurt. Charlie was someone they identified with so much. It was a slap in the face to see a queer woman gutted by a family who helped the Nazis. And it did damage to the fandom, and the series' reputation, that was extremely hard to recover from. Sure, it was where the story took the writers, and they're cruel, capricious gods. But was there really no detour you could have taken here?

Spoiler Alert: Is where the story goes worth it? I don't know. But one thing that's annoying, is that even though we find out the friggin' Frankensteins are all over the world manipulating everything, and maybe did 9/11 (WTF!?), they're never heard from again. Maybe they were eaten by the Chicago monster families we forgot about.

Death Notes: Other deaths in the series were more poignant or shocking, but Charlie's death will forever be the most upsetting and offensive. 0/10.

The Prisoner

Episode 10.22 Airdate: May 13, 2015
Written by: Andrew Dabb
Directed by: Thomas Wright
Guest Cast: Misha Collins (Castiel), Mark Sheppard (Crowley), Ruth Connell (Rowena), David Hoflin (Eldon Styne), Markus Flanagan (Monroe Styne), Conor Price (Cyrus Styne)
Synopsis: Dean takes his revenge on the Stynes, while Sam continues to try to find a cure for the mark.

Despite the last episode and Charlie's death being terrible, this episode turns out stellar. There are huge character moments for all four of our main dudes. And yes, it's kind of an inherent problem on the show that all the main emotion and drama is about four white males. But hey, that's a bigger problem than just this series. At least Rowena is still around making trouble and looking fabulous.

Sam and Crowley are a great contrast in their interactions. Sam has fully bought into the idea that he must go to any extreme to protect his family, whereas Crowley finally realizes he just has to be himself. For the first time in ages, Crowley is truly scary, and his actualization is a scene worthy of seeing Mark Sheppard with red demon eyes.

Sam and Crowley's complicated relationships to their families actually work with the Styne story, which is all about blind, violent family loyalty. For Dean though, he sees the Stynes as an example of inherent evil that can't be washed away. In destroying them, he's destroying himself and becoming the monster he feels is inevitable.

But then there's Cas, who makes it abundantly clear that he will stay by Dean's side for eternity. Cas, who is an angel, who's more human than most humans, who fell because of Dean. That's why the final fight between the two is so major. It's a mirror of their scene in "Goodbye Stranger" and once again, one can't kill the other because there's still love there. But it's fading. This makes clear to the audience that the mark has to go.

Ship Shape: The emotion and importance of that final Dean and Cas scene doesn't come from the subtext—it comes from the text. These two have been separated a lot this season and last, which sucks. Cas pretty clearly loves Dean and is the only person at times that can reach him, so he has to be "taken off the board" to allow Dean to spiral. But the result is another scene that just makes this love story more dramatic and messy.

Death Notes: Good friggin' bye, Stynes! You sucked!

Brother's Keeper

Episode 10.23. Airdate: May 20, 2015
Written by: Jeremy Carver
Directed by: Phil Sgriccia
Guest Cast: Misha Collins (Castiel), Mark Sheppard (Crowley), Julian Richings (Death), Ruth Connell (Rowena), Robert Maloney (Rudy), A large black CGI cloud (The Darkness)
Synopsis: Hello Darkness, my old friend.

Well, if saving Dean only to unleash a primordial evil, while also killing Death in the process isn't standard Winchester things, I don't know what is. Though Sam and Dean make some really good points about how they've done a lot of harm in the name of brotherhood, and yet are still good people, Dean ultimately can't kill Sam so he kills Death instead! Is this ultimately a good decision? As heroic as not killing your brother is, the immediate negative consequences here maybe not good. Wouldn't the world be better off at this point with Sam dead and Dean on the moon or whatever?

I think not killing Sam is good, because killing him would represent walking away from family, sort of how Rowena did with both Crowley and Oskar. And since the mark would have been removed whether Sam had been killed or not, it's definitely better to have him around. But not killing Sam doesn't solve the problems that the Winchesters have in their relationship. And Sam's refusal to let Dean go is what leads to the Darkness.

Overall, this finale has some good ideas and moments that don't fully land. I don't buy why Sam needs to die, and his confrontation with Dean is overwrought. I also don't buy that Dean letting a random hunter (who we've only heard of for a few episodes) die is somehow the straw that breaks the camel's back. Who the hell is Randy? Why not bring back Cole and kill him to tie off that story? It's messy and weird, but hey, at least we're back in apocalypse territory. Also, Crowley's done for, Cas is an attack dog, and Rowena has all the power. That can't be good.

Death Notes: Dean killed Death and it wasn't the craziest thing in the episode. I honestly don't like this decision, since Julian Richings was so great in this role, but not having someone in Death's role is probably important going into a season where Sam and Dean are facing cosmic forces.

SUPERNATURAL

CHAPTER ELEVEN

Keep Grinding

After a season of massive angst and comparatively intimate stories, Jeremy Carver went into his final year of showrunning ready to turn things back up to eleven. At this point though, Carver wasn't the only one running the show with Bob Singer. Long-time writer Andrew Dabb stepped up in a major way, and it's Dabb who ended up not only finishing the season, but taking over for the rest of the series' run. That's why it's somewhat hard to classify this season as "Carver era" or "Dabb era." Either way, it's a big change from Season Ten's doldrums, and generally that's for the better. There was only one new voice in the writer's room, as Nancy Won replaced Adam Glass, so things were generally steady.

If Seasons Nine and Ten were about taking the boys to the nadir of their co-dependency, Season Eleven is where they start to come out on the other side. It's a season about siblings, about balance, family, and trust, and it's about the consequences of the crazy things we do for our family to feel loved. But it also takes the show back to the largest scale possible for villains and heroes, while asking us what makes either. And if fighting is always the right course.

This very easily, like later seasons, could have been a final bow for the show, but instead functions as a bit of a reset for another new era. It has one of, if not the, best episode of the series, as well as interesting characters and journeys for most of our favorites. As always, there are some stumbles, but there are more highs than lows.

Out of the Darkness, Into the Fire

Episode 11.01. Airdate: October 7, 2015
Written by: Jeremy Carver
Directed by: Robert Singer
Guest Cast: Misha Collins (Castiel), Mark Sheppard (Crowley), Emily Swallow (The Darkness), Laci J. Mailey (Deputy Jenna Nickerson)
Synopsis: Dean and Sam have a darkness-infected town to deal with. Cas has a really bad day. Crowley has an orgy.

This premiere is surprisingly quiet, considering the rabid not-Zombies and that Dean and Sam just released a pre-Biblical evil on the world. I like that from the beginning, the Darkness is kind of ambiguous. And also, I relate to her in that if the first human I ever met was Dean, I would imprint on him too. It is somewhat a bummer that she attaches to Dean because of the mark, and not to Sam or anyone else that freed her, but hey, he's cute.

What I really like to see in this episode is Sam directly calling out how screwed up he, Dean, and their priorities are. They need to change, or they will keep breaking the world. This is the Sam I love, the one that's committed to saving people and he's been missing for a while. And yes, sometimes to do that he has to be separate from Dean.

Dean himself is doing… kind of okay, considering he killed Death a few hours before. But again, this is the Dean I love—free of the mark and saving babies… who might be the Darkness. Whoops.

Beyond some moral discussions, we get interesting character beats from Crowley and Cas. While one of them would rather get kidnapped by angels, rather than hurt humans, Crowley is content to kill and manipulate. And he's also there to remind us that the cage, Lucifer, and Michael are all still around. Cursed Cas is not a terribly interesting plot since it only serves to keep him away from the boys, but oh well.

Ship Shape: There's honestly no denying at this point that Crowley isn't pansexual, given his partaking in the orgy in Marnie's body. We've known this from the get-go, but it really does support the idea of his feelings for Dean as a love story. Cas on the other hand only really cares about Dean being okay at this point, which is sweet. He doesn't sound too happy about a primordial force of evil making moves on his man though. Can't blame him.

Familiar Faces: Does Jenna look familiar? She should! She was the Alpha Vampire's pet human in "There Will Be Blood" back in Season Seven!

Form And Void

Episode 11.02. Airdate: October 14, 2015
Written by: Andrew Dabb
Directed by: Phil Sgriccia
Guest Cast: Misha Collins (Castiel), Mark Sheppard (Crowley), Lee Majdoub (Hannah), Laci J. Mailey (Jenna), Lisa Berry (Billie)
Synopsis: Sam and Cas have really bad days and nights; Dean learns how children grow up so fast.

This episode is more like a second part to the season opener than its own independent thing, and that's fine. It finishes the job of setting up the big plot for the season, and gives us hero moments and foreshadowing. Amara is established as very scary, because heaven and hell both fear her. And she eats souls, which can't be good. She's still kinda cute and likes Dean though, so you know, complexity.

This episode honestly has Dean and Sam at their most Dean and Sam. Dean acts tough, but is secretly tender and every supernatural being that encounters him falls in love. Sam keeps fighting to save people even in the worst moments. I love that he just doesn't give up, and it's nice to see the moose get a win. It's also interesting to see him seeking out a higher power, because that's never gone badly before.

Sam and the rabids parallel what's happening with Cas, who also won't compromise his loyalty to the Winchesters. Loyalty that got him into this cursed mess, which cost three more angel lives. Generally seeing Cas sad and tortured is sad. I hope he gets a hug. We also learn that the Winchesters are facing much higher stakes this season with the old Death gone, and that maybe they will actually stay dead if they bite it now.

Fan Favorite: Billie! We have a new favorite reaper from the moment she appears, singing "O Death," which isn't the first time a song on the show had leapt from extradiegetic to diegetic. Lisa Berry is cool, badass, and terrifying.

Spoiler Alert: Billie's excellent scene with Sam is also the first time we hear mention of The Empty. I don't know if at this point the writers had decided it was an actual thing. Turns out it's where angels and demons go when they die, and contrary to Billie's assertions, Winchesters can come back too.

The Bad Seed

Episode 11.03. Airdate: October 21, 2015
Written by: Brad Buckner & Eugenie Ross-Leming
Directed by: Jensen Ackles
Guest Cast: Misha Collins (Castiel), Mark Sheppard (Crowley), Ruth Connell (Rowena), Emily Swallow (Adult Amara), Gracyn Shinyei (Young Amara)
Synopsis: The boys go after Rowena so she can end the curse on Cas.

Past the icky, racist "fortune nookie" porn bit, a few characters acting in incredibly stupid ways, and some bad underaged acting, this episode isn't too bad. But it isn't particularly good either. A lot happens to straighten up a few of the messes from the last season, but the ending is mainly the status quo.

Is there thematic stuff here? Well, there are a lot of discussions about God and why he allows suffering, and stuff that's maybe above the paygrade of a CW horror show. But there's also a few hopeful bits and nods to how Dean's feeling sad, Sam is feeling hopeful, and Cas just wants to be useful.

As with most episodes she's in, Rowena owns this one. She's so fun and spunky that we end up rooting for her, even if that means killing Crowley. She's more interesting than her son at this point, as he seems to have lost a lot of the moral complexity that defined him. Rowena will get some of that complexity herself, but even at this point she might be my favorite MacLeod.

So, Get This: This episode was directed by Jensen, and the name of the restaurant where Rowena makes her mega coven pitch, "Elta café" is a nod to his wife.

Ship Shape: That part where Dean gently cradles Cas' face in his hand, and looks at him with all the tenderness and concern in the world? Worth all the other dumb stuff in this episode. Also, Dean not letting Cas heal him because he feels guilty for beating the crap out of Cas in "The Prisoner" is peak Dean.

Baby

Episode 11.04. Airdate: October 28, 2015
Written by: Robbie Thompson
Directed by: Thomas Wright
Guest Cast: Misha Collins (Castiel), Matt Cohen (John), Baby (Herself)
Synopsis: Shown for the perspective of the Impala, Sam and Dean track a were-pire. Or is a ghoul-pire?

In a series as varied and vast as *Supernatural,* it's impossible to call anything the "best" episode, because every episode is different. From the emotions of "All Hell Breaks Loose" or "On the Head of a Pin," to the meta madness of "The French Mistake" or "Fan Fiction," there are so many different ways an episode can be great. But this is, if I had to pick, the greatest episode of *Supernatural*. It's everything that makes the show what it is: humor and horror, family, fun, creativity, and classic rock. Two brothers with an angel on their shoulder, in a big black car, fighting to save the world.

"Baby" is remarkable for its innovation and how the result is so simple and pure. The idea of setting a whole episode of television inside a car is an entirely new take on the classic "bottle episode." The results are unique and beautiful scenes that are both incredibly creative and distill the series down to its essence. As Sam and Dean drive, talk, sleep, eat and even fight in the Impala, we get faith and family, and what these boys need and want. They may have other dreams, but their home is right there, saving people and hunting things.

It's so hard to pick favorite moments from this episode, but Sam and Dean's long talk about dreams, parables, and God in the "Winchester Motel" is truly wonderful. So is Dean vs. Deputy Dumbass, with Cas on the phone (great way to integrate Cas, by the way). The head on the windshield is perfection. But honestly, the whole episode is a perfect love letter to the show—to the car that symbolizes the Winchester family. No other show could make an episode like this.

Driver Picks the Music: The "Night Moves" scene is so perfect, mainly because most of it was filmed remotely, with Jared and Jensen left to improvise as they drove around. It's such a fun, brotherly scene, and Bob Seger scores it perfectly.

So, Get This: While the Impala is extremely large, it's not actually big enough to hold two reclining hunters; for the scene where Sam and Dean are seen sleeping from above, both actor's feet were hanging out of open doors and the shot was accomplished using a deconstructed Impala with no roof.

Spoiler Alert: The entity talking to Sam is Lucifer, which is implied by the light that shines on his face at key points. Lucifer is the light bringer, after all.

Thin Lizzy

Episode 11.05. Airdate: November 4, 2015
Written by: Nancy Won
Directed by: Rashaad Ernesto Green
Guest Cast: Jared Gertner (Len Fletcher), Tess Atkins (Sydney), Yasmeene Ball (Amara)
Synopsis: Murders at the Lizzy Borden Bed and breakfast lead Sam and Dean to a crop of people who have had their souls sucked out by Amara.

"Thin Lizzy" gets back to that classic, early *Supernatural* model of starting as one thing and ending as another. What begins as a fun monster of the week that sets off Sam's nerd alarm, turns out to be really important to the mythology. This is another signal that Season Eleven is breaking pattern.

But it's also a good episode, with great guest performances and twists that give us a lot more information about Amara and what she signifies. If God is form, then she's void. She's the depressive, cynical, unattached side of existence. She's not destruction per se. She's nothingness.

And for some people, that's attractive. Especially for Dean, and maybe even Sam. There's a big parallel here between Dean going through the motions, but not feeling, while Sam is the one with the most heart. Thematically, we're still somewhat unclear, but they're trying to explain why Dean has this bond with Amara.

So, Get This: The Lizzie Borden Bed and Breakfast is a real place, and it went on sale in 2020. This episode was not filmed on location however, just in Vancouver.

Future Famous Faces: Jordie, the young boy Sam and Dean save, is played by Finn Wolfhard, who would go on to play a bigger role in another horror show popular on Netflix—*Stranger Things* where he played Mike.

Our Little World

Episode 11.06. Airdate: November 11, 2015
Written by: Robert Berens
Directed by: John Showalter
Guest Cast: Misha Collins (Castiel), Mark Sheppard (Crowley), Curtis Armstrong (Metatron), Samantha Isler (Amara)
Synopsis: Sam and Dean track Amara to where she's been staying with Crowley.

There are a lot of interesting intentions in this episode, but I'm unsure how much of it pays off. It's a good episode, but confused. The story between Amara and Crowley clearly parodies parenting a teenager, and maybe that's meant to show that he's still trying to find a way to have love and a connection with people. But that motivation is about as convincing as Crowley's plastic hand when Amara breaks his wrist.

But other things do work, like Sam trying not to kill as much because he thinks God is speaking to him—and showing him visions of Lucifer's cage! Everything with Cas and Metatron works, giving us another miserable human going through the motions.

The weirdest bit though is probably the Dean and Amara stuff. Again, it makes some sense, because of course if Dean Winchester was the first thing you saw on earth, you'd have a crush… but their "bond" just comes off as creepy with Amara in a teen body. And speaking of Amara, the rotating door of actresses playing her has made her character and motivation hard to discern.

But hey, the reveal that Amara is God's sister brings into focus one thing—sibling relationships and family. That's what the show has always been about, but maybe on a pre-Biblical scale, exploring that will help Sam and Dean get over their own issues.

Driver Picks the Music: The use of "Girl, You'll Be a Woman Soon" by Urge Overkill over the final montage is probably a reference to the use of the same song in *Pulp Fiction* and I think it works okay, but it's maybe a little on the nose.

Plush

Episode 11.07. Airdate: November 18, 2015
Written by: Eric Charmelo & Nicole Snyder
Directed by: Tim Andrew
Guest Cast: Briana Buckmaster (Donna), Brendan Taylor (New Doug), Brigid Brannagh (Rita Johnson)
Synopsis: Donna calls Sam and Dean into a case where a ghost is haunting masks and costumes.

I honestly don't know what to make of an episode where the monster of the week is essentially a "Chester the molester" joke. The fact that Chester's crimes remain ambiguous doesn't help and honestly, this is a topic that they should have stayed away from.

I like Donna's part here, and her plotline with New Doug. It's always nice to see a familiar face. I just wish it were in a better episode. But kudos to Sam for facing his fear! That's going to be a theme for the season too, insofar as Sam has a story of his own.

The moral of this little story seems to be to trust your sibling, because not trusting them makes them come back really angry. That clearly applies to what God did to Amara, whose own "evil" remains as undetermined as Chester's. But it might also apply to Sam and Dean. Dean isn't trusting Sam's visions right now, after all.

Spoiler Alert: It isn't though! Nothing good comes from the cage this season! Nothing! Lucifer gets out, and while that ultimately may lead to the world getting fixed five seasons from now… Sam's visions are still a trick. So, I don't think Dean's wrong!

Plot Hole: Cas went *to Gaza?* Cas has no wings! That means Cas got on a plane and somehow smuggled tons of ancient books out of the holy land?! That would be a much more interesting episode! I guess it's better than these same writers' last excuse for Cas being absent, which was friggin' riverboat gambling!

Just My Imagination

Episode 11.08. Airdate: December 2, 2015
Written by: Jenny Klein
Directed by: Richard Speight Jr.
Guest Cast: Nate Torrance (Sully), Anja Savcic (Reese), Dylan Everett (Young Dean), Dylan Kingwell (Young Sam), Eduard Witzke (Weems)
Synopsis: Sam's childhood imaginary friend Sully turns out to be a real creature called a Zanna, who needs Sam's help.

This episode is a treat. As the directorial debut of Richard Speight Jr., it's wonderfully done and a lot of fun, with a cute concept that has a lot of emotion. Nate Torrance is also fantastic as Sully! And it's a Sam-centric episode which is something we haven't seen in a while. I just wish that making Sam sensitive didn't translate to Dean being such a dick for most of the episode.

A lot like the last episode, this one is about sibling relationships and trust, and it emphasizes a few things: that Sam in his heart may still want a different life, and that he only goes through the motions of hunting because that's how he can be with his family. That's not good and kind of matches with some things we've seen about how the Winchester co-dependency is not good for Sam and Dean as individuals. But Sully also encourages Sam to be his brave, daring self, and to face his fears and trauma.

There's also some stuff here about trust, betrayal, and revenge. Reese wants to hurt Sully, because he left her alone after making a mistake. That applies to Amara and how she feels about God, and the fact Reese *doesn't* take revenge is interesting.

Spoiler Alert: It's also massive foreshadowing! In fact, the resolution of Sully and Reese's relationship is a lot like how Chuck and Amara work things out. What's interesting is that Sully encourages Sam to go to the cage, meaning everyone is playing into Lucifer's tricks. Whoops.

Oh Brother, Where Art Thou?

Episode 11.09. Airdate: December 9, 2015
Written by: Brad Buckner & Eugenie Ross-Leming
Directed by: Robert Singer
Guest Cast: Mark Sheppard (Crowley), Mark Pellegrino (Lucifer), Ruth Connell (Rowena), Emily Swallow (Amara)
Synopsis: With Rowena and Crowley's help, Sam head to hell to speak with Lucifer. Meanwhile Dean ignores his brother's calls to make out with Amara.

You know how I do those fun "plot hole" sections for some episodes? If I did one for this episode, it would be the whole dang thing. This episode is plot holes, nonsense, and messiness from start to finish.

Sure, there are some things that are okay, and to be nice I'll do those first. There's great acting from the boys. Jared is incredible in his scenes with Mark Pellegrino, and Jensen does admirably trying to find a motivation for Dean among all this. Emily Swallow does less well finding meaning in the self-important gobbledygook Amara gets stuck with though. Also, where is Amara, like, physically? Where are Sam and Dean? Why is the door to hell so close? Honestly, the Impala turned into a Tardis like, three years ago so… I'll ignore the location nonsense.

The stuff in hell, while corny, rushed, and over the top, is okay. What's absurd is Sam and Dean going into this without telling Cas. But Amara's stuff is so weird, and bad, because it makes no sense. Her attempts to get God's attention feel so small, and her conversations about God are freshman theology class basic. It's all woefully terrestrial and centered on a really simplistic idea of God and the universe that isn't worthy of a show that can be much smarter than this. This is what happens when they try to depict celestial concepts better left the imagination. Hell was less scary when we didn't see it, and primal darkness is better when no one tries to explain it.

What is Amara? I can't tell you at this point. She's bliss but she eats people—except Dean—and she could have created stuff, but she didn't. And she's all powerful, but not powerful enough to find God? And she and Dean have… a bond? What does that mean? It doesn't make sense, like a lot of the rushed, silly aspects of this episode.

Ship Shape: Is the Dean-Amara thing supposed to be romantic? I can see her liking him, but what does Dean feel around her? Calm? Does she represent some latent suicidal ideation in Dean? Cause that's not romantic. I think Lucifer and Rowena have better chances. Woof.

The Devil in the Details

Episode 11.09. Airdate: January 20, 2016
Written by: Andrew Dabb
Directed by: Thomas Wright
Guest Cast: Misha Collins (Castiel), Mark Sheppard (Crowley), Colin Ford (Young Sam), Mark Pellegrino (Lucifer), Ruth Connell (Rowena), Emily Swallow (Amara), Lisa Berry (Billie)
Synopsis: In hell, Lucifer tries to convince Sam to say yes, but it's Cas who does.

As ridiculous as the last episode was, this hour almost makes up for it with excellent twists and character dissection. Last week, Dean got some examination that didn't make much sense, but here we really dig into Sam. And I gotta say, Lucifer is pretty right when he looks at Sam's past. Does that mean he should have said yes? I don't know. It's unclear, but I like Jared and Pellegrino's scenes as always.

Cas however has the hardest time this episode. After failing a lot the past few years, getting cursed, and in general being just used or ignored all season, I can't really blame him for feeling like he has to make a big move. It's shocking, but it fits with how depressed he's been. And this whole season is about fighting depression.

Death Notes: Rowena! NO! This death is a shock for many reasons, which makes it actually pretty good, and it comes after such an excellent show from Ruth Connell, who can really be fun and powerful. But we also finally get to dig deep on who Rowena really is, and why she won't let herself love Fergus.

Ship Shape: Dean, where did you think Cas was gonna take your temperature? And you better learn to be more appreciative of your angel or he'll go straight to Satan!

Plot Hole: Okay, so if it's that easy to get someone out of the cage—and speaking of that, if Lucifer could have just jumped into Jimmy Novak—was there a point to Seasons Four and Five?

Into The Mystic

Episode 11.10. Airdate: January 27, 2016
Written by: Robbie Thompson
Directed by: John Badham
Guest Cast: Misha Collins (Lucifer), Shoshannah Stern (Eileen Leahy), Dee Wallace (Mildred Baker)
Synopsis: Sam and Dean hunt a banshee at a local retirement home and meet a hunter named Eileen. Casifer enjoys life outside of the cage.

Let's take a minute and give mad props, as the kids say, to Misha Collins for absolutely embodying Lucifer. There's a lot of vessel-hopping on this show, so we know how hard it can be for one actor to play another character, but Misha really nails Pellegrino's Lucifer, while doing his own thing. And on top of that, he has to play Lucifer pretending to be Cas, and that's great too! That's a highlight for me.

Our focus is balanced between Dean and Sam, with Sam recovering from the trauma of seeing Lucifer, and finally truly apologizing for not looking for Dean. Good, and good on Dean for letting him. It's a sign that Sam feels like he'll always have his brother, that he's now planning to retire with him.

Dean on the other hand is having issues that I buy less, because Dean Winchester losing his spine over a crush that could wipe out the world is weird. But we also have stuff here about forgiveness, and letting go, so if Dean can forgive Sam, maybe Amara can forgive God. Yeah, I still don't get her. Dean would be better off with Mildred who is AWESOME.

Ship Shape: So, Dean's admitting his attraction to Amara and gets called out for "pining" over her? Amara is hot, sure, but this bond is forced and nonsensical. Good ships come from chemistry, not plot contrivances that push folks out of character. And just look at the Amara weirdness in comparison to Dean and Cas. Dean is so effortlessly intimate and trusting with Cas, even when it's not really Cas! And he can tell something is off when Cas puts a hand on the wrong shoulder.

Also great: Sam and Eileen. Instant chemistry and connection.

Complete cuteness when Sam says “F you” instead of “thank you” in ASL. Eileen is perfect for Sam, and I love them together from the moment they meet.

Fan Favorite/Famous Faces: Because Shoshannah Stern was so awesome as a disabled, flirty hunter, she was immediately beloved by fandom. And yes, that’s Dee Wallace from *ET* as Mildred.

Name Game: Mixing it up, the names Osborne and Butler reference Ozzy Osborne and Geezer Butler of Black Sabbath. I like that a case at an old folks’ home includes reference to a guy named Geezer.

Don't You Forget About Me

Episode 11.12. Airdate: February 3, 2016
Written by: Nancy Won
Directed by: Stefan Pleszczynski
Guest Cast: Kim Rhodes (Jody Mills), Katherine Ramdeen (Alex), Kathryn Newton (Claire), Ben Cotton (Wheeler), Jedidiah Goodacre (Henry)
Synopsis: Claire calls in the Winchesters to help with a possible hunt, but they also find a tense home situation between Claire, Alex, and Jody.

After a few months of dealing with God's family drama, it must be nice for Sam and Dean to deal with some more human issues. It's also nice for us, because we get to see the boys as role models and mentors. And the ways they are completely useless compared to an actual adult like Jody. The family dinner scene is fantastic, with sharp writing and hysterical acting from everyone, and it's also nice to see the boys get a good home cooked meal.

Claire, Alex, and Jody really are an interesting family unit, and it's appropriate for this show that their family doesn't start or end in blood. Even so, they love and support one another, and forgive each other for their mistakes. Forgiveness is stronger than the desire for revenge, and it's a big neon sign about Amara and God.

This episode exists because the Jody-Claire-Alex dynamic and set up is so organic, and fans responded to it so well, that they were calling for a spin-off before this episode even aired. And though it took some time, we do return to these characters again and again, until these Wayward daughters get the spotlight in Season Thirteen.

Love Hurts

Episode 11.13. Airdate: February 10, 2016
Written by: Eric Charmelo & Nicole Snyder
Directed by: Phil Sgriccia
Guest Cast: Emily Swallow (Amara), Luciana Carro (Melissa Harper), Venus Terzo (Sonja)
Synopsis: A witches curse has people's deepest desires ripping their hearts out.

Finally, with a shockingly boring episode, the show begins to dig into what the hell is going on with Dean and Amara. Is the explanation adequate? No. But does it at least make things make a bit more sense? Maybe.

I think this episode represents the writers realizing the Dean-Amara thing was weird and trying to fix it by saying, no, he's not in love with her, but rather she has some sort of control over him. She is a deity after all. At least that's what Sam's going for? I think it might be better understood that Dean's darkest, deepest desire, is to stop fighting and just fall into the void. Which is really dark! But maybe I'm getting too deep for a mediocre episode.

So, Get This: This is the first time Dean's ever won Rock, Paper, Scissors against Sam. He finally broke the cycle! And that's all that matters to him!

The Vessel

Episode 11.14. Airdate: February 17, 2016
Written by: Robert Berens
Directed by: John Badham
Guest Cast: Misha Collins (Lucifer/Castiel), Mark Sheppard (Crowley), Weronika Rosati (Delphine Seydoux), Grant Harvey (Peter Giraldi)
Synopsis: Casifer sends Dean back in time to a World War 2 sub in order to retrieve an artifact touched by God.

This is an excellent episode, with incredible production values. But also as Dean notes, for pretty much all of it, they're witnesses to other stories and reveals, not themselves the heroes. That's fine and it doesn't detract from the overall episode. In fact, it emphasizes how small these two humans are in the face of wars, gods, and the machinery of fate.

There's big character moments and developments all over here. Sam has to confront his abuser, again. Cas saves the boys, again. And Dean is left devastated that Cas let himself be possessed. Not to mention Lucifer playing puppy with Crowley, which is very funny. But it also shows how much Lucifer has changed as a character. Back then he was mysterious and scary, but now he's just a sadistic little shit. It's less intimidating, but at least with Misha at the helm, it's fun to watch.

Plot Hole: Do yourself and favor and don't spend too much time obsessing over how the mythos of *Supernatural* works. At some points it takes the Old Testament literally, and everything there happened, except it didn't and none of it is accurate. There are other gods, and maybe other planets? With the same gods and alternative universes, but that's not the same, and God has a sister who is as powerful as him and… no.

Ship Shape: Oh boy am I a sucker for Cas refusing to cast out Lucifer, so he can save Dean and Dean being really sad. That's the good stuff right there.

Beyond The Mat

Episode 11.15. Airdate: February 24, 2016
Written by: John Bring, Andrew Dabb
Directed by: Jerry Wanek
Guest Cast: Misha Collins (Lucifer), Mark Sheppard (Crowley), Alex Paunovic (Gunnar Lawless), Jackie Debatin (Rio), Bethany Brown (Simmons), Aidan Khan (Duke)
Synopsis: Sam and Dean wrestle with demons. In hell, Crowley narrowly escapes Lucifer after some rod measuring shenanigans.

I wonder sometimes if the writers know how very gay things will come off on-screen. I'm not talking about Crowley and Lucifer's dueling entendres, I'm talking about Dean Winchester, bisexual disaster. This is one of those episodes that reminds us—with a few fanboy smiles and a wink from a man in spandex—that *Supernatural* is the apex of hypermasculinity transmuting into homoeroticism.

I say all of this with love, because this is a legitimately good episode. Jensen Ackles shows that he's not only capable of having chemistry with anyone, but that he's a brilliant physical comedian and a powerful dramatic actor. That's range!

Casifer, Sam and Crowley all continue to be great too. And the main storyline of Gunnar giving himself up for one win is a clear mirror, allowing Dean to process what's going on with Cas. Cas made a bad decision for good reasons, and Sam and Dean get that and already forgive him. Because that's what family does.

Spoiler Alert: Weirdly, barely anything Dean says they're going to do in his big inspirational speech at the end actually happens. They aren't the ones to get Lucifer out of Cas, they don't kill him for like, two years, and they don't shank the Darkness.

Familiar Faces: Fans of actual wrestling and *The Real World* will recognize Mike "The Miz" Mizanin as Harley. Alex Paunovic has also been in about a thousand other things, including *Van Helsing*, *Snowpiercer* and two previous appearances here.

Safe House

Episode 11.16. Airdate: March 23, 2016
Written by: Robbie Thompson
Directed by: Stefan Pleszczynski
Guest Cast: Jim Beaver (Bobby), Steven Williams (Rufus), Jane McLean (Naoki Himura)
Synopsis: Sam and Dean hunt a soul eater that Bobby and Rufus dealt with years ago.

No matter what form he's in, it's always wonderful to see Jim Beaver back as Bobby. And with Steven Williams along as Rufus, this episode is a winner. I also love the unique structure and the way that Bobby and Rufus's hunt so neatly overlays with Sam and Dean's. And of course, the lessons that Bobby and Rufus learn may be applicable to this season as well.

And what is that lesson? That sometimes you can save everyone. Again, it's subtle, but it makes more sense in the full context of the season. As I noted, Dean and Sam are attached to an awfully specific idea of what winning means—and it's all about killing and keeping up their toxic cycles since before the apocalypse. But maybe there's a different way that doesn't involve sacrifice, death and violence?

Name Game: Sam and Dean ditch the rock and movie alias and instead use "Rizer" and "Bean," which are characters from the videogame *Contra*. Bobby and Rufus go incognito as Riggs and Murtaugh, a reference to *Lethal Weapon*.

Red Meat

Episode 11.17. Airdate: March 30, 2016
Written by: Andrew Dabb, Robert Berens
Directed by: Nina Lopez-Corrado
Guest Cast: Lisa Berry (Billie), Erin Way (Michelle Tilghman), Blair Penner (Corbin Tilghman)
Synopsis: Sam almost dies so Dean does die to save him.

Welcome to the absolute apex of Winchester co-dependency. The willingness to sacrifice and make the worst decisions possible to save a brother is broken down to what it really is here—suicidal.

Sam and Dean's revolving door of death is bad, folks. Real bad! We see in Corbin and Michelle's story, how doing anything to save someone else makes you a monster. Billie calls it out explicitly—just like Lucifer did with Sam—telling Dean that he doesn't care about the world. He just can't exist without Sam. But it's also understandable at this point—all their friends are dead, disappeared, or possessed by Lucifer.

The big message of this episode is once again that the old ways don't work, and that the co-dependency is bad. There's one extreme of trying to kill someone you loved, and the other of killing for them, and neither are good. Balance, guys. You need balance.

Ship Shape: There's a case to be made that this is a very Wincest-positive episode, and I know there are fans of that ship that love it but … I gotta give that a big yikes. Yes, it's dramatic and sure, maybe romantic if you wanna see it that way.

So, Get This: In an earlier version of the script, Billie said she imagined Dean dying of "autoerotic asphyxiation" while watching *Charles in Charge*.

Death Notes: Though for a second it looked like Sam was gonna be the one passing into the veil, it's Dean who gets another point! Scores stands at Dean: 18, Sam: 6, Castiel: 4. Guys, I think Dean might win this.

Hell's Angel

Episode 11.18. Airdate: April 6, 2016
Written by: Brad Buckner & Eugenie Ross-Leming
Directed by: Phil Sgriccia
Guest Cast: Misha Collins (Lucifer/Castiel), Mark Sheppard (Crowley), Mark Pellegrino (Also Lucifer), Ruth Connell (Rowena), Emily Swallow (Amara)
Synopsis: The Winchesters try to save Cas, Rowena tries to play the odds, Crowley tries to get revenge, Lucifer tries to kill Amara, Cas just tries to watch TV in peace.

This is another one of those lots of plot, all at once, episodes that Brad Buckner and Eugenie Ross-Leming tend to specialize in. It's way more coherent than "Oh Brother, Where Art Thou?" so that's good, and we do get some big developments, including the return of Rowena, which is very welcome.

This episode at last also makes Amara a truly scary enemy, and we get some interesting development for our supporting players. Rowena may be growing a conscience, Crowley is out for blood, and poor Cas is really depressed. We don't get a lot from Sam and Dean in the writing, but it's there in the acting. Sam's flinches when Lucifer is around and Dean focuses on Cas above everything. Overall, this is a good, exciting entry that set the stage for some huge stuff.

Also, the decision to save Cas is a contrast to the Winchester revolving sacrifice door. I think in this case, they want to stop Cas martyring himself and end that cycle.

Ship Shape: Dean's entire thing here is "save Cas" and that's hella romantic. So obvious even that Lucifer makes fun of it. And it's interesting that Amara clocks that Dean's more worried about Cas. The brief moments between Dean and Cas also have, let's admit, more of a spark than the stuff Amara has had all season.

Plot Hole: Amara calls Lucifer God's first son, but that's Michael. Also, um, how did Lucifer get into heaven? And what's going on with hell now? And… never mind.

The Chitters

Episode 11.19. Airdate: April 27, 2016
Written by: Nancy Won
Directed by: Eduardo Sánchez
Guest Cast: Lee Rumhor (Jesse Cuevas), Hugo Ateo (Cesar Cuevas), Kandyse McClure (Sherriff Tyson)
Synopsis: It's Sam and Dean and two gay hunters versus evil cicada monsters.

Before we dive into this episode, let's point out the one thing that doesn't work—where this episode sits in the season. Now, every season we have instances where Sam and Dean have the old "well, the plotline is stalled, let's go die hunting a monster of the week." And that's fine. But I think there would have been more energy for the end game if this episode had happened before "Hells Angel."

But that's a quibble, and this lovely episode with a truly gross and creepy monster is otherwise great. For one, we finally meet a happy, queer couple of hunters, and they are fantastic. They're not the first, or last, queer characters on the show, but I really love Jesse and Cesar. And I especially love that they are allowed to have a happy ending, walking away from the cycle of hunting, violence, and revenge. That's excellent.

And again, we have a big, huge message that revenge isn't worth it. There's also some stuff about forgiveness for big mistakes that's going to be important. I give the show credit with this as it's appeared this season, because it's honestly huge foreshadowing. But it's also subtle enough that what's coming is still exciting. But also good work making cicadas more evil.

Fan Favorites: Though they only show up here, the #HunterHusbands made a huge impression on fandom.

Don't Call Me Shurley

Episode 11.20. Airdate: May 4, 2016
Written by: Robbie Thompson
Directed by: Robert Singer
Guest Cast: Rob Benedict (Chuck), Curtis Armstrong (Metatron)
Synopsis: God and an angel walk into a bar.

This episode is, simply put, magnificent. It's not your usual hour of *Supernatural*, because heck, Sam and Dean are barely in it. But it's the kind of big swing that only a show like this could take. It's a one act play, with Rob Benedict and Curtis Armstrong bringing an incredible script by Robbie Thompson to life, to talk about creation, music, divinity, loneliness and so much more. It's astonishing.

It almost feels impossible to point out favorite moments in this episode, because there's so much amazing stuff in here. From little things like God being bisexual and Rob's incredible ability to switch from nerdy little teddy bear to wrathful terror. But the moment I love the most, the one that makes me cry like clockwork, is Metatron's final speech to God. Telling him why he mattered, why he wanted God to come back, and why people matter. The idea that humanity is disappointing but keeps trying is the thesis of the entire series. It's beautiful and perfect.

After years of wondering where god has been—which is a big question—we finally get some answers and they're pretty satisfying. Chuck doesn't want to face failure or things he can't control. But like Metatron, he loves a good story.

Spoiler Alert: In hindsight, knowing what Chuck will do in the final season, this episode is even better because it doesn't make Chuck a hero at all. He's kind of a jerk in an Old Testament sense and that's who he remains.

Driver Picks the Music: This episode is about music, and the needle drops of "Good Vibrations" by the Beach Boys and "Gimme Shelter" by the Rolling Stones, referencing Metatron's bit about *Wouldn't It Be Nice* versus *Life*. But the show letting actual rock god Rob Benedict absolutely slay "Fare Thee Well" is one of the best uses of music in the entire series. It's beautiful, mournful, and perfectly shot it feels like a miracle.

So, Get This: The new series Chuck is working on called *Revolution* is reference to Eric Kripke's post-*Supernatural* series of the same name. Also, Dean ironing Sam's shirt with beer was improvised by Jared and Jensen.

All in the Family

Episode 11.21. Airdate: May 11, 2016
Written by: Brad Buckner & Eugenie Ross-Leming
Directed by: Thomas Wright
Guest Cast: Misha Collins (Lucifer), Rob Benedict (Chuck), Curtis Armstrong (Metatron), Osric Chau (Kevin), Emily Swallow (Amara), Keith Szarabajka (Donatello Redfield)
Synopsis: With help from Metatron and a new prophet, and even Chuck, Sam and Dean manage to rescue Casifer.

Following up a very philosophical episode like "Don't Call Me Shurley" is a hard task, but this sort of rises to the occasion. Donatello is a fun character, even though he's pretty much a retcon mixed with a plot point in a human suit. And dear Chuck, why did he have to be another white guy? Like many end-of-season episodes, this one has to do a lot of setting of the board and getting characters where they need to be, but it's fine for that.

There are really good moments, mainly between Dean and Chuck. These confrontations are different than Metatron's, but I love them. Dean is the ultimate embodiment of humanity, so it's fitting that he's the one calling out Chuck on his absenteeism and surrender. The fact that Dean is human also makes his Amara connection quite clear, because humanity does seem to want to destroy itself.

Ship Shape: Let's talk about Amara and Dean, because their connection is certainly evolving now. Amara wants the one part of humanity she likes—Dean—to be part of her. But Dean's not on board with that, and actually manages to betray her. How? Also, somehow, she has an open line of psychic communication to him? This could just be a plot hole, but the other answer is… Cas.

Somehow Amara uses Cas' connection to Dean—whatever that is—to reach him. But it's because Amara is specifically hurting Cas, while she's hurting Lucifer, that Dean actually has the motivation and strength to resist her. This is honestly the only way a kind of messy plot makes sense, so, um, yes Destiel?

Spoiler Alert: Chuck, you totally didn't send Kevin to heaven, you dick!

Plot Hole: Nothing about Donatello makes much sense. He has powers we've never seen in a prophet, he's not on the list of prophets from Season Eight, and in general it's all just confusing. Maybe he's Amara's prophet, not God's, which might make a difference. But it's still really weird.

Death Notes: Metatron! I for one am sad to see the Scribe go, because he's always been so interesting, and I love Curtis Armstrong's performance in the role. Still, I do like that he gets that last minute redemption arc because he deserved it.

We Happy Few

Episode 11.22. Airdate: May 18, 2016
Written by: Robert Berens
Directed by: John Badham
Guest Cast: Misha Collins (Castiel/Lucifer), Mark Sheppard (Crowley), Rob Benedict (Chuck), Ruth Connell (Rowena), Emily Swallow (Amara)
Synopsis: Everybody and their mother goes up against God's sister. It fails!

This episode asks, what if we did Ocean's Eleven but Biblical? It's a fun and action-packed episode, that has huge character moments and cosmic family therapy.

When it comes down to it, *Supernatural* is a show about family, and seeing one dysfunctional family (The Winchesters) counsel God and Lucifer is weirdly fitting. Parents make mistakes, even when they try to do what's best, and they act out of love. That's the core of Chuck's apology to Lucifer, and it rings pretty true. This whole season has been about doing things differently, and actually confronting underlying problems with honesty. It's good that Lucifer and Chuck talk it out, and maybe it might be a blueprint for how to deal with Amara.

Amara's motivation—what she is and what she's done—remain a bit mysterious, as does whatever Dean's got going on with her. I can't really keep straight when creation happened, or how, because there have been so many different versions of events according to everyone. Chuck created many worlds, but Amara destroyed them. But before he created creation, he created the archangels and then locked Amara away. And Lucifer had a bad opinion of humanity before he got the mark, but they were created after? And Dean wants Chuck to kill Amara, because he doesn't want her to die?

It's a lot of mental gymnastics for some major metaphysics, that's maybe above the paygrade of this show, but it still works because everything in this episode really comes down to characters and relationships that are very human and relatable. It's the emotions, not the myth, that wins out.

And finally, this episode shows actual character growth for Sam and Dean! Instead of interfering with Sam's choice to take on the mark, Dean lets him make his own decision. Even though this exercise of free will is part of God's plan, they're finally chipping away at that co-dependency. Too bad God's dying, the world is about to end!

Ship Shape: No real romantic moments for anyone here, but hey, Sam and Rowena together again and Dean visiting his ex, Crowley, to ask a favor. Cute.

Alpha and Omega

Episode 11.23. Airdate: May 25, 2016
Written by: Andrew Dabb
Directed by: Phil Sgriccia
Guest Cast: Misha Collins (Castiel), Mark Sheppard (Crowley), Samantha Smith (Mary), Rob Benedict (Chuck), Ruth Connell (Rowena), Emily Swallow (Amara), Lisa Berry (Billie)
Synopsis: It turns out the solution to all the problems is Dean having a heart to heart with Amara and helping her to forgive her brother.

This is a pretty unique season finale and episode for *Supernatural*—a show that literally killed Death last season—in that no one actually dies! The big, cosmic problems are solved, not with a bomb and suicidal plan, but by talking about feelings. Much like Dean admitting he likes chick flicks, this feels like a direct blow to toxic masculinity. It's only now that they can deal with their mommy issues and Mary's return. And English men of letters? WTF? We'll get there later.

Chuck and Amara are balanced, which they need much like Sam and Dean. Amara created lots of problems for Chuck, because she didn't want to share him. That's co-dependency. Sam and Dean caused a lot of problems, because they couldn't live without one another for the same reason. But amazingly, the moose and the pretty one actually grow emotionally and realize that they can still love someone and share them. They can respect family's choices while supporting them. That's what Dean's able to give Amara, and it's a very human perspective.

Amara didn't want Dean as a lover, so much as she wanted him to be only with her the way Chuck was, because of a bond or whatever. But there's more to the world than that kind of all-consuming love. To have that realization save the world, and allow Chuck and Amara to be at peace, is a really ballsy way to end a season. But it works so well in an episode that's emotional and beautiful.

I do have some quibbles here though, including that Sam doesn't have much to do and we've sort of dropped the ball on character stuff for Rowena and Crowley. But overall, this episode is a great conclusion to a sorta weird season. It was all about doing things a different way and not choosing revenge, so in that way, it succeeded.

Spoiler Alert: This season finale, and Sam letting Dean go, really shows that the Winchester co-dependency is better. And now they need to fix other relationships, trauma, and people, which is why Mary shows up. Sam and Dean stay on good footing for the rest of the series at this point, and that's good, but not having drama with each other will make the series different in the Dabb era.

Ship Shape: Cas is back to hug Dean and stare at him lovingly and wow I missed that angel. Kinda wish Dean didn't tell him he was a brother, which to Dean is the biggest declaration of love possible, but which Cas maybe hears with a "and that's all" addendum. Also, I kinda love Chuck, and Rowena, and Crowley and Billie.

So, Get This: There's a lot of, let's say, *interesting* fanfic out there on the internet. And one subgenre that involves kinda werewolf-ish sexy times w gender variations is what's called "Alpha Beta Omega." And it actually got its start in the *Supernatural* fandom, though it's since spread. Andrew Dabb was not aware of this when he titled the episode with what was meant as a sort of biblical reference, but boy did fans have a field day with it.

SUPERNATURAL

CHAPTER TWELVE

How They Met Their Mother

Once again, we're back to a new season, asking "where do you go after you meet God?" As is often the case in *Supernatural*, the answer to big cosmic plot points is to go inward and really dig into character stuff. And for the most part, I think this season actually makes that work, barring a few episodes that are well… spectacularly stupid.

Season Twelve sees Andrew Dabb officially in the role of showrunner, as well as a pretty big turn over in the writing staff. But the new voices of Davy Perez, Meredith Glynn, and Steve Yockey all really get *Supernatural*, and their episodes are consistently great. But as with any time the show has reinvented itself, there are some stumbles, and the season takes a while to find a consistent tone or rhythm.

The good stuff, as noted, comes from the characters. Now that the Winchesters are in a relatively good place with one another, it's time for them to deal with their past in the form of Mary. Bringing Mary back is fascinating, and her journey with the boys' relationship to her is all about memory, nostalgia, and coming to terms with how our parents are flawed people. And that's all great.

Does this fit in with our season-long antagonists? Maybe. For most of the season, we're actually dealing with two big bads—The British Men of Letters and, once again, Lucifer. Neither of these threats work great, to be honest, but they bring in other good stuff. We also have big character stuff going on for Cas that shapes the endgame of the entire series. Even Rowena continues to grow and develop. But the story that clearly stalled last season was Crowley, and he isn't particularly well served.

So, strap in a for a fascinating new kind of show that tries a lot of things to figure out what works and, as always, carries on.

Keep Calm and Carry On

Episode 12.01. Airdate: October 12, 2016
Written by: Andrew Dabb
Directed by: Phil Sgriccia
Guest Cast: Misha Collins (Castiel), Mark Sheppard (Crowley), Samantha Smith (Mary), Elizabeth Blackmore (Lady Toni Bevell), Bronagh Waugh (Ms. Watt)
Synopsis: Dean introduces Mary Winchester to the 21st century and Ooops, the British Men of Letters are here!

Sam's getting tortured, Dean's not dead, and Mom is home and I'm pretty sure no one cleaned their rooms. From the jump, Mary Winchester is not the angelic, sweet vision that Dean has held onto. She's a complicated, strong woman, who has been yanked out of heaven and thrown 33 years into the future. Just like Dean, she's badass and incredibly traumatized! Samantha Smith does an incredible job stepping into a role she began playing 11 years before, and just this first episode is a big signal that Mary is not going to be what anyone expected.

And speaking of not meeting expectations, I don't think Sam expected to meet a heretofore-unknown-to-the-Winchesters branch of the Men of Letters, only to immediately get tortured by them. Lady Toni and Ms. Watt do not make a good first impression on the Americans, and that's going to keep us suspicious of these jerks all season. But they can't break Sam Winchester. It probably helps that he thinks Dean is dead and has nothing to lose.

Cas and Crowley are of course around too, with the former motivated by love and getting back to the Winchesters, and the latter mainly focused on hate and tracking down Lucifer. Much like last season, this episode is really just part one of a story that spans two episodes, and seeing this as a first half makes the lack of resolution less jarring.

Driver Picks the Music: The mournful use of Black Sabbath's "Solitude" over the final montage is particularly good, and it sets up a season that may be about feeling alone even when the people you love are right there.

Ship Shape: We got a great Dean and Cas hug in the previous episode, but since no one is going to their death this time, this is even better. Bonus points for Mary's *look* at her boys, and just her face as she's processing that her son may be dating an angel. Also great? Dean's look when he realizes his parents did it in the back of his car.

Mamma Mia

Episode 12.02. Airdate: October 20, 2016
Written by: Brad Buckner & Eugenie Ross-Leming
Directed by: Thomas Wright
Guest Cast: Misha Collins (Castiel), Mark Sheppard (Crowley), Samantha Smith (Mary), Ruth Connell (Rowena), Elizabeth Blackmore (Lady Toni Bevell), Adam Fergus (Mick Davies), Rick Springfield (Vince Vicente)
Synopsis: Mary, Dean and Cas continue to search for Sam, who continues to get tortured. Crowley and Rowena look for Lucifer, who has taken the body of a rock star.

Like I said, this episode is really the second part of a very long season opener that digs deeper into the plot points that were seeded in "Keep Calm and Carry On." Most specifically, how friggin' awful this all is for Mary. She's doing her best, but she's been resurrected into a bit of a nightmare scenario. Even though it means a lot to her boys that she's there to save them, we also have to think about how hard this is for her. Still, I love Sam finally getting to hug his mom! Excellent acting from Jared there.

We're far less sympathetic to the British Men of Letters, with Toni basically mind-raping Sam. We meet a good-ish guy in the form of Mick, but let's take a moment to reflect that it's sorta sexist that so far, the "evil" members were women, and the nice one is yet another white dude. At least this "Mr. Ketch" is getting set up as an evil James Bond?

The BMOL should be the good guys, yet they cause Sam a lot of pain. This is kind of foreshadowing Mary's story, because like the British Men of Letters, she's really good at her job, but coming into the Winchesters life in the middle of the story. And she's not sure what to make of it. Like Lady Toni, who's a mom and still ruthless.

And then there's the side plot with Crowley, Lucifer and Rowena which is… kind of silly and a bit boring, because we've been down this road before. At least Rowena remains incredibly entertaining.

Plot Hole: When Mary is looking at John's journal, she pulls out a picture of Bobby and others from camp Chautauqua, from when Dean visited an alternate version of 2014 in "The End." This wasn't some big clue about time travel, it just happened because it was a prop that was available. It's still something that shouldn't exist in this world.

Ship Shape: Once again, what Toni does to Sam is incredibly gross! Kudos to Mick for giving Cas his number. But back off, the angel is taken.

Famous Faces: Rick Springfield?! Yes, the kind of famous actor and singer of "Jesse's Girl" coming on as the new Lucifer was sold as a pretty big deal when the season began. But he's not as good at channeling Lucifer as Misha or Mark Pellegrino.

The Foundry

Episode 12.03. Airdate: October 27, 2016
Written by: Robert Berens
Directed by: Robert Singer
Guest Cast: Misha Collins (Castiel), Mark Sheppard (Crowley), Samantha Smith (Mary), Ruth Connell (Rowena), Rick Springfield (Lucifer)
Synopsis: Mary and her boys go on a ghost hunt. Cas and Crowley hunt Lucifer

This episode is all about the moms, who the dudes of this show need to realize are allowed to be competent, but also damaged people in their own right. First there's Rowena, who faces the man who killed her and continues to abuse her—and she manages to hurt him in ways no one else on the show ever has. That's awesome and I love that while Cas and Crowley are off playing buddy cops, Rowena is getting crap done.

Mary also shows she can handle herself, despite her sons treating her with kid gloves and forgetting that she is a person. Treating women, especially mothers, as things in service to others, and not people with complex needs, emotions, and trauma, is a problem all over and I love that *Supernatural* addresses this with Mary. She's completely justified in taking time to heal and I for one feel for her and support her.

The case of the week in an interesting mirror, because in one way it's commenting on Mary keeping the idea of that her children are gone close to her in a way that's harmful. But keeping someone close who doesn't want to be, as a replacement… that's what Sam and Dean are doing. This relationship has a lot of work ahead.

Name Game: Partridge, Cassidy, and Bonaduce are all references to the Partridge family, which is great because they aren't a real family or band, they just play one on TV. Sort of like how the Winchesters are just going through the motions. Also, I love Cas completely understanding the musician names as aliases assignment.

America Nightmare

Episode 12.04. Airdate: November 3, 2016
Written by: Davy Perez
Directed by: John Showalter
Guest Cast: Christina Carlisi (Gail Peterson), William MacDonald (Abraham Peterson), Paloma Kwiatkowski (Magda Petterson), Aliza Vellani (Beth), David Haydn-Jones (Mr. Ketch)
Synopsis: Sam and Dean investigate a psychic girl abused by her religious family.

Like the previous, this episode is all about family. And like the whole series, it's also about faith. Sometimes, family can hurt you and hold you back, especially when they have extremely strict ideas about who you should be. I'm not saying what Mary and the boys' want and need are close to the things Gail does to Magda, but it's the same idea.

I also like this episode because it's seriously gothic and scary, in a way that recalls season one. It even harkens back to when Sam was a freak kid who didn't feel like he fit in. We get a lot of Sam pathos in this episode, highlighting the dichotomy of how Dean and Sam deal with stress—Sam saves people and Dean hunts things.

It's also at this point that some of our favorite themes begin to bubble, as well as longer plot developments. "American Nightmare" also has a fully human monster which is something we're going to see a lot of. Also, we learn that the BMOL are not into nuance, and just like killing people! Neat!

Name Game: In addition to being Fathers Penn and DeNiro, the boys also go by James Morrison and Ray Manzarek, referencing member of The Doors.

The One You've Been Waiting For

Episode 12.05. Airdate: November 10, 2016
Written by: Meredith Glynn
Directed by: Nina Lopez-Corrado
Guest Cast: Allison Page (Ellie Grant), Keegan Tracey (Christoph), Gil Darnell (Nauhaus/Hitler), Adam Rose (Aaron)
Synopsis: The one where Dean kills Hitler.

For an episode about Nazi necromancers, this outing is surprisingly fun. Taking a page out of *The Producers'* book and playing Hitler for laughs strikes a lighter tone in an episode that could have been much darker. And in the context of when this episode originally aired (two days after Donald Trump was elected) it did come off much darker. But in a binge now, it works great.

This early stage of the season is shaping up to be all about not just confronting the past, but literally meeting it. Things and people aren't always the way we remember. That means that sometimes Hitler is an utter boob, but you still need to shoot him in the head. This also applies to parents, with Christoph finally breaking away from his father.

All of this, as well as Ellie's stuff about not running from problems, all comments on the boys and Mary, and how much the whole clan needs to stop looking at the past and the way things were, to face the now.

Spoiler Alert: Despite the fact that it's been visible since the pilot, this is the first ever actual mention of the grenade launcher that lives in the trunk of the Impala. It's a fun bit of foreshadowing, since we'll finally see the thing get used at the end of the season. Let's call it Chekov's grenade launcher.

Celebrating The Life of Asa Fox

Episode 12.06. Airdate: November 17, 2016
Written by: Steve Yockey
Directed by: John Badham
Guest Cast: Samantha Smith (Mary), Kim Rhodes (Jody), Lisa Berry (Billie), Kendrick Sampson (Max Banes), Kara Royster (Alicia Banes), Laurie Patton (Lorraine Fox), Mac Brandt (Bucky Sims)
Synopsis: Sam and Dean join Jody at a hunter's wake in Canada where their mom and an angry crossroads demon also show up.

I love when *Supernatural* stealthily becomes an Agatha Christie mystery, that delves into the world of hunting. And when we go deep on supporting characters, it makes a big winner for me. It's an efficient and interesting story, full of fully realized characters, that works almost like a play (not surprising given that Steve Yockey's background is in theater).

Once again, we're faced with our character's relationship to the past, whether it's guilt, or nostalgia, or anger. With the memories and truth about Asa, everyone must reckon with the story that's been told and decide how they want to retell it. Even Sam and Dean have to confront the stories people tell about them. Many stories, including Asa's death, turn out to be lies, and the demon Jael shows how lying about the past has dangerous consequences.

For Mary, she's placed in an impossible situation of coming back to life and having to live up to a story that John, Dean, and later Sam told about her. She's also depressed! Billie isn't happy with another death-defying Winchester, but Mary chooses not to die. She can't just be better, but she's a Winchester so she's not giving up on life or her family.

Fan Favorites: This episode is honestly stacked with great characters we already love, like Jody and Mary, and new awesome ones like Max and Alicia Banes. New, cool, queer, nice witches? Sign us up!

Driver Picks the Music: The montage of Asa's very Canadian hunter life is set to "Roll on Down the Highway" by Bachman-Turner Overdrive, a band who, like Asa, hailed from Manitoba. We see what you did there.

Rock Never Dies

Episode 12.07. Airdate: December 1, 2016
Written by: Robert Berens
Directed by: Eduardo Sánchez
Guest Cast: Misha Collins (Castiel), Mark Sheppard (Crowley), Rick Springfield (Lucifer), Woody Jeffreys (Tommy), Kadeem Hardison (Russell Lemons), Sandy Sidhu (Constance)
Synopsis: Lucifer decides being a rock god is better than being the other kind of god.

This one is about Lucifer feeling frustrated and directionless after God has again left the building. So it's a bit meta that this episode is a bit directionless and frustrating itself. The outing isn't bad, but it's a confusing mix of cheerfully skewering LA and super dark commentary of celebrities, so tonally it's off.

One of the issues here is that Rick Springfield just isn't up to the task of embodying Lucifer. He's fine, but he's not terrifyingly petulant the way other actors have been in the role. But hey, it's kind of fun to have our core four all in one room, working together. We get some nice Sam stuff in this episode, and I love the tall one's big hero moment holding open those doors. Sam's emotional story this season is still unclear.

Lucifer's desire for love, and love based on a flawed nostalgic idea of a person, works fine. But he also asks where you go when you let go of the past, or it lets go of you. The show takes a little while to answer this, but the answer (a new future) ultimately ends up being more satisfying. But before we get there, things have to get dumb.

Driver Picks the Music: Ladyheart's big song "Bloody Messiah" was written by one of *Supernatural*'s two composers, Jay Gruska and Robert Berens.

Ship Shape: What's the opposite of a ship? Because that's what Cas and Crowley have. Honestly at this point, Crowley's need to just connect to someone and prove he's sorta good, but still scary, is kind of sad and tired.

LOTUS

Episode 12.08. Airdate: December 8, 2016
Written by: Ben Buckner & Eugenie Ross-Leming
Directed by: Phil Sgriccia
Guest Cast: Misha Collins (Castiel), Mark Sheppard (Crowley), Ruth Connell (Rowena), David Haydn-Jones (Ketch), Courtney Ford (Kelly Klein), David Chisum (President Jefferson Rooney)
Synopsis: Lucifer possesses the president. He also gets a nice lady pregnant. There's a magic egg but that has nothing to do with the pregnancy.

Remember how *Supernatural* doesn't do so well when it takes on current events? It's why the Leviathans didn't work. Well, imagine distilling everything dumb about the Leviathans down into one episode and you get… whatever this is.

Woof, this episode. There are, as always, good moments—including Crowley sweetly exploding a man for his mother, and Sam's moment of triumph expelling Lucifer—but that doesn't make up for the ridiculousness of Lucifer possessing the president. And again, it's not like ridiculous can't work on this show. This just doesn't jive with the show's vibe. Also, it's just a bad idea and this actor isn't a particularly good Lucifer.

Plot Holes: President Satan also makes zero sense in continuity. Dean has mentioned Obama, and the show will go on to mention Trump, so *who the hell is this guy*? The only way it makes sense in cannon is if Crowley not sending Gavin back to his era altered the timeline a la Balthazar unsinking the Titanic.

Spoiler Alert: What's extra insane about this episode is that it gives birth, pun fully intended, to the defining plotline to the end run of the show—Jack. I guess they can make ridiculous work. But also, Crowley screwed with the devil and damnit, made Sam's win here meaningless. Also, the next episode is just as dumb!

Fan Favorites: We do formally meet two important characters here, one who we've heard of before (Ketch) and one who will be important going forward—Kelly. Ketch is kind of silly, like the episode, but whatever. Kelly however is great, and Courtney Ford does really well with such a strange part.

You may know Ford from her many other genre roles, including a run on *DC'S Legends of Tomorrow* with her husband, Brandon Routh. *Legends* filmed right next door to *Supernatural* in Vancouver, so Ford would pop over for lunch with her hubby. If you love *Supernatural*, check out *Legends* by the way.

First Blood

Episode 12.09. Airdate: January 26, 2017
Written by: Andrew Dabb
Directed by: Robert Singer
Guest Cast: Misha Collins (Castiel), Mark Sheppard (Crowley), Samantha Smith (Mary), Lisa Berry (Billie), Adam Fergus (Mick), David Haydn-Jones (Ketch), Stephen Lobo (Sanchez), Norman Browning (Camp)
Synopsis: The boys end up in a government black site for weeks and make a deal with Billie to get out.

This episode is hard for me. On the one hand, it sets a lot of plots moving and fixes some things, like making the BMOL less terrible, pulling Mary back into hunting, and giving Cas a huge moment. But it does it in such a weird way that makes no sense in the mythology of the show.

The thematic stuff here is… iffy as well. The Winchesters are bad asses, but they have a moral compass. Yet with hunting, the cycles of sacrifice and violence are impossible to escape. Cas tries to break it by stabbing Billie in the back, and that's big. And breaking up with fate is a huge theme for the rest of the show. But again, we didn't need a weird, shadow government plot line to do this. And for it to break the lore either? No thank you.

Plot Hole: For years, we've seen that Cas can hear the boys' prayers and even sense longing. Heck, so does Billie. So why don't they just pray to Cas and give him a clue of how to find them? There's no reason for this, other than to make Cas feel really bad. And in general his ineptitude at hunting is weird. But honestly, this storyline just doesn't make sense in this world at all.

Ship Shape: You know what's good about this episode though? The Destiel of it all. We get some quality pining, some great soulful looks, and a beautiful hug. But mainly we see how much Cas loves the Winchesters. But as usual it's focused on one Winchester in particular and Cas, feeling useless, is again ready to risk cosmic consequences. This isn't even subtext, it's just text!

Spoiler Alert: And definitely keep a look out for Cas doing other rather dumb things to redeem himself later this season. Cas will die in the exact way he killed Billie in the season finale. But don't worry, he'll be fine.

Death Notes: Billie has gone bye-bye, but something tells me she'll be fine. But her death sure is a great surprise. And we have two more Winchester deaths to add to the tally! We are now at: Dean: 19, Sam: 7, Castiel: 4. No wonder Billie hates these guys.

Lily Sunder Has Some Regrets

Episode 12.10. Airdate: February 2, 2017
Written by: Steve Yockey
Directed by: Thomas Wright
Guest Cast: Misha Collins (Castiel), Alicia Witt (Lily Sunder), Ian Tracey (Ishim)
Synopsis: A woman wronged by angels a century ago is hunting Castiel's old regiment. It turns out she's justified.

This episode is brilliant, as well as entertaining, for doing so much on so many levels. For one, though it doesn't advance any season-long arcs, it makes them matter a lot more. We learn how powerful Nephilim are and why, but we also explore how Cas is feeling. There's foreshadowing here about Kelly, but also about adoptive angelic parents and human-angel couples. The fact that Lily is entirely justified that her daughter wasn't dangerous, is going to be important. But her story tells us a lot about revenge and how (in this case) it literally saps your soul.

Mainly, this episode is about the consequences and reasons for Cas killing Billie. We explore how much Cas has changed, but as Sam and Dean note, he's not weak. He's just far more human and cares about people. He cares about the Winchesters… especially Dean.

Ship Shape: Not only are Dean and Cas a bickering married couple for most of this episode, it's literally all about angels falling in love with humans, and humans loving them back. Ishim calls it out explicitly, and we're reminded that angels don't really have gender and Cas once had a female vessel. So, if it's not clear at this point that Cas loves Dean and he's a queer character, I don't know what to tell you.

Now, does Cas think he's worthy of being with Dean? Oh no. These idiots talk past each other. And when they try to show how much they care for one another, they both misinterpret things. Beautiful, lovestruck, morons.

Regarding Dean

Episode 12.11. Airdate: February 9, 2017
Written by: Meredith Glynn
Directed by: John Badham
Guest Cast: Ruth Connell (Rowena), Tirra Dent (Catriona Loughlin), Vincent Gale (Boyd Loughlin), Bunny (Herself)
Synopsis: A witch's hex makes Dean lose his memory.

The rules by which we judge what's "award worthy" or "prestige" television are stupid, because there are many episodes of *Supernatural* that deserved Emmy awards or other accolades. And I don't think there's a better case for what an incredible actor Jensen Ackles is, than this funny, heartbreaking episode. He's so good at subtly shifting to a different, lighter Dean as he loses his memories. But the scene with just him looking into the mirror slowly losing himself is a work of art. Give him awards!

This episode in general is wonderful, thanks to its humor and a surprisingly emotional return for Rowena. Like her son, she's trying to figure out how to live when all her assumptions have been upended, and that means breaking with the past.

Both this episode and "Lily Sunder Has Some Regrets" echo a theme that's familiar at this point—the limits of memory and how the past is not always what we remember it to be. The truth of what happened is subjective, and imperfect, and it all comes down to a story we tell ourselves. That's true of the past, but if the past is not what we think it was, then this applies to the future not being what we believe it has to be. Which is exactly what's about to happen.

Spoiler Alert: At this point the production for "ScoobyNatural" was underway, and so Dean's enjoyment of *Scooby-Doo* may count as foreshadowing.

Name Game: Agents Moon and Entwhistle are a reference to The Who. Or as Dean in this episode might say, the who?

Stuck in the Middle (With You)

Episode 12.12. Airdate: February 16, 2017
Written by: Davy Perez
Directed by: Richard Speight Jr.
Guest Cast: Misha Collins (Castiel), Mark Sheppard (Crowley), Samantha Smith (Mary), Mark Pellegrino (Lucifer), David Haydn-Jones (Ketch), Jerry Trimble (Ramiel), Donavan Stinson (Wally)
Synopsis: The Winchesters go after a powerful demon and things go very wrong.

This episode is an homage to the films of Quentin Tarantino, most specifically Reservoir Dogs. But it's an awesome outing even if you don't know the films it's referencing. It's an incredible outside-the box hour, with great writing from Davy Perez and expert direction from our angelic bud, Richard Speight Jr. Seriously, it's pretty impressive to be given the task of emulating one of the most well-known directors in modern cinema, but Speight hits it out of the park here.

Again, it's all about history, stories, and our different perspectives on those things. We learn a big part of Crowley's history with his ascent to the throne of hell, and expand the mythos. We learn that Mary is hiding things from her family. And we dig further into Cas as someone who feels out of place and just wants to get a win for the family he loves so much.

Ramiel is an excellent one-off villain, and the lore on the Princes of Hell finally explains who and what Azazel was. Of course those name drops are going to matter. But the big reveal is that Crowley has Lucifer, in Nick of all people, and despite the fact he saved Cas, has betrayed the Winchesters for selfish revenge. In fact, between Mary, Crowley and Cas, the focus here is a lot of different people not in sync with Sam and Dean for various reasons.

Behind the Scenes: Dean is light in this and upcoming episodes, because Jensen's wife Danneel gave birth to their twins, Arrow and Zeppelin, during filming. In fact, the reason we don't see Dean fighting the demons early in the episode is because Jensen had to leave for the birth.

Ship Shape: Watching this episode feels a bit like getting pierced by Michael's Lance, eh? Despite Dean's performative heterosexuality in front of the hunter breakfast, he's pretty broken up that his boyfriend may be dying. And oh, that part where Cas says he loves him… and also everyone else. When this aired, despite the editing to emphasize Dean, this was seen as ambiguous but… it really wasn't.

Family Feud

Episode 12.13. Airdate: February 23, 2017
Written by: Brad Buckner & Eugenie Ross-Leming
Directed by: P.J. Pesce
Guest Cast: Mark Sheppard (Crowley), Samantha Smith (Mary), Mark Pellegrino (Lucifer), Theo Devaney (Gavin), Ruth Connell (Rowena), Courtney Ford (Kelly), David Haydn-Jones (Ketch), Ali Ahn (Dagon)
Synopsis: Gavin MacLeod must return to his destined death to stop a ghost. Mary continues to work with the British Men of Letters.

This is another episode that's doing a lot plot-wise, as Buckner and Ross-Leming episodes tend to. But it actually works here, because the disparate stories with Kelly and Mary are pretty well reflected in the main story about Gavin. That's all about parenting, but also about not belonging and why it's impossible to change the past.

Lucifer and Kelly both want to protect their son in different ways, though Lucifer is selfish. But hey, Kelly has a nice demon looking out for her now? Mary's story is more reflected in the way that she, like Gavin, doesn't belong in this world and would rather be with the person she lost, who doesn't even exist anymore.

And also, there's a big lesson here about why revenge continues to be very bad! Rowena takes her revenge on Crowley, after years of waiting, and it's painful. Which should maybe tell Crowley that him taking revenge on Lucifer is also BAD.

You'll notice that there's no mention up there of Sam and Dean, who are more witnesses than main characters, and that's fine. The show has finally expanded enough that their drama doesn't need to be central all the time.

Spoiler Alert: Ultimately, Crowley will die later this season, in another futile attempt at revenge and redemption. His scene here with Rowena is the last time mother and son see each other.

Ship Shape: Ketch seems very into Mary which is… oh god… let's not.

The Raid

Episode 12.14. Airdate: March 2, 2017
Written by: Robert Berens
Directed by: John MacCarthy
Guest Cast: Samantha Smith (Mary), Rick Worthy (Alpha Vampire), Adam Fergus (Mick), David Haydn-Jones (Ketch), Aaron Douglass (Pierce Moncrieff)
Synopsis: Mary and the British Men of Letters attempt to convince Sam and Dean they're not bad guys by getting nearly wiped out by vampires!

I love when *Supernatural* goes back to its Season One roots with a mini-movie episode. This tense hour with the British Men of Letters echoes so many horror films (including its namesake, the Indonesian film *The Raid.*) It's a fun episode that moves the plot along and gives Sam some big character moments, as well as a big bad kill.

Bringing the boys somewhat into the fold of the Men of Letters is good, because it puts Sam and Dean back in the center of the mythical arc for this season. And pleasantly, this happens in a balanced way that actually allows the guys to have a difference of opinion on something.

We also finally learn why Mary is doing this. It's great to hear her articulate that she's a mother, but that's not all she is and that she's working with the Hobbits to make a better world for her sons. She wants this, because she herself is experiencing the massive trauma of not being allowed to leave hunting. She's taking back her agency and I like that.

What works less is the British Men of Letters themselves. I don't quite get how they are so good at hunting, but also so bad at it? And I think that Mick and Ketch may have worked more organically if Adam Fergus and David Haydn-Jones had switched parts. Or if the show had just swapped their accents and coded Mick as the fancy pants nerd, with Ketch as the working-class dude.

Death Notes: It's always a bit of a bummer to see a character from the past return only for them to die, but Sam taking out the Alpha with the

Colt is epic. I love Rick Worthy in this role, and his character was so fun and scary he could have been a season-long antagonist in another world. But this is a good exit.

Ship Shape: Did Ketch just take Dean on a date? Or is he doing the "mom's new boyfriend tries to make the kid think he's cool" bit? Because either way: NOPE.

Somewhere Between Heaven and Hell

Episode 12.15. Airdate: March 9, 2017
Written by: Davy Perez
Directed by: Nina Lopez-Corrado
Guest Cast: Misha Collins (Castiel), Mark Sheppard (Crowley), Mark Pellegrino (Lucifer), Angelique Rivera (Gwen Hernandez), Nathan Mitchell (Kelvin)
Synopsis: The boys and Crowley track a hellhound. Cas continue to hunt for Kelly and ends up working with angels.

Episodes like this that are about slowly moving the plot along, building on separate stories for our core four, sometimes feel disjointed, or like not a lot happens. This episode tends in that direction. Sure, some pieces on the boards move—Cas into heaven again, the boys fully into the British Men of Letters camp, Crowley into a spot that's going to screw everyone over—but it's subtle. This makes the main plot about Lucifer's hellhound (named… Ramsey? The monster created at the beginning of time is named Ramsey???) seem almost inconsequential.

I do like that it's Sam that's in the plot and emotional driver's seat. Since mid-Season Nine, it's been almost entirely Dean doing the heavy lifting, with Sam merely reacting or supporting his brother. So it's nice to see the other Winchester as a hero again. I'm more concerned about Cas, whose insecurities and the feeling that he's not loved are driving him to keep secrets.

Keeping secrets is really the theme of this episode. It fits with the season's theme about how we lie to ourselves about the past. Here, people are all lying about the present because of their emotional baggage from the past… and it's gonna screw things up, royally. Lucifer may be his bitch right now, but Crowley really is soft on the Winchesters—and they aren't gonna like that he's betrayed them.

Ship Shape: Crowley and Dean together again, friendly exes reminiscing how they rubbed off on one another and… yeah, Dean is right, that's kinda gross! But let's look at Cas from a shippy lens. Since he let Lucifer out, he's been assured that he's family, and that Dean cares for him like a brother. But he still doesn't feel like he's worthy. Maybe because, oh, he wants something different and can't have it in his mind? That would explain some of his insecurity here.

So, Get This: The bat wrapped in barbed wire that John Winchester apparently loved is a reference to another character played by Jeffrey Dean Morgan—Negan on *The Walking Dead.* The barbwire-wrapped bat, named Lucille, is his signature weapon.

Ladies Drink Free

Episode 12.16. Airdate: March 30, 2017
Written by: Meredith Glynn
Directed by: Amyn Kaderali
Guest Cast: Kathryn Newton (Claire), Adam Fergus (Mick), Matt Visser (Justin)
Synopsis: Mick joins the boys on a werewolf hunt where they run into Claire.

This episode is a great character study for an old friend, and a new one. First off, Claire is back, continuing her growth from a damaged rebel to a hunter. I really love Claire's story, because over the course of her arc it's been about her claiming her own agency. Honestly "It's my life, I get all the votes" is a sentiment more men need to respect when it comes from women.

We also finally get to know Mick better, and he's a fancy version of the way the Winchester used to see the world—back when they thought every monster had to die. Indeed, the Brits all represent a dangerous lack of empathy—an empathy that's also lacking when it comes to Kelly and her kid. And empathy that people lack for Mary. Remember that.

Thematic stuff? The Winchesters empathy comes from them actually learning from their past. And aside from empathy, we have more reminders that lying to your family is bad. And open, honest communication about your feelings and needs is good.

Name Game: McVie, Fleetwood and Buckingham are all references to Fleetwood Mac, but Claire's alias, Beatrice Quimby is a reference to Beverley Cleary's *Ramona* books.

Driver Picks the Music: The way that "Make Me Wanna Die" but The Pretty Reckless transitions from Claire's headphones to the soundtrack is great.

The British Invasion

Episode 12.17. Airdate: April 6, 2017
Written by: brad Buckner & Eugenie Ross-Leming
Directed by: John Showalter
Guest Cast: Mark Sheppard (Crowley), Samantha Smith (Mary), Mark Pellegrino (Lucifer), Shoshannah Stern (Eileen), Adam Fergus (Mick), Courtney Ford (Kelly), David Haydn-Jones (Ketch), Ali Ahn (Dagon), Gillian Barber (Dr. Hess)
Synopsis: The Winchesters and Eileen clash with the British Men of letters over how to handle Kelly.

Shocker, the British Men of Letters are bad guys after all! There are probably better ways the show could have depicted how bad unquestioning devotion to a rigid code is than… evil Hogwarts, but I guess this gets things done. At least Eileen is back to be awesome! She's the perfect hunter ally, because rather than a random character we've never met, we know her, and we care that she's in the cross hairs.

We also have someone as the face of the BMOL with Dr. Hess, who is all kinds of horrible—almost cartoonishly so. In general, that's the problem. The Brits are such an over-the-top, clichéd version of "British" in contrast to the roughness of American hunters, that they just come off silly. Again, evil Hogwarts. Very dumb.

Also dumb, and now getting really boring, is everything to do with Crowley and Lucifer. It's just repetitive filler establishing Crowley's huge hubris. And Lucifer is dangerous and wants his kid, which we already know. Kelly is more interesting, but Dagon doesn't have much of a personality beyond looking cool. At least the BMOL storyline advanced in this episode.

Death Notes: Aw, Mick, we should have known that the moment you got interesting you were bound to die. His death certainly provides shock, and its a great showcase for another person whose point of view was changed by Sam and Dean. And those people sadly happen to die a lot. RIP.

Ship Shape: I'm gonna focus on the cuteness of Sam and Eileen to distract myself from the "oh god my eyes!" of Mary and Ketch. And hey,

I'm not judging Mary for seeing to her needs, but I wish it were with a less creepy dude! Sam and Eileen are such a great couple, because there's so much respect and warmth there. I love it. Now if only Dean's angel would answer his calls there could be a double date.

The Memory Remains

Episode 12.18. Airdate: April 13, 2017
Written by: John Bring
Directed by: Phil Sgriccia
Guest Cast: David Haydn-Jones (Ketch), Ryan McDonald (Pete Garfinkle), Steve Boyle (Sheriff Brett Bishop)
Synopsis: Just another bloodthirsty goat god in the basement.

Okay this was boring. Sure, there's stuff in here about legacy and how when you try to leave that legacy behind, someone might pull you back in. And sure, that parallels Mary's arc. But despite some okay horror moments, there's not much else. It's sort of like something from Season One, down to Dean's sudden reversion into a womanizing doofus, but with none of the depth.

The highlight moment comes at the end, proving that even a mediocre episode can leave a mark—this one literal. After Ketch and the BMOL have secretly invaded their home, the boys mark it as their own by carving their initials in the table, just like they did in the Impala as kids Symbolically, it truly becomes their other home, after Baby.

Familiar Face? Moloch is played by John DeSantis, a giant of a man who has previously appeared as Freeman Daggett in "Ghostfacers," the Golem in "Everybody Hates Hitler" and the scarecrow in "Fan Fiction."

The Future

Episode 12.19. Airdate: April 27, 2017
Written by: Robert Berens, Meredith Glynn
Directed by: Amanda Tapping
Guest Cast: Misha Collins (Castiel), Mark Pellegrino (Lucifer), Courtney Ford (Kelly), Ali Ahn (Dagon), Nathan Mitchell (Kelvin)
Synopsis: Cas returns with a plan to take out Kelly and her baby, but the baby has plans of his own which include choosing Cas as his protector.

We had to wait for it, but Cas' return is incredibly worth it. "The Future" goes deep on our favorite angel and the results are spectacular. Since Cas fell in Season Four, he's been looking for purpose and a new mission. It makes sense that he goes back to heaven, but still can't be a good soldier. And it also makes sense that he cares with all his heart about protecting the Winchesters.

For Cas, being chosen by the nephilim is a big deal. It's the first time in a long time that he's had a higher purpose. Now, Cas has made big swings in the hope of bettering the world, and it has never worked out before. But this one feels different. And the idea of a future that's different, created by someone who refuses to be bound by the toxic cycles of their parents… that's what thematic elements of the series have been pointing to for years. Cas is right to hope this kid can make it happen.

But what about everything else? I do wish that Kelly had more personality, other than loving her baby, and that Dagon was more than just a scary demon. But they're entertaining this episode. Sam and Dean, having seen faith fail firsthand are not into Cas' plan. They believe in one thing—family and trusting one another. For Dean, the fact that Cas continues not to do this, is a big affront.

Spoiler Alert: This episode is even more satisfying in hindsight, because Cas is absolutely right about the baby we'll come to know as Jack. Though it takes some time, Cas' adopted son rewrites pretty much the whole universe and proves love, hope and empathy can save the day.

Ship Shape: This episode is in the Destiel hall of fame for the mix tape scene alone. It's so raw, and intimate, and painful because these are two people who really love each other just talking past one another. Dean's love language is trust, but for Cas he shows love by doing things. So, they're both trying to say how much they care, but all they hear from the other is that they don't. It's maddening and so deliciously painful.

Also, uh, can we talk about Dean saying Cas got the colt from under his pillow and Sam not batting an eye? The moose knows.

Death Notes: There are many well-done deaths in this episode. Kelly's suicide is haunting and unsettling, Joshua's instant poofing is weirdly hysterical, and Dagon's demise is very satisfying.

Twigs & Twine & Tasha Banes

Episode 12.20. Airdate: May 4, 2017
Written by: Steve Yockey
Directed by: Richard Speight Jr.
Guest Cast: Samantha Smith (Mary), Elizabeth Blackmore (Lady Bevell), Kendrick Sampson (Max), Kara Royster (Alicia), David Haydn-Jones (Ketch), Alvina August (Tasha Banes), Lind Darlow (Witch)
Synopsis: The boys help the Banes twins search for their mother, but they're too late.

This episode serves as a final thematic rest stop, before we dive into the final run of the season, and it's rich, powerful stuff. For one, we have a mother brought back from the dead—a clear mirror to Mary—and she's everything her children want. But she's not the real Tasha Banes, and she's under the control of someone evil. Mary's fight with Ketch however, is incredible.

Like the whole series, this episode is about family and the things we'll do to stay with them. Max sells his soul to keep a version of Alicia with him, and in that we can see a mirror of how the boys might be willing to give part of themselves up. This reflects all the horrible decisions they have made to save one another. But Sam and Dean have finally moved past that point when it comes to one another.

There are some racial elements that aren't really integrated, with the witch sort of racially profiling Tasha and making her, a black woman, her doll. She comes off pretty racist—so her death is extra satisfying—but it also highlights the unfortunate fact that *Supernatural*, despite its greatness in other aspects, is a very white show.

Spoiler Alert: Perhaps the most disappointing part of this episode is that we never see Max and Alicia again, to find out where their story went.

So, Get This: Jared's third child, his daughter Odette, was born during filming, meaning that both episodes Richard Speight directed, a lead actor had a baby.

There's Something About Mary

Episode 12.21. Airdate: May 11, 2017
Written by: Brad Buckner & Eugenie Ross-Leming
Directed by: P.J. Pesce
Guest Cast: Mark Sheppard (Crowley), Samantha Smith (Mary), Mark Pellegrino (Lucifer), Shoshannah Stern (Eileen), Elizabeth Blackmore (Lady Bevell), David Haydn-Jones (Ketch), Gillian Barber (Dr. Hess)
Synopsis: The British Men of Letter brainwash Mary into turning on her sons.

This episode should be a deep exploration of Mary's character, but it takes the horribleness of the BMOL to a new, really gross level, that leaves viewers with a bitter taste in our mouths. We didn't need Eileen to die, just to prove the people we already knew were bad, were bad.

There's always been a big theme in *Supernatural* about agency, autonomy, and free will. For a Winchester, the worst thing is being controlled. Mary was a pawn of fate before she died, and then her agency was taken when she was resurrected. Working with the BMOL and hunting was meant to remove monsters, and to give her and her sons a choice. But again, it's taken in a really gross, mind-rapey way.

There's a lot of hubris in this episode. Crowley's obsession with revenge finally bites him in the ass—as we all knew it would—and of course it's not a spoiler to say that Ketch leaving the Winchesters alive is a spectacularly arrogant and stupid move.

Ship Shape: I still think Ketch and Mary sleeping together is gross, and Toni and Ketch is only slightly less gross. Sam gets a good emotional beat to mourn Eileen and, to parallel that, Dean's been angsting about Cas for a while.

Death Notes: Eileen's death is right up there with Charlie's in terms of grossness. We didn't need to see a disabled woman die to advance the story, and it's a loss for the show. Crowley's "death" as well is both expected and anti-climactic.

Who We Are

Episode 12.22. Airdate: May 18, 2017
Written by: Robert Berens
Directed by: John Showalter
Guest Cast: Samantha Smith (Mary), Kim Rhodes (Jody), Elizabeth Blackmore (Lady Bevell), David Haydn-Jones (Ketch), Gillian Barber (Dr. Hess)
Synopsis: The boys take down the British Men of Letters, with some help from friends, enemies, and the grenade launcher.

This incredible episode is the culmination of stories and character development arcs that weren't just developed all season, but that have been at the core of the show for years. Yes, Dean finally gets the use the grenade launcher!

It's silly, but in all honesty the grenade launcher is a great metaphor for the emotional catharsis of this episode. First, Sammy. Since the pilot, Sam has been running away from hunting, from his own skill and power. But this episode Sam truly and fully steps into his ability as a leader and the results are fantastic. He takes down the BMOL and earns the trust of his brother. He even forgives his mom for the mistakes she made that brought him there.

Dean's emotional moments are just as massive. For one, that whole trusting Sammy and letting him go on his own thing is huge. But he also gets to confront his mom and finally destroy the fantasy that she was blameless and perfect. She wasn't—she was just a person like Dean, who did terrible things for someone she loved. Dean and Mary are so alike in the guilt they carry, so Dean getting out his anger and expressing his forgiveness is huge.

And Mary, well, she finally gets to choose to come back and be part of her boys' life. Even though it's imperfect, it's who they are. And that's parenting—accepting you'll make mistakes and showing up to be there for your kid anyway. This is a great episode for all the Winchesters, and a really strong resolution to Mary and the Brits.

Death Notes: This episode is a bit of a blood bath and interestingly, Sam and Dean only succeed in killing flat objects. It's Mary and Jody who get to take out the real bad guys. Nice. I will say as terrible as she was, Toni's death is a bit anticlimactic. Ketch's defeat is very satisfying though.

All Along the Watchtower

Episode 12.23. Airdate: May 25, 2017
Written by: Andrew Dabb
Directed by: Robert Singer
Guest Cast: Misha Collins (Castiel), Mark Sheppard (Crowley), Samantha Smith (Mary), Jim Beaver (AU Bobby), Mark Pellegrino (Lucifer), Courtney Ford (Kelly), Alexander Calvert (Jack)
Synopsis: A lot of characters die as a new one is born, and reality rips open to a whole new world.

This episode feels like the start of a new season, rather than the conclusion of one. So much happens setting up huge stories, and literal new worlds of possibility. But many stories also come to an end, and so it works both ways.

First, the moms. Mary helps Kelly through labor and Jack is born. Kelly's goodbye to her son is heartbreaking, but they remind Mary that she still would do anything for her kids. So, Mary facing down Lucifer to save Jack and her boys is the ultimate mom move, and a big moment for her that I really like.

Then we have Crowley, whose story has been idling for seasons, finally sacrificing himself in a selfless way. It's in part out of spite, but also because he does sort of love those heaps of flannel. His ending really fits, but Castiel's sudden skewering after being so solid and faithful all episode is a big shock—one that almost broke the fandom when this episode aired.

Death Notes: This episode is quite the bloodbath, even though we see almost everyone who "dies" here again… And that's good, because no one would tolerate Rowena dying off-screen. That is except for Crowley. His final moment is good and shows that the only one who could ever beat Crowley was himself. But it's immediately undercut by Kelly's emotional end, and Cas' sudden death, which is a shame. Oh, and Cas puts another on the board for a score of: Dean: 19, Sam: 7, Castiel: 5.

Ship Shape: Please look at Dean's face when Cas dies, and tell me he didn't just lose the love of his life.

Spoiler Alert/So, Get This: But luckily like a true Winchester, Cas doesn't stay dead, and it's bringing Cas back that we come to really like and trust Jack next season. A few days after this episode aired, Jared Padalecki was discussing the just-announced "ScoobyNatural" episode at a convention and mentioned recording dialogue for it with Misha, saving the fandom a summer hiatus of worry.

SUPERNATURAL

CHAPTER THIRTEEN

Jack's Three Dads

Season Thirteen is the final soft reboot, with the addition of a new major cast member in Alexander Calvert. Jack and his story—as was foreshadowed through much of Season Twelve—will be incredibly important for the overall endgame of the series, which is finally on the horizon. Andrew Dabb has a stable cadre of writers and a plan at this point, though it can and does get adjusted.

Because Jack is Lucifer's kid, he's a perfect character to explore ideas of nature versus nurture, and how that relates to the ideas of a destiny, free will, and the toxic cycles *Supernatural* is so preoccupied with. But it also puts someone on the board with the power to change all of that.

I think it's helpful to look at the final three seasons as a trilogy, in the classic vein of *Star Wars*. The show started out with Sam as Luke Skywalker and Dean as Han Solo. But now Jack is our Luke, which makes Dean… still Han Solo. Does that make Sam Chewbacca? The look fits, but he's more like Obi Wan. It definitely makes Cas Leia, who starts this season needing rescue. This may have gotten away from me.

There's a lot in this season about grief and hope, but there's also a lot about how the Winchesters change and inspire people, because this season was also setting up the spin-off series, *Wayward Sisters*. Despite that series never happening, it still works.

Lost and Found

Episode 13.01. Airdate: October 12, 2017
Written by: Andrew Dabb
Directed by: Phil Sgriccia
Guest Cast: Misha Collins (Corpstiel), Mark Pellegrino (Lucifer), Alexander Calvert (Jack), Samantha Smith (Mary), Andrea Menard (Sheriff Christine Baker), Rob Raco (Clark), Carlena Britch (Miriam aka Fries Angel)
Synopsis: The Winchesters differ on how to deal with Jack, who mainly just wants to eat nougat and find his dad — Cas.

Following an action-packed and extremely fatal season finale, this episode is all about picking up the pieces and establishing who Jack is and whether we can trust him. And the answer, after some tense, ambiguous scenes is… yes. Jack is kind of adorable. He's like a little duckling walking around, asking "are you my dad?" Making Jack basically Castiel's orphaned son is a smart move, because he becomes a link to someone we've lost, who the Winchesters have found.

The Winchesters, of course, have vastly different ideas about who Jack is and that comes down to the old debate of nature versus nurture. Sam, ever hopeful, is on the nurture side while Dean, heartbroken and hurting, is mister nature and thus mister "kill him." The whole situation is a reflection of the series long meditations on free will.

And of course, everyone—including heaven—wants to use Jack. So perhaps using people, rather than respecting them as people, will become a theme as well, with the reveal that Lucifer may want to use Mary. We'll see.

Fan Favorite: Though we saw him very briefly at the end of "All Along the Watchtower," we really meet Jack here, and his utter cuteness and sincerity is a surprising choice. Calvert was best known at this point for a role on *Arrow,* where he played the villain Anarky who ironically killed the parents of a character later played by Courtney Ford.

Ship Shape: This episode is honestly incredible for the way it focuses specifically on Dean's grief over Cas. His prayer to Chuck is a rip-your-heart-out scene, and Dean barely holding it together as he prepares Cas' body makes it pretty clear that he lost someone he loved without getting to tell them how much…

The Rising Son

Episode 13.02. Airdate: October 19, 2017
Written by: Brad Buckner & Eugenie Ross-Leming
Directed by: Thomas Wright
Guest Cast: Mark Pellegrino (Lucifer), Alexander Calvert (Jack), Samantha Smith (Mary), Keith Szarabajka (Donatello Redfield), Jeffrey Vincent Parise (Asmodeus), Christian Keyes (Michael)
Synopsis: Prince of hell Asmodeus takes a turn leading the demons and trying to nab Jack. Mary and Lucifer meet apocalypse world Michael.

If the season premiere was an elegiac meditation on grief, and a careful introduction into Jack as a character, this serves to get lots of plot balls rolling again. We have not one but three antagonists vying for attention—Lucifer, Michael and Evil Colonel Sanders, aka Asmodeus. They're all pretty intimidating, and Asmodeus' powers are impressive, but the good stuff still comes from the characters and how they relate.

Donatello returns—soulless but still entertaining—to outright articulate the nature vs. nurture argument, reminding us that part of Jack's nature is that he's both God's grandson, and the child of the ultimate rebel. So maybe it's in his nature to be nurtured to make his own choice? That's undecided, but he does seem to have imprinted on Sam and Dean as his family.

But I also love how much Sam wants to protect Jack and help him be good. After all, Sam was told for most of his life that he was a monster, and that he would be evil as Lucifer's tool. Dean doesn't have that POV—he just sees Jack as the reason a lot of people he loves are dead. But these two men are going to shape Jack.

Lucifer and Mary's story in the alternate universe also reflects on the power of choice. This is a world where Mary never made the choice to save John, so Sam and Dean were never born.

Fan Favorite? We finally meet Asmodeus, though he joins the Eileen Leahy club of characters whose names are, for some reason, pronounced differently the second episode it's mentioned. Jeffrey Vincent Parise is doing the most as this character, which makes him maybe less scary but at least he's fun to watch.

So, Get This: Jack opens the Bible to the song of Solomon, a biblical figure who controlled and trapped demons according to near-East lore (remember Sam finding The Lesser Key of Solomon way back in Season One?). One of the most powerful demons he controlled was Asmodeus.

Patience

Episode 13.03. Airdate: October 26, 2017
Written by: Robert Berens
Directed by: Robert Singer
Guest Cast: Misha Collins (Castiel), Alexander Calvert (Jack), Loretta Divine (Missouri), Kim Rhodes (Jody), Clark Backo (Patience Turner), Adrian Holmes (James Turner)
Synopsis: Dean leaves for a case involving Missouri Moseley and her granddaughter.

"Patience" has a dual task at this point in the season, one of which is no longer relevant on a binge watch. Patience as a character was added so she could become part of Wayward Sister. Unlike with Bloodlines—which introduced a bunch of new characters no one cared about—the producers introduced new characters early. Patience is smart and interested in her power, and we have more to explore from her. She and Missouri also function as narrative mirrors for Jack.

Just like James can't forgive his psychic mom for not saving his wife, Dean can't forgive Jack for not saving Cas. But James is wrong about not trusting his mom and Patience, and so is Dean about Jack. It's also important that Jody empowers Patience.

Sam wants Jack to have a choice as well, and to make the right one. It's because of Sam's history that he cares about Jack, or at least empathizes with him—and having empathy and believing that people can be good, or make good choices, is a key theme.

Ship Shape: Dean's broken up over losing his mom again, that's true. But he specifically can't get over losing Cas, which makes it hard for him to connect to Cas' kid. So once again, gay love pierces through the veil of death to save the day.

Spoiler Alert: Whatever you do, don't think about how an outburst of love from Dean leads to Cas ultimately escaping the Empty, and how a declaration of love for Dean eventually sends him back. And then Jack saves him again and for good!

The Big Empty

Episode 13.04. Airdate: November 2, 2017
Written by: Meredith Glynn
Directed by: John Badham
Guest Cast: Misha Collins (Castiel/The Cosmic Entity), Alexander Calvert (Jack), Courtney Ford ("Kelly"), Rukiya Bernard (Mia Valens)
Synopsis: Time for therapy with a shapeshifter. Also, Castiel annoys his way to resurrection.

I always love when *Supernatural* pauses for a bit of therapy, because Chuck knows all these damaged guys need some sort of catharsis—and that's what they get. Jack gets the most literal version by finally saying hello and goodbye to his mom in a really beautiful and moving scene. The added layer that is Mia—a monster trying to be good—telling Jack that he can be good if he chooses to be makes it extra great.

For Sam, he finally gets the release of just telling Dean how he feels about Mary. He really didn't have a deep relationship with her, and that sucks for him! Dean gets his real feelings out too, confessing that he's finally lost faith. Even with his brother beside him, they've grown past their co-dependency. And he's lost.

But luckily, not for long because Cas is back! And Cas gets out of the empty through, yes, catharsis. He finally rejects the idea that he's a failure and somehow not good enough. He's awake, because his faith wasn't misplaced, so he saves himself! And gets a much nicer coat for his trouble!

Ship Shape: Oh, you know who Cas loved, Cosmic Entity? Do tell. We have some guesses.

Advanced Thanatology

Episode 13.05. Airdate: November 9, 2017
Written by: Steve Yockey
Directed by: John Showalter
Guest Cast: Misha Collins (Castiel), Lisa Berry (Billie), Seth Isaac Johnson (Shawn Raider). Kayla Stanton (Jessica the Reaper)
Synopsis: A simple haunting case leads to a meeting with the new death: Billie.

This episode closes out Dean's arc of grief and loss of faith, but not before revealing how far Dean has fallen. It's dark stuff, especially for Dean who's always fought through before. There's humor in Sam trying to cheer him up, but Dean doesn't need hedonism keeping up his mask of toxic masculinity—he needs hope.

Hope means different things to different people. Sam has always been the big picture Winchester and so, because he has Jack and wants to keep saving people, he's doing okay. But Dean's hunting of things comes from a place of love, and a desire to protect. And without Cas and Mary, a big part of that motivation is now gone. The evil plague doctor is great, but I love that this episode takes a left turn in the final third to become a sort of play contemplating the nature of fate and the universe.

Dean needs a win and Cas is that. Cas coming into his life, be it in "Lazarus Rising," "Lucifer Rising" or "The Born-Again Identity," at the right moment has always been something to give Dean a boost of faith. He's defined by his family.

Driver Picks the Music: The use of Steppenwolf's "Never too Late to Start All Over Again" is really perfect for the final scenes. And that moment where Dean realizes it's Cas, and the light illuminates his face? Amazing.

Death Notes: I loved Julian Richings as Death, but this is a great way to expand the mythology and bring back the spectacular Lisa Berry. Also, I guess this means we can put another on the board for Dean. Dean: 20, Sam: 7, Castiel: 5.

Tombstone

Episode 13.06. Airdate: November 16, 2017
Written by: Davy Perez
Directed by: Nina Lopez-Corrado
Guest Cast: Misha Collins (Castiel), Alexander Calvert (Jack), Sarah Troyer (Athena Lopez), Eric Schweig (Sarge), Johnathan Cherry (Dave Mather/Ghoul)
Synopsis: Sam, Dean, Cas, and Jack play cowboy.

This episode is so fun and, much like "Hunteri Heroici" it makes me wish the whole show was the extended family solving cases. It's a shame that having everyone together and alive was something we only get once in a blue moon. These cases with all hands-on deck are so fun, and I love seeing Jack and Cas on a hunt.

The monster plot here is an interesting, distorted mirror of the family plot. Fake Dave is a toxic boyfriend, holding back the person he supposedly loves. We see that as a mirror for how Jack sees himself, but also as the toxic ideas in Jack's head.

Jack has already internalized a lot of the BS that was thrown at him, which is sad. It's really nice to see Dean come around and say he was wrong for how he treated Jack too. Of course, Dean is riding high for most of the episode because he finally got his win, and got to do some cosplay.

Ship Shape: I just love that after an emotional reunion, Dean and Cas are right back to being married, complete with references to movies nights and the fact that Cas knows Dean's an angry sleeper.

Driver Picks the Music: "Space Cowboy" by the Steve Miller band playing over Dean and Castiel's slow motion walk is a thing of beauty.

Name Game: All the aliases are actor's names from the movie *Tombstone*.

Plot Hole: In Season Nine, Gadreel healed several people like Cas and Charlie who were "dead" so it's weird that Cas can't heal the guard.

War of the Worlds

Episode 13.07. Airdate: November 23, 2017
Written by: Brad Buckner & Eugenie Ross-Leming
Directed by: Richard Speight Jr.
Guest Cast: Misha Collins (Castiel), Mark Pellegrino (Lucifer), Osric Chau (AU Kevin), David Haydn-Jones (Ketch), Jeffrey Vincent Parise (Asmodeus), Christian Keyes (AU Michael), Erica Cerra (Duma)
Synopsis: Lucifer returns to the regular world. Ketch pretends to be his own evil twin.

So many *things* happen in this episode, yet the plot really doesn't move much. And to add to that, there are hints at redemption arcs for Ketch and Lucifer, which… yikes. At least the evil twin thing turns out to be a canard, or the levels of dumb would be too high.

There are some fun scenes, for sure. I think Cas and Lucifer talking about Jack is interesting at least, and as is standard for Season Thirteen so far, the action scenes are really incredible. And hey, it's nice to see Osric Chau back, even in a wigged-out form!

But there's not a lot of character development—at least for anyone we care about. Meeting someone we know in the AU, as well as Lucifer and Ketch maybe changing, bring up some of the nature versus nurture theme. But what this hour really does is put Lucifer and Cas on ice so they can be absent for a while, putting Michael and Asmodeus on deck as big bads.

Spoiler Alert: Asmodeus taking down Cas and Lucifer, and his rather angelic powers that include disguises and trickery, make much more sense when you know that his "collection" also includes Gabriel.

The Scorpion and the Frog

Episode 13.08. Airdate: November 30, 2017
Written by: Meredith Glynn
Directed by: Robert Singer
Guest Cast: David Cubitt (Barthamus), Richard Brake (Luther Shrike), Christie Burk (Smash), Matthew Kevin Anderson (Grab)
Synopsis: A demon enlists Sam and Dean into a heist in exchange for a spell to track a nephilim.

The point of this episode is all in the name, referencing the old parable of the scorpion that stings a frog after getting a lift across a river. It does this because that's what's in its nature, and this season so far is all about Jack's struggle with that. But what about Sam and Dean? What are their natures? Or a demon's? The boys have worked with demons before and been stung, but demons have also helped them. Crowley died for them!

Though Barthamus ends up a scorpion, it's worth remembering that not everyone is. Shrike is wrong about the Winchesters, and that's true of Smash as well. The key is finding the line between when the ends justify the means and when it all goes south.

Trivia/Familiar Face: The reference to *Game of Thrones* and Shrike liking the books is a meta nod to the fact that Richard Brake played *The Night's King* in the television series—a character that doesn't exist in the *Song of Ice and Fire* books.

The Bad Place

Episode 13.09. Airdate: December 7, 2017
Written by: Robert Berens
Directed by: Phil Sgriccia
Guest Cast: Alexander Calvert (Jack), Samantha Smith (Mary), Kim Rhodes (Jody), Clark Backo (Patience), Adrian Holmes (James), Yadira Guevara-Prip (Kaia Nieves)
Synopsis: The boys find Jack, who is seeking out dream walkers like Kaia Nieves

This episode was doing double duty when it aired, as it was a mid-season finale moving the plot along, as well as a set up for the *Wayward Sisters* backdoor pilot. Since that series sadly didn't happen, we're just left with it as a regular episode of *Supernatural*. That's fine though, because it still works.

For one, the action is great and the final scene of the angels assaulting that amazing, abandoned boat is incredible. But we also get important character stuff that resonates with the overall questions of the season. Jack wants to be good, but it's easy for people to decide he's evil or just a tool. Kaia wants to be normal, but she has to decide how she'll use her gift. And all of this seems to point in the direction that the whole series leans—that it's our choices that define us, not our nature.

But other things affect choices too, like guilt and anger, and a touch of toxic masculinity. Which is exactly what happens when Dean makes the shocking choice to force Kaia to help them at gunpoint. He's always been aggressive and angry, but this is a really extreme example and certainly not a heroic moment.

Plot Hole: Kaia references "Trump's America" which doesn't make sense, given that Jefferson Rooney was supposedly the President the year before. I stand by my theory that Gavin returning put us back in a world where Trump exists. Thanks for *that*.

So, Get This: The scenes in this episode and the next on that abandoned ferry were filmed on a real abandoned ferry awaiting demolition, the Queen of Sydney.

Wayward Sisters

Episode 13.10. Airdate: January 18, 2018
Written by: Robert Berens & Andrew Dabb
Directed by: Phil Sgriccia
Guest Cast: Kim Rhodes (Jody), Briana Buckmaster (Donna Hanscum), Katherine Ramdeen (Alex), Kathryn Newton (Claire), Clark Backo (Patience), Yadira Guevara-Prip (Kaia)
Synopsis: Claire reunites with Jody and Alex, and along with Patience, Donna and Kaia, they save Sam and Dean from The Bad Place.

Watching this episode within a binge, and with the hindsight of knowing that the series *Wayward Sisters* was not picked up by the CW, is a bittersweet experience. It's a great pilot that I still think would have made a great spin-off. It didn't happen for reasons, but what we have is a really incredible story about a group of diverse women who get the work done and save the day.

We see Claire coming into her own as a hero, and even though this was meant as a pilot, it's a fitting end to her story on *Supernatural*. She's finally become a true hunter and hero. Scared by loss, she's also been shaped by her chosen family. We see that Sam and Dean's most important legacy continues to be the people they saved and inspired.

This is also a big emotional episode for Jody, where we see how brave she is—not for killing monsters, but for loving again. She takes on all her Wayward Daughters (which should have been the name of the show) despite the risk of losing them, and that's incredible.

Spoiler Alert: Because there was no series pickup, we actually don't see Claire, Alex, or Patience ever again. Though we'll hear Alex's voice. That's a shame, because Patience's story had lots of potential. We find out how things end up for Claire, but since Kathryn Newton left to conquer Hollywood after this, we don't see that on screen. Luckily, dark Kaia proves important and the some of the big stories that would have been used on Wayward do get their due.

Ship Shape: I love Kaia and Claire together. The connect in such a sweet way, and it's lovely to see two prickly characters be vulnerable with one another. That does make it hurt more when Kaia seemingly gets killed, but it works as an inciting incident for Claire.

Drive Picks the Music: The recap set to "I Am the Fire" by Haelstrom may actually be one of my favorite parts of the episode for the sheer levels of awesome.

Breakdown

Episode 13.11. Airdate: January 25, 2018
Written by: Davy Perez
Directed by: Amyn Kaderali
Guest Cast: Briana Buckmaster (Donna), Brendan Taylor (Doug), Chris William Martin (Agent Clegg), Sarah Dugdale (Wendy Hanscum)
Synopsis: Donna calls in the Winchesters for help when her niece goes missing.

After "Wayward Sisters," there was still some work to do on the core characters, so this episode was doing some work on Donna who had been mostly sunshine and rainbows until now. In that way, it succeeds, and Briana Buckmaster does great work bringing more depth to the character. But the mystery and big reveal is seriously dark, even for this show. A dark web body parts auction and implications of child abuse by a preacher? Just too much.

It's also really sad for Donna to lose Doug—not to violence, but to the inevitability of people that hunters love getting killed. We've gone from a debate of nature versus nurture with Jack, to the consequences of that choice, and weighing the costs and benefits of hunting. On the one side is the people who get saved, and on the other is the dozens of friends, lovers, and family that didn't make it.

It's interesting to see this kind of dark thinking coming from Sam at this point, but it makes sense. Everyone he's loved or cared for has been ripped away from him by hunting—even people in the life like Eileen and Mary. Dean's doing better at this point since getting Cas back (of course, no one knows Cas was imprisoned by a demon.)

So, Get This: The original concept for this episode was called "Midnight Train" but known among the production as "Stakes on a Train." It was supposed to be a vampire hunt contained on a moving train, but it was too complicated and expensive to produce. Alas, that would have been awesome.

Plot Hole: This idea that there are hundreds of thousands of monsters out there has been played with, and hinted at, since Season Six. Even explored in "Bloodlines" but the show forgets it all the time and that's good, because it makes what the Winchesters do seem utterly pointless.

Various & Sundry Villains

Episode 13.12. Airdate: February 1, 2018
Written by: Steve Yockey
Directed by: Amanda Tapping
Guest Cast: Misha Collins (Castiel), Mark Pellegrino (Lucifer), Ruth Connell (Rowena), Elsie Gatien (Jennie Plum), Jordan Claire Robins (Jamie Plum)
Synopsis: Witches enchant Dean, all part of Rowena's plan to get the book and unchain her power. Meanwhile, Lucifer and Cas escape Asmodeus' prison.

Surprising no one, our favorite witch is back and oh it's so lovely to see her, having evolved as a character from a witch who would causally kill the Winchesters to one who uses spells to save them. It's a big arc marked by trauma, but also love and growth. I love seeing Rowena and Sam open up to each other, and Sam confessing he doesn't know how to make it through. It's up to Dean in the end to remind Sam that he should have faith in them, and Rowena gets to have faith in herself.

With the Wayward girls, and now Rowena, we're seeing a different angle of the nature vs. nurture debate. All these people who are coming into their own as heroes are doing it because of the Winchesters. Jamie and Jenny aren't mirrors to Sam and Dean who need their mom to guide them—they're mirrors to who the boys used to be, before they became the guides.

This is sort of echoed with Cas and Lucifer, with Lucifer's rage coming from the fact that the Winchesters of all people have nurtured his son into a hero. It's a bit weird seeing Lucifer be kind of funny and sympathetic, while at the same time Sam and Rowena reminisce about how terrible he is.

Ship Shape: Alas, the Winchester luck with the ladies continues to be miserable. Dean just needs to stop with ladies in general maybe. And I do wonder what fifth base is.

Devil's Bargain

Episode 13.13. Airdate: February 8, 2018
Written by: Brad Buckner & Eugenie Ross-Leming
Directed by: Eduardo Sánchez
Guest Cast: Misha Collins (Castiel), Mark Pellegrino (Lucifer), Richard Speight Jr. (Gabriel), Keith Szarabajka (Donatello Redfield), David Haydn-Jones (Ketch), Jeffrey Vincent Parise (Asmodeus), Danneel Ackles (Jo/Anael)
Synopsis: Lucifer manages to survive again with the help of an ambitious angel.

Here we are, once again looking at how humanity and circumstances affect people differently. This time it's with Lucifer as the focus. Surprising no one, he's terrible. Lucifer really is just the worst. He's the personification of toxic masculinity, defining himself by violence and daddy issues. At least Jo is smart enough to manipulate him.

That also means, in a grander scheme, that Cas is the opposite of toxicity. He's defined by how much he cares. And that's interesting to think about in terms of how Jo, and Lucifer, and other angels have talked about angels not feeling things. We know Cas feels things, and that other angels maybe can too, so I think grace just dampens emotion.

Sam and Dean are just sort of along for the ride here, as well as an absolute embarrassment of other morally dubious white guys: Ketch, Donatello, Asmodeus and now even Gabriel! At least that's an exciting reveal!

Fan Favorite: Danneel Ackles, who plays Jo, is Jensen's wife. She joked years before this when it seemed like an absurd timeline that she would guest on her hubby's series in Season Thirteen. When she told Jensen early in the season that she actually would like to guest, the character of Jo was created for her.

Spoiler Alert: This episode either emphasizes or sets up big plot things that we assume will be important: Lucifer as king of heaven, angels going extinct, Ketch doing literally anything not annoying. And most of that fizzles out before it can matter.

Good Intentions

Episode 13.14. Airdate: March 1, 2018
Written by: Meredith Glynn
Directed by: P.J. Pesce
Guest Cast: Misha Collins (Castiel), Alexander Calvert (Jack), Jim Beaver (AU Bobby), Samantha Smith (Mary), Keith Szarabajka (Donatello Redfield), Christian Keyes (AU Michael), Chad Rook (AU Balthazar)
Synopsis: In our world, the demon tablet drives Donatello to madness and in apocalypse world Jack proves himself to Mary and the few humans who remain.

So, at this point in the season, we're not just looking at how a person becomes good or bad, but how that manifests, and how we judge decisions on that same paradigm. Do good intentions matter if people get hurt? What if people get hurt with any decision, how to we decide which to make? It's sort of like the trolley problem, but with giants made of sand who think Cas is pretty.

First, let's look at Jack and Mary. Mary learns that the decision she regretted the most—her demon deal to save John—actually saved the world. She made that decision out of love. Jack is able to prove it's not just his intentions that are good, but that he is, because he can't just abandon people in need. He chooses to be a hero.

In the normal world, it's not Sam and Dean's decisions we're focused on. Donatello has no soul, so he can't even have good intentions, or act from love. It's Cas that makes the scary decision to strip Donatello's mind. It's brutal, but it's the right choice as it will ultimately save the people he loves. This episode is good stuff.

Ship Shape: This episode is all about that love. Note that Cas doesn't go ballistic on Donatello until he tries to kill Dean. And also, Dean and Cas vs. Gog and Magog is the most married fight ever. Though Dean really needs to communicate with his husband.

Another great ship that blossoms this episode? AU Bobby and Mary! It's so obvious the old hunter has eyes for Mary, and I just love them as a pair.

A Most Holy Man

Episode 13.15. Airdate: March 8, 2018
Written by: Robert Singer & Andrew Dabb
Directed by: Amanda Tapping
Guest Cast: Massi Furlan (Luca Camilleri), Lean Lapp (Margaret Astor), Al Sapienza (Santino Scarpatti), Dominic Burgess (Richard Greenstreet), Fulvio Cecere (Cromarty)
Synopsis: Dean and Sam must engage in some noir chancery with the stolen skull of St. Peter in order to get a spell ingredient to open the interdimensional door.

There are many episodes where *Supernatural* plays with other genres. Heck, the episode after this is the most ambitious departure in the show's history. This episode in particular is an experiment in film noir, and if you've seen *The Maltese Falcon* or other films of that genre, this sort of works. If you haven't… well, it comes off as a bit odd.

I don't dislike this episode, truly. The guest cast is having so much fun, as were the crew, composers and writers emulating the styles of old Hollywood. And Dean and Sam have an interesting journey that serves as a moral wake-up call. They've become so accustomed to "doing whatever it takes," that they might be indistinguishable from the bad guys. Luca reminds them of what it means to live a moral life, and why it's important to keep trying to do real good.

I really like this, and Luca as a vehicle to remind the Winchesters who they are. It resets Sam back on the path he found at the end of Season Twelve—one of leadership and trying to build a new future without monsters.

Name Game: The characters of Margaret Astor and Richard Greenstreet are named after two famous noir stars who co-starred in *The Maltese Falcon*, Mary Astor, and Sydney Greenstreet.

Famous Faces: If you've watched any genre TV you'll recognize Dominic Burgess, who has been in everything from *The Good Place* to *The Magicians.*

ScoobyNatural

Episode 13.16. Airdate: March 29, 2018
Written by: Jim Krieg & Jeremy Adams
Directed by: Robert Singer
Guest Cast: Misha Collins (Castiel), Frank Welker (Fred/Scooby-Doo), Grey Griffin (Daphne), Matthew Lillard (Shaggy), Kate Micucci (Velma)
Synopsis: Ruh roh.

What other show could pull off an episode like this? Honestly, this hour of television is a true miracle because it's so bonkers and ambitious, yet it works so well. Of course, Dean, Sam and Cas get stuck in an episode of Scooby-Doo. The fact that this makes sense at all is a testament to the wildness and creativity of *Supernatural*, and the results are so fun and so worth it.

Because this script was written by independent writers long before Season Thirteen started filming, this is a true standalone. And you can kind of tell, because as funny as Dean lusting after Daphne is, it's also a pretty simplified surface reading of his character. Cas also reads more like Season Five Cas. But those are quibbles. What this episode truly is, is an incredibly meta take…on Scooby-Doo.

Honestly, the Scooby Gang having a full-on existential crisis when confronted with the actual existence of the supernatural is the funniest thing (along with Dean eating the mega sandwiches with Scooby and Shaggy). Seriously, Daphne, what did you do that you're that worried about going to hell?! It's so brilliant. So, cheers to one of the most incredible episodes of the series that seriously is in a category all its own.

So, Get This: With the dismembered body, this may be the goriest episode of *Supernatural*… all the gore just happens to be animated.

The Thing

Episode 13.17. Airdate: February 8, 2018
Written by: Davy Perez
Directed by: John Showalter
Guest Cast: Richard Speight Jr. (Gabriel), David Haydn-Jones (Ketch), Jeffrey Vincent Parise (Asmodeus), Magda Apanowicz (Sandy/Yokoth), Tiffany Smith (Ophelia Avila), Large Tentacle Elder God (Himself)
Synopsis: There's bondage and tentacles but somehow, it's not porn.

We're back to our regularly scheduled programming and it's time for more Winchesters almost breaking the world. At this point, the boys accidentally releasing an eldritch terror on a fetch quest is the least surprising thing. And honestly, as fun as Dean vs tentacles and the sassy waitress are, I think the monster stuff this week is slightly boring. Not bad, just not exciting, since we the audience know this will all be fine.

What is interesting is, and you know I hate to say this, Ketch growing a conscience to defy Asmodeus and free Gabriel. It makes sense thematically within the season, which is all about being good or bad, and the role choice plays in that. Ketch chooses to turn on the bad guy, and that's great. He does it in part out of compassion for Gabriel, but also because he doesn't like being called out as just a killer.

But once again we don't have much to say about Dean and Sam on their emotional journey. They're generally through their grief and just focused on getting things fixed. But then, of course, there will be another mess to clean up.

Ship Shape: I mean, I'm not *not* into Dean and the tentacles. But mainly this episode makes me ship Asmodeus with a slow, painful death.

Bring 'em Back Alive

Episode 13.18. Airdate: April 12, 2018
Written by: Brad Buckner & Eugenie Ross-Leming
Directed by: Amyn Kaderali
Guest Cast: Misha Collins (Castiel), Mark Pellegrino (Lucifer), Richard Speight Jr. (Gabriel), Felicia Day (AU Charlie), David Haydn-Jones (Ketch), Jeffrey Vincent Parise (Asmodeus), Danneel Ackles (Jo)
Synopsis: Dean and Ketch enter Thunderdome to save Mary and Jack but end up saving the apocalypse world's Charlie instead. Cas and Sam help Gabriel heal.

There are three very different stories happening in this episode, which is pretty standard for Buckner and Ross-Leming—but this one doesn't actually feel too crowded. In fact, it's pretty balanced and everything tonally informs everything else. It's about three men getting offered chances to rewrite their stories, or at least write different endings… and only two of them choose to do so. Well, maybe one and a half.

First, we've got Ketch, who moves along his redemption arc in snarky fits, but he really does seem to have been changed by proximity to the Winchesters. And Dean's dogged determination to fix everything is inspiring, so good on Scary Poppins for that.

Just as Dean must confront his trauma and mistakes in the form of Charlie, Gabriel takes center stage, working through his failures. It's tough, but man do I love Sam Winchester coming through with his big heart to get through to Gabe. I love seeing our favorite Trickster standing up and Kentucky frying Asmodeus.

Gabriel bolts though, at least he tries. Lucifer is a contrast to these guys because he sucks, and despite his whining about daddy, is the author of his own suckitude. It turns out we're not getting a Lucifer redemption arc—we're contrasting his complete inability to grow with other characters, setting him up not only as a final boss, but one based on the themes of this whole season: a man who is evil because of his choices *and* his inability to hold himself accountable for them.

Ship Shape: I do not care how much hurt and comfort you throw at me, show. I'm not shipping Dean and Ketch. Especially when Dean's worried husband, who was not informed of Dean's trip to another reality, is right there. I'm way more into Sam and Gabriel—a pairing that's actually quite popular in fandom. Also, bless Jo for dumping Lucifer's sorry ass and delivering an epic, blistering takedown. You know she and Dean might have some chemistry…

Funeralia

Episode 13.19. Airdate: April 19, 2018
Written by: Steve Yockey
Directed by: Nina Lopez-Corrado
Guest Cast: Misha Collins (Castiel), Amanda Tapping (Naomi), Ruth Connell (Rowena), Lisa Berry (Billie), Kayla Stanton (Jessica)
Synopsis: Rowena starts killing reapers (and also bad people) to get Death's attention in order to bring back Crowley. Cas confronts an abuser.

The season's big examination of morality and free will continues with an incredible episode, giving us Rowena at her most powerful and most vulnerable. As a character that was introduced as a villain, Rowena finally breaks out of those constraints for good. Her exposure to the Winchesters has truly changed her, and made her not only a better person, but a woman who mourns the son she loved too late. It's an incredible journey and Ruth Connell nails every delicious minute of it.

This episode sees Rowena, Billie and Jessica all talking about how choices shape our fate. It's one of those questions of free will versus determinism that's defined *Supernatural*—do we have a choice in anything? Do we have a choice in who we are? The answer is yes… but it's complicated. Because other people have choices too, and their actions and consequences define others' lives. Crowley chose his path, but Rowena was part of it.

Billie's speech to Rowena is fantastic, and it's something Sam also needed to hear. Sometimes, bad things are just bad, and we can't stop them. What matters is what you do after them. And on this show, that's what makes a hero. Rowena makes the choice to use her power for good, proving that even the deadliest witch can change.

There's a lot of other things to love here, and shout out specifically to Reaper Jessica, who is red headed, hangs out in Portland, and spends most of her time watching the Winchesters. I feel a personal connection to her for some reason.

Spoiler Alert: What works way less is the Cas in heaven stuff. Not only do I hate Cas not getting closure with his abuser, Naomi, but this "heaven is dying and there's gonna be a ghost apocalypse" story never really goes much of anywhere.

Ship Shape: I respect Rowena for acquiring a highly trained and devoted henchman in Bernard, but this episode is all about Sam and Rowena. I love their relationship and the connection they have over magic and trauma. Sam being fated to kill her adds a whole layer of deliciousness to it.

So, Get This: Writer Steve Yockey must really love the word "Funeralia" because he used it as a title for an episode of his own series, *The Flight Attendant* which debuted in 2020. It's a great show, check it out.

Unfinished Business

Episode 13.20. Airdate: April 26, 2018
Written by: Meredith Glynn
Directed by: Richard Speight Jr.
Guest Cast: Alexander Calvert (Jack), Samantha Smith (Mary), Richard Speight Jr. (Gabriel/Loki), Osric Chau (AU Kevin)
Synopsis: Gabriel seeks revenge on Loki and his sons—who sold him to Asmodeus.

This episode is a masterpiece from two artists working at their peak—Richard Speight Jr. and episode scribe Meredith Glynn. Not only is it fun, action-packed, and emotional, but it also weaves together thematic threads from pretty much the whole series! And Richard directed himself, fighting himself! That's amazing!

As you know by now from reading this book, *Supernatural* is about a lot of things: destiny, cycles of violence and how to end them, and what it means to be a good person. And all of these things come from family. Because it's family—the relationships to the people we love—that inform everything. Gabriel, like Sam and Dean, is defined by a bad relationship with his family. And that spun into a cycle of violence when he met Loki and merged with their family. Those cycles and choices seem to create destiny, but we can break them.

Gabriel gets his revenge, but it's in making the sincere choice to move on and help the world that he really breaks his cycle. Jack still has to learn this, because for this episode he's acting from a hubristic place in going blindly after Michael.

Sam and Dean play important roles here as they're now the ones who have mostly learned how pointless revenge is, and that this merry-go-round of apocalypses needs to end. Sam knows what it's like to confront trauma—he's had to continually do it with Lucifer. Will he break his cycle? And will Dean ever stop being willing to die?

Spoiler Alert: Absolutely not.

Beat The Devil

Episode 13.21. Airdate: May 3, 2018
Written by: Robert Berens
Directed by: Phil Sgriccia
Guest Cast: Misha Collins (Castiel), Mark Pellegrino (Lucifer), Alexander Calvert (Jack), Samantha Smith (Mary), Richard Speight Jr. (Gabriel), Ruth Connell (Rowena)
Synopsis: The team heads to Apocalypse world to save Mary and Jack, and even manage to trap Lucifer to do it. It all goes well until it goes terribly wrong and Sam dies. Again.

This episode has everything from dick jokes to horrific deaths, and somehow it all works. There's a lot of triumphant moments—including Rowena and Gabe hooking up to take down Lucifer—and some great humor, like the boys reacting to Rowena and Gabe.

Though it's not a big episode for him, it's good to see Cas back in the game and trying to sell Gabe on heaven, which is obviously foreshadowing bad things for the archangel. Sigh. But there's also a lot of foreshadowing about how happy and optimistic Sam is… so of course he dies!

Sam and Dean's inability to let the other stay dead has caused most of the apocalypses on this show, so it's actually character development for Dean to leave that tunnel and let Sam stay dead even for a minute. That's a slight breaking of a cycle… but the big one comes with Sam owing his life to Lucifer. Even though he's failed at everything, Lucifer is still looking for that redemption via a relationship with Jack.

Ship Shape: Gabriel and Rowena make so much sense and I sorta love it? They'd both be down for a threesome with Sam too, so go for it dudes.

Death Notes: Of the many, many Winchester deaths, this one is maybe the most shocking and probably the goriest since Dean got chomped on by hell hounds. Now, if Sam died in apocalypse world, did he go to apocalypse world heaven? Or hell? Any how, the score is now: Dean: 20, Sam: 8, Castiel: 5.

Exodus

Episode 13.22. Airdate: May 10, 2018
Written by: Brad Buckner & Eugenie Ross-Leming
Directed by: Thomas Wright
Guest Cast: Misha Collins (Castiel/Castiel), Mark Pellegrino (Lucifer), Alexander Calvert (Jack), Samantha Smith (Mary), Jim Beaver (AU Bobby), Richard Speight Jr. (Gabriel), Felicia Day (AU Charlie), Ruth Connell (Rowena), David Haydn-Jones (Ketch), Christian Keyes (AU Michael)
Synopsis: Time for a family road trip… with some stabbing.

"Exodus" is chock-full of stuff. Some of it good, some of it incredibly bad. The good stuff is, as usual, the family and character stuff. Everyone has a moment. Dean still can't manage his rage, Sam chooses revenge, and Gabriel chooses to stand and fight, calling out his big bro. Jack gives his father some empathy, which he learned from the Winchesters. Mary proves she's just as much a hero as her boys.

Cas literally confronts the worst version of himself and kills it… but not before reminding us that he thinks he's unworthy of love. And Rowena, Ketch and Charlie are big dang heroes. Everyone makes choices, good and bad. Even Lucifer seems to be trying to make the right choice…at first. But it's still just selfish.

Now the bad: Misha is often great on this show, but his accent choice for creepy Nazi torture Cas was awful. It was distracting, and undercut the drama of the moment. Also bad: the entire final confrontation where Sam, Dean, and Gabe could have literally gone through the door *at any point*, but no. Gabriel had to die for nothing.

Death Notes: Seriously! Gabriel said he'd buy time for the guys to escape or something, but then they just stand there! What was the point!? His first death was better and way less infuriating.

Plot Hole: *Why does Cas have a German accent?*

Let the Good Times Roll

Episode 13.23. Airdate: May 17, 2018
Written by: Andrew Dabb
Directed by: Robert Singer
Guest Cast: Misha Collins (Castiel), Mark Pellegrino (Lucifer), Alexander Calvert (Jack), Samantha Smith (Mary), Jim Beaver (AU Bobby), Christian Keyes (AU Michael), Katherine Evan (Maggie), Michael's Jaunty Chapeau (Herself)
Synopsis: Everything seems to be going well until it isn't when AU Michael and Lucifer get back into the regular world.

Much like season twelve, where it felt like we had two finales wrapping up two stories, this one ends a separate storyline from what was resolved in "Exodus." However, it's more cohesive than twelve. Turns out the real villain of the season—and maybe the series—wasn't Satan per se, but toxic abusive parents. That's why characters like AU Michael never quite fit, despite fine work by Christian Keyes—he's not messed up enough about his dad.

Supernatural has always been about daddy issues, but making Lucifer the ultimate narcissistic bad dad really puts a spotlight on that. Characters like Sam, Dean, and Cas all have serious self-esteem issues, most of which come from paternal abandonment and crappy parenting. Jack does too, and in the heartbreaking scene where he's crying over hurting people, we can see that. So, he thinks that maybe finding good in his dad or that relationship can make him good… but that's just not going to happen. Goodness on this show comes from individuals breaking their cycles of destiny and violence, not from succumbing to them.

After this, we immediately see how bad Lucifer is, but also how much he's degraded as a character. It's somewhat odd to compare this annoying, needy, terrible jerk to the distant, celestial, apocalyptic threat of Season Five… but his assholery then and now makes it that much more satisfying when he finally, truly dies. Take that, toxic parenting and abusers! Sam standing up to help kill his abuser? Also awesome. But that wire work fight? Um, not so much. I get what the show was trying for, but with the budget they had it just looked kinda silly.

And now Michael's in Dean doing Peaky Blinders cosplay? That can't be good. At least Dean looked way cool with wings? Overall, "there's an angel in Dean (no not the way you hope) cliffhanger is weak, but the death of Lucifer is a satisfying ending.

Ship Shape: Bobby's making some pretty cute heart eyes at Mary, and she seems into it, so good for her. We never had to deal with a Mary/Ketch reunion either, so that's a win. Cas doesn't get much to do this episode besides co-parenting Jack and looking really sad when Dean says yes to Michael. At least no accents.

And Charlie and Rowena on a cross country road trip? Love it. Perfect power couple there. And finally, my favorite ship of Lucifer and fiery death went canon.

Death Notes: Seriously, Mark Pellegrino was great in this part, which is why it was so satisfying to see Luci finally bite it.

Spoiler Alert: Dean fantasizing about retiring and going to a beach with Sam and Cas is adorable, and it's a big contrast to the Dean who thought he'd always be hunting. And it's also really sad, because he never gets to do that. My galaxy brain theory is that when this episode was written, it was assumed that *Wayward Sisters* was going to be picked up, and if that show had continued we would have seen a *Supernatural* series finale with Dean and Sam retired, not dead. Alas.

SUPERNATURAL

CHAPTER FOURTEEN

A Better World?

After a stellar thirteenth season, we're into Season Fourteen and it's… less so. This season stagnates and struggles at the start, but does eventually find its way to some very emotional and surprising stories that I love. But on the way, it veers into some extremely tiresome and annoying stories.

Yes, Nick is alive! Mark Pellegrino was signed on as a regular last season, and I guess they thought that maybe telling his story—even though it made no sense and was boring—was some sort of contrast to Dean serving as a vessel for Michael. Using Pellegrino may also have been a way to ease the burden on the leads. Nick is for sure the weakest part of the season, but the rest generally finds it way after some soul searching.

Between the wrap of Season Thirteen, and the start of work on fourteen, *Wayward Sisters* was not picked up so there's some grief and frustration in the writing. It also meant a change of plans for the world that the writers were working with. There would be no crossovers, and if they were to end, the world wouldn't continue on screen elsewhere. Though, in some ways, that allowed them to make bigger swings and changes.

And that's the other big factor here—setting up an endgame. The writers were not certain that they were building to a final season, until some point in the second half. The decision to end the show—which was a joint one between Jensen, Jared, and the writers—was officially announced on March 22, 2019. This gave the fans more than a year to emotionally prepare… little did we know that it would be an even longer final ride than anyone anticipated.

Stranger in a Strange Land

Episode 14.01. Airdate: October 11, 2018
Written by: Andrew Dabb
Directed by: Thomas Wright
Guest Cast: Misha Collins (Castiel), Alexander Calvert (Jack) Mark Pellegrino (Nick), Samantha Smith (Mary), Jim Beaver (AU Bobby), Danneel Ackles (Jo), Dean Armstrong (Kip)
Synopsis: Sam leads the search for Dean and Michael. Cas gets kidnapped.

This is the first ever episode without Dean Winchester, unless you count demon Dean as not the real deal. And just like those episodes, this hour feels lost at sea without Dean anchoring it as the emotional core. Sam is given a lot of focus to make up for Dean's absence, continuing the thread of Sam becoming great leader… but it's not terribly compelling. Maybe that's because—as empowering as it is to see Sam being such a badass—I think Sam still wants a normal life, so there's a sadness to him having so much responsibility.

Through the vessel of a rather chattier Michael, this episode is quite literally asking what people want and establishing their dreams. But that's a hard question to answer. Jack wants to be useful—that's easy—but he also wants his power. Luckily, Cas is there to remind him of the big lesson of *Supernatural*, that it's family that gives you strength.

And that's why what Sam and Cas want, is Dean. Cas is mirrored by another rebel angel Jo, who wants love and a family. He wants that too, and it's incomplete without Dean—sort of like the show. Jensen does a great job channeling apocalypse world Michael, but Michael isn't actually that interesting of a character.

Ship Shape: I wish I could ship Michael and Jo even a little bit, given that Jensen and Danneel are married… but nope! Like Kip, I know that the big story is Cas and Dean attached.

Plot Hole: Why is Nick here? Not only is his story simply weird, but it also flies in the face of all the mythology about angel vessels, and dead angels, and… ugh. It's just so strange and a waste of time. We have enough sad white men on this show, we do not need this.

Also, as a general gripe, the show cannot decide what Castiel's powers are and when they work. Cas, who once obliterated an asylum full of monsters, can't break out of some rope because… plot? Sloppy.

Gods and Monsters

Episode 14.02. Airdate: October 18, 2018
Written by: Brad Buckner & Eugenie Ross-Leming
Directed by: Richard Speight Jr.
Guest Cast: Misha Collins (Castiel), Alexander Calvert (Jack), Mark Pellegrino (Nick), Samantha Smith (Mary), Jim Beaver (AU Bobby)
Synopsis: Michael decides monsters should inherit the Earth. Cas babysits Jack and Nick and loses them both.

Another episode without Dean, and the show certainly is feeling it. Michael's monster upgrade plan is marginally interesting, but as always, I'm here for character stuff—and we get more of it here than in the season premiere, so I'm calling this a step up, albeit a small one.

Most of it is focused on Jack, who is trying to figure out who he is with no powers, or bells and whistles. What Cas lays out for him is possibly the thesis of the whole season—it's not your past that defines you, it's what you do going forward. We see this with Michael trying out new and different ways of destroying a world. We see it with Jack searching for who his mom was, and who he might be. And we even see it with Bobby and Mary adjusting back to a nicer reality.

And of course, we see the worst permutation of this with Nick. Nick can neither let go of the monster he was as Lucifer, or what happened that made him say yes. Mark Pellegrino gets to be the antithesis of everything our characters need to learn, because Nick ain't moving on.

But where does that leave Sam? Well, not anywhere right now. Same for Dean, but if this episode and the last are giving us anything, they should be considering what they're taking from their past very soon.

So, Get This: Quite often, Jared and Jensen would grow beards between seasons, because it was the one time they didn't have to shave. The production liked the idea of Sam having a stress or grief beard, so they let him keep it for the start of the season.

Plot Hole: The whole “Cas can’t come because Michael will sense him” is very dumb and has never been a problem before. Once again, it’s just putting Cas in a specific place, because the plot needs him there.

The Scar

Episode 14.03. Airdate: October 25, 2018
Written by: Robert Berens
Directed by: Robert Singer
Guest Cast: Misha Collins (Castiel), Alexander Calvert (Jack), Kim Rhodes (Jody), Yadira Guevara-Prip (Dark Kaia), Catherine Lough Haggquist (Jules)
Synopsis: Sam and Dean track down a weapon that can hurt Michael — a spear belonging to the Kaia who crossed over from the Bad Place. Cas and Jack solve a case.

Yes, here we are. Good old-fashioned Winchester angst. That's what we've been missing. And not only do we get Dean angst, we get Jack angst in the first really resonant episode of this season. And it's all about not running away from your trauma.

Jack tries to leave the bunker, maybe because he feels useless or maybe he doesn't want his three dads to know that he's dying. But he learns that running away from family doesn't solve things. You end up with unresolved trauma like a dying witch, endlessly sucking the life from you. You gotta deal with that stuff.

Dean and Jody are also both refusing to deal—Jody telling Claire the truth and Dean's horror of being used by Michael. But Dean is also called out for his anger. Keep an eye on that in the final run of episodes, because there are a lot of people who tell Dean he's just a scared, angry monster. Sam is at least there to listen to Dean when he needs it, but he can't make it better.

It's good to see Dark Kaia back, because she's a badass. And what we get here is a glimpse at the story that would have been told in *Wayward Sisters*. I can't help but see Jody's line "I just feel like I already lost before I ever even began," as a meta commentary by Robert Berens (who co-created and would have run *Wayward Sisters*) on the disappointment of that show not happening. And indeed, this whole top half is about processing loss and disappointment.

Ship Shape: I love that we get confirmation that Claire and Kaia were in love. What I don't love is that Cas being the support for Jack's story (which is important) means that he gets some soulful looks at Dean, but they're generally being kept apart, which is a bummer.

Mint Condition

Episode 14.04. Airdate: November 1, 2018
Written by: Davy Perez
Directed by: Amyn Kaderali
Guest Cast: Kurt Ostlund (Stewart), Genevieve Buechner (Samantha), Aaron Paul Stewart (Dirk)
Synopsis: On Halloween, Sam and Dean fight a ghost haunting a comic shop.

The season is finally on track with a really fun episode that lets Dean be his nerdiest self, while also doing some interesting things about his anger issues. We get some good Sam stuff too, with a fun childhood story about why he hates Halloween. And the writers get to pretty much tell the internet to stop being dicks.

In an interesting turn, Dean and Sam call out their narrative mirrors. While Dean is right that the nice, smart, forgiving Samantha in plaid is definitely Sam, I don't think that sweet, nerdy Dirk is Dean. Stewart, the angry screw-up, is Dean. Like Dean, he's kind of a mess, but has a family that loves him. I think that actually makes Dirk Cas—the guy who had a bad relationship with his dad, and found a home with Stewart. Aw.

So, what does that mean about our ghost, if this season is about confronting the past? I guess in this sense, the ghost is the past and the way it will come back to haunt us. And if we want to go deeper, the ghost—who was a friend to Stewart—manifesting in the form of something Dean loves is maybe how family can turn into a toxic cycle?

Spoiler Alert: If you want to go really galaxy brain here, and see Dirk as Cas, Jordan was more of a father to him and he's mad at the Dean mirror for not doing what he wants. That's major Chuck foreshadowing. But I might be reaching. More likely a father figure returning might foreshadow John's return.

Nightmare Logic

Episode 14.05. Airdate: November 8, 2018
Written by: Meredith Glynn
Directed by: Darren Grant
Guest Cast: Samantha Smith (Mary), Jim Beaver (AU Bobby), Katherine Evans (Maggie), Leah Cairns (Sasha), Chris Patrick-Simpson (Neil)
Synopsis: Sam and Dean run into Mary and Bobby on a case where a Djinn is bringing nightmares to life.

This episode takes the "confronting the worst nightmares of the past" really literally, and along the way we get good character stuff for Sam and Bobby, which I like. Less so for Mary, but I'll get to that. In the background, Dean isn't letting go of his past and continues to give people good advice he can't take himself.

First, Sam is dealing with the burdens of leadership and confronted with his worst nightmare—a hunter dead on his watch (and this one isn't an illusion). Sam's goal to make a full network of hunters to save the world is admirable, and heroic, but it worries me for his own emotional health. He's stopped putting Dean's perceptions and needs ahead of his own—now he's doing that for everyone. He's become obsessed with being the ultimate hunter he was supposedly born to be. Is that good?

What's really interesting is the emphasis on learning AU Bobby's history, and how much the wars and hunting has cost him. He's a contrast to Sam, as they both lost everything to hunting. So it's good for them to get away. But I'm also disappointed that, since Mary had her big moments with Dean at the end of Season Twelve, she really hasn't been part of her sons' lives.

Name Game: Agents Byrne and Harrison is a reference to The Talking Heads.

Spoiler Alert: Much like Eve and her armies of monsters in Season Six, Michael's hunter traps and super monsters just… don't matter after a little while?

Optimism

Episode 14.06. Airdate: November 15, 2018
Written by: Steve Yockey
Directed by: Richard Speight Jr.
Guest Cast: Alexander Calvert (Jack), Felicia Day (AU Charlie), Maddie Phillips (Harper Sayles)
Synopsis: Jack and Dean hunt a necromancer librarian, while Charlie and Sam track a giant half fly monster.

So, is the musca the grossest monster ever on *Supernatural*? Maybe. I put it up there with the gross spider monsters from "Unforgiven." What? I don't like bugs. The musca storyline, and Sam convincing Charlie to give people a chance, is sweet though, despite the monster. And it reminds us that family, and finding your people, is what this show is all about.

Dean and Jack's adventure however, is more interesting. These two aren't necessarily alike—aside from the fact they feel the weight of the world on their shoulders—but it's their contrast that makes them a great pair. Opposed to bitter old man Dean, Jack is generally adorable. The image of Jack hiding in the bathroom, asking Dean all he knows about sex, is gold.

But their plot is also about not letting go of the past, how hanging onto notions about how someone should be is toxic. You have to be realistic, but if we add Charlie's story into this mix, it becomes shouldn't let your realism make you cynical.

Name Game: Dean and Jack go by Agents Berry and Charles, referencing Chuck Berry and his son Charles.

So, Get This: After fourteen years, someone finally used "Christo" again to see if someone was possessed! I think in this case, the writers maybe wanted fans to stop tweeting about that.

Unhuman Nature

Episode 14.07. Airdate: November 29, 2018
Written by: Brad Buckner & Eugenie Ross-Leming
Directed by: John Showalter
Guest Cast: Misha Collins (Castiel), Alexander Calvert (Jack), Mark Pellegrino (Nick), Ruth Connell (Rowena), Dimitri Vantis (Sergei)
Synopsis: As Jack's condition worsens, his family tries to save him and comfort him.

This episode is the definition of a mixed bag, because everything with Jack's decline, and his three dads trying to save him, is fine to great. And everything with Nick is either annoying or completely horrible. Also, Cas' stuff with Sergei is fine, but it's weird that Sam is just in the background this episode.

We'll get Nick out of the way first, as he continues to exemplify the absolute worst way to deal with trauma. Unable to move on, he would rather go back to being the devil's meat suit. It's thematically on point I guess, but it's gross and boring to watch. We don't care about this horrible person.

On the other hand, Dean and Jack are paragons of making the most of a short, fleeting moment of happiness. The two of them fishing is one of the most beautiful scenes in the season, and I love how tender and heart felt it is. Indeed, everything with the guys and Rowena trying bravely to save Jack is really moving, and I just love that they're a bunch of dads (and a vodka aunt) worried about their kid. And he's a great kid!

Spoiler Alert/Plot Hole: Dean's getting dizzy for the same reason that the Djinn couldn't whammy him—Michael is still around. Which you think Dean's boyfriend the angel might have sensed??? Also, how did Nick wake up something in the empty, when it took Jack—the most powerful being on the show behind God—to do it before?

Driver Picks the Music: Dean and Jack cruise along to "Let It Ride" by Bachman-Turner Overdrive and it's perfect. Pure dad, but also pure Dean.

Byzantium

Episode 14.08. Airdate: December 6, 2018
Written by: Meredith Glynn
Directed by: Eduardo Sánchez
Guest Cast: Misha Collins (Castiel), Alexander Calvert (Jack), Amanda Tapping (Naomi), Courtney Ford (Kelly), Erica Cerra (Duma), Veronica Cartwright (Lily Sunder), Sean Amsing (Anubis)
Synopsis: Jack dies, but with help from Lily Sunder, the boys find a way to bring him back. In heaven, the empty wants Jack, but Cas makes a deal to save him.

So much happens this episode that it almost feels like a little movie. Heck, Jack dies before the title card! While he semi-quotes Peter Pan! Jack gets to truly meet his mom! Cas actually saves heaven and his son! It's so much!

The answer to bringing Jack back is typically Winchester. They solve one problem by potentially (spoiler: very definitely) creating a new, bigger problem, by letting Jack diminish his soul. And a deal is made. But these deals and the cheating of death is different, because it's not Sam and Dean's co-dependency driving it. They've expanded their world and family in a different way—they're rewriting the story by saving their kid, and not each other.

That's what Lily does as well. She's damned because of what she's done in the past, but she changes that by making a selfless, compassionate choice in the present. It's empathy that makes her do the right thing. That's going to be important as we move through the endgame of the series.

Driver Picks the Music: Jack's wake, full of nougat and booze set to "Please Come Home" by the Alman Brothers, is one of many incredible moments. Though it's hard to tell if we're watching Sam, Dean, and Cas, or Jared, Jensen, and Misha.

Famous Faces: Veronica Cartwright is an incredible guest star here, and you may recognize her from *Alien* or *The Witches of Eastwick.*

Ship Shape: Cas and Dean pair off for most of the episode, while Sam is on his own in grief. That separation does lead to the solution though. But let's talk about Cas' deal. It all feels very much like Angel's curse on *Buffy the Vampire Slayer*, where he would lose his soul in a moment of happiness. The obvious thing that's going to make Cas happy… is Dean.

Spoiler Alert: But it turns out it's even more painful than just Dean.

The Spear

Episode 14.09. Airdate: December 13, 2018
Written by: Robert Berens
Directed by: Amyn Kaderali
Guest Cast: Misha Collins (Castiel), Alexander Calvert (Jack), DJ Qualls (Garth), David Haydn-Jones (Ketch), Yadira Guevara-Prip (Dark Kaia), Felisha Terrell (Michael)
Synopsis: Michael launches his plan for a monster apocalypse, and it includes a trap for the Winchesters and taking back Dean's body.

This episode is like a mini version of Cas' deal and contemplates how it's often right when you let go to let yourself be happy, that everything can go to crap. That's certainly what happens to Dean, who dares to be optimistic. But as Cas tells Jack—hunting is rarely happy.

There's a lot going on in this episode, which is sort of trying to be an homage to *Die Hard*, but doesn't quite hit that note. It's nice to see Garth back, and it's good to know that the network of hunters is out there doing good. Not that it looks good for them with Michael doing his best impression of Thanos.

Michael wanting to use Jack is an interesting bit of actual character development, as is his fussing over his pose before the attack. It took a while for Michael to be more than just scary, but I like it. What I like a bit less is that Sam continues to have less of an emotional stake compared to Dean, Cas, Jack, Dark Kaia and even Garth.

Ship Shape: Dean and Cas together in front of giant piles of garbage is probably symbolic of something, but I'm just going to focus on Cas' look at Dean when he says Jack is back.

Driver Picks the Music: The slow-motion hero walk set to Beethoven's "Ode to Joy" is a reference to *Die Hard*.

Nihilism

Episode 14.10. Airdate: January 17, 2019
Written by: Steve Yockey
Directed by: Amanda Tapping
Guest Cast: Misha Collins (Castiel), Alexander Calvert (Jack), Thunderbird Dinwindle (Pamela), Lisa Berry (Billie), Katherine Evans (Maggie)
Synopsis: Michael traps Dean in his own mind, but it's fine, he shoves him in a mental walk-in freezer.

"Nihilism" has the kind of deep character stuff mixed with action and magic, that we love from *Supernatural*. It's all about Dean, while also giving us important beats for everyone else. Good stuff. Michael ends up on ice, literally in Dean's head, but not after getting figuratively into Jack and Cas' heads.

We've always known that Dean, at heart, just wants to be with his family, so his little prison of contentment in Rocky's Bar is interesting. It's not quite paradise, or everything Dean would want, but it's the most he thinks he deserves—booze, bullets, and a bar. We get a reminder of how much trauma Dean's been through, and boy howdy it's amazing that he even lets himself have this. But his family gets him out, because you do anything for family.

That's the lesson Jack has internalized from the Winchesters, for better or worse. He uses up his soul, and that's a commentary on how Sam and Dean saved each other repeatedly throughout the years, at the cost of some moral compass.

Spoiler Alert: Michael's assertion that the many different worlds out there are all Chuck's failed drafts, turns out to be pretty much correct. Although this world seems to be the original. But it's an interesting perspective to see Chuck as a heartless dick trying to get to the ending he wants. And it's massive foreshadowing for Chuck's return and his reveal as the final boss of the series.

Damaged Goods

Episode 14.11. Airdate: January 24, 2019
Written by: Davy Perez
Directed by: Phil Sgriccia
Guest Cast: Mark Pellegrino (Nick), Samantha Smith (Mary), Briana Buckmaster (Donna), Nelson Leis (Abraxas)
Synopsis: Dean decides to take boxing up his problems to a whole new level. Nick tracks down Mary as part of his hunt for vengeance.

This episode is fine, but doesn't quite work thanks to Nick continuing to be the absolute worst. It's also weird to see Dean giving up, even when his family wants him to fight. I love seeing the tenderness and healthy relationship between Dean and his mom. Donna is also great, but something is missing.

Thematically, we're still about dealing with the past, but now we're looking at it from the perspective of fate and being angry at the why. Nick's family, like Sam and Dean's, were sacrificed as part of Lucifer's greater purpose. It was pointless and terrible, but Nick let it turn him into a monster.

Billie's guidebook for Dean is no less terrible. As Sam notes, it's uncharacteristic for a Winchester to roll over for fate. Their entire existence has been about not following the story, and making it up as they go. So it's fair for Sam to not be down with Dean's terrible "throw myself in a box in the ocean" plan. Dean, of course, isn't doing this for himself, but to save the world, because self-sacrifice is also a Winchester special.

Spoiler Alert: I think it's fair not to trust Billie, since death books have been rewritten before. Also, she's not really team Winchester. We know that Billie's ultimate plan will be to be a new god, so her trying to get Dean in that box feels like manipulation. But also, Jack is being set up as the one who will rewrite fate in the end, ignoring Billie's and Chuck's stories.

So, Get This: Dean telling Sam "I love you for trying" is the first time either brother has told the other "I love you." And it's the first time Dean has said those words to someone other than Mary. Add that in to the "we don't hug" thing, and wow do these boys need to get better at sharing loving feelings.

Prophet and Loss

Episode 14.12. Airdate: January 24, 2019
Written by: Brad Buckner & Eugenie Ross-Leming
Directed by: Thomas Wright
Guest Cast: Misha Collins (Castiel), Mark Pellegrino (Nick), Keith Szarabajka (Donatello)
Synopsis: As Dean persists with his plan to lock himself in the Ma'lak box, Sam convinces him to take a case. The result is that the team saves Donatello from the prison of his own mind.

This is an episode about giving up and why that's just not an option for a Winchester. In a way, it's about suicide and depression, which is seriously dark, but not out of bounds. Given Jared Padalecki's public "Always Keep Fighting" campaigns for mental health awareness, and that Jensen and Misha were the public face of a campaign to fund suicide prevention hotlines, this topic is very much at the heart of the show on a super-textual level.

Despite the rather disturbing serial killer vibes of this episode, I like it. It's about Cas and Sam giving Dean reasons to keep fighting, echoing many of the themes of "Point of No Return." But since that was two hundred episodes ago, I think it's fine for the show to repeat itself.

Just like that episode, it's a combination of Castiel's action to do what he can, and Sam's faith to Dean, that turn the tide. The fact that Cas is able to save Donatello, is the seed of hope that Sam's "I believe in us" speech helps grow and take root. And it's a good metaphor for helping someone at rock bottom find something to hold onto.

Ship Shape: Oh boy is it a lot to see Cas' anger and sadness, as the person he loves just gives up. The fact that Cas was the one to break Donatello for Dean, and also saves him, is big. And their conversation about Dean's decision is significant.

Lebanon

Episode 14.13. Airdate: February 7, 2019 (Episode 300)
Written by: Andrew Dabb & Meredith Glynn
Directed by: Robert Singer
Guest Cast: Misha Collins (Castiel), Jeffrey Dean Morgan (John), Samantha Smith (Mary), Kurt Fuller (Zachariah)
Synopsis: In the series' 300th episode, John Winchester returns for one family dinner and a lot of catharsis

In old-school *Supernatural* style that's fitting for a milestone episode, "Lebanon" is all about the sudden turn into something unexpected. What starts as a story about how the town of Lebanon sees the boys, turns into an emotional journey about family and forgiveness.

That forgiveness thing is key here. John Winchester is, to put it lightly, not a popular character in fandom. He's seen as an abuser, and a jerk, and in general a monster. But he's the foundation to who Sam and Dean are, and what the show is. And despite his flaws, he's family and the boys love, and forgive him. In a season that's all about dealing with your past, John's return makes sense. And everyone makes the best of it.

Sam and Dean make peace with their past and recognize that, for all its pain, it made them who they are. They have a family and they're the guys that save the world. That wouldn't be the case without John, but they're also okay without him.

Not only do they want to be who they are, but they want their world to stay the same. Seeing Cas returned to factory settings (along with a fabulous return from Zachariah), remind them of the impact Sam and Dean made. And it matters.

Ship Shape: As much as I ship Mary and AU Bobby, seeing John and Mary (husband and wife) reunited at last, gets me right in the feels. And his departure seems to hit Mary the hardest, as so many things have done since she was brought back.

Ouroboros

Episode 14.14. Airdate: March 7, 2019
Written by: Steve Yockey
Directed by: Amyn Kaderali
Guest Cast: Misha Collins (Castiel), Alexander Calvert (Jack), Ruth Connell (Rowena), Katherine Evans (Maggie), Philippe Bowgen (Noah Ophis)
Synopsis: The whole gang hunts a pansexual gorgon. Oh, and Jack burns off most of his soul to kill Michael.

Once again, we're using my favorite formula of a massive left turn, as an all hands on deck monster hunt suddenly turns into Michael's shockingly ultimate defeat. And a big power up for Jack. But it all works, because the first parts with Noah the Gorgon inform the latter half. Noah is sort of like Michael—a monster that can out think and paralyze everyone, until Jack just cuts him off.

First, there's a clear connection between Noah's prophecy and the story of the black snake. Jack, as Cas explained, kills the thing he loves to defeat the thing he hates—he gives his very soul to save the world and his family. His declaration that he is a Winchester is really heroic, and doing something dumb and self-destructive to save the world is a very Winchester thing to do. See: literally the entire series.

Michael's sudden demise is great and so shocking, and Ruth Connell is amazing as Michael's final host. And there are so many other great moments here too. From poor Jack's undercover assignment as a yorkie, to Cas' fantastic speech about what it means to love mortals as an immortal being. Everyone is amazing this episode and it's a big winner for the season.

Death Notes: Michael's death gets points for its shocking nature, because no one expects the big bad to die in episode fourteen. He was also a dick, so good riddance! Serious RIP to poor Maggie though, who has been nothing but a plot punching bag for almost a year.

Ship Shape: It's hard to look at how queer this episode is, and not see some relevance to that one big queer ship, but I think it's more important to just look at the text and not the subtext. Noah isn't really a mirror to Dean or Cas. Instead, he's just a prompt for Cas to give us a beautiful speech about love and the impermanence of human life. Maybe this implies that the ultimate conclusion for his love would be a relationship where both beings aren't worried about dying? Like… in heaven?

Peace of Mind

Episode 14.15. Airdate: March 14, 2019
Written by: Meghan Fitzmartin (Story & teleplay), Steve Yockey (story)
Directed by: Phil Sgriccia
Guest Cast: Misha Collins (Castiel), Alexander Calvert (Jack), Keith Szarabajka (Donatello Redfield), Caitlin Ashley-Thompson (Sunny Harrington), Bill Dow (Chip Harrington)
Synopsis: Sam and Cas go on a hunt that takes them back to the 50s and see Sam in a cardigan. Dean takes Jack to a soulessness tutorial with Donatello.

Written by Andrew Dabb's long-time assistant, Meghan Fitzmartin, this is one of those episodes that seems light and full, and delightful. And it is. But it's also super-layered, telling us a lot about the season. Also, we get Cas being completely frustrated and confused for a whole episode, while being badass saving Sam, and yelling that God has a beard. Perfection.

This episode follows up on a lot from "Ouroboros," but not what we'd expect. It gives focus to Sam's trauma for once, and his need to escape his guilt. His stint as a leader, which had such build up, ends bloody like most cracks at happiness that these boys try. Sam, who has run away from his life before, wants to retreat to a dream world. Poor thing.

Jack isn't sure what he wants, or if that black hole (visualized so well in that shot of the cream in the coffee, swirling like a galaxy) is in him. But Chip Harrington is a mirror that tells us a lot of scary things for him. Chip at first used his power reflexively to protect his family, like Jack. But his power and need for control made him a monster. The townspeople who Chip tried to make happy are victims, just like poor Felix the snake. And that's because Jack (and Chip) has power and ideas about making people happy, but lacks empathy. And it's all about empathy.

Name Game: The characters named Griffin and Justin are a reference to Griffin and Justin McElroy, of the podcasts *My Brother, My Brother, And Me,* as well as The Adventure Zone. But don't worry, completionists, Fitzmartin made sure to get a character named Travis into her next episode, "Drag Me Away from You."

Cas and Sam pose as agents Scholz and Delp, references to members of the band Boston, who wrote the song "Peace of Mind."

Don't Go in the Woods

Episode 14.16. Airdate: March 21, 2019
Written by: Davy Perez & Nick Vaught
Directed by: John Fitzpatrick
Guest Cast: Alexander Calvert (Jack), Skylar Radizon (Max), Zenia Marshall (Stacy), Cory Gruter-Andrew (Eliot), Adam Beach (Sheriff Mason)
Synopsis: Sam and Dean leave Jack alone while they hunt an extra-gross monster.

This episode is all about information and knowledge, and who gets to have it. After Cas saw Jack kill poor Felix, he took off which turns out to be a very bad thing. He's not sharing information, just as Sherriff Mason failed to do. Sam and Dean do too, but most frighteningly, Jack doesn't tell his dads that he revealed his powers and nearly killed someone.

If this season is all about dealing with the past and how trauma affects you, the key lessons is that you have to talk about it. The whistling slime monster is proof of that, because when information about the past was lost, people stopped learning from it and died.

It's also interesting, because for the first time we see Jack trying to fit in and be a person with "other kids." It's telling how much of his personality is based on things Dean likes, but his showing off ends with someone getting stabbed, which is an interesting little parable about stupid things teens do to impress one another.

Spoiler Alert: We never hear from Max, Stacy, or Eliot again, which is weird because they know a lot. And they're fun characters I would have liked to see more of.

Game Night

Episode 14.17. Airdate: April 4, 2019
Written by: Meredith Glynn
Directed by: John Showalter
Guest Cast: Misha Collins (Castiel), Alexander Calvert (Jack), Mark Pellegrino (Nick), Samantha Smith (Mary), Keith Szarabajka (Donatello Redfield), Danneel Ackles (Jo/Anael)
Synopsis: Jack, Mary and the boys try to save Donatello from Nick and prevent Nick from resurrecting Lucifer. Cas tries to contact God.

If this episode has one moral, it's "listen to your mom." Also, how important empathy continues to be. A soul on this show means empathy, which is why Sam and Dean, despite having every reason to kill Nick, don't. Sam especially still has some hope that Nick can stop clinging to the past and turn back. But he can't. Jack on the other hand is so powerful, that he's lost his soul. That power allows him to save the day at a violent cost, but that's not the only cost.

Mary's apparent (spoiler: it's real) demise is seriously foreshadowed all episode, because she gets really great moments with both her sons individually. I love her connecting with Dean, who's so much like her, but it's her moment where she tells Sam how proud of him she is, that's my favorite. And the things she's so proud of are the things that makes Sam Sam—that compassion and empathy for even the worst monster.

On Cas' side of things, another character's having trouble facing reality, though not as badly as Nick or Jack. And thanks to Anael, Cas comes to realize that he should tell the Winchesters his fears about Jack, instead of looking to someone else.

Death Notes: I think Mark Pellegrino sets a record here for having two of the fieriest and satisfying deaths on the show. And props to the effects on Nick's hand. We've come a long way from Crowley's plastic hand in "Our Little World." Yes, Nick's death was maybe over the top, and definitely a display that Jack's gone kinda bad.

Absence

Episode 14.18. Airdate: April 11, 2019
Written by: Robert Berens
Directed by: Nina Lopez-Corrado
Guest Cast: Misha Collins (Castiel), Alexander Calvert (Jack), Mark Pellegrino (Jack's Hallucifer), Samantha Smith (Mary), Ruth Connell (Rowena), Erica Cerra (Duma)
Synopsis: Sam, Dean, Jack, and Cas grapple with Mary's death.

"Absence" is about mourning. It's about the huge hole a person leaves when they pass. In a season about learning to cope with grief, this installment looks at grief at its most raw and painful. As our heroes remember how Mary was such a mother and comfort to them, it's that pain that reminds them how much they loved her.

Each of our four Winchesters are in one of the five stages of grief, with all of them reaching some kind of acceptance. Dean of course is anger, and the target of his anger can't be Sam—and Jack isn't there—so it all falls on Cas. Jack is in the bargaining phase, trying desperately to make things better.

That leaves Sam with denial, and Cas with his old friend depression. Jack gave Cas back his faith, and Sam has been losing battles all season. Losing Jack spiritually, and Mary literally, is a huge blow and another instance of the season testing our heroes.

Death Notes: Now that we know Mary is truly dead, let's talk about it. While I do think that Mary's own story got lost this season, this episode was a loving and fitting tribute to her with a satisfying goodbye. Her story ended the way it should have, with her at peace with John. I like it.

Ship Shape: So, this is definitely not a good episode for Dean and Cas at all. In fact, it's the start of a major rift for them that will open (and reopen) all sorts of wounds. But you can't be this mad at someone unless you love them, and finding a way past his anger is gonna sorta be a big thing for Dean.

Spoiler Alert: With another mention of Chuck last week, and a death that's pretty much a senseless act of God, we're getting into some serious foreshadowing. We're also expanding on the season's question of "how do we respond to bad things" with "why are there bad things and can we control them." Which brings in Chuck.

Jack in the Box

Episode 14.19. Airdate: April 18, 2019
Written by: brad Buckner & Eugenie Ross-Leming
Directed by: Robert Singer
Guest Cast: Misha Collins (Castiel), Alexander Calvert (Jack), Mark Pellegrino (Hallucifer), Jim Beaver (AU Bobby), Erica Cerra (Dumah)
Synopsis: Jack tries to get into the Winchester's good graces by playing God, but all the want to do it lock him in a box.

This penultimate episode is very literal about bad ways to deal with problems. There's Jack, just sort of pretending they aren't problems and not accepting responsibility, and we have Dean who wants to lock up the bad things and feelings, ignoring them until they explode. As we see with a heartbreaking scene of Dean crying alone in the woods, this guy is and always has been about keeping his pain and vulnerability hidden.

I personally prefer Sam and Cas' approach, which is more emotionally mature, and less driven by anger and trauma. Sam's viewpoint is driven by compassion for Jack, but he's still overpowered by grief so, he's all in on the put Jack in the box (honestly that's such a bad pun). But Cas still has faith—not in Jack or God, but in family and in love. Bless him.

There's a lot here reminding us that heaven and Biblical justice are cruel, and manipulative, which is why it's certainly better to have Cas and Sam's brand of faith. I guess Jack making new angels also resolves that whole, "heaven is going to implode" thing. But in general, this episode proves that ignoring problems ends up with a pissed-off nephilim listening to his devil hallucinations.

Spoiler Alert: This may be the last we hear about Naomi, ever, which is a weird and very unsatisfying resolution to that story.

Moriah

Episode 14.20. Airdate: April 25, 2019
Written by: Andrew Dabb
Directed by: Phil Sgriccia
Guest Cast: Misha Collins (Castiel), Alexander Calvert (Jack), Rob Benedict (Chuck), Lisa Berry (Billie)
Synopsis: Chuck returns to deal with Jack but God was never on their side.

In terms of finale twists, this is one of the absolute best—which it sort of has to be, as it's less of a season finale than a lead into the final season of the show. Thematically, Chuck's return works great. We've segued from "how do you deal with your past and your pain" to "how do we confront the world and circumstances that caused it?" Well, you do that by confronting God.

The idea of free will and fate is in the DNA of *Supernatural*, but so is the fourth-wall-busting idea of authorship and how that relates to the audience and fandom. God is a writer who gets blamed for every bad thing, because it was where the story took him. That's not just Chuck, but the showrunnners. They hurt "people" for good drama. Chuck is an audience that enjoys that pain and won't let these boys rest. There's no better set up.

But Sam, Dean, and Cas are the characters that don't do what they're told, evolving beyond the parameters of the story. The audience is also complicit and involved in that, but these three really are Team Free Will—with Jack being the ultimate agent, because he's the only real threat to God. Chuck wants to take him off the board with the one ending he's never got out of these guys—one family member killing the other.

Think of all the times we've come close, and neither Sam, Dean, or Cas can do it. And this is going to be unpacked as the author and Winchesters end the story for good.

Driver Picks the Music: Motorhead's "God Was Never on You Side" is maybe a little on the nose, but that final sequence is so powerful I'll forgive it.

SUPERNATURAL

CHAPTER FIFTEEN

Lay Your Weary Head to Rest

As Chuck would say when he wasn't being an asshole—endings are hard. And ending a beloved series in a way that's dramatic and satisfying, while staying true to the characters people have loved for 15 years? That's even harder. So, did Andrew Dabb and his writers succeed in bringing this one home? Well, yes and no. It's complicated.

There's a lot of really great stuff in Season Fifteen that attempts to honor the past, while also telling a meta story about authorship and the nature of free will. There are certainly some early stumbles, but the overall story of the boys finding real freedom is really good. But factors outside of the writers' control made it extremely hard for this season to be great—especially the last two episodes.

The COVID-19 pandemic shut down filming of *Supernatural* in March of 2020, only one day into shooting episode 19, "Inherit the Earth." It wouldn't be until August that the cast and crew would return to finish the show, but under intense safety protocols and limited resources. COVID meant that many story elements that might have been resolved just didn't happen. It also meant a six-month gap in the middle of airing that did no one any favors.

Watching this season as binge is a much better experience, but it still doesn't make up for the other thing the writers can't control—how we feel about the show and how we wanted to see it end. There's lots of foreshadowing this season pointing to the final outcome for Sam and Dean, but if that's not an outcome you like, it's hard to see and swallow. With that in mind, let's do this one more time.

Back and to the Future

Episode 15.01. Airdate: October 10, 2019
Written by: Andrew Dabb
Directed by: John Showalter
Guest Cast: Misha Collins (Castiel), Alexander Calvert (Belphegor)
Synopsis: The guys deal with a rift that's releasing all the souls in hell.

After a shocking and emotional finale, the final season begins sadly with a whimper—not a bang. While the first chaotic scenes of Team Free Will fleeing from the zombie horde are nice and scary, the fact that the rest of it was filmed in bright summer sunshine is incredibly jarring. Add in, like, four ghosts straight out of a Spirit Halloween discount sale paired with slow, boring action scenes, and nothing sets up anything close to scary, let along an apocalypse.

What I do like is that we're setting up where the boys will be emotionally this season, and how they're coping with their loss of faith. As usual, Dean is angry and feels helpless, while Sam is hopeful as long as he's got his brother. Cas' grief is more personal, as he reels from losing his son and Dean's refusal to forgive him. At least he and Sam get to save people, while Dean has to deal with a creepy, kinda horny demon in his dead kid's body.

The best part of this episode is Dean and Sam trying to figure out if they ever had free will, which is a major question of life. I do also like the call back to the pilot, ending on "We've Got Work to Do." But the other references to previous episodes, monsters and plots feels a bit forced.

Ship Shape: Dean and Cas continue to be in a bad place, but it's right at the forefront of their stories, especially Cas', and that certainly matters this season.

Raising Hell

Episode 15.02. Airdate: October 17, 2019
Written by: Brad Buckner & Eugenie Ross-Leming
Directed by: Robert Singer
Guest Cast: Misha Collins (Castiel), Alexander Calvert (Belphegor), Rob Benedict (Chuck), Osric Chau (Kevin Tran), Ruth Connell (Rowena), Emily Swallow (Amara), David Haydn-Jones (Ketch), Lane Davies (Francis Tumbelty)
Synopsis: The gang tries to stop the flood of ghosts from the fissure in hell. Chuck seeks help from Amara.

This episode is better than the premiere, though it still suffers from the problem of shooting ghosts in bright sunlight and how incredibly not scary that is. At least it gives us a lot of information about what's going on, and why it's not worse. Most importantly, it explains why Chuck hasn't wiped out the planet yet. Chuck and Amara's scenes are interesting, but not earthshaking. That said, there's maybe too much inconsequential plot stuff and not enough emotion.

There are, however, some interesting mirrors. One is Sam's leadership being mirrored by… Jack the Ripper? Tumblety and Sam take up identical roles, and neither are too successful. But perhaps the losses Tumblety faces foreshadow some dark choices for Sam. Kevin being there is less a mirror and more a highlight of how cruel Chuck really is and… message received. His fate has somehow become more and more tragic since his death.

The best moment here is between Dean and Cas, with Cas' awesome assertion that what's real is the bonds between them. As Dean told him way back in "Lucifer Rising," it's people and families that are real, and the love we feel for them despite their flaws. That's pretty important. Too bad Dean's too angry to hear it. I could put this in the ship section, because it is hella romantic, but it's also more than that and incredibly important for the rest of the season and series.

Spoiler Alert/Death Notes: This turns out to be the final time we see Kevin Tran on screen, and that's maybe the first casualty of the finale's changes due to the COVID-19 shutdown. When Jack fixes everything at the end of the season, we should assume that Kevin finally, really got to heaven. And we probably would have seen him there.

Ship Shape: Rowena and Ketch seem to be here to show that all hands are on deck, but also to absurdly flirt. It's incredibly weird and the humor doesn't quite fit, but okay. Less gross than Ketch and Mary, but Rowena and Sam will always be superior.

The Rupture

Episode 15.03. Airdate: October 24, 2019
Written by: Robert Berens
Directed by: Charles Beeson
Guest Cast: Misha Collins (Castiel), Alexander Calvert (Belphegor), Ruth Connell (Rowena), David Haydn-Jones (Ketch)
Synopsis: The team tries to seal up help. After Belphegor betrays them, Rowena gives her life to save the world.

Now this is the good stuff. The first genuinely great episode of the season moves the plot and rips your heart out. If you're Ketch—that's literal! But Ketch's death actually illuminates our themes, which we see writ large with Rowena's following death. Finally breaking toxic cycles and finding redemption.

After a lifetime of violence, Ketch chooses his friends, while after centuries of evading death and only looking out for herself, Rowena chooses self-sacrifice in order to save the world. But she does it in a Rowena way, placing her faith in Sam and the friends she loves. It's beautiful, powerful, and fantastic, and a great sendoff that sets up a season of send offs.

Rowena changes, but Dean, and Cas don't. This crisis has sent Dean and Cas into their worst patterns, with Dean lashing out in anger and falling back into co-dependency. Meanwhile, Cas once again feels like he was tricked and put his faith in the wrong place. Killing Belphegor is cathartic for Cas after Jack's death, but it feels like another failure. So, he does the most Cas thing and just leaves, because Dean won't ask him to stay.

And then there's Sam, who has a huge moment killing Rowena. But his place in all this remains murky. His destiny seems to be violence and to lose people. His connection with Rowena was special, and now he's particularly alone.

Ship Shape: Honestly, Dean and Cas have a genuine break up scene here, and their relationship is one of the titular ruptures. Sam also loses someone he could have loved, and it's heart breaking. We'll continue to see Dean and Cas paralleled to Sam.

Death Notes: RIP Ketch, you were surprisingly not horrible at the end of your life, proving anyone can be redeemed in some way. But it is Rowena's final sacrifice that's the standout demise.

Atomic Monsters

Episode 15.04. Airdate: October 31, 2019
Written by: Davy Perez
Directed by: Jensen Ackles
Guest Cast: Rob Benedict (Chuck), Emily Perkins (Becky), Ty Olsson (Benny), Burkely Duffield (Billy Whitfield), Andrew Airlie (Henry Whitfield), Anne Marie DeLuise (Janet Whitfield)
Synopsis: The boys take on a case that leads to a family trying to protect a vampire son. Meanwhile, Chuck goes to Becky for help with writer's block.

There are two very different stories happening in the episode. The main story—with the vampire team who has to die—mirrors the loss of Jack and gives Sam and Dean some time to process what it means to be parents to a monster. Sam's continuing depression and exhaustion with the life is troubling. What's far more interesting is Chuck in direct dialogue with a fan whose work has surpassed his own.

Supernatural has always had a pretty positive relationship to fan fiction. Although there's been teasing, there's still respect and love for it. Having Becky be the mature person who has learned to love herself, while the "real" author of the show is just sort of obsessed with monsters and tragic endings is the writers' way of saying fans are valid and probably better adjusted in some ways. And they're just as legitimate authors of the story.

So, Get This: This is Jensen's sixth and final time directing, and like all of his episodes it was filmed first. In this case, that meant Jensen kept his hiatus beard for the alternate reality sequence. Also, Benny's cameo wasn't written to be Benny, but Jensen thought it would work. Also, many of the collectibles in Becky's office are gifts made by actual fans on the show, given to the cast and crew.

Driver Picks the Music: Continuing the Jensen theme, the song which plays over the montage of Billy dying is "Sounds of Someday" by the band Radio Company, which is made up of Jensen and Steve Carlson. This song was off the band's debut album.

Proverbs 17:3

Episode 15.05. Airdate: November 14, 2019
Written by: Steve Yockey
Directed by: Richard Speight Jr.
Guest Cast: Anna Grace Barlow (Ashley/Lilith), Luke Camilleri(Josh May), Markian Tarasiuk (Andy May*)*
Synopsis: A simple werewolf case turns out to be a trap orchestrated by Chuck, starring Lilith.

Five episodes into the final season, and we've got another return of a long-lost character with two flashes to alternate realities. These devices are a great way to pay tribute to, and commentate on, the series. In this case, the monster of the week mirroring the brothers is incredibly on the nose, but that's on purpose. Like every other plot element the boys have encountered, it's designed to push them a certain way.

But what happens when the characters become self-aware? This is a really interesting question for the actual writers of the show! And it's a meta commentary as Eric Kripke's original ending was one brother killing the other in "Swan Song." But who the Winchesters and Cas became changed all of that. Now they can see when they're being manipulated by the story around them.

It's fun to finally see Lilith in all her power and glory, and it's sad to see the boys so upset that Chuck was never gone. So now they need to fight God, which should be easy.

Ship Shape: It's interesting to note that Chuck missed mentioning Cas in the story he wrote with Becky, and that Cas never shows up in any of these alternate worlds. Is that because Cas is the one thing about this world that's different and won't conform?

Golden Time

Episode 15.06. Airdate: November 21, 2019
Written by: Meredith Glynn
Directed by: John Showalter
Guest Cast: Misha Collins (Castiel), Shoshannah Stern (Eileen), Keegan Conor Tracy (Witch Mother), Jodelle Ferland (Emily)
Synopsis: Ghost Eileen and Sam encounter some witches at Rowena's old place. Cas works a djinn case and realizes he needs to go home.

A big triumph requires taking heroes to their lowest points, before watching them rise up. We've seen *Supernatural* do this before—especially in Season Seven—but it's not all loss and longing this time. We get to see our boys find some hope and something to fight for. Well, at least Sam and Cas do. Dean's hope is still a work in progress.

Just like Cas returning in Season Thirteen was a win for Dean, the resurrection of Eileen is a win Sam sorely needed. Also the fact that Sam is able to save her in a way that honors Rowena and relies on how he's always been different is a bonus. It's empowering and Sam's no longer alone thanks to her return, and I love it.

I also love Cas successfully working a case and solving it in his own angelic way. His powers are fading, but he still saves people. This whole family is stronger together, and that's the only way they have a shot at taking down, you know, GOD.

Spoiler Alert: Just like with the werewolf brothers last week, the witch sisters are very Winchester parallels of messed up families repeating Winchester mistakes. That makes more sense when you get that Eileen's resurrection is also a Chuck "story." Even so, I like Eileen and Sam.

Ship Shape: As much as I love Rowena and Sam, whose relationship is lovingly treated this episode, I adore Sam and Eileen and that they are finally getting a chance. They've been through the same trauma, and have the same sort of humor and strength. They're sort of perfect together.

Also, they're paralleled a lot to Dean and Cas, whose one interaction this episode is absolute gold. Only someone you love can annoy you that much.

Driver Picks the Music: The opener set to Cobra Ramone's "So Quiet" is outside of the box for *Supernatural*, but I really love it.

Last Call

Episode 15.07. Airdate: December 5, 2019
Written by: Jeremy Adams
Directed by: Amyn Kaderali
Guest Cast: Misha Collins (Castiel), Shoshannah Stern (Eileen), Dimitri Vantis (Sergei), Christian Kane (Lee Webb)
Synopsis: Cas comes home with a plan to track down Chuck, which doesn't go to well for Sam. Dean goes on a case alone and it turns out his old friend is the monster.

This episode is weird, with half of it just plot stuff with no emotion. Sam's situation gets Sergei back in the mix, who along with Donatello has become the preferred white guy information maguffin. And we learn that Chuck is weak. It's all fine, and it's nice to see Cas be sorta ruthless. And Eileen is just cool.

But then we have Dean's story. Lee is living Dean's dream life that we saw in "Nihilism," but with one important thing missing—hunting. The message here is very clear: Hunters who refuse the call to help people become monsters. Of course, it's more subtle than that, but Dean specifically cannot walk away from who he is. Seems pretty important. The thing is, Dean sees himself as just the hunter, with saving people as a bonus. But really, it's the other way around.

Lee brings out a lot of interesting things in Dean. He allows him to be himself or, if you look at it differently, encourages Dean's more performative version of himself. And so, it's also important that Dean rejects this and heads home where he belongs—with his brother and his real bestie, hunting God.

Spoiler Alert: This episode not only foreshadows that Dean can't and doesn't want to retire, but it's also a dry run for the finale in heaven we never saw because of COVID. In that finale, it would have been all the good parts of Swayze's—a band, beer, and all the people Dean had lost together again.

Ship Shape: If Lee and Dean aren't ex-boyfriends, I don't know what to say. They even apparently had a fivesome together?

Driver Picks the Music/So, Get This: After years of "Dean can't sing" jokes, it's awesome to see him on stage belting out the Dukes of Hazard theme. The song Lee sings when he's introduced is called "House Rules" which Christian Kane actually wrote. Oh, and the house band? That's "The Impalas," a band made up of *Supernatural* crew members (Perry Battista, Tracy Dunlop, Dave Webb, Cam Beck, and Chris Glynn Jones) that has been playing together since at least the 100th episode party.

Famous Faces: Christian Kane, who many will know from *Angel* and *Leverage* is a good friend of Jensen Ackles.

Our Father, Who Aren't in Heaven

Episode 15.08. Airdate: December 12, 2019
Written by: Brad Buckner & Eugenie Ross-Leming
Directed by: Richard Speight Jr.
Guest Cast: Misha Collins (Castiel), Rob Benedict (Chuck), Jake Abel (Adam/Michael), Ruth Connell (Rowena), Shoshannah Stern (Eileen), Keith Szarabajka (Donatello Redfield)
Synopsis: The plan to defeat God starts with a trip to hell and ends with Michael opening a door to Purgatory.

This episode functions best as the first half to a longer story that's wrapped up in "The Trap." In that way, much of it is laying groundwork for what's to come, but also tying up a plot thread that's been dangling since Season Five—Adam.

It's actually great to see Adam and Michael back, doing relatively well. And Michael's grappling with Chuck using Sam and Dean as entertainment is really good. Jake Abel does excellent work switching between personas. It's fantastic, but not at all surprising, to see Rowena rising to her rightful position as Queen of Hell. This is a perfect resolution for her that I adore, and she uses her new role to have Sam get her drinks and to give Dean and Cas marriage counseling.

Sam and Dean's main emotional arcs in this episode are interesting, because they want to defeat Chuck, and they deal with how they failed Adam, but they're also dealing with their relationships to others—namely Eileen and Cas. These relationships actually say a lot about who Dean and Sam are, and what they want to be. Sam may want to try to have a family, and Dean, well… he needs to grow enough to forgive Cas and look at why he's so mad.

Spoiler Alert: This episode ends up being the final appearances for both Rowena and Donatello. I don't know if there were plans to check on Donatello one more time before COVID changed things, but Rowena was very much intended to show up in the finale, ruling fabulously.

Ship Shape: This episode is all about couples, from Dean and Cas being bitchy, to Sam being cute and over-protective with Eileen. Also, I'm kinda shipping Adam and Michael? Is that weird? Actually, don't answer that.

Driver Picks the Music: Just as Jensen got to feature his band and music when he directed, the song playing when Michael and Adam talk is "Going Straight" by Richard's group, Dick Jr., and the Volunteers.

The Trap

Episode 15.09. Airdate: January 16, 2020
Written by: Robert Berens
Directed by: Robert Singer
Guest Cast: Misha Collins (Castiel), Alexander Calvert (Jack), Jim Beaver (AU Bobby), Rob Benedict (Chuck), Kim Rhodes (Jody), Lisa Berry (Billie), Shoshannah Stern (Eileen)
Synopsis: Dean and Cas head back to purgatory as Chuck shows Sam the future to get him to lose hope.

"The Trap" is one of the major highlights of the final season, because it plays a literal "what if?" and gives us a big quest. There's also huge emotional, character stuff. Let's talk about Chuck and Sam first.

The thing that makes Sam the hero he is has always been hope. So, taking that away even for a minute, is a low—if not the lowest—point for Sam. It also games out what could have been the rest of the season, reminding us how freaking dark the "Butch and Sundance" ending is. Is doesn't matter if Sam and Dean still have each other if the world is dead. And also, the vampire effects and acting in their big death scene are kinda terrible, so I get Sam not wanting that future.

This is still about free will, and the same determinism that Billie traffics in. It's a paradox of sorts that telling someone they can make choices, but that once said choice is made, there's no changing the outcome. But Chuck's version of the future doesn't account for Jack. So… we'll see.

Ship Shape: We have Dean and Cas, and holy crap guys. Previous rifts and sins in their relations relationship were repaired in purgatory, so it's fitting that it's here that Cas redeems himself and gets a win for Dean.
Dean, on his knees praying to Cas and giving him forgiveness is incredible. Not just for Jensen's acting, but because it gets to Dean's deepest wounds and how he compensates for them. He reacts to pain with anger, and that makes him a hero and a hunter—but it also makes him, in his eyes, a monster and a killer. The fact that he lets Cas into this intimate pain is so romantic and beautiful and… I'm gonna need a minute.

Eileen and Sam do much worse here, but like Cas told Dean at the start of the season, how they got there doesn't matter. What's between them and how they feel is real.

Spoiler Alert: This is another unintended final appearance of a character on screen. We likely would have seen Eileen again in the finale with Sam, but it didn't happen. At least Shoshannah got a high-quality smooch before her departure.

The Heroes' Journey

Episode 15.10. Airdate: January 23, 2020
Written by: Andrew Dabb
Directed by: John Showalter
Guest Cast: DJ Qualls (Garth), Sarah Smyth (Bess)
Synopsis: Sam and Dean find out what life is like when they aren't the heroes of God's story. Also: Dean dream tap dances.

This installment goes meta in a way that fits a very meta season. Not only do writers want their characters to behave a certain way, they also don't want to bother with all the normal stuff. This episode basically points out the plot holes inherent in most TV and stories.

Heroes don't get colds, or flat tires, or go to the dentist. Life is brutal for Sam and Dean—who are basically part of God's own version of monster fight club. But what happens when they aren't part of it? Someone else takes out the bad guys. The results are pretty fun, with the guys doing some great comedy.

Garth has always been a great character, but he's extra great here showing that maybe the supporting characters have it best. Also, maybe a normal life after hunting is possible, with a few tweaks—and when you're not the protagonist of course. That's not something we've seen before, but it's certainly a possibility that shouldn't be ignored. But what's important is that Garth saves the day, proving that you don't need plot armor to be a hero.

So, Get This: Also, Dean tap dances? This sequence is wild and weird, but it also sort of works because it means that not being the hero is allowing Dean to be vulnerable. That's actually according to the choreographer of the tap sequence, Gordon Hart. What's most amazing is that DJ and Jensen learned that dance in a day.

The Gamblers

Episode 15.11. Airdate: January 30, 2020
Written by: Meredith Glynn (story & teleplay), Davy Perez (story)
Directed by: Charles Beeson
Guest Cast: Misha Collins (Castiel), Alexander Calvert (Jack), Lynda Boyd (Fortuna), Hanneke Talbot (Evie)
Synopsis: Sam and Dean try to win back some luck in a pool game against the goddess of luck herself. Cas finds Jack has returned.

This episode has some excellent moments, but it does feels like an odd detour. There are no emotional revelations about the manner of Jack's return, though it's great that Cas is the one who gets to find him. And the boys win their luck by just sort of existing, making a good case to Fortuna and not so much in an actual act of heroism.

But maybe that's the point, that their inherent heroism and willingness to save people is what eventually saves the day. Maybe that's because it's not the story that defines them, but the choices they make within said story.

The pool games echo "The Curious Case of Dean Winchester" which itself was all about Dean being able to trust Sam. It comes much easier here, and that's important as the guys are older and wiser now. I also like that we finally get an explanation of how gods worked when God himself is a thing.

So, Get This: All the pool shots made by Sam and Dean are real, including Dean's trick shot which Jensen filmed in one take.

Galaxy Brain

Episode 15.12. Airdate: March 16, 2020
Written by: Robert Berens (teleplay and story), Meredith Glynn (story)
Directed by: Richard Speight Jr.
Guest Cast: Misha Collins (Castiel), Alexander Calvert (Jack), Rob Benedict (Chuck), Kim Rhodes (Jody), Lisa Berry (Billie), Yadira Guevara-Prip (Kaias), Sandra Ferens (Merle)
Synopsis: Jack is back with orders from Billie, which he instantly ignores to help Kaia.

"Galaxy Brain" continues what we first saw in "The Gamblers," which is what made Sam and Dean heroes. They make the dumb, right choice, rather than the safe one. Cas and Jack doing the thing that's morally right for them against Death's orders is a continuation of just that. It's pretty telling on both sides, especially for Jack as he reintegrates into his family.

Despite having no soul, Jack still knows what's right thanks to his family. Doing the moral thing means not listening to Billie. Billie wants them to do the same thing as Chuck—to just play their roles in a pre-written story. But that's not what Winchesters do, and that's good because free will isn't just about choices. It's about the right choices.

This episode also wraps up a plot that would have been the center of *Wayward Sisters'* first season, with Kaia's return (she lives!) and reunification with Claire. Spoiler, but this is the final time we see Jody on screen, and it's a satisfying end to the Wayward story. It's pretty meta that Chuck mentions canceling shows and failed spin-offs, in the episode that wraps up the failed spin off.

But what we really have to pay attention to is Billie. She says God wove himself into the fabric of the universe, and what that means is the library. Everyone has a fate, a story, created by determinism. There's some choice, yes, but it's still all rules and what must be. So, Billie and her rules are just more… Chuck? In that case, we need to rip up all the endings to be free.

Spoiler Alert: We were never going to see Claire on screen, due to Kathryn Newton's thriving career. But not actually seeing how important characters' stories end turns out to be the norm for *Supernatural*.

So, Get This: The song playing in the Radio Shed at the top of the episode is "Pop Tart Heart" by Louden Swain, Rob Benedict's own band.

Destiny's Child

Episode 15.13. Airdate: March 23, 2020
Written by: Brad Buckner & Eugenie Ross-Leming
Directed by: Robert Singer
Guest Cast: Misha Collins (Castiel), Alexander Calvert (Jack), Genevieve Padalecki (Ruby), Rachel Miner (The Empty), Danneel Ackles (Jo/Anael)
Synopsis: Various Winchesters jump around realms and realities and eventually Jack gets his soul back.

So much happens in this episode, and not much of it makes much sense, but at least it's fun and we get final appearances by three of our favorite actresses. Does it reflect anything more than a lot of plot nonsense though? Well, yes. Because again, this story is about our heroes being heroes, and what makes them just that. It's Cas who does the dumb, right thing here, saving the day and Jack's soul because of it. It's definitely good to have original Jack back.

I love seeing Rachel Miner and Genevieve Padalecki back, as well as Danneel Ackles. Rachel has made a huge impact on the *Supernatural* fandom, so bringing her back (and in a way that accommodated her) was so special. The same goes for Genevieve, who got a whole family out of her work. In general, the returns work from an emotional point of view, and give us more of the show coming full circle.

I honestly don't really get the point of the Fancy Winchesters who hop over in their Mini Cooper, other than humor. They don't seem very broken up about their entire universe dying, but hey. We get Sam in a manbun being kinda fussy about stuff?

Plot Hole: The connection between Ruby and Jo is kind of a cool way to get the leads' wives together, but it makes *zero* sense. Jo wasn't doing her businesswoman thing until after the fall in Season Nine. In fact, she should have been rounded up by Castiel and Hannah in Season Ten. And what happened to her angel name? Why do we have two Jos on this show?!

It's a huge error, in an episode of big errors. Honestly, everything about hell and the empty has slowly been thrown out or revamped, which is sort of a reminder that the lore on the show has been stretched so much that maybe it's okay the story is ending.

Spoiler Alert: Cas never follows through helping Ruby, but that might have been something that would have been resolved in the series finale.

Ship Shape: Cas and Dean's love language is calling one another idiots and I love it. Also, it's kind of pointed how the "then" segment emphasizes that Cas is into the pizza man, and then shows Dean eating lots of pizza? Since Cas watches over Jack, that makes him the babysitter, right?

Death Notes: I'm giving Cas a point for style! Dean: 20, Sam: 8, Castiel: 6.

Last Holiday

Episode 15.14. Airdate: October 8, 2020
Written by: Jeremy Adams
Directed by: Eduardo Sánchez
Guest Cast: Alexander Calvert (Jack), Meagen Fay (Mrs. Butters), Kavan Smith (Cuthbert Sinclair)
Synopsis: Sam and Dean activate the bunker's wood nymph who just wants to cook, clean, and maybe kill Jack.

"Last Holiday" is all about bringing Jack back into the fold and making him feel like less of a monster. That's rather hard to do when there's a rogue wood nymph calling him a monster. Like Jack, Mrs. Butters is a supernatural creature that was adopted into a family… and yeah, she goes bad, but it's not because of her nature—it's because she was trying to save the people she loved.

That's exactly what happened to Jack when he lost his soul, so, it's important that Mrs. Butters isn't killed or trapped. She's just a reminder of what's important and what the mission is. I like that, and it bodes well for Jack given all that he has left to do. And his family is with him, as Dean's actions show at the end with making that cake.

This episode isn't perfect though. Dean's a little too goofy for most of it, and Sam has once again just sort of disappeared in terms of his own emotional plotlines. But the biggest offense is of course that Cas is just not there.

So, Get This: This was the first episode to air of the final run, after a nearly-seven-month hiatus due to the COVID-19 pandemic. That also was the show's longest hiatus between new episodes. This installment works much better in the context of a season when it doesn't come after a huge, unplanned break. So enjoy, binge watchers!

Ship Shape: It's good to know that Sam and Eileen are still a thing and are giving it a try. Sam actually dressing up for a date is adorable.

Gimme Shelter

Episode 15.15. Airdate: October 15, 2020
Written by: Davy Perez
Directed by: Matt Cohen
Guest Cast: Misha Collins (Castiel), Alexander Calvert (Jack), Emily Swallow (Amara), Steve Bacic (Pastor Joe), Nicole Muñoz (Sylvia)
Synopsis: Cas and Jack solve a murder while Dean and Sam look for Amara.

This final season has brought a lot of the big ideas of *Supernatural* to the forefront, like free will and family, and what even makes a person good. We have all of that, with more of Billie's very Chuck-like plan, as well as Cas and Jack solving the case. But we also dive into faith. When you've made God your bad guy—and he's always been the ultimate bad father—how do you deal with people who do good and terrible things in God's name?

Chuck, for all his modern flair, is a very Old Testament god. But Pastor Joe (Jeez, another Joe!?) and his flock believe in tolerance, service, and taking care of one another. Their faith isn't in waiting for God, it's in themselves as instruments of God. And that's what inspires Cas to testify, I think, reminding us how he found a new faith in family. This idea that God is more than a bad dad is important for Jack's story going forward.

What's also important is Dean and Amara's discussion of Mary and Dean's anger. Despite the murkiness of their "connection" in Season Eleven, Amara does understand Dean, and sees how much his rage and frustration holds him back from happiness. The same went for his ideas about his mom, but it's the mention of his anger that calls back to his prayer to Cas in purgatory. He won't be at peace until he's released from the rage that makes him a killer.

Sam is here too I guess, but for this episode it's not really clear what he's defined by. What he clearly wants is a life of his own, making his own choices and story.

Familiar Faces: This episode is full of alumni! We have Doctor Sexy himself as Pastor Joe, and the little girl from "Everybody Loves a Clown" as Sylvia. And the episode was direct by Matt Cohen, aka young John Winchester!

Ship Shape: Cas is great all episode, but a particular highlight is him being utterly frustrated when Dean mentions he and Amara kinda used to have a thing. And Dean's big lie to Amara is maybe not a great sign.

Drag Me Away from You

Episode 15.16. Airdate: October 22, 2020
Written by: Meghan Fitzmartin
Directed by: Amyn Kaderali
Guest Cast: Lisa Berry (Billie), Paxton Singleton (Young Dean), Christian Michael Cooper (Young Sam), Kelsey Crane (Adult Caitlin), Elle McKinnon (Young Caitlin)
Synopsis: Dean and Sam return to the scene of their first case together as kids.

This is the final "regular" episode of the show, as from here on out it's all endgame stuff before the series finale. And so, it's fitting that the last case we see Sam and Dean take on echoes one of their first—literary symmetry and all that. But finishing something they started as kids, that wasn't as finished as they thought, is pretty key to how things are going to end.

The flashback here reminds us of who Dean and Sam were. Sam just wanted a normal life, and Dean, well, he put on a brave face to protect Sammy and do as his dad wanted. And now in the present, we have Sam repeating that they do what they do to save people, and Dean consumed by rage at Chuck for taking away his freedom.

But it wasn't just Chuck, it was his whole story and choices. It was John, and Sam, and Mary's death. Dean thinks that all of these things defined him into a killer. His rage is at what Chuck and the story made him into. And that's his tragedy. And the continued tragedy is that he's just buying into another story—Billie's. Billie wants to use Dean and Jack as weapons, and she's using Dean's anger at Jack over Mary to manipulate them both.

Driver Picks the Music: The title of the episode comes from Toto's "Africa" and of all the songs used for titles that we don't hear in episodes (and there are a lot) not hearing this, the greatest song of all time, is perhaps the greatest disappointment.

Unity

Episode 15.17. Airdate: October 29, 2020
Written by: Meredith Glynn
Directed by: Catriona McKenzie
Guest Cast: Misha Collins (Castiel), Alexander Calvert (Jack), Rob Benedict (Chuck), Rachel Miner (The Empty), Emily Swallow (Amara), Alessandro Juliani (Adam), Carmen Moore (Serafina)
Synopsis: Amara tries to convince Chuck not to end the world, as Dean and Jack prepare the spell that will kill him. Sam and Cas look for another way.

Much in the way that the final three seasons make up a sort of "Jack Trilogy," the final episodes of this season make up their own that wraps up not only the season, but the series. And much like how this episode divides its focus on different characters, each of these episodes builds to a big moment for one of our core three, while Chuck and Jack evolve and devolve beside them. This episode has such a moment for Sam; "Despair" is all about Cas; and Dean is left with the emotional pay off that carries "Inherit the Earth."

This episode launches us in the darkest moments with an installment that digs into the questions *Supernatural*, and humanity have asked from the beginning—what is choice and why does it matter? It's revealed here that Billie wants to be the next Chuck, making sure everyone fulfills their predetermined story. She's not a writer though. She's just a pedantic reader who likes the early seasons and doesn't want innovation or rule-breaking stories. In a way, that's worse than Chuck, who at least enjoyed the entertainment of people trying. Sam has arguably been the most victimized by fate throughout the series, so it's important that he's the one who says no.

And Chuck himself is still at it, manipulating the outcome based on who he thinks the Winchesters are—especially Dean. He's counting on that rage that's been getting so much focus. But that brotherly bond comes through again, thanks to Sam's big speech. Dean won't kill Sam, and that means he won't let Jack die. Sam wins the day with his faith in Dean and family. It's perhaps his biggest moment, because it rewrites the story.

And that's good. Because as we see with Adam and Serafina, Jack dying to kill Chuck is just part of another deterministic story. It's the same as Michael and Lucifer, way back in Season Five. But that was wrong, and so is Adam. Because God created characters so defined by their love for one another, that they ceased being defined by what he wanted. And God should be in everything, and loving everything, not just obsessed with one story.

Familiar Faces: Alessandro Juliani is our final familiar face and so it's fitting it's another *Battlestar Galactica* alum!

Death Notes: Amara doesn't really die, but she does cease to exist alone, and honestly that's sort of nice for her. She never quite made sense when you thought too much about her, but the idea that she's finally in balance is a satisfying ending.

Ship Shape: Not only does Dean look right at Cas when Sam mentions everyone that's been brought back will die, but... let's talk about this Cas. He's the one that didn't do as he was told. He's the variable where Sam and Dean also don't. This Cas is, perhaps, the thing setting this world apart, and it's because he fell, in every way, for Dean. I do not think this was at all the plan when the character was introduced, but just like with Chuck, these characters do their own thing.

Despair

Episode 15.18. Airdate: November 5, 2020
Written by: Robert Berens
Directed by: Richard Speight Jr.
Guest Cast: Misha Collins (Castiel), Alexander Calvert (Jack), Jim Beaver (AU Bobby), Rachel Miner (The Empty), Felicia Day (AU Charlie), Briana Buckmaster (Donna), Lisa Berry (Billie)
Synopsis: Gay love pierces through the veil at death to save the day. Sorta.

We will get to Cas, I promise. But first, there are some really important things for all the players. Jack feels like failure, but Cas in their final conversation on earth, reminds him that he is loved because of who he is, not his destiny and power. Sam loses the woman he loves (off screen!), and his leadership skills are affirmed just in time for everyone to disappear on his watch. Billie goes full bad guy and tries to take down one of the only guys who could save the world, and we get our second death of Death. The title "Despair" is very on point.

But the real point of this episode is not actually despair. It's love—Castiel's love for Dean. Cas saves Dean within one of the most moving scenes of the entire series, made more so by the fact that there's more than a decade of history and tension between these two. Sam and Dean is the story *Supernatural* was always meant to be about, and it begins and ends with them. But Dean and Cas? They're the story that was never supposed to happen. It just did.

Having romantic love (and, trust me, it's romantic!) be canon? It's almost meta, especially for this season, because it's characters living their truth contrary to some original intentions.

Cas telling Dean what we all know—that he's the most loving man on earth—is massive. It's massive for Dean, but also for Cas. Love defined him, because he loved Dean and defied heaven, expressing that love—queer, selfless, accepting love—saves Dean. It's a perfect way for this part of Cas' story to end. Just the way it started, with Dean Winchester and a handprint.

So, Get This: The final scene with the handprint, and the shot echoing Cas' first appearance showing his wings, were some elements developed by Richard Speight Jr., Jensen, and Misha.

When this episode aired, it was a wild night on social media. "Destiel" began to trend on special media just as the state of Georgia went blue in the 2020 presidential election. And as false rumors that Vladimir Putin was stepping down also trended.

Death Notes/Spoiler Alert: We have a lot of final appearances in this show, most of which were not intended to be like Donna and Charlie. Billie's end is final, and it's a pretty epic goodbye for a great character. Lisa Berry was also extremely pregnant when she filmed her final scene. But just know everyone, including Cas, is fine eventually. We just won't see them on screen. Cas gets a final point in, but he can't pull ahead. It's Dean: 20, Sam: 8, Castiel: 7.

Inherit The Earth

Episode 15.19. Airdate: November 12, 2020
Written by: Brad Buckner & Eugenie Ross-Leming
Directed by: John Showalter
Guest Cast: Alexander Calvert (Jack), Rob Benedict (Chuck), Jake Abel (Michael), Mark Pellegrino (Lucifer), Lexi the Terrier Mix (Miracle)
Synopsis: Chuck's story ends.

How do you keep fighting against God, when you've lost nearly everyone? In the fallout of "Despair," Sam, Dean, and Jack are left alone on Earth and still victimized by Chuck's manipulations. This comes in the forms of Lucifer and Michael that are played out, strained, and heavy-handed. But maybe there's a meta element to Chuck going back to his classic story of brother versus brother, and it being boring and unsatisfying. A cycle of violence and revenge is like that.

While the guys spend some of the episode trying to work with a pre-written story, they ultimately win by writing their own. That's the part I love about this episode. Sam and Dean ignore the book, and they ignore Chuck's ideas allowing the world to come back with a new God in the form of Jack.

Rather than being "hands off" with the world by leaving, Jack internalizes everything that he's learned from his adventures and places his divinity everywhere. But mainly, he puts it in people. I love that the ultimate point of the whole series, is that people can be good. They can do the right thing out of love. Jack gives the world free will, because Sam and Dean Winchester taught him it was important to love people and family.

Sam, Dean, and Cas end up not just saving the world through their actions, but remaking it by simply being a loving family. Cas' faith in Jack is finally rewarded and it turns out that the paradise he saw was real. That's a really wonderful, final resolution to the over-arching series' theme.

But what about the actual characters? Well, Sam and Cas have had their big moments, so we finally get one for Dean and it's in not doing something that we find his final actualization. When Chuck calls him the ultimate killer, and Dean responds "That's not who I am," he finally sees himself the way Cas does. Cas really did save him. His family's love freed him from the story he wrote about himself. This guy has grown so much that he lets his inner softie out and tries to steal a dog! Oh, and lets the biggest villain of his existence live.

Chuck doesn't die. And the cycle of violence is finally broken. Jack takes over and we get a nice montage. Cas and Jack's names sit beside Dean, Sam, and Mary's initials, and it's the highest tribute possible. These are all great endings. Could they have been better? Yeah. We were supposed to see all of the characters we lost in "Despair" come back, but for reasons unknown—probably related to COVID and money—we didn't get that. But we got an ending that pretty much worked.

Ship Shape: If somehow the end of the last episode left you doubting that Dean doesn't care about Cas, just look at the way this dork *runs* up the stairs when he thinks he's back. And that whole thing where Cas changed how Dean saw himself.

Is my biggest regret with this episode, the fact that Jack doesn't bring Cas back? Yeah, that would have been nice, but I don't think anything would match the fanfic we have in our hearts of what that reunion would be like. But that's not so for the other big Season Fifteen romance—Sam, and Eileen. She doesn't get a mention, which is pretty annoying, but at least we know that she and everyone else are fine.

Driver Picks the Music: The first montage to "Get Together" by the Youngbloods is corny, but I love it. This world deserves some corny. But what really gets me in the series-spanning recap set to Jackson Browne's "Running on Empty."

Carry On

Episode 15.20. Airdate: November 19, 2020
Written by: Andrew Dabb
Directed by: Robert Singer
Guest Cast: Jim Beaver (Bobby), Lexie the Terrier Mix (Miracle)
Synopsis: Dean and Sam go to a pie festival.

There's actually a lot of good in this episode. Incredible acting from Jensen and Jared, that's almost as good as Sam's old man wig is bad. But… yeah. There's also stuff that's divisive. We're gonna need a bit more room, so meet me in the next chapter.

Drive Picks the Music: The needle drops are really perfect. From Van Morrison's "Ordinary Life" over the, ordinary life montage, to Dire Straits' "Brothers in Arms" over Sam moving on without Dean. And of course, we have "Carry on Wayward Son" which doesn't just anchor the final montage—it gives the episode its title and guiding ideas. And we end with a perfect version of the "Americana" theme.

Ship Shape: The way Dean smiles when Bobby tells him "Cas helped," means Cas is there and waiting for him. That's the whole enchilada, right there. Dean and Cas, together in heaven forever is a happy ending I never anticipated! It's better than Sam and his blurry wife. In my mind and heart that's Eileen, but that's not definitive.

Name Game: Agents Singer and Kripke reference Eric Kripke and Bob Singer, who created and shepherded the show. When Sam shoves the pie in Dean's face, that's Bob Singer behind Dean laughing. And there's a Dabb's pies in the background too.

Death Notes: Both Winchesters score final points in the last round, but there was never any question who would take the win! But oh boy, is it a sad death. Dean: 21, Sam: 9, Castiel: 7. At least everyone is together at the end? Does that make it better?

Seriously, let me make it better, guys.

How Do We "Carry On?"

The final episode of *Supernatural* aired on Thursday, November 19th to mixed reactions to say the least. It survived network and time slot changes, bugs, cast turnover, bad ratings, dick jokes, ship wars, a pandemic, several presidents, and more. The fandom that supported the show for a decade and a half had built orphanages, campaigned for mental health, spread kindness, and built a community. But the end of the on-screen story of Sam and Dean was as complicated as it was controversial, and the fandom is in many ways still processing it, with "Carry On" currently being the worst reviewed episode of the entire series. And that's a bummer, because no one wants to end a journey like this in disappointment and anger.

So, we're going to talk about why the show ended the way it did, why it wasn't so bad, and what we would have seen had it not been for that pesky pandemic. I love this show, and if you're reading this book, you probably do too. So I want there to be some peace now that we're done. Let's do this.

Why *This* Ending?

After beating God, and the devil, and everyone in between, Dean Winchester dies on a random hunt. That's the big twist. And his goodbye to his little brother is a truly incredible scene—one that makes me sob watching it. There's just so much real emotion in both Jensen and Jared's performances, and why wouldn't there be? These guys were Sam and Dean for 15 years. That's a long time. And it's different than any death or goodbye we've seen on the show before, because these two have finally, finally, broken out of their cycles of rage, grief, violence, and suffering. They're both able to finally let go and that's huge for them.

And that's one reason why the death was so shocking. For fans, this went against everything we expected. Sam doesn't give up! Winchesters don't just die! How could they have escaped Chuck's ending, only for Dean to just bite it thanks to a piece of rebar? What many of us—myself included—expected from the final episode of *Supernatural* was getting to see Sam and Dean drive off into the sunset, or close the trunk with a final "we've got work to do." But no, that was the penultimate episode. Here, we get the real ending, and it's not open-ended. It doesn't allow for us to fanfic out the rest of the journey. It's definitive and it's painful.

Why did Dean have to die? That's the biggest question we're left with. Sam goes on to live a full, happy life with his blurry wife and a son named Dean. But why? How could this happen after these boys went through so much? Here's why.

For one, Dean dying while saving people and hunting things, with Sam living on to be happy and fulfilled, is the ending Dean always saw for himself. It's what he wanted. We talked about this in "Trial and Error," and what happens in "Carry On" is almost verbatim what Dean envisioned. But wait, you say, isn't this just more determinism!? How could Dean and Sam have escaped fate, only to get the ending they foresaw.

Because this is their ending.

It's not Chuck's, or the fans', it's theirs. All through the last season, especially in "Last Call," we were reminded that Dean could never walk away from saving people. It's just who he is and it's how he knew he would die. Yes, a few times he fantasized about retiring, but that was in a world with no monsters, which just wasn't the case here. And from an extradiegetic point of view, a retired Dean and Sam was only going to happen if *Wayward Sisters* had gone forward to open things up for cameos. But the *Supernatural* universe (supposedly) ended with this finale, so Sam and Dean's stories needed to end too. We had to close that book.

Of course there's a big appeal to an open-ended story, but I think this finale was very much guided by the words of "Carry on Wayward Son." There needed to be peace for these boys. They needed to be done and Heaven waited for them. After 15 years of scripts ending with "To Be Continued," this one ended with "The End." And I think Dabb, Singer, and the writers felt that these characters deserved the peace of a full, definitive ending that gave the boys what they wanted.

For Sam, as we were reminded in "Drag Me Away from You," he always wanted a normal life. And Dean wanted to die hunting, to be at peace with the people he loved. In this show, death is not an ending and saying that Dean could only lay down his burdens and find peace in death isn't as sad or dark as it sounds. He let Sam go, and he moved on. That's growth for him and a good end.

It's also a beautiful end for Cas. After confessing his love and saving Dean—and thus the world—the person he put all his faith into, Jack, comes through. He gets to help create the paradise he saw in "The Future" and gets to share it with Dean. When Bobby says, "Cas helped," that's his happy ending. Because he finally saves his family and his home. He always just wanted to help, and he wanted that because of Dean. I love this ending for them better than Cas returning to earth, or something like that, because this is something permanent and eternal.

All of our heroes get the ending they would write for themselves, and it's not because it was some inevitable story written for them by Chuck. It's because of their choices. Does that mean you have to like it? Well, no. Of course not. But I'm just trying to give you a point of view from which it works.

What Could and Should Have Been

There are a lot of crappy things about this finale though! I can't deny that. In the original plan for the finale, Dean wouldn't just have been driving around heaven in Baby, he would have entered Harvelle's to see a huge party filled with all the people he loved, with the actual band Kansas playing "Carry on Wayward Son." (Does this mean someone killed Kansas?!) A call was to have gone out to anyone who had been on the show to show up and be part of the crowd.

We would have seen Rowena in hell. We would maybe even have seen Ruby rescued from the Empty as Cas had promised, along with lots of angels we loved and missed. Eileen might have truly been Sam's blurry wife. Heck, his son might have been played by one of Jared or Jensen's own kids. It would have served as a prelude to a wrap party to end all wrap parties …

But the coronavirus pandemic had very different ideas. Not only did everyone who appeared in the final two episodes have to quarantine alone for two weeks, but there were strict protocols in place for crowds and actors. Not only did that lead to weird choices like the vampires wearing masks (yup, that's a COVID thing), but it meant there could only be one familiar face at the end.

Bobby's return works, overall. Jim Beaver is fantastic and plays that scene perfectly. Yes, of course I would have liked to SEE Castiel there for a moment, but it wasn't in the cards or the budget. The same goes for Eileen and every other familiar face. But these changes don't affect the overall story. And no, there was no other secret ending that the network somehow squashed for being too gay. This is the story as it was meant to be told, just without a party. This makes me sad for the show, but this ending makes me even sadder for the cast and crew who never got to celebrate the series and say goodbye.

At least no one had to kill Kansas for this scenario.

That's It?

Is the finale perfect? No. Would any episode be able to meet the expectations built up over all these years? Also no. Is there some laughably bad stuff in there? Well, yeah. But there's also great stuff. The show ends with Sam and Dean saving a pair of brothers. It calls back to the pilot and the first season in small and big ways. It proves that Dean getting his pie means death is near. It shows incredible growth in these men and gives us a beautiful, final goodbye on earth, with peace for everyone we love in heaven.

There is some ambiguity in this ending, with parts of the story left for the audience to fill in. But in many ways it's very final and that's what these writers wanted. And I respect that. But the thing about this show is that they have their ending, and if you don't like it, you can have yours.

There's always fanfic. There's always imagination. This is a story and it can end however you want it to in your heart. And this show recognizes and respects that. If one story doesn't serve, there are a million others that might.

There's a part in Willian Goldman's novel *The Princess Bride* that discusses how the Grandson eventually read the epilogue of the book—a part that his grandfather didn't read him. In it, Buttercup gets old, Inigo dies, and it's sad and disappointing because these characters just go on and live, and die, like normal people. Because that's what people do. This is very much the same. It's an epilogue. And you don't have to read it or accept it if you don't want to.

Jack exists in everyone. Cas lives on having changed Dean. Dean tells Sam he's with him forever. These stories and characters live on in us, in the ways they inspire and comfort us. Whenever we're having a bad day and turn on an episode or think "What would the Winchester do?" Sam, Dean, Cas and everyone else is right there.

Even if the story ends, the parts that mattered still do. The family that don't end in blood, the promise to always keep fighting, the faith and the love, that all stays right there. They all carry on in us.

My Favorite Episodes

It's almost impossible to pick one episode out of three hundred and twenty-seven, so I'm going to cheat. If there's one episode that I think fully embodies the show in its tone, themes, creativity, and characters, it would be "Baby." It's funny, innovative, and it truly understands who Sam, Dean and Cas are. But there are lots of other essential episodes, and there are also my personal favorites, so I'll spread the love through all the seasons.

Here are 15 essential episodes that perfectly represent the series:

Season One: Pilot

- Season Two: In My Time of Dying
- Season Three: Mystery Spot
- Season Four: The Monster as the End of This Book
- Season Five: Changing Channels
- Season Six: The French Mistake
- Season Seven: Death's Door
- Season Eight: Sacrifice
- Season Nine: First Born
- Season Ten: Fan Fiction
- Season Eleven: Baby
- Season Twelve: The Future
- Season Thirteen: ScoobyNatural
- Season Fourteen: Byzantium
- Season Fifteen: Despair

But I also have some personal favorites that, well, I just love the most.

Season One: Scarecrow

- Season Two: Tall Tales
- Season Three: Bad Day at Black Rock
- Season Four: On the Head of a Pin
- Season Five: The End
- Season Six: Clap Your Hands if You Believe
- Season Seven: The Girl with the Dungeons and Dragons Tattoo
- Season Eight: Huteri Heroici
- Season Nine: Meta Fiction
- Season Ten: The Executioner's Song
- Season Eleven: Don't Call Me Shurley
- Season Twelve: Regarding Dean
- Season Thirteen: Unfinished Business
- Season Fourteen: Ouroboros
- Season Fifteen: The Rupture

And while I'm here, two more lists. First, the essential brothers episodes, for drama and, uh, brotherly love.

Season One: Hell House

- Season Two: Playthings
- Season Three: A Very *Supernatural* Christmas
- Season Four: When the Levee Breaks
- Season Five: Swan Song
- Season Six: The Man Who Knew Too Much
- Season Seven: Plucky Pennywhistle's Magical Menagerie
- Season Eight: The Great Escapist
- Season Nine: Road Trip
- Season Ten: Soul Survivor
- Season Eleven: Red Meat
- Season Twelve: Who We Are
- Season Thirteen: Beat the Devil
- Season Fourteen: Prophet and Loss
- Season Fifteen: Carry On

And because this is my book, here are the best Dean and Cas episodes! And yes, Cas is not in three of them!

Season One: Faith

- Season Two: Houses of the Holy
- Season Three: Red Sky at Morning (They say his name, okay!)
- Season Four: Lazarus Rising
- Also Season Four: Lucifer Rising
- Season Five: Free to Be You and Me
- Season Six: The Man Who Would Be King
- Season Seven: The Born-Again Identity
- Season Eight: Goodbye Stranger
- Season Nine: Heaven Can't Wait
- Season Ten: The Things We Left Behind
- Season Eleven: Hell's Angel
- Season Twelve: Stuck in The Middle with You
- Season Thirteen: Tombstone
- Season Fourteen: Absence
- Season Fifteen: The Trap

After You've Watched

So, you made it through 327 episodes of angst, meta weirdness, homoeroticism, and monsters. What now? Well first, please go outside and take a walk or see the sun. It might be needed. But when you're ready to dive into other shows that will scratch that *Supernatural* itch, I have some suggestions.

I've actually mentioned most these shows in the episode guide, because all of them are from *Supernatural* alumni or star them. And that's not a coincidence. The people who made this show made other excellent shows. Here are just a few.

Looking for shows staring *Supernatural* guest stars? If you want biblical crime solving and a devil with daddy issues, go for *Lucifer*. Want just demons and plots that, uh, kind of make no sense but hey, siblings? Try *Wynonna Earp* (at least the first two seasons, it goes off the rails after that). Or would you like absolute bonkers weirdness, with a wealth of queer characters and another unicorn that kills people? Watch *DC's Legends of Tomorrow*.

And speaking of weird superheroes, two former *Supernatural* showrunners have made two incredible superhero shows that are both wild, raunchy, and as meta and weird as you would expect. There's Eric Kripke's *The Boys*, which has a bunch of former *Supernatural* cast members on it including one Jensen Ackles, who joined in Season Three. And then there's Jeremy Carver's incredible *Doom Patrol*, which features many familiar faces, most notably Mark Shepperd. And then there's Sera Gamble, who gave us more *Supernatural* actors, magic, and queer stories with *The Magicians*. All three of these are incredible.

Other *Supernatural* writers have done great things too though. Steve Yockey runs *The Flight Attendant*, and Jenny Klein works over on *The Witcher*. These are two very different shows, but they're both pretty great! And hey, if you like that Jared Padalecki fellow, he's still saving people over on *Walker*.

But if you want to stay in this world, I heartily recommend looking up Archive of Our Own and reading some fanfiction. *Supernatural* has the most works of any fandom, so you're sure to find something to your liking. I even have a few up there myself, if you know where to look.

Want to do more? Check out one of the *Supernatural* conventions run by Creation Entertainment that run throughout the year, or contribute to one of the many charities the cast supports, especially Random Acts which Misha Collins founded. And if you need more Misha, you can always join Misha's wild scavenger hunt, GISH!

And of course, there's one way to always enjoy the show, and to make sure Sam, Dean, Cas, and the rest are always with you—watch it again. And if your spouse, or friends, or parents complain about it, just remember: Driver picks the music, shotgun shuts his cakehole.

About the Author

Jessica Mason lives near Portland, Oregon with her wife, daughter, and corgi. She's a journalist and author of nonfiction, fiction, and fan fiction. She hosts the podcast Reel Magic, and when she's not writing or being a fangirl, she enjoys gardening, writing other things, music, and witchcraft.

Other Riverdale Avenue Books Binge Watcher's Guides You Might Like

The Binge Watcher's Guide to Doctor Who:
A History of the Doctor Who and the First Female Doctor
By Mackenzie Flohr

The Binge Watcher's Guide to the Films of Harry Potter
An Unauthorized Guide
By Cecilia Tan

The Binge Watcher's Guide to The Handmaid's Tale
An Unofficial Companion
By Jamie K. Schmidt

The Binge Watcher's Guide to Black Mirror:
An Unofficial Companion
By Marc W. Polite

The Binge Watcher's Guide to The Twilight Zone:
An Unofficial Journey
By Jason Trussell

The Binge Watcher's Guide to Riverdale
By Melissa Ford Luken

www.ingramcontent.com/pod-product-compliance
Lightning Source LLC
Chambersburg PA
CBHW071012280326
41935CB00011B/1323

* 9 7 8 1 6 2 6 0 1 5 9 8 2 *